Te Witer's Craft

ANNOTA TEACHER'S EDITION

SENIOR AUTHOR

RIDAN BLAU
University California at Santa Barbara

NSULTING AUTHOR

TER ELBOW
Universi Massachusetts at Amherst

SPE CONTRIBUTING AUTHORS

on Killgallon
Baltin County Public Schools

bekah Caplan
Oaklan Unified School District

IOR CONSULTANTS

Arthur Applebee
State Unisity of New York at Albany

Judith Langer
State Univsity of New York at Albany

McDougal Littell
A HOUGHTON MIFFLIN COMPANY
Evanston, Illinois • Boston • Dallas

ISBN95-86384-8
Copt © 1998 by McDougal Littell Inc.
All i reserved.

Pri in the United States of America.

5 6 7 8 9 10–VJM–02 01 00 99

Contents of the Annotated Teacher's Edition

Excellence in Three Parts

The Writer's Craft presents a perfect blend of literature, writing, and grammar. But the real value of the series lies in its flexible approach to teaching. This flexibility results from a unique three-part arrangement.

The Writer's Workshops

Real-world writing experiences show students how writing can help them affect and make sense of their world. References to the two Handbooks help them solve any writing problems that arise.

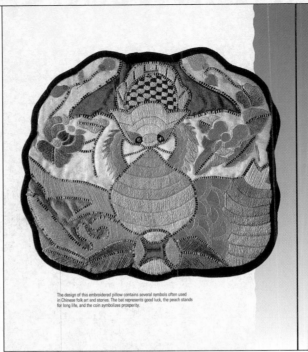

The design of this embroidered pillow contains several symbols often used in Chinese folk art and stories. The bat represents good luck, the peach stands for long life, and the coin symbolizes prosperity.

Writer's Workshops

This yarn drawing is an example of the artistry of the Huichol people, who live in a mountainous region of central Mexico. The deer, cow, cactus, and sun symbols commonly appear in Huichol textiles.

Writing Handbook
MINI-LESSONS

Grammar and Usage Handbook
MINI-LESSONS

The Writing Handbook

Mini-lessons on the writing process, style, and academic skills allow both teachers and students to find just the right help at just the right time.

The Grammar and Usage Handbook

...ong grammar instruction is taken out ...isolation and presented in the context ...drafting, revision, proofreading, and ...erature. Students apply their skills ...mediately after learning them.

Writer's Workshops

Each Writer's Workshop explores a writing mode or skill through one Guided Assignment and one Related Assignment.

Guided Assignments Hands-on activities provide in-depth suggestions and strategies for each stage of the writing process.

Related Assignments These streamlined writing experiences build on and extend the skills presented in the Guided Assignments by allowing students to problem solve within motivating, less traditional formats:

- Collage
- Children's Book
- Field Notes
- Graphics
- Commercials
- Oral History
- Song
- Script
- Magazine

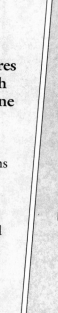

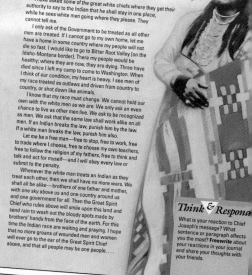

The following are panels from the student book:

Guided ASSIGNMENT — Supporting Opinions

Starting from LITERATURE

Think of a time you were treated unjustly. Try to remember how you felt. How did you express your feelings? Did you argue? Did you fight? As you read this selection, notice the language Chief Joseph uses to express his deep feelings and convince people to feel as he does.

In the late 1800s, the United States government took over the land of the Nez Percé Indians and ordered them to live on reservations far from their homes. Chief Joseph refused to accept this order and set out for Canada with a small band of his people. However, thirty miles from the Canadian border the U.S. Army surrounded them, and they were forced to surrender. The chief traveled to Washington, D.C., and tried to persuade President Hayes to set his people free.

Chief Joseph Speaks

I have seen the Great Father Chief [the President], the next Great Chief [Secretary of the Interior], . . . and many other law chiefs [members of Congress], and they all say they are my friends, and that I shall have justice; but while their mouths all talk right, I do not understand why nothing is done for my people. I have heard talk and talk, but nothing is done.

Good words do not last long unless they amount to something. Words do not pay for my dead people. They do not pay for my country, now overrun by white men. They do not protect my father's grave. . . . There has been too much talking by men who had no right to talk. Too many misrepresentations have been made, too many misunderstandings have come up between the white men about the Indians.

If the white man wants to live in peace with the Indian, he can live in peace. There need be no trouble. Treat all men alike. Give them the same law. Give them all an even chance to live and grow.

All men are made by the same Great Spirit Chief. They are all brothers. The earth is the mother of all people, and all people should have equal rights upon it. You might as well expect all rivers to run backward as that any man who was born a free man should be contented when penned up and denied liberty to go where he pleases. If you tie a horse to a stake, do you expect he will grow fat? If you pen an Indian up on a small spot of earth and compel him to stay there, he will not be contented, nor will he grow and prosper.

I have asked some of the great white chiefs where they get their authority to say to the Indian that he shall stay in one place, while he sees white men going where they please. They cannot tell me.

I only ask of the Government to be treated as all other men are treated. If I cannot go to my own home, let me have a home in some country where my people will not die so fast. I would like to go to Bitter Root Valley [on the Idaho-Montana border]. There my people would be healthy; where they are now, they are dying. Three have died since I left my camp to come to Washington. When I think of our condition, my heart is heavy. I see men of my race treated as outlaws and driven from country to country, or shot down like animals.

I know that my race must change. We cannot hold our own with the white men as we are. We only ask an even chance to live as other men live. We ask to be recognized as men. We ask that the same law shall work alike on all men. If an Indian breaks the law, punish him by the law. If a white man breaks the law, punish him also.

Let me be a free man—free to stop, free to work, free to trade where I choose, free to choose my own teachers, free to follow the religion of my fathers, free to think and talk and act for myself—and I will obey every law or submit to the penalty.

Whenever the white man treats an Indian as they treat each other, then we shall have no more wars. We shall all be alike—brothers of one father and mother, with one sky above us and one country around us and one government for all. Then the Great Spirit Chief who rules above will smile upon this land and send rain to wash out the bloody spots made by brothers' hands from the face of the earth. For this time the Indian race are waiting and praying. I hope that no more groans of wounded men and women will ever go to the ear of the Great Spirit Chief above, and that all people may be one people. . . .

Think & Respond

What is your reaction to Chief Joseph's message? What sentence or paragraph affects you the most? **Freewrite** about your reactions in your journal and share your thoughts with your friends.

140   Workshop 6

Related ASSIGNMENT — Advertisement

Starting from ADVERTISING

With so many similar products on the market today, what makes you buy one brand rather than another? Sometimes you buy things because you're used to them or because your friends recommend them. Many times, though, you buy a product simply because you've seen a catchy ad for it. As you read this ad, notice how the writer used persuasive language to deliver the ad's message.

Blade through the day with Roller Bran

Start your day off on the right foot with the newest cereal to hit the streets. This unique blend of supersoluble oat bran and corn gives you all the nutrition and energy you need to glide through the day and perform your best. And the taste leaves other breakfast cereals by the side of the road.

And grab it while you can—this cereal's on the move.

Roller BRAN Healthy Whole Grain Flakes

Watch for Roller Bran on your grocer's shelf.

Think & Respond

What audience was the advertiser trying to reach? Do you think you would buy the cereal? Why? What words or pictures in the ad are most persuasive?

152   Workshop 6

Guided Assignment

Comparison and Contrast

Guided ASSIGNMENT

Starting from LITERATURE

Our solar system has nine planets, each with its own unique characteristics. What would life be like on another planet—Mars, for example? Brad Darrach and Steve Petranek wondered too, and decided the simplest way to explain the red planet would be to show how it was similar to and different from the earth. As you read their informative essay, from *Life* magazine, notice how they compare and contrast these two planets in our solar system.

Oh, what a fascinating walk you could take near the Martian equator next December, in the middle of a summer day. The weather would be perfect—high 60s and a bright orange Creamsicle-colored sky—but shirtsleeves would be out. You'd be wearing a light space suit to keep your blood from boiling because the "air" on Mars is so thin, about the same density as Earth's at 20 miles above sea level. The space suit would help with two other problems—the deadly ultraviolet light from the Sun, and the unbreathable Martian atmosphere, which is 95 percent carbon dioxide, with traces of nitrogen and argon.

The physical act of walking would seem effortless; you could endlessly hop, skip or jump along because gravity is only about a third of what it is on Earth. A 100-pound woman would feel as if she weighed 38 pounds, and a world-class athlete could run 100 meters in less than five seconds. The vista would remind you of the Arizona and California deserts—fine sand littered with rocks and boulders. But the sand would be pink and reddish-brown, because Martian soil is about 13 percent iron, much of which has turned to rust. Of course, there wouldn't be any cacti or scrub plants like tumbleweed, any darting lizards or rabbits. The terrain would be much drier than any desert on Earth, so dry that an ice cube placed on the ground would quickly disappear, evaporating before it could melt, going straight from solid to vapor.

You could walk just about anywhere you wanted on

A LAND OF STAGGERING PROPORTIONS

by
Brad Darrach
and
Steve Petranek

Mars, because the entire surface is land; there are no lakes, rivers or oceans. All the water is underground or frozen at the north and south poles. There's as much land on Mars as there is on Earth, even though Mars is only half as big as Earth and weighs only a tenth as much. Because of its weaker gravity, Mars is not as dense as Earth; it's puffed up. A thousand feet below the surface of Earth you would probably hit solid rock, but a thousand feet below the crust of Mars you would find porous material, perhaps even a gravelly slurry of rock and ice.

A day's walk on Mars would offer about as much Sun time as on Earth; Mars rotates once every 24 hours, 37 minutes. But the summer would last twice as long because Mars takes 687 days to orbit the Sun.

A trek to any of Earth's natural wonders would pale by comparison to what can be seen on Mars. Mount Everest, at just over 29,000 feet, would seem a foothill compared to the Tharsis bulge, a broad raised equatorial plain the size of the United States. On Tharsis sit extraordinary volcanoes, among them Olympus Mons, at 90,000 feet the highest known elevation in the solar system. The mighty Colorado River's cut through the Grand Canyon would seem a drainage ditch next to Valles Marineris, a gorge that would stretch from Seattle to Miami.

You could spend a lifetime on the surface of Mars and never run out of new formations to see . . . Just one thing, though. You would want to get back to base before dark. Most nights, even in summer, the temperature drops to about -125° F.

Think & Respond

What aspects of the Martian environment do you find most intriguing? Why? Give some examples from the essay that show how the authors help you to understand the environment of Mars.

116   Workshop 5

Starting from Literature

The authors of *The Writer's Craft* believe that writing is an exciting journey of discovery where students explore ideas, examine options, problem solve, and share what they have done with others. Every assignment in each Writer's Workshop builds upon these ideas.

Literary and Professional Writing

Each Guided and Related Assignment begins with a model that focuses on a specific writing type or strategy. The introduction to the model presents the writing type to be covered, previews the literature, and sets a purpose for reading.

- **Models** cover a wide range of writing types, from traditional and contemporary literature, to newspaper and magazine articles, to consumer reports and TV scripts. Topics often lead to strong cross-curricular ties, and students gain a sense of how writing functions in the real world.

- **Think and Respond** questions allow students to respond to what they have read and prepare them to begin writing a piece of their own.

One Student's Writing

Thor!
The Wonder Dog?

By Rick Shen

When my mom announced at dinner one night that our family was finally getting a dog, I couldn't have been happier. I'd been listening to my friend Laura brag about her dog, Sam, forever. Sam's parents were national champions. Sam was faster than a Corvette. Sam could leap 10 feet in the air to catch a Frisbee. Sam brought the newspaper in every night. Listening to Laura, you'd think Sam did her math homework too. I decided my dog would do anything Sam could do, only better.

The next day, Mom brought Thor home from the animal shelter. I named him Thor even before I saw him because I remembered from English class that Thor is the Norse god of thunder, and I wanted my dog to be powerful and fast. Mom told us that Thor had been abandoned by his owners and had fallen off a bridge into the river. I guess I should have realized right then that he wasn't going to be the most coordinated dog in the world. But I didn't—at least not until Mom brought him in the front door. I looked at Thor and my heart sank. This was going to be my wonder dog? How was I ever going to face Laura and Sam?

You see, Sam is a golden retriever. Golden retrievers are sporting dogs. You can take them hunting, for companionship and to bring back any game birds you've brought down. Like all golden retrievers, Sam has long, silky, reddish-golden hair, a long tail, and a happy face. Sam always looks like she's smiling. Golden retrievers are great with little kids and make terrific pets.

Thor, on the other hand, is a dachshund, a hound. About all he has in common with Sam is that both dachshunds and golden retrievers are used for hunting. Instead of long, silky, golden hair, Thor has short, wiry, blackish-brown hair. His legs are about two inches long, and his stomach practically sits on the ground. Even with his head raised up, he can't be more than 12 inches tall. Thor looks sort of like a sausage with legs. Dachshunds are also good with little kids, although when Thor howls I think a little kid would get scared. Thor howls because dachshunds don't bark exactly like other dogs do.

When I told Laura I had gotten a dog, she suggested we take our dogs to the park to play one Saturday morning. That's when I realized how else Thor was different from Sam.

Laura threw the Frisbee and Sam ran after it. At the last second Sam jumped up high and grabbed it out of the air. Now it was our turn. I threw the Frisbee and Thor ran underneath it. At the last second, it hit Thor in the head. He had tried to jump up, but dachshunds just weren't made for jumping.

Then Laura asked Sam to sit and shake her hand. Sam did both things easily. I told Thor to sit. Dachshunds don't sit like other dogs. Thor sort of leans over until the back part of his body flops on the ground. Then he tries to keep his front half steady. Shaking hands in this position isn't easy. We finally gave up. By the end of the afternoon, I think Thor was better friends with Sam than I was with Laura.

That was last year. By now I've grown to love Thor a lot. He'll never chase sports cars or catch Frisbees like Sam, although he has learned to shake hands. I guess people will always ask about his funny shape. And I don't let him get anywhere near the river. Thor will never be a wonder dog, but we've become really great buddies, and that's good enough for me.

Is This
How to Choose Right Veterinarian

THE DOG-OWNERS MAGAZINE

Bow Wow

Think & Respond

Respond as a Reader
▶ Do you think Rick's first impressions of Thor are understandable? Why?
▶ Did you ever dream big dreams for one of your own pets? Did your dreams come true?

Respond as a Writer
▶ How does Rick lead up to his comparison of golden retrievers and dachshunds?
▶ How does Rick organize his comparison and contrast?

Reading Student Writing

A student-written paper follows the opening model, demonstrating to students the importance of their own writing and the usefulness of the skills they will be learning.

Student Models

Each student model shows students the importance of becoming invested in their writing. A variety of publishing formats suggests the many ways writing can be shared.

- **Placement** of the complete model at the front of the lesson allows teachers to use the whole-to-part teaching strategy so successful with middle school students.

- **Think and Respond** questions focus on both reader response and on analyzing the writer's technique.

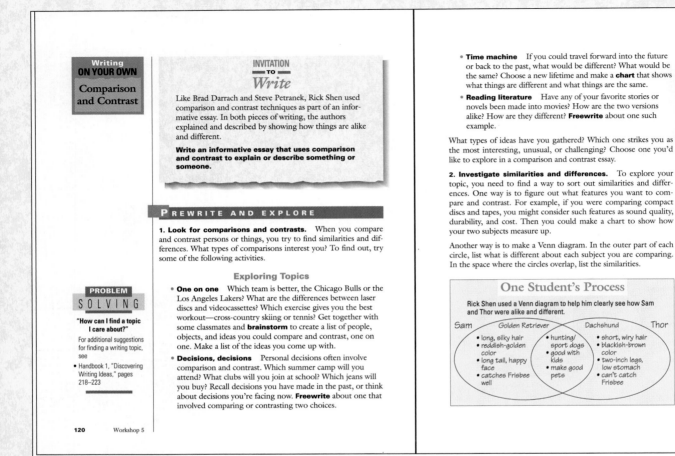

Writing
ON YOUR OWN

Comparison and Contrast

INVITATION
—TO—
Write

Like Brad Darrach and Steve Petranek, Rick Shen used comparison and contrast techniques as part of an informative essay. In both pieces of writing, the authors explained and described by showing how things are alike and different.

Write an informative essay that uses comparison and contrast to explain or describe something or someone.

PREWRITE AND EXPLORE

1. Look for comparisons and contrasts. When you compare and contrast persons or things, you try to find similarities and differences. What types of comparisons interest you? To find out, try some of the following activities.

Exploring Topics

• **One on one** Which team is better, the Chicago Bulls or the Los Angeles Lakers? What are the differences between laser discs and videocassettes? Which exercise gives you the best workout—cross-country skiing or tennis? Get together with some classmates and **brainstorm** to create a list of people, objects, and ideas you could compare and contrast, one on one. Make a list of the ideas you come up with.

• **Decisions, decisions** Personal decisions often involve comparison and contrast. Which summer camp will you attend? What clubs will you join at school? Which jeans will you buy? Recall decisions you have made in the past, or think about decisions you're facing now. **Freewrite** about one that involved comparing or contrasting two choices.

PROBLEM
S O L V I N G

"How can I find a topic I care about?"

For additional suggestions for finding a writing topic, see
• Handbook 1, "Discovering Writing Ideas," pages 218–223

• **Time machine** If you could travel forward into the future or back to the past, what would be different? What would be the same? Choose a new lifetime and make a **chart** that shows what things are different and what things are the same.

• **Reading literature** Have any of your favorite stories or novels been made into movies? How are the two versions alike? How are they different? **Freewrite** about one such example.

What types of ideas have you gathered? Which one strikes you as the most interesting, unusual, or challenging? Choose one you'd like to explore in a comparison and contrast essay.

2. Investigate similarities and differences. To explore your topic, you need to find a way to sort out similarities and differences. One way is to figure out what features you want to compare and contrast. For example, if you were comparing compact discs and tapes, you might consider such features as sound quality, durability, and cost. Then you could make a chart to show how your two subjects measure up.

Another way is to make a Venn diagram. In the outer part of each circle, list what is different about each subject you are comparing. In the space where the circles overlap, list the similarities.

One Student's Process

Rick Shen used a Venn diagram to help him clearly see how Sam and Thor were alike and different.

Sam — Golden Retriever
• long, silky hair
• reddish-golden color
• long tail, happy face
• catches Frisbee well

(overlap)
• hunting/ sport dogs
• good with kids
• make good pets

Dachshund — Thor
• short, wiry hair
• blackish-brown color
• two-inch legs, low stomach
• can't catch Frisbee

120 Workshop 5

Comparison and Contrast 121

Moving to Writing

After discussing the model, your students are invited to write on their own. The detailed Guided Assignments lead students through each stage of the writing process, where they are presented with different strategies and encouraged to experiment, problem solve, and collaborate with others.

Writing on Your Own

A variety of features helps students make the transition from reading to writing.

• **Invitation to Write** refers to the professional and student models and describes the assignment students are to complete.

• **Exploring Topics** provides creative activities to help students find writing ideas they can care about.

• **Problem Solving** notes appear throughout the lesson and offer cross-references to the Handbooks. This provides you with ideas for mini-lessons and shows your students where they can look for additional help.

• **One Student's Process** follows a student writer through every stage of the assignment.

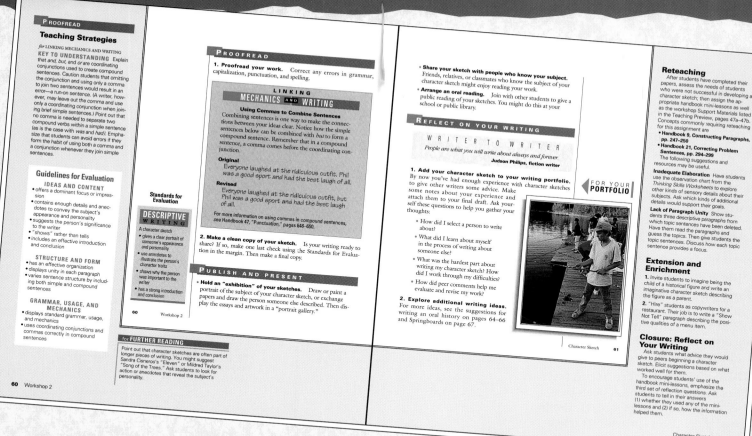

- **Guidelines for Evaluation**
Rubrics for evaluating student papers.

- **Reteaching Suggestions**
Suggestions for providing additional instruction in areas where students were not successful.

- **Extension and Enrichment**
Ideas for moving students beyond the assignment.

- **Reflect on Your Writing** Ideas that help students learn from each assignment and build writing portfolios.

- **For Further Reading** Other readings that are related to the model.

Other Features

Answer Keys Answers or suggested responses to all student activities.

Professional Notebook Quotes and suggestions from experts on teaching and the writing process.

Multicultural Connections Opportunities to broaden learning to include a variety of cultures.

Spice Box Motivating quotes and activities.

Teacher's Lounge Humor from the bulletin boards to you.

Teacher's Resource File

Motivation, reinforcement, creative approaches to writing, and practical teaching support are the hallmarks of the Teacher's Resource File.

Transparency Pack

A wealth of transparencies enhances all of your writing lessons.

- **Fine Art Transparencies** Classic and contemporary art reproductions offer springboards to writing. Worksheets provide writing prompts for a variety of modes.

- **Thinking Skills Transparencies** These graphic organizers can be used to help students find or develop ideas. Worksheets provide practice with each device.

- **Elaboration, Revision, and Proofreading Transparencies** Transparencies and worksheets give students extra experience with three key writing skills.

Guidelines for Writing Assessment and Portfolio Use

This booklet includes evaluation guidelines; models of strong, average, and weak student responses; and materials to aid in portfolio building.

Sentence Composing Copy Masters

These activities provide additional practice in composing sentences based on literary models.

McDougal, Littell
Starting Points for Writing

Another Vanishing Cowboy (1988), Stephen Rosser.

Stephen Rosser (1954–) is an Oklahoma arti... bright colors, bold shapes, and a playful style to... the horror movies and television programs he w... A movie character called the Invisible Man insp... this "invisible" cowboy... realized that he was als... pearing from the West...

McDougal, Littell
Thinking Skills
Problem-Solution

Problem: **What** *Choice: track team or community theater*
Why *Not enough time for both and homework*

Possible Solutions
1. *Choose track*

Results—Pros and Cons
Pro *Lots of friends on the te... May get to go to region...*

...e to earn money for ...ck shoes

...to perform before ...e

...ve to get a ride to ...ing practice ...nly lasts 4 weeks

Informative Writing: Explaining **What**
Elaboration

(1) When you sleep, something strange happens
beneath your eyelids. (2) While your lids are closed,
your e...
sign...
sleep...
plac...
It takes...
90 ...
Your hear...
slow dow...
but you...

Informative Writing: Explaining **What**
Elaboration

The following paragraph is from the beginning of a definition of *REM sleep.*
Use the **Suggestions for Elaboration** to develop the paragraph further by
adding information to sentences or by making up new sentences. You may find
details and other ideas in the **Data Bank**. Write your paragraph on a separate
sheet of paper.

First Draft

(1) When you sleep, something strange happens beneath your
eyelids. (2) While your lids are closed, your eyeballs sometimes move.
(3) The movement is a sign that you are in REM, or Rapid Eye
Movement, sleep. (4) During REM sleep, other changes also take place
in your body. (5) REM sleep occurs about every 90 minutes. (6) It's
during REM sleep that you dream.

Data Bank

■ eyelids closed ■ eyeballs dart ■ move back and forth rapidly ■ as if
watching fast game of tennis ■ occurs about every 90 minutes ■ takes up
25% of sleep time ■ heart rate and breathing often speed up or slow
down ■ slight twitching of muscles ■ body seems paralyzed

Suggestions for Elaboration

- Elaborate on Sentence 2 by adding details and a comparison that shows how the eyeballs of a person in REM sleep move.
- Support Sentence 4 by adding examples of other changes that occur in the body during REM sleep.
- Following Sentence 5, add information telling how much of an average night is taken up with REM sleep.

Elaboration: Informative Writing/Explaining What 9

Writing from Personal Experience
Strong Response

A Perfect Bunt

I've always talked about giving people a chance, but I'd
never tested my belief until one hot, dusty Saturday on the
ballfield near my house. We were choosing up sides for the
weekly softball team, and I was one of the captains. I
noticed a new kid, Raul. He was short and skinny. Let
Daryl choose him for his team, I thought. I want to win!
I chose Luiza, who was fast as a sprinter, Rob, who had
a powerful arm, and five others. Soon it was down to Raul
and Loren. I wanted Loren, but I stopped before calling her
name. Should I give the new kid a chance?
My palms sweated as I thought. *Raul might* lose the
game for us. I had to decide quickly, though. "Raul!" I
shouted, swallowing hard. "You catch."
Raul struck out twice before the ninth inning. Then w...

The introduction establishes the setting and personal nature of this narrative. It encourages the reader to continue.

Specific details help show the writer's feelings.

Paragraphs a... used effectiv... to present dialogue and ... show the next... scene in the narrative.

Subject–Verb Splits: Phrases

Put a phrase between subject and verb to add details about the subject and
give variety to your sentences. Here are examples of phrases as S–V splits.

Model A The other six, two brothers and four sisters, lived with
their parents in a spacious house at 426 Twenty-Ninth
Street, in Oakland.
Frank B. Gilbreth, Jr., and Ernestine Gilbreth Carey,
Cheaper by the Dozen

Model B The boy, regaining his balance, dragged Sounder off the
porch and to the corner of the cabin.
William H. Armstrong, ***Sounder***

Model C Johnny, trained in a silver shop to do such work, made a
bullet mold.
Esther Forbes, ***Johnny Tremain***

A. Combining Sentences At the caret (‸) in the first sentence, insert
the underlined part of the second sentence as an S–V split. Add commas.

1. Mafuto ‸ heard a scornful laugh. He was standing tense in the shadows.
Armstrong Sperry, ***Call It Courage***

2. The voice of a different frog ‸ croaked from the nearest bank. This voice
was hoarser and not so deep.
Natalie Babbitt, ***Tuck Everlasting***

3. A long table ‸ took up almost the whole dining room. The table was
loaded with food.
Norma Fox Mazer, "I, Hungry Hannah Cassandra Glen . . ."

4. Mr. Lema ‸ greeted me and assigned me a desk. He was the sixth grade
teacher.
Francisco Jiménez, "The Circuit"

Peer Response Guides

Students are given prompts to guide them through peer response sessions for each Guided Assignment.

Writing Resource Book

Practice and reteaching exercises are provided for each Writer's Workshop and each section of the Writing Handbook.

Grammar and Usage Practice Book

A variety of practice and reteaching exercises reinforce concepts taught in the Grammar Handbook. A special section of Proofreading exercises helps students improve proofreading skills.

Spelling and Vocabulary Booklet

Ten spelling lessons and thirty-six vocabulary lessons improve student vocabulary through activities and word lists based on SAT and ACT examinations.

Tests and Writing Assessment Prompts

This complete testing and assessment package offers Pretests and Mastery Tests for all grammar, usage, and mechanics concepts. Writing Prompts for Assessment are provided for each Guided Assignment in the text to help prepare students for evaluation situations.

Writing from Literature

Writing prompts designed to accompany fourteen frequently taught literary selections provide students opportunities to practice the types of writing covered in the Guided Assignments.

Standardized Test Practice

Provides practice and teaches students strategies for standardized test question formats such as spelling, vocabulary, usage, and reading comprehension.

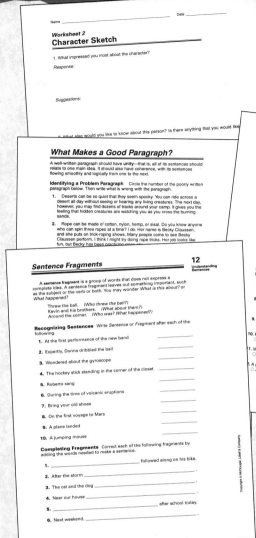

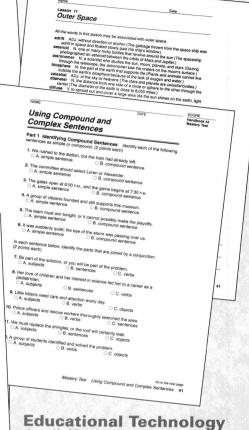

Educational Technology
(available separately)

- *Writing Coach* (word-processing program)
- The *Writer's DataBank* (computer software)
- *Grammar Test Generator* (computer software)
- *Electronic English Handbook* (computer software)
- *On Assignment!* (interactive videodisc program)
- *The McDougal Littell Home Page* at http://www.mcdougallittell.com

What makes my students different?

Teaching Young Adolescents: The Middle Years

Author:

Susan Hynds, Associate Professor and Director of English Education, Syracuse University, Syracuse, New York

Middle school students are, indeed, *in the middle* of childhood and young adulthood. But rather than living in some nether world between the two, they seem to be straddling them. Sometimes they tip more to the side of childhood, at other times to the side of young adulthood. That very quality is what makes them a delight to teach on one day, and an exercise in hair-pulling exasperation the next.

Physically, socially, intellectually, and emotionally, young adolescents seem more different from each other and seem to change more dramatically in four short years than children of almost any age. For example . . .

Physically . . .

Middle school students have three main characteristics: energy, energy, and energy! Just stand in a middle school hallway at the change of classes and feel the vibrating chaos as hundreds of spirited young bodies stream from classrooms, banging their lockers, flying up stairways, screaming at their peers and streaming past their teachers. But this seemingly endless reservoir of energy is fluctuating and unpredictable. The same students who were just screaming and hitting each other in the hallways can be seen a few minutes later, lounging in their desks in a near-catatonic state the minute classes begin again.

Because they always seem poised on the brink of hyperactivity or boredom, middle school students need to be invited to read about, write about, and explore topics that are personally meaningful and easily related to their own worlds in some way. They also need language activities that allow them to get up out of their desks, to switch intellectual gears, and to interact with other students.

Socially . . .

There is no question that middle school students are very social creatures. Often, it's only through the support of their peers that they discover and develop their own personal identities. Their social identities, like their moods, are in a perpetual and dramatic state of flux.

To move from the safe, self-contained classroom of the elementary school to the middle school with its changes of classes and teachers makes young adolescents needy of little touches that say they are cared about and part of a classroom family. If you are a middle school teacher, you know how often you seem to be dispensing paper clips, pencils, hall passes, hugs, and bandaids.

Young adolescents need to belong in another way as well. The friends of elementary school are often quickly forgotten, but middle school students are beginning to forge the bonds of friendships that can last a lifetime. At the same time, they are beginning to think of themselves as members of a society. They are curious about how issues of race, gender, poverty, and crime touch their own lives or neighborhoods.

They are also becoming aware of social and cultural differences. For this reason, they need to be presented with situations that allow them to explore a variety of human relationships and cultural perspectives. Teachers need to invite them to write and talk about these perspectives with others, and to capitalize on their irrepressibly social natures.

Intellectually . . .

For many years, it was assumed that students between the ages of ten and fourteen were beginning to move from what Piaget called "concrete operations" into what he called "formal operations"—basically, that they could think abstractly about themselves and the world. For that reason, many instructional materials for junior high school students were geared to lead students up through the ranks from concrete to more abstract levels of thinking.

Today, we know that most middle school students—indeed, many high school students, and even adults—have not yet moved fully into formal operational thinking in the purest sense of that term. This doesn't mean that middle school learners can't think abstractly. It means that they need teachers who can help them make concrete connections between abstract ideas and their own personal worlds.

A middle school student writing about one of the Greek myths might remark: "He's just a male chauvinist!" or "She's just stupid!" They don't typically gravitate to more abstract comments like: "Greed is a common human characteristic," or "People should follow the spirit and not the letter of the law." Because young adolescents often believe that all eyes are on them, it's hard for them to look past their own viewpoints.

This doesn't mean that middle school learners can't think abstractly about people and events; it means that they need to be invited to think beyond themselves. They need to be challenged with statements like, "Tell me all the reasons that

you believe this solution is a good one," or "Does this historical event remind you of anything in today's world?" or "How could your experience be turned into a story with meaning for everyone?" They need to be led back and forth from the world of concrete, personal experience, into the realm of imagining, speculating, and hypothesizing.

Emotionally . . .

Middle school students are intense! Perhaps because life seems so intense for them, middle school students have a powerful need to be recognized, listened to. They need to have opportunities to perform, to be at center stage, and to express their feelings and concerns. A wide range of writing and speaking activities—journals, songs, scripts, opinion pieces, discussion groups, and storytelling—are all excellent ways for students to sort through and share all of the new emotions they are experiencing.

At the same time, because they are so intense, they have a very strong need for routine. This does not mean a need for boring drill and practice exercises, but for comfortable rituals which invite them to take risks and be creative. They need little routines that say "we are a classroom family, and we do things this way in *our* room." Providing predictable structures for portfolio conferences and writers' and readers' workshops will give students this sense of safety and comfort.

The Nineties: Harsh Realities

Unfortunately, there are many issues that may not have faced us in the days when we went to junior high school. We are beginning to see some of the effects of parental substance abuse, sexual abuse, and domestic violence on the intellectual and emotional capacities of young adolescents. These problems of abuse and neglect know no racial, ethnic, or socioeconomic lines. They are as present in suburbs as they are in cities.

There is also a great deal of media openness which treats virginity as a social disease, which promotes materialism, and makes a life of crime seem like a glamorous occupation. On top of this, young adolescents are reaching puberty earlier than their cohorts did at the turn of the century, and, perhaps regrettably, many of them are experimenting with issues and experiences that once were considered beyond the realm of children their age.

Finally, as productive members of society, middle school students are, quite literally, useless. Years ago, young people worked on farms or in the village when they weren't in school. They were an integral part of the larger social community. Today, although they might be loved, they aren't needed for much of anything. And so, they often become consumers of junk food, video games, or other kinds of mindless diversion.

Teachers need to realize that the teaching of literature and writing can provide a way for students to deal with sensitive or personal issues that may have no other outlet. They need to offer a range of topics for writing and discussion so that students who are uncomfortable with certain subjects can maintain a comfortable distance, while others can be free to explore those topics. Teachers also need to help young adolescents to feel integral and involved in their community and the larger world.

The Writer's Craft invites young adolescents to explore a whole array of personally meaningful topics and issues through a variety of different formats, both written and oral. A host of language activities invites students to work collaboratively or individually, moving beyond their own perspectives and considering the viewpoints of others. Best of all, *The Writer's Craft* invites you to create a sense of classroom community and to give your middle school students the self-confidence to become more involved in the world beyond the walls of school.

Related Reading

George, P. S.; Stevenson, C.; Thomason, J; & Beane, J. (1992). *The middle school and beyond*. Alexandria, VA: Association for Supervision and Curriculum Development.

Hester, J. P. & Hester, P. J (1983). Brain research and the middle school curriculum. *Middle School Journal 15* (1), pp. 4–7.

Johnson, J. H. & Markle, G. C. (1986). *What research says to the middle level practitioner*. Columbus, OH: National Middle School Association.

Lawrence, V. (1988). The teacher in the middle school. *Early Adolescence Magazine, 2* (3), pp. 19–21.

Silvern, S. B. (1990). Connecting classroom practice and research. *Journal of Research in Childhood Education, 5* (1), pp. 85–86.

Wiles, J. & Bondi, J. (1986). *Making middle schools work*. Alexandria, VA: Association for Supervision and Curriculum Development.

accountable for successful group process, for their own learning, and for that of other group members. Options for using grades to reward students for group learning include

- averaging individual scores within each group;
- giving a single score to all group members who have worked cooperatively on a single product;
- giving individual scores plus bonus points for successful group performance and the development of social skills.

Students should share in the assessment process by evaluating their own performance and that of their group. Students may judge that they've been successful if they have met the designated goals of the collaborative learning session. In evaluating group process, they might consider such questions as, "Did I feel supported? challenged? confronted? Were feelings hurt or were ideas shared and feedback given in an encouraging, supportive way? How might we improve the process next time?" Teachers and students should discuss what works and what doesn't work in group process and brainstorm together on ways of improving collaborative learning skills.

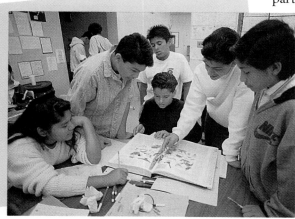

Ideas for Collaborative Learning

The Writer's Craft encourages students to work together in groups to explore concepts and ideas, problem solve, brainstorm, and collaborate during all phases of the writing process. The collaborative learning activities that follow can be effectively adapted for use in the English classroom.

Collaborative planning While students working alone during the planning stage rarely go beyond deciding what information to include in their texts, students planning in pairs or small groups consider the full range of writing variables and keep them in mind throughout the writing process. Developed at the Center for the Study of Writing at Berkeley and Carnegie-Mellon University under co-director Linda Flower, collaborative planning helps students learn to monitor their own learning about writing.

Before students begin to draft a writing assignment, divide the class into pairs or groups of three; have them take turns in the roles of writer and partner, talking through their writing ideas. While the writer talks about his or her ideas for content, audience, purpose, and form, partners help the writer by acting as a sounding board, listening carefully, asking for clarification or elaboration, and suggesting alternatives.

Jigsaw projects Students may choose to work collaboratively on any large or complex project, dividing the assignment into "pieces" and assigning each student to a piece. Students creating a video, for example, could divide the project into such "pieces" as research, scriptwriting, direction, and production. Students would then work together to meld the pieces into a coherent whole.

Learning partners After presenting new information on a topic or giving an assignment to the entire class, have students review the material out loud with a peer, using their notes as necessary to summarize or explain. For example, students could meet in small groups after grammar instruction. They could take turns paraphrasing the new rules out loud, presenting examples of the concept at work, or finding examples in their reading. The whole group can then complete or review the answers to the practice activities together, make necessary corrections, and submit a single set of answers for grading.

Research groups Students may conduct research on a topic and pool information into a written or oral report. Students will need to divide the workload equally, with each person responsible for researching a particular aspect of their outline. Students will join the pieces of information into a cohesive whole; one grade can be assigned to the entire group.

Team teaching Teachers from different subject areas may work together to develop theme-based projects that can lead to student learning and involvement across the curriculum. Because of their scope, such projects are ideal for collaborative learning activities. The Project Files preceding each Workshop in this Teacher's Edition provide detailed guidelines for this type of project. If team teaching is not utilized in a particular school, the projects can still be executed within the language arts classroom.

Are tests the only way to check progress?

Assessment and Response to Student Writing

Authors:

Arthur N. Applebee, Professor of Education, State University of New York at Albany

Judith A. Langer, Professor of Education, State University of New York at Albany

Traditionally, much of the work in the teaching of writing has occurred in the process of responding to and assessing what students write. Teachers have given students topics to write about, and then have spent a great deal of time marking the papers that result—giving grades, making suggestions for ways the writing could have been improved, and correcting errors.

Such an approach is exhausting for teachers —the paperload quickly becomes overwhelming—and discouraging for students—whose papers "bleed" with the teachers' red penciling. Such an approach also works against what we know about the writing process. When students write about topics that have substance and depth, we can expect their work to be characterized by growth and change over time. They will try out and abandon ideas. They will reorganize sections. This is the "normal" state of affairs among the best of writers, and characterizes the *process* of crafting a text.

Response and Assessment

For students to engage in the kinds of thoughtful exploration described above, evaluation—judgments about how well the work has been done—needs to be separated from response—reactions to the paper and ideas for further development that come from an interested reader. This is because evaluation, although well-intentioned, can become too much a focus of ongoing instruction, and therefore inhibiting to students; it teaches them not to take risks, not to try new forms, not to draft and redraft, but to concentrate on letter-perfect work that says little and goes nowhere.

Response is the critical feature in writing instruction; it helps students know what works, what doesn't, and how to go about improving what they have written. The ideal writing environment invites students to engage in exploratory writing and offers response to work-in-process. Evaluation and grades are postponed until later.

Providing Effective Response

Teachers can use a number of strategies to ensure that students receive sufficient and helpful response to their work. The most powerful is the use of peer readers and peer response groups (see pages T32–T33). The following suggestions should also be kept in mind:

1) Limit the amount of writing to which you, the teacher, respond.

Writers need frequent responses from interested readers, but that does not mean that the teacher needs to read everything that is written. Instead students may be asked to share with each other initial brainstorming about a topic, to reflect upon one another's notes and journals, and to respond to early drafts.

These early drafts and explorations have served their purpose once they have been discussed with an interested reader or mined for the nuggets that will become part of later drafts. Therefore, there is no reason for the teacher to read them, too: indeed, the teacher can become a bottleneck and may inadvertently turn students back toward thoughts already abandoned.

2) Respond to work in progress as a collaborator rather than an evaluator.

Teachers can, of course, be very helpful while students are working on their drafts. They can show new ways to solve writing problems, suggest other issues to consider, and offer their own responses as readers about what parts are clear, what parts are interesting, and what parts fail to convince. These kinds of responses are instructional in the best sense: the teacher's suggestions about work in progress can become part of the developing writer's repertoire of strategies and models, available for use in other contexts.

Exploring Assessment

Reader response is certainly the most productive way to respond to student writing, but evaluation is, of course, necessary. Report cards demand grades, and students want to know how they are doing. But there are a number of ways in which evaluation can be managed so it supports rather than subverts the processes of teaching and learning.

Choose criteria carefully. Since writing should be considered a process for exploring ideas and sharing them with others, it follows that conventions of writing should be treated as part of this process rather than as the focus of instruction. It is easy, however, for both writers and teacher to get bogged down in usage and mechanics.

Therefore, to prevent both writers and evaluators from losing track of the key issues of writing, it is important to have clear, consistent standards about what "writing well" will mean in your class. If "writing well" is to mean exploring ideas and experimenting with ways to share them effectively, then students who try to do this should be rewarded with higher grades—even if their experiments lead them to make mistakes. A new and difficult task, completed with some uncertainty, may reflect much more growth in writing achievement than a simple task completed with little thought and no "error."

Use a variety of evaluation methods. In recent years, teachers have developed a number of different ways to formalize their evaluations of student writing. Most of these have been used in the context of large-group assessment, where the concern is with how well students are doing *relative to* one another or to some external criterion. Using such procedures (for example, general impression [or holistic] scoring, analytic scoring, or primary trait scoring) is generally inappropriate within a classroom when used in a formal sense, but can be extremely helpful when used informally to guide teachers' and students' mutual understandings of the goals of the writing task. These methods, however, should be used sparingly and combined with more flexible techniques such as peer response and portfolio assessment.

For those occasions when holistic or analytic evaluations are desired, the Writer's Workshops in *The Writer's Craft* include specific criteria for evaluation of various types of writing, as does the booklet *Guidelines for Writing Assessment and Portfolio Use* in the Teacher's Resource File. Underlying these criteria are a few broad questions that can be used in assessing how well the writing succeeds:
- Is the writer's purpose clear? Has it caught my interest?
- Is there enough detail for me to accept or reject what the writer has said?
- Does the writing carry me through clearly from beginning to end, or are there places where I get lost or miss the point?
- Do the drafts indicate the student is learning to use the responses of readers effectively, or are successive drafts little more than neater versions of the same text?
- Has the writer taken care in the final draft to avoid distracting, careless errors in presentation?

Using Portfolios

Writers vary in how well they write from topic to topic and day to day. Again, this is normal and natural, but we often forget about it when judging how well a writer writes. To offer a well-grounded evaluation of a student's writing skills, we need to examine a broad sample of that student's work.

Portfolios of student work offer one of the best vehicles for classroom-based assessment for two reasons: 1) They typically contain a variety of different samples of student work, and 2) they make it easy to separate evaluation from the process of instruction. Evaluation can be based on the diverse samples of work in the portfolio rather than on the day-to-day progress of an individual piece of classroom work.

Portfolios take almost as many forms as there are teachers and can be tailored to virtually any classroom situation. The major options involve the form that portfolios take, what is included in them, and how they are evaluated.

continued

Portfolio Options

Form. Portfolios are a cumulative collection of the work students have done. The most popular forms include
- a traditional "writing folder" in which students keep their work
- a bound notebook with separate sections kept for work in progress and final drafts
- a looseleaf notebook in which students keep their drafts and revisions
- a published collection of carefully selected and hand-bound work

Content. Portfolios provide an ideal way to illustrate how a student's work has developed over time, and will give students, parents, administrators, and other teachers a much stronger sense of what students can do. Portfolios may contain
- everything a student writes for a particular class
- a selection of "best work" representing the diverse kinds of writing that a student has done
- selections chosen to represent each of the types of writing a student has done during a grading period
- a diverse collection of a student's performance including drawings and illustrations, tape recordings or videotapes of group work, and readings or dramatic presentations of the student's writing
- drafts and revisions
- a selection of finished work, chosen by the student, the teacher, or the student and teacher working together

Students can also be encouraged to reflect further upon their own progress as writers, providing an introductory essay summarizing their work as they see it in the portfolio. Like the reflective activities included at the end of each workshop in this textbook, such reflection can help students become aware of and take control over their own growth as writers.

Evaluating Content. Just as teachers vary in the form and content of the portfolios they ask their students to build, they also vary in how they use portfolios to determine students' grades.

An approach that many teachers have found to be particularly effective is to base grade a selection of work from the portfolio— chosen to reflect the range of types of writing that students have done during the grading period. Students can be asked to select the pieces to be graded, making the choice themselves or in conjunction with the teacher. With this approach, they should be given guidelines for what to choose: a narrative, an expository piece, and a persuasive essay, perhaps, plus an additional piece of their own choosing. The particular guidelines should reflect the goals and assignments in the writing program during the grading period.

The ability to choose works to be graded —rather than being graded on everything—can be a powerful motivational device as well. Many teachers give their students the opportunity to work further on the selections they want to have graded. Returning to these writings at a later point, students often recognize for themselves ways to make their writing more effective, and may reshape them substantially before offering them for evaluation.

The students' own impressions of their work should not be left out of the evaluation process. Young writers should be encouraged to comment on each piece added to their portfolios and to comment on their progress over time. Forms and guidelines in *Guidelines for Writing Assessment and Portfolio Use* in the Teacher's Resource File can help both students and teachers complete effective evaluations of finished pieces.

Weaning students from excessive evaluation. Many teachers who are new to such a workshop approach—postponing evaluation rather than interjecting it into the writing process—worry that students want quicker grades. If they aren't graded, will they do the work? One transitional device that works well in many classrooms is to give points when students have completed each separate part of the work. Everyone who completes a first draft, for example, might get a point, with another for doing a revision. These points can be totaled across the marking period to become part of the final grade.

If evaluation is separated from instruction, if criteria for evaluation are kept consistent with those stressed during instruction, and if response becomes a responsibility shared with students as well as the teacher, assessment can become an effective complement to the process of learning to write.

How do I meet the needs of different students?

Teaching Writing to Language-Minority Students

Author:

Marguerite Calderone, Associate Professor of Education in Psychology, University of Texas, El Paso

Increases in the immigrant population during the past two decades have dramatically transformed the cultural makeup of many American classrooms. Not since the great wave of immigrations around the turn of the last century have English teachers in American schools been so challenged to meet the special language needs of their students.

Few veteran English teachers are likely to feel professionally prepared to operate successfully in a multicultural, multilingual classroom. What follows here are some strategies for teaching writing to language-minority students—strategies that research has shown are especially effective with non-English speaking students but which are equally applicable to all students.

Developing Prior Knowledge

The more experience a writer has with the concepts and terms associated with a topic for writing, the easier it will be to write about that topic. Similarly, the more knowledge a teacher has of the culture and background of minority students, the easier it will be to adapt teaching strategies and writing assignments to meet their needs.

Hold class discussions. Clarify cultural references and provide general information to the entire class. Encourage language-minority students to comment on similarities to and differences from their own cultures.

Explore teaching alternatives. The use of visual aids and hands-on experiences are effective strategies for building prior knowledge and student confidence.

Encourage students to write about their native customs, holidays, geography, and foods. Such topics will be more comfortable for language-minority students. Additionally, the felt-pride from sharing their native culture will act as strong motivation for writing.

Provide opportunities for reading popular American magazines and newspapers. These activities will familiarize language-minority students with American people, places, and events. Television, movies, theater, and similar cultural activities will have the same impact.

Developing Vocabulary and Genre Knowledge

Mastering English vocabulary and patterns of discourse is essential to building writing proficiency among language-minority students. Students who are asked to write about a school or government election, for example, must be familiar with the terms and concepts of the subject, such as *parties, platform, campaign, run-off, running mate,* and so on. Ideally, preteaching vocabulary would become a regular part of each assignment.

Similarly, students who are asked to write a mock political campaign speech will feel entirely unable to do so unless they know what one looks and sounds like. All students should be given the opportunity to read a number of models of whatever type of writing they are being asked to produce.

Peer Interaction

Through group discussion, students with limited-English proficiency can build a repertoire of concepts, phrases, and rhetorical strategies by trial-and-error, questioning, and modeling. Whenever possible, divide the class into small discussion groups. Each group should include at least one language-minority student. Establish a protocol that requires all students to speak within the group. In this way language-minority students will be exposed to vocabulary and rhetorical strategies they can model and be encouraged to try out their developing English proficiency.

Writing in the Primary Language

There is strong research evidence showing that limited-English proficiency students in American schools can make significant progress toward literacy in English by reading and writing for some time in their primary language, making the transition to writing exclusively in English as they acquire English fluency. Allowing students to write in their primary language during the early stages of English acquisition offers the following advantages:

• It establishes a firm basis for acquiring universal reading and writing skills that are easily transferred from one language to another.

• It promotes success, enhances self-esteem, and builds students' confidence in their abilities as readers and writers.

• It enables students to function at the highest levels of their cognitive abilities, unhampered by their limited-English proficiency.

How can writing in languages other than English become a realistic instructional strategy in classes where teachers don't speak the primary language or languages of their non-English speaking students? Following are some strategies for implementing this instructional strategy:

• Encourage students to write in their primary language whenever they encounter a particularly demanding or complex writing assignment. This will enable them to clarify their thinking about the topic even if no one else can read what they've written.

• Have students write in their primary language only during the prewriting stage. Allowing them to focus their topic, generate ideas, and organize their material in a familiar language will lead to enhanced comprehension and increased motivation.

• Seek out individuals fluent in the student's primary language to act as responders. Such individuals might be teacher aides, parents, or classmates who speak the student's primary language but who are also fluent in English. Of course, if there are several students who share the same primary language, they can act as peer reviewers for one another.

• Invite students to translate their own primary language essays. Such translations should not be treated as final drafts, however, but as rough draft translations produced for the benefit of the teacher. Teachers who receive these translations can respond to the ideas contained in the translated essay rather than on problems in English language usage.

Additional Strategies

Following are some additional strategies for working with language-minority students:

• Preview the assignment to spot potential areas of difficulty—with cultural concepts, language requirements, research needs, and so on. Provide preteaching as necessary.

• Read aloud difficult parts of the assignment or lesson, allowing time for questions and clarification.

• Precede writing activities with similar oral activities to allow students to separate the task of clarifying ideas from that of translating them into written form.

• Provide guided practice, especially with prewriting and revising techniques.

Increased, individualized feedback and monitoring will enhance student comprehension and offer support—both of which lead to more successful writing experiences.

References

Calderone, M.; Tinajero, J.; & Hertz-Lazarowitz, R. (1990). "Effective Transition into English Reading Through CIRC." Baltimore, MD: Center for Research on Effective Education for Disadvantaged Students, Johns Hopkins University.

California State Department of Education (1981). *Schooling and Language Minority Students: A Theoretical Framework.* California State University, Los Angeles, EDAC.

Cummins, J. (1986). *Empowering Minority Students.* Sacramento, CA: California Association for Bi-Lingual Education.

Damon, W. (1984). "Peer Education: The Untapped Potential." *Journal of Applied Development Psychology:* 5, 331–343.

Stevens, R. J.; Madden, N. A.; Slavin, R. E.; & Farnish, A. M. (1987). "Cooperative Integrated Reading and Composition (CIRC)." Baltimore, MD: Center for Research on Elementary and Middle Schools, John Hopkins University.

How do I meet the needs of different students?

Addressing Different Learning Styles

People of all ages perceive and process information in different ways. A familiarity with learning styles can help educators develop teaching strategies to meet the needs of all students in the classroom.

The Types of Learners

Research on left- and right-brain functions has led to a variety of theories about preferred learning styles. The left brain is thought to be the center for analytical, logical, verbal, sequential, and convergent thinking, while the right brain is thought to be the center for emotion and visual, spatial, creative, experiential, and divergent cognitive styles. Left-brain students, who have traditionally been rewarded by the educational system, tend to excel in such school subjects as reading, mathematics, and computer programming. Right-brain dominant students tend to excel in art, dance, music, and geometry.

In addition to left/right-brain classification, students are often categorized according to three learning styles: visual, auditory, and kinesthetic.

Visual learners best comprehend and retain information presented in the form of graphs, charts, diagrams, and other visual images, such as fine art and photographs. Often, they benefit from a multimedia approach to learning.

Auditory learners, like visual learners, often benefit from a multimedia approach to learning. They need not only to read it and see it, but to hear it and discuss it.

Kinesthetic learners process information through tactile sensations, learning from activities that enable them to work with their hands or create meaning through movement and physical expression.

Harvard psychologist Howard Gardner has taken the analysis of learning styles and left- and right-brain dominance to yet another level in his theory of multiple intelligences.

The Seven Types of Intelligence

Linguistic	Verbal excellence, reading and writing skills
Logical-Mathematical	Conceptual, logical, abstract thinking
Spatial	Interest in visual images and pictures; designing, building, and inventing
Musical	Sensitivity to rhythm, singing, moving to and playing music
Bodily-Kinesthetic	Communicating with body language; processing information through bodily sensations
Interpersonal	Organizing, communicating, socializing, understanding others
Intrapersonal	Preferring to work alone and being independent, private, and self-motivated

Everyone has multiple intelligences and different styles of learning. However teachers, who tend to be left-brain oriented and strong in linguistic and logical-mathematical intelligences, often teach primarily in the modes most comfortable for them. They may therefore be unconsciously leaving a number of students out of the learning process. Yet how can any teacher adequately address the bewildering array of learning styles that may be present in any one classroom?

With its integrated approach to the development of writing, *The Writer's Craft* helps solve this problem by providing students with opportunities to work in a variety of learning modes. Teachers need only encourage students to take advantage of various learning strategies to maximize their intellectual and creative potential.

Applications in *The Writer's Craft*

Teacher's notes throughout the text point out the following learning opportunities:

Fine Art and Illustrations The art program throughout *The Writer's Craft* provides visual or spatial learners with an engaging and entertaining way into the material. Invite students to consider how the art enhances and reflects concepts in the text, and use the illustrations as springboards to creative writing.

Workshops and Related Assignments At each grade level, Workshops and Related Assignments include a broad range of activities, not all of which are writing based. Visual and spatial learners, for example, will particularly enjoy creating collages, graphic aids, and picture books. Auditory and musical learners will especially like creating videos, writing lyrics, and making oral presentations.

Exploratory Activities Workshops begin with a wide range of Exploratory Activities, providing students with options for entering writing assignments comfortably and naturally. The teacher can encourage students to experiment with the options until they find those that work best.

Graphic Organizers Graphic devices such as clusters, idea trees, flow charts, and pie graphs can be a tremendous boon to visual and kinesthetic students who learn from the physical act of writing ideas, organizing them spatially, and seeing and making the connections among them. Left-brain dominant students can organize their information with time lines, charts, and analysis frames.

Publishing Options The wide variety of publishing options offered throughout the Workshops allows students to tailor their work to their own learning styles. In different assignments, for example, students may be encouraged to include photographs or drawings, build models, incorporate music, or use videotapes, recordings, slides, or photos in a multimedia presentation.

Collaborative and Independent Learning Auditory and interpersonal learners may enjoy working collaboratively to brainstorm solutions to problems, discuss ideas, and share their writing. (See pages T34–T35.) Peer response sessions are also ideal for these kinds of learners. However, each lesson is so complete that the intrapersonal, or solitary, learner can succeed with little help from others.

Special Help with Learning Disabilities

Learning disabled students typically have average or above-average potential; however, specific areas of deficiency (which vary from student to student) make the processing of information and the acquisition of skills more difficult.

Students with learning disabilities often display some or all of the following characteristics:

• Low reading level

• Low motivation

• Difficulty organizing work or ideas

• Poor memory

• Difficulty sequencing and processing information

• Difficulty following directions and completing assignments

• Difficulty thinking, reasoning, and generalizing

• Hyperactivity and distractibility

• Poor fine-motor coordination and handwriting

It is essential to remember that learning disabilities are often physiologically based and beyond the student's control. What can appear to be inattentiveness or an uncooperative attitude may, in fact, reflect an inability to learn through conventional channels.

Whenever possible, teachers should provide opportunities for LD students to process information in their own preferred learning style. This approach will allow them to maximize their intellectual and creative potential in school. The following general strategies, along with any of the alternative strategies described in the section on learning styles, will help students get the most from classroom experiences:

• Seat students toward the front of the classroom where there are no obstructions to seeing or hearing.

• Present essential directions or material from the text both orally and in writing.

• Supply visual aids whenever possible to reinforce material from the text.

• To help students compensate for poor short- and long-term memory, repeat important ideas frequently and begin each lesson with a summary of material covered the previous day.

• When giving an assignment, model sample problems on the board, breaking the process down into clearly ordered steps.

• Encourage collaborative learning. Carefully monitor sessions to make sure they take place in an atmosphere of care, empathy, and support.

• Occasionally pair students according to ability for special peer-review sessions. For example, pair an LD student who has difficulties with sequencing and ordering events with a student who is particularly strong in those areas.

How can I integrate technology?

Using New Technology in the English Classroom

Author:
Jeffrey N. Golub, Assistant Professor of English Education, University of South Florida, Tampa

The idea of using technology as part of your instructional plan is not simply the latest passing fad. Instead, it reflects continuing revelations about what is worth knowing and how students learn. For this reason, it promises to change the nature of classroom instruction.

Why is technology so important? Primarily because the use of computers is not a "spectator sport." Rather, computers require users to do the work themselves instead of passively sitting back and watching or listening to someone else—typically a teacher—dispense information. Thus, using technology enables students to become active participants in their own learning. Similarly, the teacher's role changes to that of a "designer" and "director"—one who designs innovative and worthwhile instructional activities and then directs students as they work through these activities.

Here are some ways technology is being used in English classrooms across the country.

Taking the Fear Out of Writing

In probably their most familiar function, computers offer terrific opportunities for writing because (1) they provide students with more efficient and effective means of drafting, revising, editing, and publishing their writing efforts, and (2) they allow new kinds of opportunities for peer response, collaboration, and sharing.

More Enthusiastic Writers Research has shown repeatedly that students tend to be more fluent and less inhibited when they work at computers: the many editing features and on-line resources make revision easy. In addition, publishing programs allow students to create products far more exciting than words on paper have ever been. Computers can also make portfolio building simpler and cleaner: journal entries, drafts and revisions, and finished products are easy to store, categorize, and retrieve on computers or disks.

Easier Collaboration If you have access to a writing lab, you will find that, with readily available software programs and by networking, or linking, the computers, students can be more easily encouraged to collaborate on their planning and writing efforts. When students can compose and comment on-screen, they often become much more articulate and less reserved.

Making Connections

One of the most commonly heard complaints among teachers is that they seldom have a chance to network with each other and share ideas. Through the wonders of the Internet, this problem has all but disappeared. Education sites exist where teachers can find information ranging from developments in state assessments to projects that have worked well in other classrooms. Through the Internet, teachers can also set up classroom exchanges with other schools across the country, allow their students to go on electronic field trips, and plan interactions between the class and famous authors, scientists, and other professionals.

Developing Information Literacy

The use of technology in the English classroom enables teachers to help their students develop what will become one of the most basic skills needed for the 21st-century—media and information literacy. Students need to learn how to access information from a wide variety of both print and electronic sources; how to select appropriate information from the vast array of available resources; how to analyze and evaluate information that they read, see, and hear daily; and how to communicate their conclusions and insights clearly, completely, ethically, and persuasively. In particular, the growth of the Internet presents students with numerous opportunities to actively seek pertinent information and to engage in the processes of selection, analysis, and evaluation.

Conclusion

These are just some of the ways in which technology can make learning happen for your students. But they help demonstrate that, if used creatively, technology can bring new excitement and high levels of success to any English classroom—even while helping us achieve the same goals we have always had: to make our students solid readers, thinkers, and communicators.

Assignment Chart

Concept Development in *The Writer's Craft*

Varied, real-life writing assignments grow more sophisticated as your students do and provide opportunities for writing across the curriculum. **Guided Assignments** are listed in bold, followed by Related Assignments in each strand below.

Writing Strands	Grade 6	Grade 7	Grade 8
Personal and Expressive Writing	• **Writing from Your Journal** • Friendly Letter	• **Writing from Personal Experience** • Collage	• **Autobiographical Incident** • Song
Observation and Description	• **Describing People and Places** • Cultures and Customs	• **Character Sketch** • Oral History	• **Eyewitness Report** • Field Notes
Narrative and Literary Writing	• **Personal Narrative** • Writing a Poem	• **Short Story** • Children's Book	• **Writing a Poem** • Developing a Script
Informative Writing: Explaining *How*	• **Directions** • Explaining with Graphics	• **Problems and Solutions** • Group Discussion	• **Cause-and-Effect Explanation** • Describing a Process
Informative Writing: Explaining *What*		• **Informing and Defining** • Comparison and Contrast	• **Comparison and Contrast** • Consumer Report
Persuasion	• **Sharing an Opinion** • Public Opinion Survey • Writing for Assessment	• **Supporting Opinions** • Advertisement • Writing for Assessment	• **Argument** • Social Action Letter • Writing for Assessment
Responding to Literature	• **Personal Response** • Book Review	• **Interpreting Poetry** • Focusing on Media	• **Analyzing a Story** • Oral Storytelling
Informative Writing: Reports	• **Report of Information** • Family History	• **Multimedia Report** • Feature Article	• **Research Report** • I-Search

The Writer's Craft

Dear Pat,

We pitched our tent a few yards from a stream, and yesterday I saw two deer come down to get water. Birds like the ones in the photo are all around our campsite. They wake me up at 5:00 in the morning!

Chris

The Writer's Craft

SENIOR AUTHOR

SHERIDAN BLAU

University of California at Santa Barbara

CONSULTING AUTHOR

PETER ELBOW

University of Massachusetts at Amherst

SPECIAL CONTRIBUTING AUTHORS

Don Killgallon

Baltimore County Public Schools

Rebekah Caplan

Oakland Unified School District

SENIOR CONSULTANTS

Arthur Applebee

State University of New York at Albany

Judith Langer

State University of New York at Albany

McDougal Littell
A HOUGHTON MIFFLIN COMPANY
Evanston, Illinois • Boston • Dallas

SENIOR AUTHOR

Sheridan Blau, Senior Lecturer in English and Education and former Director of Composition, University of California at Santa Barbara; Director, South Coast Writing Project; Director, Literature Institute for Teachers

The Senior Author, in collaboration with the Consulting Author, helped establish the theoretical framework of the program and the pedagogical design of the Workshop prototype. In addition, he guided the development of the spiral of writing assignments, served as author of the literary Workshops, and reviewed completed Writer's Workshops to ensure consistency with current research and the philosophy of the series.

CONSULTING AUTHOR

Peter Elbow, Professor of English, University of Massachusetts at Amherst; Fellow, Bard Center for Writing and Thinking

The Consulting Author, in collaboration with the Senior Author, helped establish the theoretical framework for the series and the pedagogical design of the Writer's Workshops. He also reviewed Writer's Workshops and designated Writing Handbook lessons for consistency with current research and the philosophy of the series.

SPECIAL CONTRIBUTING AUTHORS

Don Killgallon, English Chairman, Educational Consultant, Baltimore County Public Schools. Mr. Killgallon conceptualized, designed, and wrote all of the features on sentence composing.

Rebekah Caplan, Coordinator, English Language Arts K–12, Oakland Unified School District, Oakland, CA; Teacher-Consultant, Bay Area Writing Project, University of California at Berkeley. Ms. Caplan developed the strategy of "Show, Don't Tell," first introduced in the book *Writers in Training,* published by Dale Seymour Publications. She also wrote the Handbook lessons and Sketchbook features for this series that deal with that concept.

SENIOR CONSULTANTS

These consultants reviewed the completed prototype to ensure consistency with current research and continuity within the series.

Arthur N. Applebee, Professor of Education, State University of New York at Albany; Director, Center for the Learning and Teaching of Literature; Senior Fellow, Center for Writing and Literacy

Judith A. Langer, Professor of Education, State University of New York at Albany; Co-director, Center for the Learning and Teaching of Literature; Senior Fellow, Center for Writing and Literacy

MULTICULTURAL ADVISORS

The multicultural advisors reviewed the literary selections for appropriate content and made suggestions for teaching lessons in a multicultural classroom.

Andrea B. Bermúdez, Professor of Multicultural Education; Director, Research Center for Language and Culture, University of Houston —Clear Lake

Alice A. Kawazoe, Director of Curriculum and Staff Development, Oakland Unified School District, Oakland, CA

Sandra Mehojah, Project Coordinator, Office of Indian Education, Omaha Public Schools, Omaha, NE

Alexs D. Pate, Writer, Consultant, Lecturer, Macalester College and the University of Minnesota

STUDENT CONTRIBUTORS

The following students contributed their writing.

Alyce Arnick, Aurora, CO; Gil Atanasoff, Kenosha, WI; Jaime Carr, York, PA; Celeste Coleman, Clovis, CA; Kara DeCarolis, Golden, CO; Jason Edwards, Clovis, CA; Ben Everett, Charleston, IL; Doug Frieburg, Lisle, IL; Jeff Hayden, St. Louis, MO; Latoya Hunter, Mt. Vernon, NY; Alisa Monnier, Arlington Heights, IL; Jonathan Moskaitis, Easton, PA; Vanessa Ramirez, Santa Barbara, CA; Dave Smith, Brookfield, WI; Tim Stanley, Las Vegas, NV; Melissa Starr, Houston, TX; Anna Quiroz, Kenosha, WI

The following students reviewed selections to assess their appeal.

Joseph Blandford, Barrington, IL; Janet Cheung, Chicago, IL; Andrea Dobrowski, Kenilworth, IL; Stephen Malcom, Chicago, IL; Utíca Miller, Evanston, IL; Andrea Ramirez, Kenosha, WI; Joy Rathod, Chicago, IL; Debra Simmet, Zion, IL; Elizabeth Vargas, Chicago, IL

TEACHER CONSULTANTS

The following teachers served as advisors on the development of the Workshop prototype and/or reviewed completed Workshops.

Wanda Bamberg, Aldine Independent School District, Houston, TX

Karen Bollinger, Tower Heights Middle School, Centerville, OH

Barbara Ann Boulden, Issaquah Middle School, Issaquah, WA

Sherryl D. Broyles, Language Arts Specialist, Los Angeles Unified School District, Los Angeles, CA

Christine Bustle, Elmbrook Middle School, Elm Grove, WI

Denise M. Campbell, Eaglecrest School, Cherry Creek School District, Aurora, CO

Cheryl Cherry, Haven Middle School, Evanston, IL

Gracie Garza, L.B.J. Junior High School, Pharr, TX

Patricia Fitzsimmons Hunter, John F. Kennedy Middle School, Springfield, MA

Mary F. La Lane, Driftwood Middle School, Hollywood, FL

Barbara Lang, South Junior High School, Arlington Heights, IL

Harry Laub, Newark Board of Education, Newark, NJ

Sister Loretta Josepha, S.C., Sts. Peter and Paul School, Bronx, NY

Jacqueline McWilliams, Carnegie School, Chicago, IL

Joanna Martin, Thompson Junior High School, St. Charles, IL

Karen Perry, Kennedy Junior High School, Lisle, IL

Patricia A. Richardson, Resident Teacher-Trainer, Harold A. Wilson Professional Development School, Newark, NJ

Pauline Sahakian, Clovis Unified School District, Clovis, CA

Elaine Sherman, Curriculum Director, Clark County, Las Vegas, NV

Richard Wagner, Language Arts Curriculum Coordinator, Paradise Valley School District, Phoenix, AZ

Beth Yeager, McKinley Elementary School, Santa Barbara, CA

Printed in the United States of America.

ISBN 0–395-86370-8

1 2 3 4 5 6 7 8 9 10 – VJM – 01 00 99 98 97

Table of Contents

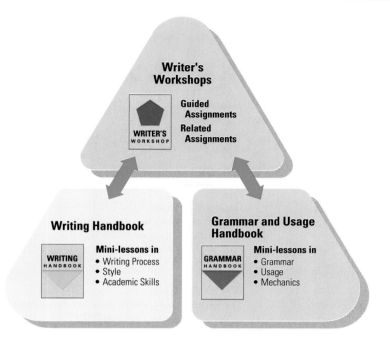

You are special. You think and act in ways that are uniquely your own. This book recognizes the fact that you are an individual. On every page you will be encouraged to discover techniques best suited to your own personal writing style. Just as important, you will learn to think your way through every writing task.

In each of the Writer's Workshops, you will experiment with ideas and approaches as you are guided through a complete piece of writing. Cross-references to the Handbooks will allow you to find additional help when you need it. Then, as you write, you will discover what you think about yourself—and about the world around you.

v

Grammar and Usage Handbook

MINI-LESSONS

The **Grammar and Usage Handbook** presents grammar mini-lessons with the context of writing.

Instruments to gauge student learning are provided in the **Skills Assessment** pages, which include a pretest, a post-test, and four proficiency tests. A standardized test format, like that often found in state assessment examinations, is used for the Skills Assessments.

Each Handbook includes Concept Checks; Drafting, Revision, and Proofreading activities; Applications in Literature; and Applications in Writing.

Exercises focus on writing themes; these themes can become springboards to writing ideas.

xvii

Checkpoints provide a mixed review of concepts and are interspersed after every few mini-lessons.

Additional Practice and **Review** exercises can be used for a variety of purposes: as refreshers, for review, for more practice, or to check student mastery.

Writing Connections enables students to integrate grammar and writing as they elaborate upon, revise, and proofread a draft. Each Writing Connections feature reinforces skills introduced in a specific Writer's Workshop.

Resources that writers commonly use are located in the **Access Guide,** along with tips for reading and writing across the curriculum and ideas for applying technology.

The **Glossary for Writers** contains definitions of key writing terms.

xix

ART NOTE Ask students to look carefully at the wall hanging shown on this page. It is the first of many pieces of folk art from around the world that they will find in this book.

Explain that folk art varies from culture to culture because it usually stems from the crafts and traditions of the particular society in which it is produced. Folk artists often don't even consider themselves artists—or their products works of art since they usually create them as part of performing a function. For example, a craftsperson might create a wall hanging to tell a story, or a bowl to perform a ritual.

This contemporary Peruvian wall hanging by an anonymous artist depicts a scene from daily life in a village near Lima, Peru. Ask someone to locate Peru on a map.

You might ask students to imagine that they are anthropologists, social scientists who study the way people live. Then ask students what they can tell about life in this particular Peruvian society, from the wall hanging. Tell students to base their guesses only on what they see in the illustration. (They may conclude that the people live in a fertile valley or plain near mountains; that they are agricultural people who grow apples, carrots, and potatoes [purple strings]; that the climate is dry [prickly pear cactus]; that they use llamas for transportation; that they live in brick or stone houses with thatched roofs.)

Ask students to think like folk artists themselves: What objects or scenes would they choose for a wall hanging depicting the daily life of their community?

This Peruvian wall hanging illustrates the daily life of people in the mountains near Lima, Peru. The apple, carrot, potato, and prickly pear (fruit-bearing cactus) images represent some of the staples in the people's diet. They use the llamas to transport goods through mountains to the markets in Lima.

Starting Points

D o you write only when you have to? If so, you may be surprised to learn that writing isn't just a way of showing teachers what you know or telling your parents where you'll be after school. Writing is also an amazing tool that can help you in all kinds of everyday situations.

The Writer's Craft will help you discover all the possibilities of writing. It will show you how to use your pen or word processor to sort through your thoughts and feelings, to explore the answers to problems, and even to invent new worlds with words. All *you* have to do is read on—and start writing.

Starting Points

This introductory chapter is designed to help teachers create a classroom atmosphere in which students will want to write and will have an opportunity for initial success in writing. The Starting Points chapter includes the four sections described below.

- **Getting Ready** motivates students and emphasizes writing as discovery and as a source of personal satisfaction. It also acquaints students with journal writing, freewriting, and writing with peers.

- **Understanding the Writing Process** provides an overview of the stages of the writing process. This section presents explanations and examples of the kinds of activities that characterize each stage and stresses the nonlinear and recursive nature of the process.

- **Using This Book** offers students an overview of the textbook. It describes the content of the Writer's Workshops and the Handbooks and also explains how the sections are related.

- The **Discovery Workshop** invites students to experience the joy and personal satisfaction of writing, as they work on an open-ended assignment. In this workshop, students choose their own goals and learn that the content of writing can shape its form, as they experiment with the stages of the writing process.

Getting Ready

WHY SHOULD I WRITE?

Writing can help you with just about anything—from remembering the important details of a conversation to making sense of the changes going on inside you and around you. What's more, in the process of writing you can make all sorts of discoveries about yourself and the world—about what you know and what you might like to learn more about. Think for a minute about all the special purposes you can use writing for.

To Discover

Writing can help you discover what you think and feel. If you have a question or a problem, writing about it can lead you to an answer. If you have a feeling you can't quite pin down, putting that feeling into words can help you identify it. If you've had a confusing experience, writing about it may help you to make sense of it.

To Remember

Are there people, places, and experiences you never want to forget? memories you treasure? Writing in a journal about what you've seen, heard, tasted, touched, smelled, thought, and felt can capture these experiences on paper. Even when you've forgotten the events you've recorded, your writing will bring everything back to you. In this way, a journal can be your own personal time capsule. Years from now, it can give you gifts from the past.

To Explore and Invent

When you write, you can create your own world. You can go anywhere you want and do anything you want—anything you can imagine. You can explore ancient pyramids in Mexico or figure out what an eleven-year-old might do if he could pick up cellular-phone conversations on his braces. You can predict the future, change the past, invent a special gadget—even dance on the moon.

To Plan and Prepare

Putting your ideas on paper can help you plan what you'll do next Saturday afternoon or how you'll spend that money you've been earning by recycling cans. Jotting down a few key phrases or ideas can help you prepare for that all-important phone conversation with someone special. You can even use pen and paper to plan a party by making lists of the friends you want to invite and the foods you will serve. Writing is an ideal way to organize your thoughts.

To Learn

When you're reading or studying, do questions pop into your mind? Writing down those questions can remind you to look for the answers later. When you're reading a book or watching television, do you find yourself talking back to the characters? Why not write down your comments instead? Writing your reactions can help you tune in to what you're thinking and feeling.

Taking notes on what you're reading or hearing can also help you fix the information in your mind. If the information is confusing, writing it down can even help you make better sense of it. So whether you're covering a student council meeting for the school newspaper or listening to your grandfather talk about what life was like during the Great Depression, keep a pen and some paper handy.

FREEWRITING

Point out the reference to freewriting in paragraph 3 and give students an opportunity to try it out. Assure them that their efforts at freewriting are for their eyes only. Then invite students to write for three minutes about whatever comes into their minds, no matter how trivial it seems. Tell them not to erase or stop to make corrections. If they can't think of anything more to say, they can repeat the last word until they think of another idea.

When the time limit is up, suggest that students reread what they have written and underline the parts that they particularly like. Tell them to save their freewriting because they might want to use some of the ideas in future writing assignments.

Everyone has different moods. For example, sometimes you want to be alone, and at other times you want to be around people. In the same way, sometimes you'll want to write on your own, and at other times you'll prefer to write with others. This book gives you opportunities to do both.

Writing on Your Own

Whether you want to explore very personal thoughts and feelings or you just want to experiment with some new ideas and ways of expressing yourself, try writing on your own. In private writing you can take risks and say whatever is on your mind, because no one else ever has to read what you've written.

There are many ways to get started writing on your own. For instance, you might begin by writing in your journal or by freewriting. **Freewriting** is a way of exploring ideas or feelings by writing freely for a specific length of time. The activities in Handbooks 1 and 2 on pages 192–202 can also help you get started.

Writing with Others

You *may* choose to write alone and keep your writing to yourself. However, writing with others as well as sharing your writing can be very enjoyable, encouraging, and helpful. You and your classmates can help one another by

- brainstorming together to find topics
- listening to one another's ideas
- sharing ways you've solved writing problems
- responding, if you wish, to one another's work

Understanding the Writing Process

Every time you write, the experience is different. On one occasion, all your ideas might come out in a rush. Another time, you might need more help getting started. You might need to read, sketch, freewrite, or discuss your ideas with others. Most times you write, however, you will find yourself doing some or all of these activities: prewriting, drafting, revising, proofreading, publishing, presenting, and reflecting.

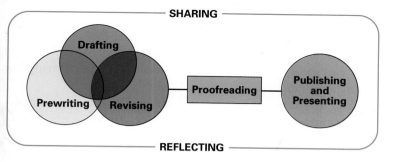

PREWRITE AND EXPLORE

Prewriting is what you do to find your topic and material for writing. You might draw pictures, talk with friends, freewrite, read, or daydream. You might even take a walk or rummage through a cluttered closet. Prewriting is whatever you do to figure out what you care about, what you think, what you know, and what you need to find out.

There may be times when you need to do very little prewriting before you draft. However, when you do want to explore your ideas to discover a topic or gather details, you may find the prewriting techniques in Handbooks 1–5 on pages 192–214 very helpful.

UNDERSTANDING THE WRITING PROCESS

As you read this page with students, focus on the diagram. Point out that the prewriting, drafting, and revising stages are shown as overlapping circles because they can be done at any time during the process and are not three steps that follow one after the other in a neat pattern.

Explain that in the next few pages, they will become better acquainted with the stages of the writing process. Then students will have an opportunity to try out what they have learned, in the Discovery Workshop on pages 13–23.

P REWRITE AND EXPLORE

Invite students to share favorite strategies for finding ideas for writing. Remind them that a wide range of activities, including just sitting and thinking, can be sources of things to write about.

DRAFT AND DISCOVER

Remind students that *draft* is another word for *write*. Tell students that when they are drafting, they are beginning to form their ideas into sentences and paragraphs.

Direct students' attention to the Writer to Writer quotation. Explain that they will see similar quotations throughout the book; these quotations are ideas and suggestions from other student writers, as well as from professional writers.

REVISE YOUR WRITING

Assure students that writers—even professional ones—often draft and revise a number of times as they work on a piece of writing. It is not unusual for writers to draft and revise, then draft and revise again, as their ideas become clearer.

DRAFT AND DISCOVER

WRITER TO WRITER

Just try to write continuously—flow.

**Tonia Lowe, student
Hummlestown, Pennsylvania**

The process of **drafting** involves putting your ideas down on paper. It's a time for experimenting—for trying out ideas and seeing where they lead you. As you write, you may find that a new idea takes you in a surprising direction. That's all right. Just get everything down on paper. Later, you can go back and smooth out any rough spots.

After you finish a draft, it's a good idea to put your writing away for a while. Just a little time away from your work can help you see if there are words or ideas you want to change or develop further.

You may want to share your writing with your classmates—**peer readers.** Sharing the discoveries you've made during drafting helps you enjoy your writing and understand it better. Sometimes you will want to get responses to your writing. At other times you may just want to hear how your words sound. In any case, sharing your writing helps you see your work the way your readers do. You can then tell what's working and what needs changing.

REVISE YOUR WRITING

After drafting, you're ready to **revise,** or improve, what you've written. Usually the first step is taking a fresh look at your writing to see how it's working. Peer comments can help you with this. What you do next, though, depends on the kind of improvements you decide to make. For example, to clear up a paragraph a reader found confusing, you might add information or rearrange your sentences. To make a description clearer, you might add transitions or replace some words with more vivid or specific ones. As you revise, you might also take new directions and make additional changes you hadn't thought of before.

PROOFREAD

Proofreading means carefully checking your writing and correcting any errors in grammar, usage, spelling, and punctuation. The symbols in Handbook 18, "Proofreading," on page 262 can help. After you've corrected any errors, you can make a final copy of your work.

PUBLISH, PRESENT, AND REFLECT

Although you've probably shown your writing to others as you've worked, **publishing and presenting** involves *formally* sharing your finished piece of writing with an audience. In this book you'll find many suggestions for publishing and presenting.

After you've finished your writing, it's helpful to think about what you've written and what you've learned about your topic and yourself as a writer. This kind of thinking, or **reflecting,** may involve asking yourself the following questions. How have my feelings about the subject changed since I started working on this piece? Did I write differently from the way I usually write? How? Why? What helped me to do a good job, and what got in my way?

Understanding
the Writing Process **9**

Using This Book

Tell students that pages 10–12 provide a guide to what is included in this textbook. Have students note the diagram of the three main sections of the textbook. Tell them to note how these sections differ and how they work together.

Using This Book

Think of this book as your own personal writing coach, ready to offer you the advice, support, and direction you need to become a better writer. Like a good coach, *The Writer's Craft* tries to understand your needs, offers you helpful suggestions, and provides you with a variety of enjoyable and interesting opportunities for writing.

As you go through *The Writer's Craft,* you'll find that it is divided into three sections: **Writer's Workshops,** a **Writing Handbook,** and a **Grammar and Usage Handbook.**

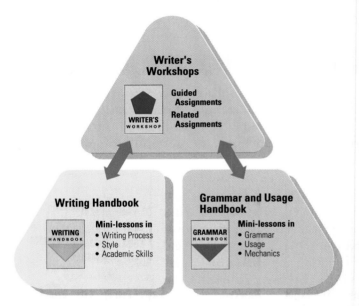

WRITER'S WORKSHOPS

The Writer's Workshops invite you to try many different kinds of writing—descriptions, stories, poems, jokes, family histories. Each Writer's Workshop consists of one Guided

Assignment and one Related Assignment. Special features that appear just before and after each Writer's Workshop—and in other places throughout *The Writer's Craft*—offer additional opportunities for writing.

Guided Assignments

Each Guided Assignment introduces you to a certain kind of writing—personal writing, writing to explain, writing about literature—and then guides you through the process of creating that kind of writing. Along the way, you get to see how a professional writer and another student have approached the same kind of writing assignment. As you work, **Problem Solving** notes in the margins point you to other parts of the book that can help you solve writing problems you may face.

Related Assignments

A Related Assignment follows each Guided Assignment. It gives you a chance to apply the skills you've just learned by experimenting with a related type of writing—a poem, perhaps, or a public-opinion survey. In the Related Assignments, you have the freedom to develop your writing in your own special way.

Additional Writing Opportunities

In addition to the workshops, throughout this book there are many other opportunities to write. For example, if you just want to play with your writing skills, you can turn to one of the Sketchbooks that appear before the workshops. These **Sketchbooks** offer "no-risk" writing warm-ups. To apply your writing skills to other school subjects or to find additional ideas to write about, you can flip to the **Springboards** at the end of each workshop. Springboards suggest interesting ways to use the writing skills you've learned.

Finally, if you like experimenting with words and phrases, you may like the **Sentence Composing** activities. In these activities you learn new ways to vary your sentences by imitating sentences written by professional writers. In the process you may discover your own personal style.

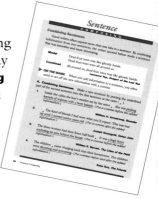

THE HANDBOOKS

The Writing Handbook and the Grammar and Usage Handbook offer the special help and practice you need to carry out the assignments in the workshops. Although Problem Solving notes in the workshops point out when certain handbook sections may be useful, you may also want to explore the handbooks on your own.

The Writing Handbook

This handbook is made up of mini-lessons that offer help and practice in everything from finding ideas and making your writing sound like you to using the library. Literary, professional, and student models show you how other writers use the skills and strategies you are learning. For example, the model on this page shows you how one author uses dialogue in his writing.

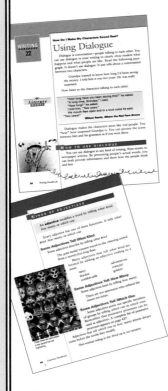

The Grammar and Usage Handbook

When you want a better understanding of how the English language works, the mini-lessons that make up this handbook can help. These lessons explain everything from the parts of speech to capitalization and punctuation. The page shown here, for example, teaches about adjectives.

Discovery Workshop

Maggie Sl...

Whenever you want to learn to do something new—whether it's planting a garden or painting a picture of one—you probably ask someone to show you how to do it. The Writer's Workshops in this book give you that kind of guidance. Each one tells you what form of writing you will work on and offers you suggestions on how to create that particular form.

One of the most wonderful things about writing, though, is that there isn't just one way to do it. In fact, when you let yourself write freely, writing can be a series of fascinating surprises.

In this Discovery Workshop, you'll have a chance to experience writing as an adventure. In addition, from the blue notes in the margins you'll learn how to use the sections and features of the Writer's Workshops that follow.

13

Discovery Workshop

The Discovery Workshop is different from the other workshops in this text, and this difference makes it uniquely valuable. All the workshops allow students to choose their own topics, but only the Discovery Workshop guides students in selecting their own form.

Author Peter Elbow explains: "The Discovery Workshop comes at the beginning for a reason. It provides a writing framework in which a student can start with anything that's on his or her mind, explore the issue, and watch it evolve, so that content ultimately leads to form. Learning to let content determine form gives students an important skill that they'll use in many other writing situations—in this book, in other classes, at work, in life."

As students develop their piece of writing, they also discover the many variables in the writing process. More importantly, they learn that writing can have personal meaning, as they begin to identify and respond to their own goals. Thus the Discovery Workshop provides students with a strong foundation that enables them to approach writing tasks with confidence and flexibility. This foundation can extend beyond the classroom and help make students lifelong writers.

The Discovery Workshop begins with a Student Model. Because this workshop centers on the process of writing, rather than on one form, the Student Model is actually several "discovery" drafts on the same topic. Teaching suggestions offer ways to use the model as a springboard to students' own writing.

The Discovery Workshop can also offer students a chance to see something they don't often experience—you, their teacher, as a writer. If possible, write along with students during this workshop. Share your experiences and responses with them and encourage them to share theirs.

Starting from LITERATURE

Motivate

Share with students the story of a time when you did something because you felt pressured by others to do it. What was the situation? How did you feel about it? How did it end? What were your feelings then? Invite students to share similar stories. (If some of the situations that students describe seem dangerous, you might want to remind them that blindly following the crowd can have negative consequences.)

BUILD ON PRIOR KNOWLEDGE

Ask students what forms of writing are shown on these pages. (journal entry, poem, postcard, story) Ask students when someone might use each form. Encourage them to identify which of the four forms they prefer to use and to offer reasons for the choice.

SET A PURPOSE

Tell students that all writing pieces on these pages were created by the same student, Maggie Skeffington. Then read Starting from Literature with them. Point out the purpose-setting suggestion ("look for similarities and differences") and question at the end of the box. Remind students to think about these issues as they read Maggie's journal entry, poem, postcard, and story.

Guided ASSIGNMENT

Writing to Discover

Starting from LITERATURE

Where do you get your writing ideas? A journal entry gave Maggie Skeffington the idea to write about her first jump from a high board. As you read the different forms Maggie's writing took, look for similarities and differences between them. Why would she have written about the same experience in so many different ways?

The *Starting from Literature* and *Reading a Student Model* boxes give you important information about the professional and student models.

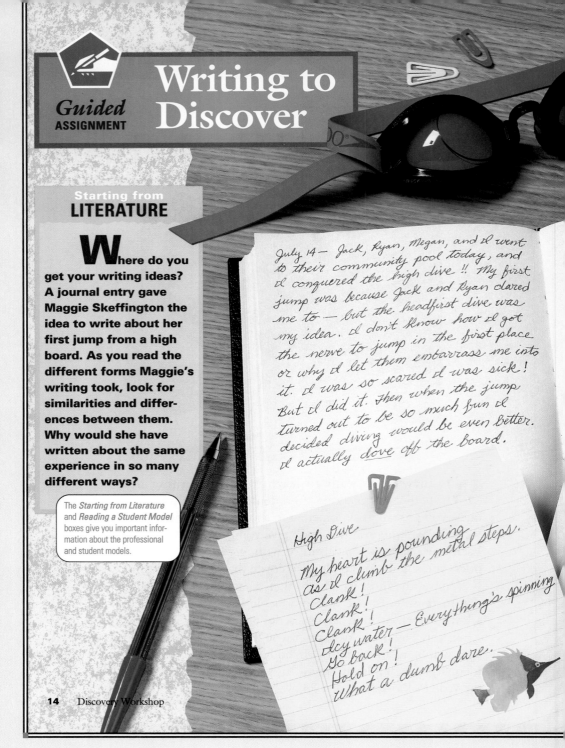

> July 14 — Jack, Ryan, Megan, and I went to their community pool today, and I conquered the high dive !! My first jump was because Jack and Ryan dared me to — but the headfirst dive was my idea. I don't know how I got the nerve to jump in the first place or why I let them embarrass me into it. I was so scared I was sick ! But I did it. Then when the jump turned out to be so much fun I decided diving would be even better. I actually dove off the board.

> High Dive
>
> My heart is pounding
> as I climb the metal steps.
> Clank !
> Clank !
> Clank !
> Icy water — Everything's spinning
> Go back !
> Hold on !
> What a dumb dare.

Maggie Skeffington
English 7
November 3

The Last Dare

"Clank! Clank! Clank!" The metal steps echoed in the cool morning air as I climbed up and up and up. Then, halfway up the ladder, with my heart pounding so hard I thought everyone could hear it, I froze. I was too scared to keep climbing. Would I ever make it home to see my mom and dad again? I wanted to go back down, but of course I couldn't. I would never hear the end of it. So, instead, I stood there shivering, thinking of how unbelievably stupid I was for accepting Jack and Ryan's latest dare.

The day before, my older brother, Jack, and I had arrived by plane in Omaha, Nebraska, to visit our friends Megan and Ryan. Since then, all any of us kids had talked about was going to swim at the Omaha City pool. We were looking forward to spending the day at the pool so much that even this morning's five-minute car ride seemed more like five hours. Finally, though, we challenged and jumped into the icy water. Then Jack and Ryan the next thing I knew, I was standing in line with beside me, explaining how to do a "suicide." I just at him, thinking, I don't have to try to do a All I have to do is walk off the board

Dear Annie,
I'm having a great time. You were right— I had no reason to worry. We're all getting along great. You won't believe what I did yesterday. I went off the high dive! (First I jumped and then I dove !!!) Actually, Jack and Ryan teased me into the first jump— and I was really scared— but it was a blast! Well, gotta go.
Love,
Maggie

POSTCARD

Annie Lee
670 Sheridan Rd.
Gainesville, GA
30506

Think & Respond

Which version of Maggie's writing interests you most? How is Maggie's journal entry different from the other pieces she wrote? Which of these forms have you tried? Would one of these forms fit something you want to say?

Think and Respond questions like these help you reflect on what you read.

Think & Respond

ELICIT PERSONAL RESPONSES

Before students respond to the questions, ask them to answer the purpose-setting question on page 14: "Why would she have written about the same experience in so many different ways?" (Sample: It was an experience that was very important to her.)

As students respond to the first question, have them explain why a particular version of Maggie's writing interested them.

For the second question, ask students to list as many differences as possible. Write their responses on the board. (Samples: The audience is Maggie; it doesn't have the specific details of the story.)

Have students respond in writing to the final two questions. Tell them that these responses are for themselves. If after beginning their writing assignment they decide that the form doesn't work, they do not have to stick with it.

The Invitation to Write creates a bridge between the model and the writing assignment. In this instance, you might remind students that Maggie chose an event in her life that was very important to her. By writing about it in several forms, Maggie discovered more about what her topic meant to her. Then point out that, like Maggie, students are invited to choose topics that they care about and to try several forms of writing as they follow their own processes of exploration and discovery.

P REWRITE AND EXPLORE

Objectives
• To use prewriting techniques to discover and explore a topic
• To identify several possible writing forms

Teaching Strategies

GENERAL NOTE

KEY TO UNDERSTANDING Remind students that the more Maggie wrote about the dive, the more its importance became clear to her. Tell students that the more they write, and the more forms of writing they try, the more clearly their thoughts will come into focus. For these reasons, encourage students to try following all the suggestions in this workshop.

**Writing
ON YOUR OWN
Writing to Discover**

This is an invitation especially for you! It asks you to explore a topic that interests you.

Discover and explore exciting writing ideas by trying the activities in this section.

Problem Solving features help you find answers to your writing questions. When you feel stuck, these features will point you to helpful mini-lessons.

PROBLEM
S O L V I N G

"How else can I find ideas?"

For more information on finding writing ideas, see
• Handbook 2, "Finding a Starting Point," pages 197–202

16   Discovery Workshop

**INVITATION
═ TO ═
*Write***

Each time Maggie Skeffington wrote about her high-diving experience she made new discoveries. Some were about the experience. Others were about herself. Now you have the chance to make your own discoveries through writing.

Write to explore something you care about—an experience, a feeling, or an idea that matters to you. Then see where your thoughts lead you.

P REWRITE AND EXPLORE

1. Find something worth spending time with.   The topics you'll most enjoy writing about are the ones that matter to you, so look for experiences and ideas you really care about. The following activities can help you find a topic.

Exploring Topics

• **Freewriting**   What's on your mind? What have you been thinking about lately? What are you feeling right now? To find out, just start writing about your thoughts. Then, as your first idea leads to others, write more about the things that interest you most.

• **Flash back**   Take a few minutes to look through your journal entries or family photographs. Dig out any toys, collections, or souvenirs that you've saved. What memories and feelings do they bring to mind?

• **Favorite things**   Is there someplace you love to go? The beach? An amusement park? Is there someone or something that never fails to cheer you up? Make a list of your favorite people, places, things, and activities.

2. Explore your ideas. Jot down the most interesting ones you've found. Then talk about them with others, or freewrite about one or two possibilities for a while.

One Student's Process

When Maggie was looking for writing ideas, a short poem she'd written reminded her of the time she conquered the high dive. She then did some freewriting to recall more about the experience.

> I remember that climb. My heart really was pounding hard. Worse, though, was that halfway up I just froze on the ladder. I was too scared to keep climbing, but I knew I couldn't go back. If I had, Ryan and Jack would never have let me hear the end of it. So I just stood there feeling terrified, wishing I hadn't taken their stupid dare.
>
> Talk about your dumb dares. That one was certainly at the top of the list. I'm never _ever_ going to let myself be pushed into doing anything I'm that scared of doing again. I'm just glad everything worked out OK.

In One Student's Process, you'll see the prewriting, drafting, and revising done by a student writer like yourself. Your own writing process may be similar—or it may be very different.

3. Take stock. Think about all the ideas you've just explored. Have you discovered one that you'd like to spend some time with? If not, look at some other journal entries or at some of the items you've paused over, or try more talking or freewriting.

4. Gather details. Once you've found a topic you like, begin gathering details you can use to flesh out a draft. If you've done some freewriting, you may already have a lot of material. Otherwise, you can simply spend some time thinking about your topic or create lists or graphic organizers. For example, you might list the facts or background information you know about your topic. You might also list sensory details—how things looked, sounded, smelled, tasted, and felt.

PROBLEM SOLVING

"How do I find details?"

For information on finding details, see

• Handbook 4, "Developing a Topic," pages 205–210

GENERAL NOTE
HELPFUL HINT Maggie used a journal entry as the basis for her story. Not all students keep journals, however. If you have students who do not have journals, suggest they do an exercise in guided imagery: a mental tour of an event, a game, or an experience, noting details, as if the tour were real. After they have finished their mental tours, they can write about them.

for ONE STUDENT'S PROCESS
KEY TO UNDERSTANDING The One Student's Process feature provides a sample of a student's work at various stages of the writing process. When you discuss this feature, be sure students understand that they do not have to use the technique that is illustrated, but are free to choose other strategies.

The accompanying teaching notes for this feature suggest ways to link the sample to students' own work. For example, you might point out that in her freewriting, Maggie starts by trying to remember the details of what happened. She ends up by writing about accepting dumb dares. Assure students that jumping from one subject to another as Maggie did is fine in freewriting. Among the many ideas, writers can generally find several that capture their interest..

Personal and Expressive Writing

Guided Assignment
Writing from Your Journal

Related Assignment
Friendly Letter

Do you ever wish you could keep track of what you do every day—the places you go, things you see, conversations you have? Do you ever feel shy about telling someone how you feel? Keeping a journal may be the answer. You can discover what you think and how you feel by writing in this safe and private place.

In this workshop you'll keep a private journal. Then you'll learn how you can take an idea from your journal and turn it into a piece of writing to share with others. In a related assignment, you'll have a chance to write a letter to a friend or relative.

27

Links to **THE LANGUAGE OF LITERATURE**

Literature For examples of personal and expressive writing in different writing forms, see *The Language of Literature,* Grade 6:
• Gary Paulsen, from *Woodsong*
• Gish Jen, "The White Umbrella"
• Norma Fox Mazer, "Tuesday of the Other June"

Writing This Guided Assignment may be used as an extension of the Guided Assignment "Write a Poem" on page 564 in *The Language of Literature,* Grade 6.

Personal and Expressive Writing

Objectives

Guided Assignment

Writing from Your Journal To respond to samples of personal writing, to keep a journal, and to use journal entries as the basis of a piece of personal writing to share with an audience.

Related Assignment

Friendly Letter To respond to a friendly letter by a well-known author and to write a letter to a friend or relative.

Teacher's Choice

Use the following guidelines to choose the assignment that best suits students' needs.

Writing from Your Journal This assignment will benefit all students by providing an outlet for expressing personal feelings and observations, as well as an opportunity to learn how a piece of public writing can be developed from personal writing. Have students begin writing in their journals as soon as the school year starts. You may want to have students write in their journals for several weeks before they begin the drafting phase of this assignment.

Friendly Letter This assignment will motivate most students by providing a specific, familiar audience for their personal writing. You may want to suggest this assignment as an alternative when students choose a form for writing in the Guided Assignment.

ASSIGNMENT RATIONALE

Journal writing is one of the most useful forms of personal writing; it helps students develop the habit of expressing and reflecting on their feelings, observations, and ideas. Drawing on material from their journals for writing assignments that can be shared with others increases students' sense of personal investment in schoolwork and reinforces the fact that their personal point of view is of value.

Starting from LITERATURE

Motivate

Ask students whether they think most adults remember what it is like to be a child or a teenager. Then ask whether they have read any fiction or nonfiction in which an adult author captures the feelings of a twelve-year-old. Have them discuss authors they admire for this reason.

BUILD ON PRIOR KNOWLEDGE

Ask students if they have ever experienced a conflict between the way they feel and the way adults expect them to act. Invite them to discuss their experiences. Then read aloud the excerpt from Anne Frank's *The Diary of a Young Girl* in the Literature Connection at the bottom of this page. Have students discuss whether people have more than one side to their personalities. Lead students to see that Anne Frank was able to express in her diary the different sides of her personality. Point out that Jean Fritz recaptured her childhood conflicts in her autobiography (see More About the Model on page 29).

Guided ASSIGNMENT Writing from Your Journal

Starting from LITERATURE

Jean Fritz was born in Hankow, China. She lived there until she was twelve years old, when her family decided to move back to the United States. In *Homesick: My Own Story*, she writes about her last two years in China.

As you read this excerpt from Jean Fritz's autobiography, notice the way she shows how she felt about herself and her name. Have you ever had any of the thoughts or feelings Jean Fritz describes? How would you write about such feelings in a diary or journal?

from

Homesick: My Own Story

by Jean Fritz

I always thought I would feel more American if I'd been named Marjorie. I could picture a girl named Marjorie roller-skating in America (I had never roller-skated). Or sled riding (there was neither snow nor hills in Hankow). Or being wild on Halloween night (I had never celebrated Halloween). The name Jean was so short, there didn't seem to be enough room in it for all the things I wanted to do, all the ways I wanted to be. Sometimes I wondered if my mother had picked a short name because she had her heart set on my being just one kind of person. Ever since she'd written in my autograph book, I was afraid that goodness was what she really wanted out of me.

"Be good, sweet child," she had written, "and let [those] who will, be clever."

Deep in my heart I knew that goodness didn't come natural to me. If I had to

Literature Connection

Students can compare Jean Fritz's feelings as a young girl to those Anne Frank expressed in *The Diary of a Young Girl*: ". . . I have, as it were, a dual personality. . . . I'm awfully scared that everyone who knows me as I always am will discover that I have another side. . . . I'm afraid they'll laugh at me, think I'm ridiculous. . . . If I'm quiet and serious, everyone thinks it's a new comedy and then I have to get out of it by turning it into a joke. . . . I start by getting snappy, then unhappy, and finally I twist my heart round again, so that the bad is on the outside and the good is on the inside. . . ."

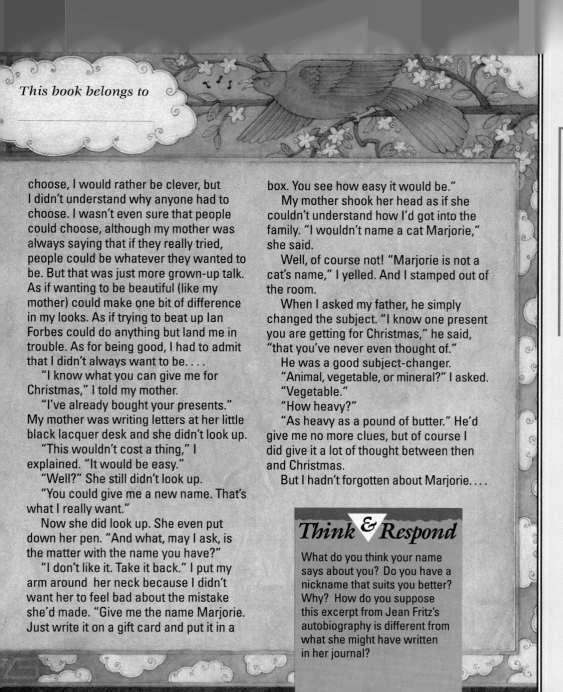

This book belongs to

_____

choose, I would rather be clever, but I didn't understand why anyone had to choose. I wasn't even sure that people could choose, although my mother was always saying that if they really tried, people could be whatever they wanted to be. But that was just more grown-up talk. As if wanting to be beautiful (like my mother) could make one bit of difference in my looks. As if trying to beat up Ian Forbes could do anything but land me in trouble. As for being good, I had to admit that I didn't always want to be. . . .

"I know what you can give me for Christmas," I told my mother.

"I've already bought your presents." My mother was writing letters at her little black lacquer desk and she didn't look up.

"This wouldn't cost a thing," I explained. "It would be easy."

"Well?" She still didn't look up.

"You could give me a new name. That's what I really want."

Now she did look up. She even put down her pen. "And what, may I ask, is the matter with the name you have?"

"I don't like it. Take it back." I put my arm around her neck because I didn't want her to feel bad about the mistake she'd made. "Give me the name Marjorie. Just write it on a gift card and put it in a box. You see how easy it would be."

My mother shook her head as if she couldn't understand how I'd got into the family. "I wouldn't name a cat Marjorie," she said.

Well, of course not! "Marjorie is not a cat's name," I yelled. And I stamped out of the room.

When I asked my father, he simply changed the subject. "I know one present you are getting for Christmas," he said, "that you've never even thought of."

He was a good subject-changer.

"Animal, vegetable, or mineral?" I asked.

"Vegetable."

"How heavy?"

"As heavy as a pound of butter." He'd give me no more clues, but of course I did give it a lot of thought between then and Christmas.

But I hadn't forgotten about Marjorie. . . .

Think & Respond

What do you think your name says about you? Do you have a nickname that suits you better? Why? How do you suppose this excerpt from Jean Fritz's autobiography is different from what she might have written in her journal?

MORE ABOUT THE MODEL

Author Note The daughter of missionaries, Jean Fritz (1915–) spent the first twelve years of her life in China. As a child, she loved her parents' stories about life in the United States and even felt homesick for a country she had not known. Needing an outlet, Fritz began a journal at an early age. At first, she recorded quotations from books she liked, but soon she began to record her private thoughts and feelings. This journal provided material for her later books, including her autobiography, *Homesick: My Own Story.*

---

from Literature box, have them read the excerpt from Jean Fritz's autobiography *Homesick: My Own Story.* Encourage students to compare Jean Fritz's feelings with their own.

Think & Respond

ELICIT PERSONAL RESPONSES

Have students consider the questions in the Think & Respond box. You might ask them to do some freewriting, expressing their feelings about their own names or names they wish they had.

Students may enjoy imagining what Jean Fritz might have written in her diary on the day she asked her mother for a new name. You might ask students to write an imaginary diary entry from Jean Fritz's point of view.

EXPLORE THE AUTHOR'S TECHNIQUES

The excerpt from Jean Fritz's autobiography is full of specific details remembered from her childhood. The details show readers ways in which her childhood was different from that of children in the United States ("I had never celebrated Halloween") and ways in which it was typical (wanting to change her name, feeling that her parents did not understand her, worrying about the contradictory parts of her personality and her mother's feelings, and wondering what her Christmas present would be). Point out to students how Fritz uses dialogue and creates a scene with conflict and suspense, shaping her memories into a good story that will hold readers' attention and move them emotionally.

Reading a
STUDENT MODEL

This student model includes excerpts from the diary of a contemporary twelve-year-old who captured her feelings and experiences so well that her diary was eventually published. In the workshop pages that follow, students will see how these private journal entries could have formed the basis of a short story.

Motivate

Ask students if they have ever kept a diary and if they let anyone read what they wrote in it. Then ask whether they can imagine using any entries from their diaries as the basis of a short story, a personal narrative, or any other piece of writing that they might share with friends.

BUILD ON PRIOR KNOWLEDGE

Have students describe diaries they have seen. They might describe leather-bound books with locks, having designated spaces for writing about each day of the year. You might mention that a journal can be simply a blank book or notebook in which a person jots down ideas, feelings, or observations. Journals may also include drawings, photos, and clippings from other people's writing. Diaries, on the other hand, are usually more like daily records of whatever is important to the writer.

SET A PURPOSE

If your students have entered junior high school this year, have them meet in small groups to complete charts with the following heads: *What I Expected* and *What It's Really Like.* Then have the class discuss their charts. Later, as they read Latoya Hunter's diary entries, they can compare their expectations and experiences with hers.

If your students will not change schools until next year, have them discuss just their expectations, comparing them with Latoya's.

One Student's Writing

Reading a
STUDENT MODEL

Writers sometimes keep their journals and diaries private. At other times, though, writers want to share the experiences they've written about. Twelve-year-old Latoya Hunter revised and published the diary she kept during her first year in junior high school. As you read these excerpts from *The Diary of Latoya Hunter: My First Year in Junior High School*, ask yourself whether you have ever had the kinds of experiences Latoya writes about.

September 10, 1990
Dear Diary, It is hard to believe that this is the day have anticipated and looked forward to for such a long tim . . . This may sound funny but somewhere in the back of m mind I thought the world would stop for my first day J[unior] H[igh]. The day proved me wrong and I've grown t realize that nothing will be quite as I dreamed [it]. . . .

Diary, there isn't much of a welcoming committee at th school. However, there's a day eighth and ninth graders s out to show freshmen how they feel about us. They call Freshman Day. It may sound sweet but it's not at all. Wh they set out to do is terrorize us. They really seem to want hurt us. It's a tradition I guess. I hope with God's help tha I'll be able to make it through without any broken bones. . .

September 11, 1990
Dear Diary, I never thought I'd get desperate enoug to say this but I envy you. . . . You don't have to go to J.H and watch the clock, praying for dismissal time to come. Yc also don't have to go through a situation like sitting in cafeteria watching others laughing and talking and you do know anyone. To sit there and eat the food that is ju terrible because there's nothing else to do.

You don't do any of those things. All you do is listen pathetic twelve-year-olds like me tell you about it.

I guess you can tell how my day went. Diary, what am going to do? My best friend left to go to another school. wish she could be with me. We had so much fun togethe

12

MORE ABOUT THE MODEL

When Latoya Hunter's class at P.S. 94 in the Bronx graduated from the sixth grade, the event was described in an article in *The New York Times*. An editor at a publishing company read the article and was struck by Latoya's teacher's praise of the girl's "incredible writing talent." The editor got in touch with the teacher to ask if Latoya would be interested in keeping a diary of her first year at junior high school. Latoya was willing, and her diary was published in 1992.

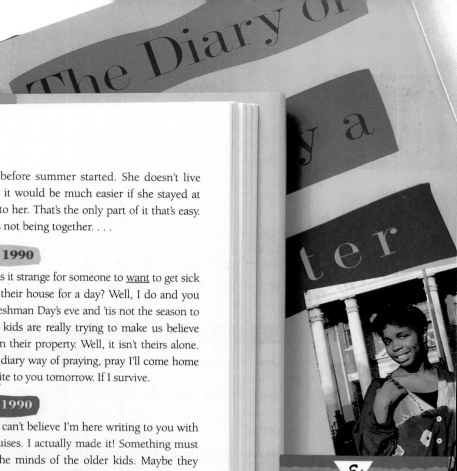

...e moved right before summer started. She doesn't live ...ywhere close so it would be much easier if she stayed at ...e school closest to her. That's the only part of it that's easy. ...e hardest part is not being together. . . .

...ptember 13, 1990

...ar Diary, Is it strange for someone to <u>want</u> to get sick ...they can't leave their house for a day? Well, I do and you ...ow why—it's Freshman Day's eve and 'tis not the season to ...jolly. The older kids are really trying to make us believe ...'re trespassing on their property. Well, it isn't theirs alone. ...here is a special diary way of praying, pray I'll come home ...one piece. I'll write to you tomorrow. If I survive.

...ptember 14, 1990

...ar Diary, I can't believe I'm here writing to you with ...scratches or bruises. I actually made it! Something must ...ve snapped in the minds of the older kids. Maybe they ...nembered when they were freshmen themselves because ...re were only a few fights today. . . .

In the morning, Mr. Gluck, the principal, announced ...t if anyone even thought of touching us it would mean ...spension. Maybe that was why this Freshman Day was so ...ch calmer. Whatever [the] reason why, I appreciate it.

Well Diary, what I assume was the worst week of J.H. is ...er. I hope things will get better next week. It has to. It ...'t get any worse . . . or can it?

13

Think & Respond

Respond as a Reader
▶ Why do you think Latoya wrote about Freshman Day more than once?

▶ Why do you think Latoya calls her diary "you," as if it were a real person?

Respond as a Writer
▶ What do you think Latoya might have learned by keeping a diary?

▶ Latoya knew that other people would read her diary. How do you think that might have affected her writing?

Think & Respond

RESPOND AS A READER
▶ Freshman Day was on Latoya's mind for several days. Have students point out details that show how worried she was.

▶ Students who have kept diaries may be able to explain that writing in a diary is like talking to a close friend. Tell students that some diary writers even give their diaries a person's name; Anne Frank called her diary "Kitty."

RESPOND AS A WRITER
▶ Students might say that Latoya learned to describe and to reflect on her feelings. To help them consider other benefits of diary writing, students should try to imagine how Latoya might react if, later in the school year, she reread her entries for this week. (Sample: She might be surprised at how worried and unhappy she had been at the time.) Ask what people can learn by looking back at their personal writing later on. (Samples: how to keep things in perspective, how experience and time affect how you feel)

▶ Students may say that Latoya might have left out incidents that were too personal or embarrassing, that she might not have expressed all her negative feelings about people, or that she might have been more careful about her language and grammar.

Word Puzzles

If you have ever eaten a sausage, onion, mushroom, green pepper, olive, and pepperoni pizza, you probably know what this is:

> **everything**
> **pizza**

Since *everything* is sitting on top of *pizza,* this word puzzle says "pizza with everything on it."

Now see if you can figure out what popular phrase or expression each of these word puzzles says. Try inventing some of your own and sharing them with friends.

> **league**

> **every   right   thing**

> R
> G rosie I
> N

> ```
>     T   M
>   A       U
>   H       S
> W         T
> ```

> **new leaf** *(printed upside down)*

> **wear**
> **long**

> ```
> F            F
> R            R
> I            I
> E  standing  E
> N    miss    N
> D            D
> S            S
> ```

Answers: Little League; right in the middle of everything; ring around the rosie; what goes up must come down; misunderstanding between friends; turn over a new leaf; long underwear.

Students might enjoy collaborating on a book of these and other word puzzles. Encourage them to submit their puzzles for publication in a school or local newspaper or to include them in their letters to friends.

Imitating Sentences

Objectives
- To analyze sentences by dividing them into meaningful "chunks"
- To recognize sentences with similar patterns
- To implement the techniques of professional writers through sentence imitation

Teaching Strategies

for CHUNKING SENTENCE PARTS

SPEAKING AND LISTENING To help students identify the correctly chunked sentences, ask volunteers to read each pair of choices aloud, pausing slightly at the slash marks. Have listeners decide which version is easier to understand. Afterward, lead students to see that a sentence part set off by commas usually makes up a single chunk.

Additional Resource

Sentence Composing Copy Masters, pp. 1–2

Answer Key
A. Chunking Sentence Parts
1. b
2. b
3. a
4. b

Imitating Sentences

Life would be boring if you did the same things every day. Likewise, writing can be boring if you write every sentence the same way. You can learn new ways to vary your sentences by imitating sentences written by professional writers. Notice how each sentence in the description below is different.

Model A	The sword Dyrnwyn, blazing white with flame, leaped from Taran's hand and fell beyond his reach.
Model B	The Horned King stood over Taran.
Model C	With a cry, Eilonwy sprang at the antlered man.
Model D	Snarling, the giant Horned King tossed her aside.

Lloyd Alexander, *The Book of Three*

▶ **ON THE MARK** Use commas to set off information that breaks up the flow of a sentence.

A. Chunking Sentence Parts   People read and write sentences in meaningful "chunks." That is, they break down sentences into groups of words that work together. Choose the sentence in each pair below that is divided into chunks of words that work together.

1. a. The sword / Dyrnwyn, blazing white with / flame, leaped from Taran's / hand and fell beyond his reach.
 b. The sword Dyrnwyn, / blazing white with flame, / leaped from Taran's hand / and fell beyond his reach.

2. a. The Horned / King stood over / Taran.
 b. The Horned King / stood / over Taran.

3. a. With a cry, / Eilonwy sprang / at the antlered man.
 b. With a / cry, Eilonwy sprang at the antlered / man.

4. a. Snarling, the / giant Horned / King tossed her aside.
 b. Snarling, / the giant Horned King / tossed her aside.

B. Identifying Imitations Divide the sentences below into chunks. Then decide which sentences have chunks that match the models on page 46.

1. Choose the sentence that imitates Model A.
   a. Crashing over the rocks, the raft bounced and swirled as it sped through the rapids.
   b. My brother Bob, smiling broadly with pride, crossed over the finish line and waved to the crowd.

2. Choose the sentence that imitates Model B.
   a. The third baseman walked toward home plate.
   b. The dog and cat, usually enemies, became friends.

3. Choose the sentence that imitates Model C.
   a. In a flash, the horses bolted from the starting gate.
   b. The toddler peered up with a cute grin, charming everyone.

4. Choose the sentence that imitates Model D.
   a. As the game ended, the fans ran out onto the court.
   b. Diving, the shortstop snared the line drive.

C. Writing Imitations Break each of the following model sentences from *The Book of Three* by Lloyd Alexander into meaningful chunks. Then write your own sentences made up of chunks that imitate the structure of the chunks in each model.

1. She unstrung the bow and picked up the arrows she had dropped.

2. To save his energy, he lay down on the straw and tried to relax.

3. He clambered easily to the top and perched there like an enormous crow, scanning the land in the direction they had traveled.

Grammar Refresher To learn more about sentence parts and how they work together, see Handbook 34, "Understanding Sentences," pages 338–373.

B. Identifying Imitations
Chunks may vary slightly but should represent logical sentence divisions. The asterisked items are the ones that match the models.

1a. Crashing over the rocks, / the raft bounced and swirled / as it sped through the rapids.
*1b. My brother Bob, / smiling broadly with pride, / crossed over the finish line / and waved to the crowd.
*2a. The third baseman / walked / toward home plate.
2b. The dog and cat, / usually enemies, / became friends.
*3a. In a flash, / the horses bolted / from the starting gate.
3b. The toddler peered up / with a cute grin, / charming everyone.
4a. As the game ended, / the fans ran out / onto the court.
*4b. Diving, / the shortstop / snared the line drive.

C. Writing Imitations
Chunks may vary slightly but should represent logical sentence divisions. Imitative sentences will vary as well but should follow the basic pattern.

1. She unstrung the bow / and picked up the arrows / she had dropped.
2. To save his energy, / he lay down on the straw / and tried to relax.
3. He clambered easily to the top / and perched there like an enormous crow, / scanning the land / in the direction they had traveled.

2
Observation and Description

Teaching Preview

Overview

Observation and description skills provide a solid foundation for informative, narrative, and persuasive writing. In this workshop students sharpen their powers of observation and learn to choose details that show, rather than tell, what they have observed. Workshop 2 includes the following Guided Assignment and Related Assignment, as well as the interdisciplinary project described on pages 47c–47d.

1. Guided: Describing People and Places calls on students to closely observe a person or place and then choose precise sensory details, examples, and comparisons to bring the subject to life for readers. This assignment encourages students to make judgments about their main impression of a subject, to select details that support their impression, and to classify and organize those details in an effective way.

2. Related: Culture and Customs invites students to observe and share details of an ethnic or religious tradition and to explain the custom's significance.

Preparation Guide

1. Use the Overview on this page and the Teacher's Choice descriptions on page 49 to decide which assignments to teach.

2. Preview the assignments and the teacher's notes and identify concepts that may require preteaching or extra support.

3. Preview the chart below for support materials in the Teacher's Resource File that may be used with this Workshop. Resources are for use with the Guided Assignment unless otherwise noted.

Support Materials

WRITER'S CRAFT RESOURCES

Prewrite and Explore
Thinking Skills Worksheets, pp. 1, 9
Thinking Skills Transparencies, pp. 1–1a, 9–9a
Writing Resource Book, pp. 3–4

Draft and Discover
Elaboration, Revision, and Proofreading Practice, pp. 3, 17–19
Elaboration, Revision, and Proofreading Transparencies, pp. 5–6, 31–34
Writing Resource Book, pp. 5–7

Revise Your Writing
Elaboration, Revision, and Proofreading Practice, pp. 4, 17–19
Elaboration, Revision, and Proofreading Transparencies, pp. 7–8, 31–34
Guidelines for Writing Assessment and Portfolio Use, pp. 15, 25–27
Peer Response Guides, pp. 9–10
Writing Resource Book, p. 8

Assessment
Tests and Writing Assessment Prompts, p. 2

Extension Activities
Sentence Composing Copymasters, pp. 3–4
Starting Points for Writing, pp. 27–30, 37, 39
Writing from Literature, pp. 1–2, 9–10, 13–14, 17–20, 25–26
Standardized Test Practice

 Educational Technology
(available separately)
Writing Coach
Writer's DataBank
Electronic English Handbook
On Assignment! (videodisc)
The McDougal Littell Home Page at http://www.mcdougallittell.com

• •

OTHER RESOURCES

Books and Journals
Cisneros, Sandra. *The House on Mango Street.* Arte Publico, 1985.
Gustaffson, J. "Design a Character." *Reading Teacher.* 44 (Sept. 1990): 86–87.

 Films and Videos
Pool Party. Fast Forward/Gary Soto, 1992.

Educational Technology
"Character Sketch/Language Delight." *Write On! Series.* Humanities Software, Apple.
Rain Forest. Image Entertainment. (videodisc).
Where in the World Is Carmen Sandiego? Broderbund. PC, PC/CD-ROM.

Linking Literature, Writing, and Grammar

The following options may be used to provide students with an integrated language experience. Begin by assigning and discussing any of the recommended pieces of literature. Use the suggested strategy to provide a link to the Guided Assignment.

LINKING LITERATURE AND WRITING

Option 1

Starting Point: "The Monkey Garden" by Sandra Cisneros on pages 50–51 of *The Writer's Craft*.

Strategy: Use the teaching suggestions on pages 50–51 to lead students into the Guided Assignment.

Option 2

Starting Point: "Ibrahima" by Walter Dean Myers on pages 257–267 of McDougal Littell's *The Language of Literature*, Grade 6. (Additional suggestions for using *The Language of Literature* can be found on page 49.)

Strategy: Have students read the biographical selection. Then ask them to describe their main impressions of Ibrahima and his African homeland. Have them find descriptive details that support their impressions. Use the discussion to introduce the Guided Assignment.

Option 3

Starting Point: "A Backwoods Boy" by Russell Freedman.

Strategy: Have students read the biographical selection. Ask what impression of Lincoln the biography gave them and what details Freedman used to create that impression. Use the discussion to introduce the Guided Assignment.

LINKING WRITING AND GRAMMAR

Before the drafting or revision stages of this assignment, tell students that when they describe people and places, they may want to combine several descriptive details in one sentence. Write the following sentences on the board and ask how students might combine them in one sentence.

My Uncle Jeff is muscular. He is very tanned. He is also as tall as a mountain.

Show how the sentences could be combined, using a series of adjectives. Point out the commas that are needed to separate items in a series.

My Uncle Jeff is muscular, very tanned, and as tall as a mountain.

Suggest that students occasionally use a series of adjectives, verbs, or nouns in their descriptions.

Go over pages 574–580 of the Grammar and Usage Handbook. If problems in using commas persist, assign the exercises on those pages for reteaching. Additional practice can be found in the *Grammar and Usage Practice Book* on page 96.

Management Guidelines

The chart below indicates the number of days recommended for each phase of the Guided and Related Assignments. These numbers are an estimate of the total time needed for each phase. In practice, of course, students may not complete each phase in one continuous session, nor will they necessarily progress from stage to stage in the linear order shown here. Stars indicate portions of the assignment that may be completed outside the classroom if time is limited or if teachers wish students to work independently.

WRITING FROM PERSONAL EXPERIENCE

Starting from Literature .... 1 day
Prewrite and Explore .... 1–2 days
Draft and Discover .... 2 days*
Revise Your Writing .... 1 day*
Proofread .... 1 day*
Publish and Present .... 1 day
Reflect on Your Writing .... 1 day
Extension and Enrichment .... open*

CULTURE AND CUSTOMS

Exploring Customs .... 1–2 days*
Describing a Custom .... 2 days*
Reviewing Your Writing .... 1 day*
Publishing and Presenting .... 2–3 days
Sentence Composing .... open*

Project File

Celebrating Diversity: An International Fair

Overview

In this project, students will choose cultures to study in depth. They will then organize an international fair to present aspects of the cultures they have investigated. During the course of the project, students will learn about and come to appreciate many different cultures.

Students will participate in the following activities:

- Choose a culture and study it in depth
- Write a description of a specific aspect of a culture
- Create an exhibit presenting an important aspect of a culture they have studied
- Plan and put on an international fair
- Use language arts, science, social studies, math, and art skills to complete their research and develop materials

Preparation Guide

Tell students that appreciating and understanding cultural variety can make the difference between peace and conflict both in world politics and in interactions with neighbors. Students should understand that the term *culture* refers to all the elements—including traditions, customs, arts, crafts, and ways of life—that characterize a group of people.

Tell students that by presenting an international fair, they will learn more about their own cultures and those of others.

Stage 1
Explore Ideas

1. Invite students to discuss ethnic fairs they have attended or heard about. Encourage them to recall the kinds of exhibits and activities featured.

2. Propose that students organize an international fair. Ask students to brainstorm lists of the aspects of cultures that interest them most. They might list such items as the following:
   - toys and handicrafts
   - foods and customs related to food
   - songs, dances, and music
   - games, stories, plays, and books
   - clothing
   - holiday traditions
   - fine arts
   - interpretations of natural phenomena
   - famous people

3. Have students share customs and traditions from their own backgrounds with the class.

TEAM TEACHING

The following activities may be used for team teaching or as enrichment and extension activities by the language arts teacher.

Social Studies Have students investigate how historians and other scholars study cultures. Have them read books about cultures and study how museum exhibits are put together (see *Resources, Stage 1*).

Math Estimate how many people will attend the fair and calculate the approximate area needed. Study math tools, like the abacus, that are used by specific cultures.

Language Arts Read stories about cultural traditions and customs.

TEACHING TIPS

- Plan for the class to attend a local ethnic fair or an "international" picnic or field day held by a student-exchange organization such as the American Field Service (see *Resources, Stage 1*).

- Invite exchange students to speak to the class about their countries and cultures.
- Encourage students both to explore their own cultural heritages and to investigate cultures they know little about.

Stage 2
Research and Describe Cultures

1. Tell students to form groups and to choose the cultures they will present at the fair.

2. Direct the groups to research their chosen cultures in preparation for the fair, focusing specifically on the subjects of the exhibits they wish to develop, such as foods, crafts, costumes, and music (see *Resources, Stage 2*).

3. Have students write detailed descriptions of the exhibits they are planning.

TEAM TEACHING

Science Learn how traditions such as harvest and food-storage customs relate to the ecology of a specific area. Explore the nutritional values of traditional foods. Study holidays and traditions linked to solstices and equinoxes.

Social Studies Investigate the history, geography, and climate of a country or cultural area. Learn about daily life, religion, and customs.

Art Examine the fine arts of a particular culture. Learn about traditional costumes and find or create costumes for the exhibits.

Music Learn traditional songs and dances and prepare to perform them at the fair (see *Resources, Stage 2*).

Language Arts Learn descriptive-writing skills (see *Resources, Stage 2*).

TEACHING TIPS

- This project could involve a number of classes or perhaps the whole school.

- **Illustrate your description.** Re-create your subject in a sketch, painting, or sculpture. Then, on a bulletin board or in a special area of your classroom, display your artwork beside your written description.

- **Submit your description to a local newspaper.** Neighborhood newspapers often publish articles about special local people and places. So if you have described a person or a place in your community, consider submitting your description to the local paper.

Mt. Fuji, with an elevation of 12,388 feet, is the highest mountain in Japan.

REFLECT ON YOUR WRITING

WRITER TO WRITER

If you can first get away from worrying about spelling and following grammar rules, you'll find that your imagination is free to write.

Paul Zindel, novelist

1. Add your writing to your portfolio.   In a note to yourself, jot down what you've learned in writing your description. Then attach your note to the final copy of your description. Thinking about the following questions may help you focus your thoughts:

- What did I notice or realize about my subject that I had never noticed or realized before?
- Did my attitude toward my subject change? If so, how?
- What would I have liked to get across more vividly?
- What helped me the most in doing this assignment? What got in my way?

2. Explore additional ideas.   See the suggestions for writing a description of a cultural custom on pages 64–66 and Springboards on page 67.

FOR YOUR
PORTFOLIO

Describing People and Places   **61**

Reteaching

After students have completed their papers, assess the needs of students who were not successful in developing an effective description; then assign the appropriate handbook mini-lessons as well as the Workshop Support Materials listed in the Teaching Preview, pages 47a–47b. Concepts commonly requiring reteaching for this assignment are:

- **Handbook 11, Show, Don't Tell, pp. 239–242**
- **Handbook 19, Appealing to the Senses, pp. 266–273**

The following suggestions and resources also may be useful.

Weak Beginnings Locate in books or stories several introductory paragraphs that begin with vivid descriptions. Read each of these introductions aloud and have students explain what main impression they get and what details help them see the scene or the person.

Lack of Specific Details Have students use the Observation Chart from the *Thinking Skills Worksheets* to list details about their topics. Students working in pairs should ask each other questions and make suggestions that will flesh out their topics.

Extension and Enrichment

1. Ask students to imagine that they are entering a magazine contest. To win, they must describe their dream rooms in two hundred words or less.

2. Challenge students to describe a familiar object so that it can be identified without being named. Have students read their descriptions aloud to find out whether their classmates can guess the object.

Closure: Reflect on Your Writing

Have students meet in small groups to discuss their answers to the questions before writing them down. Encourage students to also discuss how working with peer readers helped them revise their drafts.

Related ASSIGNMENT

Starting from LITERATURE

Objectives
- To respond to and analyze a piece of writing that describes a culture and its customs
- To create a piece of descriptive writing about a culture and its customs

Motivate
Before directing students to read Starting from Literature, ask them to name their favorite holiday and tell why they like it. Encourage students to describe favorite holidays from their family's cultural traditions. Tell students that in this assignment, they will have a chance to describe one of their favorite holidays or customs and to show what makes it special.

BUILD ON PRIOR KNOWLEDGE
Have students describe some of the ways in which people celebrate holidays; for example with certain foods, costumes or fancy clothes, colors, decorations, the exchange of presents, songs, games, and the lighting of candles. Tell students that they are going to read about a holiday in the country of Nepal, near India. Ask them to speculate about what a holiday in Nepal might be like.

SET A PURPOSE
Explain to students that they will be reading a description of a holiday with which they probably are not familiar. Remind them to look for details that describe the holiday, the people who observe it, and the place where it is observed. Urge students to look for sensory details and comparisons that help them picture the event.

Related ASSIGNMENT
Culture and Customs

Starting from LITERATURE

What are some of the customs of your family or group? When you lose a tooth, do you sleep with it under your pillow? Do you take part in special religious ceremonies? Is there a day each year when you dress up in special clothing?

In this excerpt, Elizabeth Murphy-Melas describes a festival in Nepal (nə pôl') known as Yomarhi Purnima (yō mä' dē poo ñe' mä). As you read her description, think about what the details reveal about the people of Nepal and the way they live.

YOMARHI PURNIMA
by Elizabeth Murphy-Melas

Tiny Nepal is an enchanting land of deep, picturesque valleys surrounded by the rugged, snowcapped Himalayas. In the heart of the country lies the beautiful Katmandu Valley. There, the Nepalese till the rich soil as they have for generations. . . . And each December, the people of the Katmandu Valley celebrate a special festival called Yomarhi Purnima in thanksgiving for their bountiful harvest. . . .

Yomarhi Purnima begins on the day of the full moon in December. Yomarhi is a Nepali word formed from yo ("fig") and marhi ("cake"); purnima is a Sanskrit word meaning "full moon." The Yomarhi cake is a sweet cake the Nepalese eat during the harvest celebration, just as Americans eat fruitcake at Thanksgiving and Christmas.

for FURTHER READING

Books to Read Students curious about different thanksgiving celebrations around the world might read *The Thanksgiving Book* by Lucille Recht Penner. It describes the history and customs of Thanksgiving in the United States and of similar holidays in other countries. Students also might enjoy *The Book of Holidays Around the World,* a 365-day calendar of festivals with a brief description of each, by Alice van Straalen.

On the eve of the full moon, also called the harvest moon, the women and girls of the household spend all day baking Yomarhi cakes in brick ovens. The small cakes, about the size of a child's fist, are molded by hand into the shapes of animals, people, and Hindu gods and goddesses. In the evening, the family says prayers and visits local temples and shrines, making

offerings of the cakes. The scent of incense from the shrines fills the streets.

The family then returns home for an evening of feasting and merrymaking. Children dress in their best festival clothes —the boys wearing trousers, high-necked tunics, and soft cotton topis; the girls, bright, colorful saris with bracelets and earrings. Because it's a special occasion, chicken or eggs are cooked. The Nepalese also eat rice mixed with dal, a thick sauce made from peas or lentils.

It's fun to sit upon woolen rugs on the floor, sip tea, and savor the meal!

That night, two special Yomarhi cakes—one shaped like Ganesh, the elephant-headed Hindu god of good luck, and one shaped like Laxmi, the goddess of wealth— are locked away in a cupboard. There they will remain for the four days of the harvest celebration. According to tradition, a miracle will occur, increasing the size of the cakes and bringing blessings to the family. At the end of Yomarhi Purnima, a family member unlocks the cupboard, and the cakes are enjoyed by all at a final feast.

Yomarhi Purnima is also a time of thanksgiving for merchants in the villages. They place Yomarhi cakes in their safe-deposit boxes, shops, and offices, hoping Laxmi will be pleased with their generosity and bring prosperity in the coming year. Students often wedge a few cakes in between their textbooks to bring them good luck in passing their school examinations!

Think & Respond

Which Yomarhi Purnima customs do you like best? How are the customs described here similar to or different from your own holiday traditions? Point out some of the ways Elizabeth Murphy-Melas brings the Yomarhi Purnima festival to life by showing it rather than just telling about it.

Think & Respond

ELICIT PERSONAL RESPONSES

Have volunteers tell which Yomarhi Purnima customs appeal to them most and why. How do these Nepalese customs compare to others they know about? (Sample: The Nepalese have a thanksgiving feast that celebrates the harvest, just as Americans do, but the traditional foods are different. People sit on the floor, not around a table.)

EXPLORE THE AUTHOR'S TECHNIQUES

Examples of showing details that students might mention include the brick ovens; the Yomarhi cakes, which are "molded by hand" into many shapes; the scent of incense that fills the streets; the costumes; the foods; sitting on "woolen rugs on the floor"; what people do with the special cakes; and how students carry the cakes in between their textbooks for luck. They might also mention the comparisons that the author makes between the Yomarhi cakes and fruitcake and between the cakes and the size of a child's fist.

You also might ask students to point out details that the author includes to explain things that her readers might not otherwise know. (Samples: what the words *Yomarhi* and *purnima* mean, what *dal* is, who Ganesh and Laxmi are, and why merchants put cakes in their safe-deposit boxes) Students should note that the description would be much less clear without these details. As students prepare to write, encourage them to think about what information their audience needs to know.

MULTICULTURAL Connection

Many cultures have similar holidays, including a new year festival, a festival of lights in midwinter, a celebration of renewal and rebirth in the spring, and a harvest festival or thanksgiving in the fall. Most countries also celebrate an independence day, as well as holidays associated with heroes or national leaders. Invite students to compare the celebration of some of these kinds of holidays with similar ones in the United States.

Remind students of the way Elizabeth Murphy-Melas used details about Yomarhi Purnima to help her readers picture the festival in far-off Nepal. Then note that this assignment will help them observe and record details and then use them to show their readers a holiday or custom, as Murphy-Melas did.

Handbooks for Help and Practice

The following handbooks may be used as mini-lessons before students begin writing or as resources when problems arise.
- **Show, Don't Tell, pp. 239–242**
- **Introductions, pp. 247–249**
- **Conclusions, pp. 250–252**

Teaching Strategies

for FIND A CUSTOM

HELPFUL HINT Tell students that all cultures have what are called rites of passage. Generally, these relate to birth, the taking on of adult responsibilities, marriage, and death. Invite students to consider, as topics for writing, their experiences with these customs.

for INTERVIEW

SPEAKING AND LISTENING Discuss questions interviewers might ask, such as "What holidays and special occasions do you celebrate?" or "Do you eat special foods then?" and so on. You might mention the *who, what, when, where, why,* and *how* questions, explaining how these questions can help them collect useful information in interviews. Pair students and have them use their questions to interview each other briefly about customs. Then bring students together as a class to discuss the ideas they got from these mini-interviews. You might direct students who would like to know more about interviewing skills to page 107, "Guidelines for Interviewing," in the *Writing Resource Book.*

Writing
ON YOUR OWN
Culture and Customs

The *Mani Rimdu* festival takes place each May in the Khumbu region of eastern Nepal. Monks dressed in colorful masks enact ancient legends that are based on the theme of good triumphing over evil.

INVITATION
TO
Write

In the process of describing Yomarhi Purnima, Elizabeth Murphy-Melas brings her readers into the homes and hearts of the people of Nepal.

Now write a description of an ethnic or religious custom that's familiar to you or one that you would like to learn more about.

E XPLORING CUSTOMS

1. Find a custom.   Can you think of a cultural or religious tradition you'd like to understand better or help someone else to understand? This tradition might come from your own culture or from any culture that interests you. Freewrite to come up with ideas, or try doing some of the following activities:

- **Holiday hop.**   Make a list of holidays that have special meaning to you and your family—one, for example, might be Rosh Hashana, Cinco de Mayo, Tet, or Easter. Create a **cluster** that explores the traditions associated with each holiday.

- **Interview.**   Talk with someone who has visited or lived in a culture different from yours. Ask questions and take notes on the customs of that culture.

- **Consider do's and taboos.**   What have you been taught about the traditions and customs of your culture? Do you always wear a head covering? Do you bow when you meet someone? Do you wear traditional clothing? Create a list of your customary practices and ways of behaving.

Music Connection

Many holidays have special music that is commonly sung during the festivities. Encourage students to investigate music associated with their topic. If possible, they might bring in tapes and records and play them for the class. Suitable songs might be taught to the class for a songfest.

After exploring for a while, choose a custom that you would like to describe. Freewriting can help you discover which custom you want to describe and even what you want to say.

 Writer's Choice   You may write about a custom of your own culture or one from another culture. Similarly, you may choose to describe a religious tradition that you know well or one you're interested in learning about.

2. Observe the custom and record details.   If possible, become familiar with the traditional practice first hand by watching it or by doing it yourself. If that isn't possible, "observe from memory" by recalling the practice as vividly as possible. Then record the details of the custom in a **list** or a **cluster** or by creating an **observation chart** or a **sketch**. Be sure to include plenty of sensory details.

DESCRIBING A CUSTOM

1. Start your draft.   Using your prewriting notes and your mind's eye, describe the sights, sounds, smells, tastes, and feelings you associate with the custom you've chosen. As much as possible, show rather than tell. Also, try to get yourself to write at top speed, without worrying about your word choices, grammar, or punctuation.

2. Consider your audience.   Think about what your readers will need to know to understand the custom you are describing. Then make sure to include this information. For example, Murphy-Melas explains, "The Yomarhi cake is a sweet cake the Nepalese eat during the harvest celebration, just as Americans eat fruitcake at Thanksgiving and Christmas."

3. Think about your draft.   Look for ways to improve your description. If you're comfortable sharing your draft, ask peer readers to comment on your description too.

PROBLEM SOLVING

"How can I show rather than tell?"

For help in turning telling into showing, see

- Handbook 12, "Show, Don't Tell," pages 239–242

Writing **TIP**

Comparisons of unfamiliar practices with familiar ones can help your readers better understand the unfamiliar practices. Similes (comparisons with *like* or *as*) can also help.

Culture and Customs   **65**

for OBSERVE THE CUSTOM . . .

MODELING   To help students get started gathering details, model creating a cluster diagram or filling in an observation chart with observations from your own memories of a holiday celebration or custom.

for START YOUR DRAFT

CRITICAL THINKING: ANALYZING   Suggest that before they start to write, students look over their notes to see whether they have collected enough material. They might compare the number of specific details they have gathered with those Elizabeth Murphy-Melas included in her description. Ask them which of the senses their details involve. If students decide that they need more material, they might try brainstorming or freewriting.

for THINK ABOUT YOUR DRAFT

PEER RESPONSE   Suggest that students ask a peer to read their descriptions aloud to them while they listen to see whether their main impression comes through clearly and whether their showing details are vivid and sharp. If students are not sure, urge them to question their peers about specific sentences, paragraphs, or ideas.

PROFESSIONAL NOTEBOOK

James Beane comments on the ideal middle school curriculum: "Early adolescents have the same concerns as people in general, regardless of their developmental stage. Moreover, their questions about themselves are often personal versions of larger-world questions. . . . The emerging vision of a middle school curriculum, then, is one that is organized around these rich and provocative themes. . . . Imagine, for example, a unit . . . in which students examine how self-perceptions are formed, how culture influences their self-concepts, how various cultures express their identities, and how increasing cultural diversity promises to reshape politics and the economy."

CRITICAL THINKING: ANALYZING

Have students look again at Elizabeth Murphy-Melas's first paragraph and identify the questions that the author answers. (Samples: Where is Nepal? What is it like? What do people do there? What holiday do they celebrate? Why? When?) Ask students why these would be good questions to consider. (Sample: They give readers the basic information they need in order to understand the description.) Encourage students to consider answering such questions in their introductions.

Guidelines for Evaluation

AN EFFECTIVE DESCRIPTION OF A CUSTOM

- conveys a vivid impression of the culture described
- uses sensory images and details
- shows, rather than tells
- considers its audience's knowledge of the topic
- has an effective introduction and conclusion

GENERAL NOTE

MANAGING THE PAPER LOAD

You might share the Guidelines for Evaluation (above) with students before they turn in their papers. Then limit your comments to those items on the list.

PROBLEM SOLVING

"How do I write an effective introduction and conclusion?"

For information on introductions and conclusions, see

- Handbook 14, "Introductions," pages 247–249
- Handbook 15, "Conclusions," pages 250–252

REVIEWING YOUR WRITING

1. Rework your description. Look at your own notes and your peers' comments. What needs improvement? Remember that adding sensory details, showing instead of telling, and replacing general words with more specific ones can all help bring a description to life.

2. Check your beginning and ending. In your introduction you should interest your readers in your subject and tell them what they will be reading about. To do this, you might begin by vividly describing an important feature of the custom. Another good way to begin is by pointing out a mistaken idea people have about the custom. You could also start by briefly telling about your first encounter with the tradition.

Your conclusion should leave your readers with a clear understanding of the custom you have described. Therefore, you may want to end by summarizing the important details you presented. You may also want to share what the custom means to you or what it taught you.

PUBLISHING AND PRESENTING

- **Compile an anthology of cultural customs.** Include illustrations or photos. A brief biography of each writer also would be a nice touch.
- **Create a multicultural calendar.** Meet with classmates who wrote about holiday traditions. Then, for each month of the year, create an illustrated description of how one or more cultures celebrate holidays in that month. For some months, you may need to create a collage of illustrations.
- **Reenact customs.** Create short skits about the customs you and your classmates have described. Perform your skits in class or at a school assembly.

2. Choose an idea for your narrative. Which of your ideas do you care most about? You might want to exchange story ideas with some of your classmates. Do other people's experiences give you any new ideas?

3. Think with your pencil. Freewrite about one or two of your favorite experiences. Just keep your pencil moving and see where your writing takes you.

Writer's Choice Do you want to write about something that happened to you, or do you want to write about something that happened to someone else? The important thing is to choose a story that means a lot to you.

4. Explore your story. Begin gathering facts and feelings for your narrative. Try to relive the experience. Go there in your mind and write what you see, hear, smell, taste, and feel. You might want to freewrite for a few minutes about why this experience stands out in your memory. You could also explore your ideas in a cluster or make a time line listing the events of your story in the order in which they occurred.

One Student's Process

Tim Stanley wanted to write about his grandfather's death because his grandfather had meant so much to him. He made a cluster to help him explore his feelings.

- What time was it?
- Why did she wake me?
- What happened to Grandpa?
- confused
- What would I do without Grandpa?
- MOM WAKING ME UP
- afraid
- can't believe it
- Would Grandpa be OK?

PROBLEM
SOLVING

"How can I find an idea I care about?"

For help discovering the story you want to tell, see

- Sketchbook, page 70
- Springboards, page 89
- Handbook 2, "Finding a Starting Point," pages 197–202

Teaching Strategies

GENERAL NOTE
HELPFUL HINT Tell students that the Sketchbook activities on pages 70 and 140 may help them find writing ideas.

for CHOOSE AN IDEA . . .
STUMBLING BLOCK Some students may be worried because they think other students have had more "interesting" or more dramatic experiences than they. Stress that any experience has value as long as it has personal meaning to the writer.

for THINK WITH YOUR PENCIL
CRITICAL THINKING: ANALYZING After students explore an experience in freewriting, have them reread what they have written. Then suggest that they write some more and explore *why* the experience is important to them. Have them consider such questions as these: Why do I remember this experience? What did I learn from it?

for EXPLORE YOUR STORY
HELPFUL HINT: GRAPHIC DEVICES Point out that another way to gather details for a narrative is to make a chart that answers these questions: *Who? What? When? Where? Why?* and *How?* Students can put each question at the top of a column and then list details in the appropriate columns. Direct students to the *Thinking Skills Transparency Pack* in the Teacher's Resource File for other graphic devices that can help them explore the events of their narratives.

Objectives

- To draft a personal narrative
- To organize a draft into a beginning, middle, and end
- To respond to one's own draft and to that of a peer

Teaching Strategies

for START WRITING

INDIVIDUALIZING INSTRUCTION: LD STUDENTS Consider having students tape-record their first draft. Then have them work with a peer to transcribe the tape.

for THINK ABOUT USING DIALOGUE

INDIVIDUALIZING INSTRUCTION: LEP AND ESL STUDENTS Students may wish to include dialect or foreign words in the dialogue to enliven their narratives.

for ORGANIZE YOUR DRAFT

KEY TO UNDERSTANDING Help students to see that although it is important to make the sequence of events clear in a narrative, a good narrative is more than a string of events presented in chronological order. The importance and impact of the events must be made clear. As an example, remind students of how Sheyann Webb included in her narrative what she was thinking and feeling as she marched from Selma to the Edmund Pettus bridge.

PROBLEM

S O L V I N G

"How can I make my narrative interesting to readers?"

For help finding lively details, see

- Handbook 12, "Show, Don't Tell," pages 239–242
- Handbook 19, "Appealing to the Senses," pages 266–273

1. Start writing. A good way to begin is just to tell what happened. Feel free to explore new ideas as you put your thoughts down on paper. You also might begin thinking about what you want your readers to understand or to feel after they read your narrative.

2. Think about using dialogue. Sometimes letting people speak for themselves can help readers experience events along with you. For example, notice how Tim Stanley records the conversation he had with his mother, telling most of the first part of his story in dialogue. In her narrative, Sheyann Webb uses a quotation to show how vulnerable she felt during the march. "I looked up at Mrs. Moore, and I wanted to say, 'I want to go home,' but I didn't."

3. Organize your draft. Once you have put your ideas down on paper, you can start arranging them. Your narrative should have the following parts:

- **beginning**—sets the scene, or possibly tells why the experience was important to you
- **middle**—usually tells the story in chronological order (the order in which things happened)
- **end**—sums up the story or explains why it was important to you

Notice how Tim begins his narrative with dialogue that sets the scene: it's late at night, and he's in bed. He then tells the events in the order in which they happened. Tim ends his narrative by summing up the story and explaining why it was important to him.

4. Think about your draft. Look over your draft. How do you feel about it? Do you want to continue working on it, or are you ready to get some feedback from your classmates now? The questions on the following page can help you review your draft and get the information you need to make it better.

PROFESSIONAL NOTEBOOK

Advice from the Authors Encourage students to be adventurous during drafting. "We want to try to train them to take risks in drafting," says Peter Elbow in *Writing with Power*. Remind students that when they are drafting, they are writing for themselves. "There needs to be this element of safety . . . [of] not thinking about quality and readers' needs all the time."

Questions for Yourself

- How can I help readers share my experience?
- What part of my story do I like best? What makes it so interesting?
- Have I forgotten to mention any important details? How can I work them into my narrative?

Questions for Your Peer Readers

- What part of my narrative was most interesting to you? Tell me why.
- How did reading my story make you feel?
- Did you have any trouble following the events in my story? If so, where did you get lost?
- What would you like to know more about?

One Student's Process

Tim decided to ask some classmates to read and comment on the beginning of his draft. Read their comments. What would you say about Tim's draft?

"Wake up, Tim. What time is it?
About eleven-thirty."
"Eleven-thirty?" That's when I sensed something was definitly wrong.
"Why'd you wake me up?"
"Grandma just called."
"Which one?"
"Grandma Coberly."
She said that Grandpa was in the hospital.
"Is he OK."
"It doesn't look good." I remember thinking why does everyone always say it doesn't look good. Why don't they just say that someone's dying?

Peer Reader Comments

Your beginning makes me want to know what happens, but I'm not sure who's talking.

Can you say more about why you felt something was wrong?

Yeah, I agree! People should just say what they mean.

Personal Narrative **79**

---

for QUESTIONS FOR YOURSELF
HELPFUL HINT Point out that students don't need to answer all the questions at once. They may want to focus on a different question each time they read their drafts.

for QUESTIONS FOR YOUR PEER READERS
PEER RESPONSE You may wish to have students use the *Peer Response Guide* for personal narrative on pages 11–12 in the Teacher's Resource File.

for ONE STUDENT'S PROCESS
KEY TO UNDERSTANDING Draw students' attention to the peer comments. Reinforce the point that it is important for readers to share with their peers how the writing affects them— what it makes them think and how it makes them feel as they are reading.

PROFESSIONAL NOTEBOOK

Advice from the Authors Peter Elbow writes, "It's crucial to think of peers not as fixers but as *audience*. There has to be an emphasis on peer questions that will help the relationship between writer and reader, build trust, promote discussion, find out what happens inside readers' minds."

Objectives

- To evaluate responses to a draft of a personal narrative and to revise with those responses in mind
- To evaluate the personal dimension of the narrative
- To analyze the structure of a draft, paragraph by paragraph

Teaching Strategies

for GET PERSONAL

HELPFUL HINT Point out that one way for students to achieve a personal tone is to imagine they are talking to a close friend about their experiences.

for PARAGRAPHS AT WORK

HELPFUL HINT Draw students' attention to the first sentence in each paragraph of Sheyann Webb's narrative. Point out that each sentence signals a change in the action. Her transitions make the order of events clear.

---

for DECIDE WHAT CHANGES . . .

INDIVIDUALIZING INSTRUCTION: ADVANCED STUDENTS As students revise, encourage them to experiment with techniques that break up the chronological progression of the narrative, such as flashback or flash-forward.

PROBLEM
S O L V I N G

"How can I make my writing sound like me?"
For help with finding your personal style, see

- Handbook 21, "Personal Voice," pages 276–277

COMPUTER
═ TIP ═

Try different ways of expressing an idea by moving your cursor down a line and typing in different wording. Keep the version you like best.

---

1. Think about the responses to your narrative. What good things did you or your peer readers notice about your narrative? Did your readers help you to see your draft in new ways? If you want to add more information or make parts of your draft more clear, check your prewriting notes. You may have jotted down details you can use as you revise.

2. Get personal. Since this is a personal narrative, help your readers get to know you. Does the writing sound like the way you speak now or spoke when the event took place? Have you showed how you felt about the experience?

For example, Sheyann Webb shows how she felt as an eight-year-old child during the march. "I began to hold Mrs. Moore's hand tighter, and the person's hand on the other side of me. My heart was beginning to beat real, real fast."

 Paragraphs at Work In a personal narrative, paragraph breaks will help your readers follow your story. Divide your narrative into separate paragraphs to make the flow of events clear. As you revise, remember these tips:

- Begin a new paragraph whenever the scene or action changes.
- Begin a new paragraph when a different person begins speaking.
- Use transitional words and phrases such as *first, next, later, at the same time,* and *finally* to make the order of events clear.

3. Decide what changes you want to make in your draft. You may want to make only minor changes. Don't be afraid, however, to make major revisions or even to start over again. Do whatever is needed to turn your writing into something you care about and want to share with readers.

Grammar Connection

Remind students to use verb tense consistently. Ask students to identify the tense Sheyann Webb used in her narrative. (past tense) Then demonstrate how shifts in tense can be confusing by reading a portion of Webb's narrative, changing verb tense from past to present.

One Student's Process

After reviewing his draft and his peer readers' comments, Tim decided to make the following changes in his draft. He would change it even more before he was satisfied with his story.

"Wake up, Tim. ," said Mom. ¶ "What time is it?" I asked.

"About eleven-thirty, ," she answered.

"Eleven-thirty?" That's when I sensed something was definitely wrong.

"Why'd you wake me up?"

"Grandma just called."

"Which one?"

"Grandma Coberly."

She said that Grandpa was in the hospital. He had a heart attack.

"Is he OK?"

"It doesn't look good." I remember thinking why does everyone always say it doesn't look good. Why don't they just say what they mean? that someone's dying?

¶ My heart went into my throat. My Grandma and Grandpa Coberly were the older grandparents I had. They were also the more frail.

Personal Narrative **81**

PROOFREAD

1. Proofread your work. When you proofread a personal narrative, make sure that you have spelled the names of people and places correctly. If you used dialogue, make sure you punctuated it properly. Then check for other errors in grammar, spelling, punctuation, and capitalization.

Personal Narrative **81**

---

for ONE STUDENT'S PROCESS

COLLABORATIVE OPPORTUNITY
Point out how the changes Tim made in this draft respond specifically to the peer comments on page 79. Then ask groups of students to discuss further changes that Tim might consider as he continues to revise his narrative.

PROOFREAD

Teaching Strategies

for PROOFREAD YOUR WORK

HELPFUL HINT Point out that one technique students can use to discover misspelled words is to read their narrative backwards, one word at a time. Such a reading will force them to slow down and look at each word separately.

HELPFUL HINT Draw students' attention to the revised dialogue to make sure they understand that commas and periods almost always belong inside the quotation marks. Have them look for examples of dialogue in newspaper and magazine articles and observe how the dialogue is punctuated.

Guidelines for Evaluation

IDEAS AND CONTENT
- tells an engaging story
- expresses why the story is meaningful to the writer
- uses descriptive details and dialogue to show the writer's experience

STRUCTURE AND FORM
- draws readers in with an interesting introduction
- uses chronological order effectively
- uses transitions to make the order of events clear
- has a satisfying conclusion

GRAMMAR, USAGE, AND MECHANICS
- uses verb tenses consistently
- punctuates dialogue correctly
- spells proper names correctly

LINKING
MECHANICS AND WRITING

Writing Dialogue

When you write dialogue, be sure to indicate clearly who is speaking. Enclose the exact words of the speaker in quotation marks. Place commas, periods, and question marks inside the quotation marks as needed. Also, remember to begin a new paragraph each time the speaker changes.

Notice how Tim corrected his use of quotation marks when he revised his writing.

Original

"Wake up, Tim. What time is it? About eleven-thirty."

Revised

"Wake up, Tim," said Mom.
"What time is it?" I asked.
"About eleven-thirty," she answered.

For more information about using quotation marks, see Handbook 43, "Punctuation," pages 586–588.

Standards for Evaluation

PERSONAL
WRITING

A personal narrative
- tells a story that is important to the writer
- has an introduction that draws readers in
- presents events in an order that makes sense
- makes it clear why the story is meaningful
- has a satisfying conclusion

82   Workshop 3

---

2. Make a clean copy of your narrative. Take a last look at your narrative, using the Standards for Evaluation shown in the margin as a guide. Then make a final copy of your work.

PUBLISH AND PRESENT

- **Make a class booklet.** Collect stories in a booklet that can be displayed in class or in the school library.
- **Read your narrative aloud.** If possible, add music, photographs, or other props.

- **Submit your narrative to the school magazine.** If the school does not have a magazine, your class could start one.
- **Turn your story into a dramatic skit.** Act out your story with the help of your classmates.

REFLECT ON YOUR WRITING

WRITER TO WRITER

The story's about you.

Horace, Roman poet

1. Add your writing to your portfolio. You have now read two personal narratives and written one of your own. Think about what you have learned from this experience. Then write your thoughts in a paragraph and attach it to your narrative.

▶ FOR YOUR **PORTFOLIO**

Think about questions like these:

- How did writing about my experience help me to understand the event? What new thoughts or memories came to me while writing?

- What was easiest about writing my narrative? What was hardest?

- How did sharing my writing with my peers help me? How could I have gotten more help?

- What would I do differently if I wrote about the same experience again?

2. Explore additional writing ideas. See the suggestions for writing a poem on pages 86–88 and Springboards on page 89.

Personal Narrative **83**

Reteaching

After students have completed their papers, assess the needs of students who were not successful in developing an effective personal narrative; then assign the appropriate handbook mini-lessons as well as the Workshop Support Materials listed in the Teaching Preview, pages 69a–69b. Concepts commonly requiring reteaching for this assignment are:

- **Handbook 7, Organizing Details, pp. 217–221**
- **Handbook 13, Creating Longer Pieces of Writing, pp. 243–246**

The following suggestions and resources also may be useful:

Weak Sentences In retelling events, students may produce run-on or stringy sentences. Handbook 23, "Correcting Sentence Errors," pages 281–284, can help students revise their writing.

Show, Don't Tell Remind students that they want their readers to be able to imagine themselves experiencing the events of the narrative. Direct students to "Showing an Experience" on page 13 of the *Writing Resource Book* for more practice using sensory details in personal narratives.

Extension and Enrichment

1. Suggest that students write stand-up comedy routines in which they retell humorous personal experiences.
2. Challenge students to write a fictional narrative. They might start with a real experience and then use their imaginations to change and develop the sequence of events and the outcome.

Closure: Reflect on Your Writing

As students consider the questions, encourage them to think about the unexpected twists and turns their writing took as they drafted.

Objectives

- To respond to three poems
- To experiment with expressing feelings and ideas creatively
- To draft, review, and present a poem

Motivate

Ask students to discuss characteristics of poetry. Use the discussion to correct any misconceptions students may have about poetry (e.g. all poems must rhyme). Explain that poetry is a form that gives writers great freedom: it offers many options and has few rules. Tell students that this assignment will give them a chance to play with language and experiment with ways to express their thoughts and feelings.

BUILD ON PRIOR KNOWLEDGE

Ask students to name their favorite singing groups. Then ask them to explain what they like about those performers' songs. Prompt students to recognize that one important aspect of any song is the lyrics—the words that have been set to music. Point out that lyrics are a form of poetry. Song lyrics, like the poems students are about to read, use language creatively to express feelings and ideas.

SET A PURPOSE

Point out that writing poetry is another way in which writers share their personal reactions to the world around them. As students read the poems on these pages, suggest that they notice any particularly vivid words and phrases.

Related ASSIGNMENT

Writing a Poem

A poem can capture a thought, a feeling, a scene, or any other experience. Writing poetry gives you a chance to play with language. You can think about how words sound and look, as well as about what they mean. You can be silly or serious, simple or sophisticated. As you read these poems, notice the different ways the poets use language.

Rain

Rain hits over and over
on hot tin,
on trucks,
on wires and roses.
Rain hits apples, birds, people,
coming in strokes of white,
gray, sometimes purple.
Rain cracks against my eyelids,
runs blue on my fingers,
and my shadow floats on the sidewalk
through trees and houses.

Adrien Stoutenburg

MORE ABOUT THE MODEL

Author Notes Adrien Stoutenburg and Eloise Greenfield have written many books of poetry for young people. Stoutenburg has worked as a writer, librarian, political reporter, and editor. She once said, "I always . . . desired to be a poet and write reams of poetry in my spare time." Greenfield worked as a clerk-typist for the U.S. Patent Office before becoming a writer. She said that having her first writing projects rejected taught her that writing was "not the result of talent alone, but of talent combined with skills that had to be developed."

Scrapyard

Old, old cars, rusting away,
Some cars whole—in these we play.
Now I am swerving round a corner,
Streaking round a bend,
Zooming past the finishing line
To the checkered flag—
Finishing a perfect first,
Ready for the autograph hunters.

Michael Benson

Reggie

It's summertime
And Reggie doesn't live here anymore
He lives across the street
Spends his time with the round ball
Jump, turn, shoot
Through the hoop
Spends his time with arguments
    and sweaty friends
And not with us
He's moved away
Comes here just to eat and sleep
    and sometimes pat my head
Then goes back home
To run and dribble and jump and stretch
And stretch
And shoot
Thinks he's Kareem
And not my brother

Eloise Greenfield

Think & Respond

What feeling do you get from reading each of these poems? Which poem do you like best? Why? What words strike you the most? What ideas do these poems give you for your own writing?

Think & Respond

ELICIT PERSONAL RESPONSES

Before students answer the questions in Think & Respond, ask these questions about the poems: Why does Stoutenburg say that rain "hits"? (to show that rain can strike forcefully) What is Michael Benson pretending to be in the scrapyard? (a race-car driver) What emotion does Eloise Greenfield describe? (Sample: sadness or loneliness)

EXPLORE THE AUTHORS' TECHNIQUES

You may wish to begin by pointing out some of the ways in which poetry differs from other types of writing:

- Poetry is written in lines, not in sentences. The length of each line is part of the effect of the poem. For example, Eloise Greenfield draws attention to some words by placing them in very short lines.
- Poets play with the sound and rhythm of words. Notice how Adrien Stoutenburg uses the phrases "Rain hits . . ." and "Rain cracks . . ." to give her poem a distinct visual and sound pattern. Michael Benson repeats words ending in *-ing* to give his poem a lively rhythm, contrasting motion with rest.
- Poems are condensed; poets make every word count.

PROFESSIONAL NOTEBOOK

Poet Georgia Heard shares this advice with students: "Poems have to be about something that is *so* important to me, I have a physical feeling of that topic inside me. You know how when you are scared, really scared, you can feel it in your body, or when you are so, so happy, and your body sings? . . . Feelings are the source of a poem, but you can't just write the feelings onto paper. Instead of trying to tell the reader my feelings, I go back in my mind's eye and locate the feeling in specific concrete things that we see and hear. I get a picture in my mind and then re-create that picture so the reader can feel what I felt."

Remind students that each of the poems on the previous two pages is a personal look at something that was important to the poets. Tell students that they can write a poem about anything that is interesting to them. The subject can be large or small, important or trivial, funny or sad.

Handbooks for Help and Practice

The following handbooks may be used as mini-lessons before students begin writing or as resources when problems arise:
- **Appealing to the Senses, pp. 266–273**
- **Personal Voice, pp. 276–277**

Teaching Strategies

for LOOK INSIDE YOUR HEAD

HELPFUL HINT Another useful way to begin gathering ideas for a poem is to make a cluster diagram. In the center of a piece of paper, students should write a subject, circle it, and then see how many related ideas, words, and phrases they can generate from it.

for EXPLORE IDEAS

HELPFUL HINT The images in the *Fine Art Transparency Pack* in the Teacher's Resource File can be good starting points for poetry ideas. Students can use the suggested prompts or simply free-write their personal reactions to the images.

Writing
ON YOUR OWN

Writing a Poem

PROBLEM
SOLVING

"How can I turn my ideas into a poem?"
To help bring your ideas to life, see
- Handbook 19, "Appealing to the Senses," pages 266–273

INVITATION
=== TO ===
Write

A poem can be about a subject as common as rain or as personal as your brother. The only limit to what you say—and how you say it—is your own imagination.

Write a poem about something you've seen, felt, thought, or dreamed.

EXPLORING YOUR WORLD

1. Look inside your head.   Close your eyes and try to focus your thoughts inward. What images or ideas come to mind? Also check your journal for subjects you've been thinking about lately.

2. Explore ideas.   You might try freewriting about your observations and feelings. Write down or sketch words and images that occur to you, no matter how odd they seem. Look for these kinds of details:

- **Sensory images**   What do you see, hear, smell, taste, and feel when you think about your subject?
- **Words and phrases**   What words, phrases, or sounds remind you of your subject?
- **Comparisons**   Is your subject like anything else? Look for unexpected or unusual comparisons.

For example, notice the strong sensory images Stoutenburg uses to help readers see and feel the rain—"hot tin," "strokes of white, /gray, sometimes purple," "cracks against my eyelids," and "my shadow floats on the sidewalk."

TEACHER'S LOUNGE

DRAFTING YOUR POEM

1. Write and rewrite. You actually started writing your poem when you began exploring your world. Now begin experimenting with images, ideas, words, and meanings. Keep the ones you like best and try out new ones. Many poets write their poems over and over before they really discover what they want to say.

2. Play with language. As you write, read your drafts aloud. Listen to the sound of the words. Try using words that use sound in an interesting way.

Words and Sounds

Words can

- begin with the same sound (slippery snow)
- end in the same sound (dark ink)
- have the same vowel sound (gray lake)
- sound like what they mean (buzz, crackle)

Writer's Choice Some poems rhyme and some don't. Experiment with your poem to see if rhyming the last words of lines makes your poem seem more rhythmic, more musical.

3. Think about the rhythm and shape of your poem. Notice the rise and fall of your voice as you read your poem. Also notice the way the poem looks on paper. Experiment with different words and ways of arranging them. Try short lines and long lines and different stanzas, or groupings of lines.

Notice how both Stoutenburg and Greenfield repeat certain words to give their poems rhythm. Stoutenburg repeats the word *on:* "on hot tin, / on trucks, / on wires and roses." Greenfield repeats the word *and:* "To run and dribble and jump and stretch / And stretch / And shoot."

---

for WRITE AND REWRITE
PERSONAL TOUCH You may wish to write a poem along with the class. By doing so, you can impress on students the value of experimenting and reworking drafts in order to hone ideas and language. Unless you model the process, students may stop working once they have completed a draft.

for PLAY WITH LANGUAGE
INDIVIDUALIZING INSTRUCTION: ESL STUDENTS The sensory images that make poetry so expressive can be difficult for ESL students to compose on their own. Urge these students to sketch their ideas in words and images. Then work with them to find precise words and phrases to convey the ideas and images they have drawn.

for THINK ABOUT THE RHYTHM AND SHAPE . . .
SPEAKING AND LISTENING You may wish to break the class into small groups and have students read their drafts aloud to one another. Encourage students to respond to the way the poems sound (the rhythm of the words) as well as to what the poems say.

Music Connection

You might want to give students the option of writing a song setting their poetry to music. For example, they could write new lyrics to a melody they already know.

note pads, or manila folders. You'll want to identify the tracks you find. You can get field guides to track identification at a library or bookstore. Bring a book with you when you're out looking for tracks. . . .

Carry the plaster in a tightly sealed container.

A canteen will do for toting water. You can mix the water and plaster in an empty tin can, but make sure it's clean.

When you find a track, make a one- to two-inch-high circular collar around it with the paper. Secure it with a piece of tape or a paper clip. Then combine the plaster and the water in the can and stir. This is the tricky part: the

mix cannot be too thick or too thin. It should be slightly more fluid than pancake batter. You can follow the directions that come with the plaster, or figure on two parts plaster to one part water.

Mix quickly because plaster thickens and sets fast. When the mixture is ready, carefully pour it into the track. Make sure it fills the track entirely, and even overflows a little. Next, wait for the plaster to completely harden. It takes at least a half hour, so be patient. While you're waiting, you may want to make some notes. Describe the surroundings of the track—the vegetation, and whether the print was in mud, sand, or some other kind of soil. If there is a trail of tracks, make notes about its path.

When the cast is hard, dig around it with a pocket knife or garden trowel. Be careful not to cut into the

plaster. Then remove the cast from the ground. You can clean it later with water and a toothbrush. . . .

If you spend enough time scouting around for tracks, you can build a nice collection, and at the same time, you'll learn about the habits of wildlife.

Think & Respond

Did Ricciuti's directions tempt you to try collecting tracks? Do you think you could follow Ricciuti's directions successfully? Why or why not? Can you think of activities you know how to do well enough to explain them to someone else?

for FURTHER READING

Books to Read Students interested in natural history might enjoy the following books:
- Sterling North, *Rascal*
- Bill Peet, *Cappyboppy*
- Molly Burkett, *The Year of the Badger*
- Joy Adamson, *Elsa*
- Gavin Maxwell, *Ring of Bright Water*

SET A PURPOSE

Read Starting from Literature with students; call their attention to the purpose-setting statement. Ask, "How would you make plaster casts of animal tracks? What materials would you need?" Have them check their guesses as they read.

Think & Respond

ELICIT PERSONAL RESPONSES

If students respond to the first question in the Think & Respond box with a flat "Yes" or "No," invite them to discuss why. Ask how making plaster casts of animal tracks does or does not fit in with their interests. Students considering the second question may say that the writer should have provided more information about plaster of Paris and where it can be purchased. (It's the material used to make casts for broken bones; it's sold in hardware stores and art supply stores.) For the third question, students may wish to freewrite or brainstorm in small groups to generate a list of possibilities.

EXPLORE THE AUTHOR'S TECHNIQUES

To help students identify some of Ed Ricciuti's techniques for making a complicated process easy to follow, explain that his article is organized like a recipe. Ask students to find the place near the beginning where he lists "ingredients" and equipment. (paragraph 4) Point out that Ricciuti breaks his process into steps, just as recipe writers do. Ask students to identify the steps. (making a collar, mixing the plaster, pouring it, letting it set, taking notes, removing the cast, cleaning the cast)

Then point out how Ricciuti's article differs from a recipe: He gives interesting background information; he explains how readers can benefit from his ideas; he offers warnings and advice about tricky parts. Encourage students to keep these techniques in mind as they write directions of their own.

Ed Ricciuti introduces readers to an interesting hobby. Student Doug Frieburg offers more "practical" advice. Both writers, however, give specific how-to information in a step-by-step format. Doug's "How to Clean Your Room in Ten Easy Minutes" is the final draft of the work in progress that appears on the pages of this workshop.

Motivate

Tell students that everyone has trouble following directions at one time or another, whether it's a matter of following a recipe, assembling a bicycle, or using a friend's map to find a park. You might recount one of your worst frustrations in following directions. Then ask students to share some of their experiences. Encourage students to speculate about why the directions were hard to follow.

BUILD ON PRIOR KNOWLEDGE

Ask what students' least favorite household chores are. Encourage them to elaborate on what makes the chores unpleasant. Then ask them to share any methods they have for getting these chores out of the way quickly.

SET A PURPOSE

To help students identify similarities between Doug's directions and Ed Ricciuti's, tell them to look for similarities in the structures of the essays. For example, both Ricciuti and Doug use the beginnings of their essays to get readers interested. Have students look for other similarities in the beginning, middle, and end sections of the two essays. Ask students also to look for similarities in the use of words such as *next, then,* and *while* to signal steps in a process.

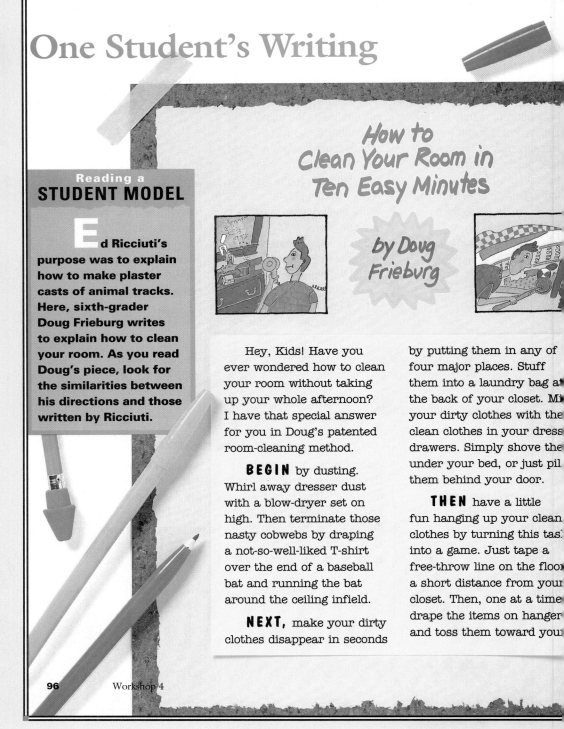

One Student's Writing

Ed Ricciuti's purpose was to explain how to make plaster casts of animal tracks. Here, sixth-grader Doug Frieburg writes to explain how to clean your room. As you read Doug's piece, look for the similarities between his directions and those written by Ricciuti.

How to Clean Your Room in Ten Easy Minutes

by Doug Frieburg

Hey, Kids! Have you ever wondered how to clean your room without taking up your whole afternoon? I have that special answer for you in Doug's patented room-cleaning method.

BEGIN by dusting. Whirl away dresser dust with a blow-dryer set on high. Then terminate those nasty cobwebs by draping a not-so-well-liked T-shirt over the end of a baseball bat and running the bat around the ceiling infield.

NEXT, make your dirty clothes disappear in seconds by putting them in any of four major places. Stuff them into a laundry bag a[t] the back of your closet. Mi[x] your dirty clothes with the clean clothes in your dress[er] drawers. Simply shove the[m] under your bed, or just pil[e] them behind your door.

THEN have a little fun hanging up your clean clothes by turning this tas[k] into a game. Just tape a free-throw line on the floo[r] a short distance from your closet. Then, one at a time drape the items on hanger[s] and toss them toward you[r]

96   Workshop 4

set rod. How many
ngers can you land on the
without losing the piece
clothing in the process?

NEXT, maximize your
elf space. Do you have
accumulation of thing-a-
-bobs you need to get rid
out can't bear to part
h? Well, you can keep
erything and still make
r room look neat and
anized just by putting
se items into containers.
d your mom's stash of
plastic containers and
rgarine tubs. Old coffee
s work well too.

FINALLY, relax on your
bed while you let the vacuum
run. The noise of the vacuum
will fool any parent into thinking that you have actually
vacuumed your room. After
about five minutes, shut off
the vacuum. Then go back to
whatever you were doing
before you started cleaning.

Many kids think cleaning
their room is boring and a
waste of time. However, if
you follow my patented room-
cleaning method, not only will
you have fun cleaning your
room, but you'll also be done
in record time.

Think & Respond

Respond as a Reader
▶ Did you enjoy reading Doug's
directions? Why or why not?
▶ What parts did you like best?

Respond as a Writer
▶ How does Doug get your
attention in his opening
paragraph?
▶ How are Doug's directions
similar to Ricciuti's? How are
they different?

Think & Respond

RESPOND AS A READER
▶ Ask students how they liked Doug's
first sentence and first paragraph. Point
out that students' initial responses can
color their reactions to the rest of the
piece.
▶ Students should identify the parts they
found particularly funny or clever. (For
example, some students may enjoy the
tips that turn tasks into games.)

RESPOND AS A WRITER
▶ Students may say that the catchy
"Hey, Kids!" opener shows that the
writer is speaking directly to them.
Students may also say that Doug's
tempting offer of a shortcut to a tiresome
chore and the humorous line "Doug's
patented room-cleaning method" also
captured their attention.
▶ Students may note that both sets of
directions use steps, get readers interested in the topic in the first paragraph,
and address the reader directly as "you."
Two differences are that Doug doesn't
list needed equipment at the beginning,
whereas Ricciuti does; and that Doug
devotes a paragraph to each step,
whereas Ricciuti combines steps in
some paragraphs. In addition, Doug uses
humor to engage his readers.

Draw Conclusions
To check students' understanding of
this introduction to informative writing
that explains *how,* ask them to list the
characteristics they have noted thus far.
Responses may include the following:
• explains how to do something
• catches readers' interest
• tells what materials are needed
• breaks the process into logical steps
  and illustrates each step with details

Point out that in making an activity clear to their readers, students can learn more about it themselves. Invite them to choose an activity that promises to be fun to write about. Remind them that Ed Ricciuti and Doug Frieburg captured their audiences' attention in the first paragraph, then presented the steps in the process in a clear and logical order.

Handbooks for Help and Practice

The following handbooks may be used as mini-lessons before students begin writing or as resources when problems arise:
- **Organizing Details, pp. 217–221**
- **Transitions, pp. 234–238**

PREWRITE AND EXPLORE

Objectives
- To use prewriting techniques to identify a topic for a set of directions
- To generate a list of steps, tools, and materials for an activity

Teaching Strategies

for LOOK FOR TOPICS

KEY TO UNDERSTANDING Remind students that Doug chose an activity he disliked, but his imagination and sense of humor made it fun. Urge students to consider writing ideas that arise from their less favorite as well as their preferred activities.

for TAKING STOCK

HELPFUL HINT After students generate a list of activities, hobbies, and skills, suggest that they organize these items into other categories, such as "most fun," "requires most equipment," "hardest," and "most familiar." Doing so can help students begin the evaluation process that will eventually lead to picking a topic.

Writing
ON YOUR OWN
Directions

INVITATION
TO
Write

Although Ed Ricciuti and Doug Frieburg explain how to do very different activities, both make their directions clear.

Now it's your turn. Write directions that explain an activity you know how to do well.

PREWRITE AND EXPLORE

1. Look for topics. What are your favorite games or hobbies? What tasks do you do so often that you could probably do them in your sleep? To find a topic, freewrite about some of the things you do in a typical day or try doing some of the following activities.

Exploring Topics

- **Taking stock** Are you the high scorer on a tricky video game? Do you bake cakes for special occasions? Are you a caretaker of fish, gerbils, or other pets? Take a moment to list your favorite activities, hobbies, and special skills.

- **Making a game of your search** Get together with a few classmates and pick a subject. Then spend a few minutes alone, listing everything about that subject you know how to do. For example, if you picked bicycles, you might list "riding with no hands," "patching inner tubes," and "changing flats." Then compare your list with those of your classmates. Who has the longest list? Did others think of any entries that you might add to your list?

98 Workshop 4

MULTICULTURAL Connection

Encourage students to consider topics related to their cultural heritage. For example, they might write directions for doing a craft, performing a dance, playing a musical instrument, or preparing a food that is linked to a tradition or holiday in a particular culture. Remind them to define terms and include background information that will help readers understand the activity.

- **Completing sentences**   Brainstorm alone or with friends or classmates to complete one or more of the following sentences. If you prefer, you can try completing a sentence of your own.

  "I know how to win at . . ."

  "You too can succeed at . . ."

  "Making a _____ requires some planning."

  "Being a good _____ takes know-how."

2. Pick a topic.   The activity you pick may be the one you know how to do best, one you think others should learn how to do, or one you think you'll have fun explaining. For help in making a selection, freewrite about your favorites to see which one interests you most.

3. Think about your activity.   If possible, carry out your chosen task or project. Then jot down the steps you follow. If performing your activity is not possible, simply imagine yourself doing the task. Also, note any materials and tools you need to perform your activity.

COMPUTER TIP

Listing your steps on a computer can make it easier to rearrange them or insert missed steps.

One Student's Process

Doug Frieburg thought about how he could add some fun to an unpleasant task as he imagined himself going through the motions of cleaning his room. Then he jotted down the following notes.

Steps	Tools and Materials
pick up dirty clothes	vacuum cleaner
put away clean clothes	blow-dryer
play closet "free throw"	laundry bag
dust	baseball bat
get rid of cobwebs	old T-shirt
vacuum	

HELPFUL HINT   Tell students that the Sketchbook activities on pages 48 and 92 may help them find writing ideas.

for COMPLETING SENTENCES

MODELING   Show students how you would complete some of the sentences in the text. Demonstrate that the sentences can be changed slightly to fit students' needs. To complete the first sentence, for example, you could say "I know how to win at Monopoly," "I know how to avoid having a dead car battery on a cold morning," "I've been taught how to give the cat its medicine," and so on.

for PICK A TOPIC

CRITICAL THINKING: MAKING COMPARISONS   If students are having trouble deciding on a topic, suggest that they freewrite briefly about each contender and then compare the freewritings. Doing so can help students see which topic they enjoy the most or know the most about.

for THINK ABOUT YOUR ACTIVITY

INDIVIDUALIZING INSTRUCTION: LD STUDENTS   Sequencing the steps in a process can be especially difficult for some students. Encourage students to number the steps in the process as they visualize following them. Some students might also benefit from drawing each step in the process.

for ONE STUDENT'S PROCESS

KEY TO UNDERSTANDING   Point out that the steps in Doug's prewriting notes aren't in the same order as those in his final draft on pages 96–97. Explain that before he began his draft, he probably numbered the steps to show which comes first, second, and so on. Tell students that they can use the same technique in their own prewriting.

Science Connection

Students interested in ecology might consider "How *not* to" topics, such as "How *Not* to Destroy the Ozone Layer," "How *Not* to Pollute Groundwater," and so on. Alternatively, students can try a tongue-in-cheek approach, writing directions on topics such as "How to Destroy the Ozone Layer" and "How to Wipe Out the Rain Forests in Just a Few Short Years." Encourage students to work with science teachers if possible.

For Your Eyes Only!

If you want to send a private message to a friend, write it in a secret code. Try these codes, then make up one of your own.

Tick-Tack-Toe Code

Did you know 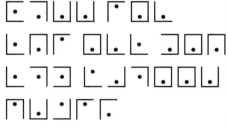 spells *theater?* The tick-tack-toe board below is your guide to this alphabet of symbols.

To write the letter **T**, for example, draw the outline of the part of the tick-tack-toe board that holds the letter: ⌐. Then place a dot in the middle part of the outline where the letter **T** is shown: ⌐•.

A •	J •	S •
B •	K •	T •
C •	L •	U •
D •	M •	V •
E •	N •	W •
F •	O •	X •
G •	P •	Y •
H •	Q •	Z •
I •	R •	? •

Can you read this message?

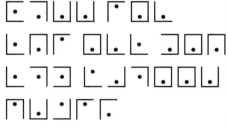

Letter Scramble

If you want to send the message *Meet me after the show,* scramble the letters by rewriting the sentence as two words. Put the first letter, **M**, at the beginning of the first word and the second letter, **e**, at the beginning of the second word. Build each of the two words from every other letter of the message.

Meet me... Mem... ete...

You end up with

Mematrhso etefetehw

If you wish, divide your two-word letter scramble into more words: **Mem atrh so ete fetehw.** To decode the message, divide the total number of letters in half. Write the second half directly below the first, and then read the letters from top to bottom.

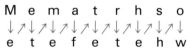

M e m a t r h s o
e t e f e t e h w

What does this message say?

Ia et gfih hvsa ergt

Ask students if they have ever used codes to send secret messages to friends. Have students describe some of their codes. What else do they know about codes? You might point out that probably thousands of codes have been used throughout history. Leonardo da Vinci, for example, protected his ideas by writing his notes backward. Military communications are often sent in code during wartime, and other codes, such as the Morse code and semaphore, were invented to send messages over long distances.

After students read the feature, have them form small groups. Ask each group to write a brief message using one of the two codes shown. Then have each group write its coded message on the board. Challenge the other groups to see who can decode each message first.

111

Sentence Openers

Objectives
- To identify sentence openers
- To compose and correctly punctuate sentences that begin with sentence openers

HELPFUL HINT: COMMAS To help students understand how and why commas are used with sentence openers, ask volunteers to read each of the model sentences aloud. Point out that students pause naturally after the openers. The pause often signals the need for a comma. If students need additional practice, refer them to "Commas That Set Off Special Elements" in Handbook 43, "Punctuation," pages 576–577.

Additional Resource

Sentence Composing Copy Masters, pp. 7–8

Answer Key

A. Combining Sentences
1. Without the slightest hesitation, he went to the door on the right and opened it.
2. After Uncle Daniels had finished with his lamb-chop dinner, I set the cream puffs on the coffee table and stood back looking at them.
3. Still angry, still outraged by his attempt to betray me, I looked at him with scorn and hatred, unable to imagine what I had ever seen in him.
4. When she got to her door, she dragged the boy inside, down a hall, and into a large kitchenette-furnished room at the rear of the house.

Sentence

COMPOSING

Sentence Openers

You can use single words or groups of words as sentence openers to add emphasis and to vary the rhythm of your writing.

Model A   <u>Outside</u>, he murmured to himself.
William H. Armstrong, *Sounder*

Model B   <u>Hobbling on one foot</u>, Wanda opened the closet door and turned on the light.
Betsy Byars, *The Summer of the Swans*

Model C   <u>Ever since I can remember</u>, I had wanted to know about the Land of the Golden Mountain, but my mother had never wanted to talk about it.
Laurence Yep, *Dragonwings*

▶ **ON THE MARK**   Put a comma after a sentence opener to separate it from the rest of the sentence.

A. Combining Sentences   Make a new sentence by adding the underlined part of the second sentence to the first sentence as a sentence opener. Write the complete sentence, putting a comma after the sentence opener.

1. He went to the door on the right and opened it. He opened it <u>without the slightest hesitation</u>.   **Frank R. Stockton, "The Lady, or the Tiger?"**

2. I set the cream puffs on the coffee table and stood back looking at them. This was <u>after Uncle Daniels had finished with his lamb-chop dinner</u>.
Rosa Guy, *Edith Jackson*

3. I looked at him with scorn and hatred, unable to imagine what I had ever seen in him. I was <u>still angry, still outraged by his attempt to betray me</u>.
James Gould Cozzens, "The Animals' Fair"

4. She dragged the boy inside, down a hall, and into a large kitchenette-furnished room at the rear of the house. She did this <u>when she got to her door</u>.   **Langston Hughes, "Thank You, M'am"**

B. Unscrambling and Imitating Sentences   Unscramble each set of sentence chunks below. Create a sentence that has a sentence opener, the same order of chunks, and the same punctuation as the model. Then write a sentence of your own that imitates each model.

1. Model   <u>With his remaining strength</u>, he dragged himself from the swirling waters.   **Richard Connell, "The Most Dangerous Game"**

onto their shoulders / the girls lifted their coach / after their stunning victory

2. Model   <u>Barely touching my waist and my fingers</u>, he began to dance with me.   **Alice Munro, "Red Dress—1946"**

to cross above us / the tightrope walker started / carefully keeping her balance and her concentration

3. Model   <u>When we arrived home</u>, we took a cold shower underneath a water hose.   **Francisco Jimenez, "The Circuit"**

the scouts told stories / as the stars twinkled above / around the campfire

C. Expanding Sentences   Use your imagination to add a sentence opener, followed by a comma, where the caret (∧) appears in each sentence below.

1. ∧ We could hear axes ringing in the woods, voices, and sometimes the fall of a tree.   **Alexei Panshin, *Rite of Passage***

2. ∧ Ralph laid the small end of the shell against his mouth and blew.   **William Golding, *Lord of the Flies***

3. ∧ Mama Bellini picked him up by his antennae, tossed him into the cricket cage and locked the gate behind him.   **George Selden, *The Cricket in Times Square***

Grammar Refresher   Some sentence openers are prepositional phrases. To learn more about prepositional phrases, see Handbook 40, "Understanding Prepositions and Conjunctions," pages 502–525.

5

Persuasion

Overview

Persuasive writing is used to convince readers that they should accept the writer's opinion on an issue. In this workshop, students apply observation, analysis, problem-solving, and research skills to write about issues that concern them. Workshop 5 includes the following Guided and Related Assignments, as well as the interdisciplinary project on pages 113c–113d.

1. **Guided: Sharing an Opinion** invites students to identify an issue they care about, formulate an opinion about it, and support the opinion with convincing facts, examples, and statistics in a persuasive paper aimed at a particular audience.

2. **Related: Public Opinion Survey** guides students through the steps of designing, administering, and reporting the results of a survey of opinion.

3. **Related: Writing for Assessment** helps students apply their persuasive writing skills in responding to a writing prompt like those that appear in writing tests.

Teaching Preview

Preparation Guide

1. Use the Overview on this page and the Teacher's Choice descriptions on page 115 as a basis for deciding which assignments to teach.

2. Preview the assignments and the teacher's notes and identify concepts that may require preteaching or extra support, given your class's abilities. The handbook mini-lessons suggested within the lesson may also provide guidance.

3. Preview the chart below for support materials in the Teacher's Resource File that may be used with this Workshop. Resources are for use with the Guided Assignment unless otherwise noted.

Support Materials

WRITER'S CRAFT RESOURCES

Prewrite and Explore
Thinking Skills Worksheets, p. 5
Thinking Skills Transparencies, pp. 5–5a
Writing Resource Book, pp. 22–23

Draft and Discover
Elaboration, Revision, and Proofreading Practice, p. 9
Elaboration, Revision, and Proofreading Transparencies, pp. 17–18
Writing Resource Book, pp. 24–26

Revise Your Writing
Elaboration, Revision, and Proofreading Practice, p. 10
Elaboration, Revision, and Proofreading Transparencies, pp. 19–20
Guidelines for Writing Assessment and Portfolio Use, pp. 18, 34–36
Peer Response Guides, pp. 15–16
Writing Resource Book, p. 27

Assessment
Tests and Writing Assessment Prompts, p. 5

Extension Activities
Sentence Composing Copymasters, pp. 9–10
Starting Points for Writing, pp. 31–32, 37–40
Writing from Literature, pp. 1–2, 5–12, 15–22
Standardized Test Practice

 Educational Technology
(available separately)
Writing Coach
Writer's DataBank
Electronic English Handbook
On Assignment! (videodisc)
The McDougal Littell Home Page at http://www.mcdougallittell.com

• •

OTHER RESOURCES

Books and Journals
Caplan, Rebekah. "The Argumentative Essay." *Writers in Training*. Palo Alto: Dale Seymour, 1984"
Rybczynski, M. "Audience Adaptation and Persuasive Strategies." *Journal of Research and Development in Education.* 26 (Fall 1992): 15–23.

 Films and Videos
Join the Resistance. Carousel, 1992.

 Educational Technology
Ace Inquirer. Mindplay. Apple Series.
Fact or Opinion: Smart Shopper. Mindscape/SVE. Apple II.

Management Guidelines

The chart below estimates the number of days needed for each phase of the Guided and Related Assignments. Students may not complete each phase in one continuous session, nor necessarily progress from stage to stage in the linear order shown here. Stars indicate portions of the assignment that may be completed outside the classroom if time is limited or if teachers wish students to work independently.

SHARING AN OPINION

Starting from Literature ....1 day
Prewrite and Explore ....3 days
Draft and Discover.......................3 days*
Revise Your Writing......................2 days*
Proofread ....1 day*
Publish and Present..................1–2 days
Reflect on Your Writing................1 day
Extension and Enrichment ....open*

PUBLIC OPINION SURVEY

Finding a Focus ....1 day
Creating Your Survey................2–3 days*
Completing the Survey.............4–5 days*
Sharing Your Results ....1 day

WRITING FOR ASSESSMENT

Reading the Question ....1 day*
Getting Ready to Answer
    and Writing Your Answer ....1 day
Reviewing Your Answer...............1 day
Sentence Composing......................open*

Linking Literature, Writing, and Grammar

The following options may be used to provide students with an integrated language experience. Begin by assigning and discussing any of the recommended pieces of literature. Use the suggested strategy to provide a link to the Guided Assignment.

LINKING LITERATURE AND WRITING

Option 1

Starting Point: "Video 'Web' Weaves an Inadequate Tale" by Barbara Brotman on pages 116–117 of *The Writer's Craft.*

Strategy: Use the teaching suggestions on pages 116–117 to lead students into the Guided Assignment.

Option 2

Starting Point: The excerpt from *A Long Hard Journey* by Patricia and Fredrick McKissack on pages 329–337 of McDougal Littell's *The Language of Literature,* Grade 6. (Additional suggestions for using *The Language of Literature* can be found on page 115.)

Strategy: Have students read the selection. Then ask their opinions of George Pullman and the Pullman porters. Have students give reasons for their opinions. Use the discussion to introduce the Guided Assignment.

Option 3

Starting Point: "If I Were in Charge of the World" by Judith Viorst.

Strategy: Ask a student to read the poem aloud. Then ask which of Viorst's ideas students agree with and why. What things about the world would they change if they could? Use their ideas to introduce the Guided Assignment.

LINKING WRITING AND GRAMMAR

Before the drafting or revision stages of this assignment, tell students that mistakes in grammar and usage can distract readers from the ideas a writer is trying to present and can even make a piece of writing less persuasive. One common usage problem is subject-verb agreement. Tell students to ignore the nouns in prepositional phrases when they are deciding whether to use a singular or plural verb. Put the following examples on the board and have students select the correct verb. If they have difficulty, cross out the prepositional phrases.

The causes of this problem (is, *are*) hard to figure out.

The cause of these problems (*is,* are) a lack of money.

Go over pages 526–541 of the Grammar and Usage Handbook. If problems with subject-verb agreement still appear in students' papers, assign the exercises on those pages for reteaching. Additional practice can be found in the *Grammar and Usage Practice Book* on pages 78–83.

Right On! A Students' Bill of Rights

Overview

During this project, students will investigate the rights, responsibilities, and restrictions placed on students by society. They will study the Bill of Rights in the U.S. Constitution, and they will write a Students' Bill of Rights to address what they believe should be the rights of students. The project will culminate with students' publication of their document and with feedback from the school community.

Students will participate in the following activities:

- Examine the Bill of Rights
- Research minors' legal rights
- Draft and revise a Students' Bill of Rights
- Solicit feedback on the draft from other students
- Write essays explaining their opinions about one item covered by their Students' Bill of Rights
- Use language arts, math, social studies, and art skills to complete their research and to develop their materials

Preparation Guide

Ask students what they think some of their legal rights are. Ask them to share what they remember about court cases involving students. For example, students have been involved in protesting school dress codes and administration censorship of school newspapers. Lead students to see that an understanding of their rights can empower them to make changes.

Explain that for this project students will learn about the legal status of people their age and will use persuasive writing skills in creating a Students' Bill of Rights.

Stage 1
Focus on Students' Rights

1. Have students read the Bill of Rights, the first ten amendments to the U.S. Constitution.

2. Ask students if they think that the Bill of Rights applies to them. Encourage them to discuss situations in which they do, and do not, seem to have the freedoms supported by the Bill of Rights. They may bring up any of the following issues:
   - curfews
   - censorship of music or books
   - movie ratings
   - restrictions on skateboarding or in-line skating
   - dress codes
   - parental restrictions on television viewing
   - equal access to protection under the law

3. Propose that students brainstorm a list of rights that they would like to include in a Students' Bill of Rights.

4. Instruct students to design and administer a survey to find out which rights are important to the other students in the school (see *Resources, Stage 1*). Have students add items to, or cut items from, their list, as indicated by survey results.

TEAM TEACHING

The following activities may be used for team teaching or as enrichment and extension activities by the language arts teacher.

Social Studies Learn about the history of the Bill of Rights. Learn the legal definition of *child* and study laws regulating the behavior of children.

Language Arts Learn techniques for devising and conducting surveys (see *Resources, Stage 1*).

Math Compile and tabulate survey results.

TEACHING TIPS

- Suggest that when students read the Bill of Rights, they paraphrase it to enhance comprehension.
- Invite an attorney to speak to the class about children's civil rights and civil liberties.
- Have students use interviews or other research to learn whether they have the same rights as adults.

Stage 2
Draft a Bill of Rights

1. Direct students to create broad categories of rights that concern them. For example, they might make categories such as "rights at home," "rights at school," and "rights in the community." Then have them create subcategories such as freedom of dress (under rights at school) or freedom to choose their own friends (under freedom at home). Suggest that each subcategory be addressed in a section of the Students' Bill of Rights.

2. Ask students to work in groups to research their existing legal rights in each category and to develop proposals for the wording of the corresponding section of the Students' Bill of Rights.

3. Have students present their proposals for the class to discuss.

TEAM TEACHING

Social Studies Research how the Supreme Court has viewed the rights of children; study how the Supreme Court's views affect the law (see *Resources, Stage 2*).

Language Arts Learn research skills. Practice oral presentation techniques (see *Resources, Stage 2*).

TEACHING TIPS

- Schedule a library tour focusing on information about the judicial and legal systems.
- Challenge students developing proposals to avoid "We want" statements, such as "We want to be allowed to wear earrings to school." Have them use statements involving subcategories instead, such as "Students should be free to dress as they wish."

Stage 3
Publish and Evaluate

1. Direct students to revise their proposals based on the class discussion, to make a final draft of their Bill of Rights, and to publish it by posting it in a central area or delivering a copy of it to each homeroom.

2. Have students hold hearings or a vote to get the reactions of students and teachers throughout the school.

3. Instruct students to use the information they have collected to write essays in which they express their opinion of one item in the Students' Bill of Rights (see *Resources, Stage 3*).

TEAM TEACHING

Art Create a design for the finished document.

Math Tabulate votes or chart reactions to the Students' Bill of Rights.

Language Arts Learn techniques of writing to share opinions.

TEACHING TIPS

- During hearings, encourage students to explain and defend their views. Be sure all viewpoints have a chance to be heard.
- Have students vote on the Student Bill of Rights as if it were a constitutional amendment. (At least three-fourths of all students must vote yes for the Bill to be approved.)

Resources

STAGE 1

The Bill of Rights: How We Got It and What It Means by Milton Meltzer paraphrases the Bill of Rights and examines its history and implications.

Your Legal Rights by Linda Atkinson and *You Have a Right* by Leland S. Englebardt outline children's civil rights.

In *The Writer's Craft,* Grade 6, Workshop 5, "Persuasion," pages 128–132, teaches students how to create and conduct a public opinion survey.

STAGE 2

Blue Jeans and Black Robes: Teenagers and the Supreme Court by Peter P. Sgroi reviews Supreme Court rulings relating to the rights of teenagers.

Your Rights, Past and Present by James Haskins examines changing views of the rights of minors.

Up Against the Law: Your Legal Rights as a Minor by Ross Olney and Patricia Olney discusses the rights of minors under the law and gives many examples of actual and hypothetical cases.

In Defense of Children: Understanding the Rights, Needs, and Interests of the Child: A Resource for Parents and Professionals by Thomas Nazario reviews the rights of children.

The Writer's Craft, Grade 6, Handbook 25, "Study and Research Skills," pages 294–297 teaches research techniques. Handbook 32, "Oral Reports," pages 324–325 provides guidelines for effective oral reports.

STAGE 3

The Writer's Craft, Grade 6, Workshop 5, "Persuasion," pages 114–127, teaches students how to write about their opinions.

I Am Not a Short Adult! Getting Good at Being a Kid by Marilyn Burns deals with various aspects of childhood, including legal rights.

Additional Projects

Presenting Popcorn Have students participate in an ongoing class popcorn sale, with the proceeds to be used for a field trip or celebration at the end of the year. They should use persuasive techniques as they create an advertising campaign to publicize their product. Tell students to create ads, make posters, write product descriptions, and find other ways to persuade buyers. Ask students to track the effects of their advertisements by using sales records and customer surveys to discover which advertisements are most effective. Students should change their ads regularly in response to their findings.

Community Safety Ask students to identify community safety issues that they are concerned about. For example, they might focus on a dangerous intersection in need of a stoplight or on a neighborhood lacking a safe place for children to play. Encourage students to use interviews, surveys, and other research to learn more about the issues and about other people who share their concerns. Have students create multimedia presentations including posters and videos to increase awareness of the issues. Also have them write persuasive letters that explain their concerns and urge action on the issues. Students could mail their letters to community leaders and local newspapers.

- **Turn your opinion into a poster.** Create headlines and illustrations to present your opinion.

- **Hold a class discussion.** Get together with your classmates and present your papers orally. Then share your reactions to each other's work.

- **Present your case.** Deliver your opinion personally to someone in a position of authority who might be able to help.

REFLECT ON YOUR WRITING

WRITER TO WRITER

One role of the writer today is to sound the alarm.

E. B. White, American writer

1. Add your writing to your portfolio. Include a note, to be attached to your paper, in which you reflect on your experience in writing your opinion paper. In this note you may want to write about the following questions:

- How did I find a topic to write about?

- How did my opinion change as I thought and wrote about my topic?

- What happened when my classmates read my paper? How did their responses help me or get in my way?

- How would I change my essay now, if I were to revise it again?

2. Explore additional writing ideas. See the suggestions for writing a review on pages 130–132, and Springboards on page 137.

FOR YOUR **PORTFOLIO**

Reteaching

After students have completed their papers, assess the needs of students who were not successful in developing an effective opinion essay and assign the appropriate handbook mini-lessons as well as the Workshop Support Materials listed in the Teaching Preview, pages 113a–113b.

Concepts commonly requiring reteaching for this assignment are

- **Handbook 7, Organizing Details, pp. 217–221**
- **Handbook 30, Thinking Skills, pp. 320–322**

The following suggestions and resources also may be useful:

Lack of Supporting Reasons, Facts, and Examples Use page 7, "Analyzing," of the *Thinking Skills Worksheets* to help students generate reasons for an opinion. Then suggest working with partners to list facts and examples that support these reasons.

Ignoring Opposing Views Have students compare and contrast the Strong Response and the Weak Response on pages 34 and 36 of *Guidelines for Writing Assessment and Portfolio Use* in the Teacher's Resource File. Point out passages in which the writer responds to or ignores opposing views.

Extension and Enrichment

1. If students could make any change at school, what would it be? Ask them to write a persuasive letter that outlines the change and deals with at least one possible objection.

2. Supply this scenario: You are in charge of publicity for a rock group. Design a poster to advertise a concert. The poster must persuade middle school students to attend but also appeal to parents.

Closure: Reflect on Your Writing

As students reflect on what to include in their note, encourage them to give special consideration to the final question. Explain that even professional writers think about ways in which they can improve a finished piece of writing.

Reading a
PUBLIC OPINION SURVEY

Objectives
- To analyze and respond to a public opinion survey
- To identify a purpose and audience for a survey
- To create and complete a survey and write a report on the results

Motivate

Informally administer the survey on page 128 to your students, reading the directions and the questions and writing the qualities on the board. Tally the results; then list the qualities in the order in which your class ranked them. Tell students that they will compare their answers with those of another group of students.

BUILD ON PRIOR KNOWLEDGE

Ask students to share any experiences they have had with taking or reading the results of public opinion surveys. Then share your experiences, perhaps with market research surveys, political surveys, or opinion surveys given by schools, government groups, or organizations. Discuss the type and purpose of the survey, and the likely use of the results.

SET A PURPOSE

After students have read Reading a Public Opinion Survey, explain that they now will find out how their results compare with Tina's. Remind students to think about a question on which they would like to know others' opinions.

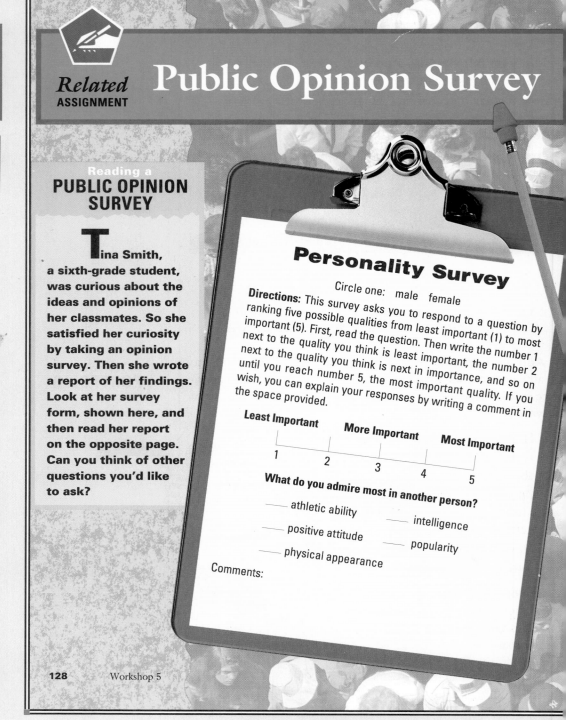

Related ASSIGNMENT
Public Opinion Survey

Reading a
PUBLIC OPINION SURVEY

Tina Smith, a sixth-grade student, was curious about the ideas and opinions of her classmates. So she satisfied her curiosity by taking an opinion survey. Then she wrote a report of her findings. Look at her survey form, shown here, and then read her report on the opposite page. Can you think of other questions you'd like to ask?

Personality Survey

Circle one: male female

Directions: This survey asks you to respond to a question by ranking five possible qualities from least important (1) to most important (5). First, read the question. Then write the number 1 next to the quality you think is least important, the number 2 next to the quality you think is next in importance, and so on until you reach number 5, the most important quality. If you wish, you can explain your responses by writing a comment in the space provided.

Least Important | More Important | Most Important

1   2   3   4   5

What do you admire most in another person?

—— athletic ability   —— intelligence

—— positive attitude   —— popularity

—— physical appearance

Comments:

Mathematics Connection

If possible, you might invite a math teacher who is familiar with statistics to talk informally about designing and analyzing surveys. The teacher can explain the importance of the size of the sample in analyzing the results. For example, with a large sample, very small differences in numbers are not statistically significant. With a small sample, however, such differences can result in a markedly different interpretation.

Personality Survey

Question

I've often wondered why my friends like some people more than others. I started asking them what they admired most in a person. Some said intelligence was most important. Others mentioned good looks or personality. Sometimes, though, I wasn't sure they were being honest. So I decided to take an opinion survey. I wrote down five qualities that people mentioned the most. Then I made up a questionnaire.

Method

I conducted this survey at my school in March. I gave the survey form to 100 sixth-grade students, 50 girls and 50 boys. When I got the forms back, I added up all the numbers. If someone ranked a quality as number five, I gave that answer five points. The second choice got four points, and so on. Here are the choices the students made and the total points each quality got.

SURVEY RESULTS

Quality	Girls	Boys	Total
Positive Attitude	236	222	458
Intelligence	193	189	382
Athletic ability	117	132	249
Physical appearance	122	118	240
Popularity	81	89	170

Results

The most important quality of the five turned out to be a positive attitude. Out of the 100 students, 39 girls and 32 boys put it at the top of the list. The next most important trait was intelligence. It was rated number 2 by 35 girls and 26 boys. Almost one-fourth of the boys even gave it the highest rating. Third place was pretty close to a tie, but athletic ability came out a little ahead of physical appearance. Popularity came in last.

Conclusion

This survey tells me that boys and girls admire similar things. Both think a positive attitude and intelligence are most important. Girls seem to value physical appearance a little more than athletic ability, and with boys it's the other way around. Everyone put popularity last. I learned that most kids value more lasting things.

Think & Respond

What do you find to be the most interesting result of Tina's survey? Can you think of any reason why girls and boys disagreed about what to rank third? How do Tina's findings compare with your own experience?

Think & Respond

ELICIT PERSONAL RESPONSES

Have students freewrite responses to the questions in the Think & Respond box. Then discuss students' responses. If there are major differences between Tina's findings and their statistics, ask students why the results differ.

EXPLORE THE AUTHOR'S TECHNIQUES

Point out that Tina's survey has two main parts—the survey itself (page 128) and the report of her findings (page 129). Ask students what makes the survey easy to complete. (Samples: clear directions, a scale showing how to respond, and a fill-in-the-blank format for responding) Also, point out that Tina wanted to look at the differences between the responses of girls and those of boys; therefore, she asked respondents to indicate their gender. Then focus attention on the organization of the report, emphasizing the four sections and the presentation of the statistical information. You might mention that the format of the report is similar to the format of laboratory reports in science.

Grammar Connection

Students may not know how to deal with numbers in their reports—that is, whether to use numerals or spell out the numbers as words. In actuality, style for treating numbers varies. Refer students to the "Method" and "Results" sections of Tina's report. Note that numbers under 10 and fractions are spelled out. Numbers with more than one digit are written as numerals. Point out that in a chart or other graphic aid, numbers are always written as numerals.

Remind students of the features that made Tina's survey easy to complete and to tabulate (clear directions and format, the use of a numerical scale for responses). Suggest that students consider Tina's approach as they plan their own public opinion surveys.

 Handbooks for Help and Practice

The following handbooks may be used as mini-lessons before students begin writing or as resources when problems arise:
- **Finding a Focus, pp. 203–204**
- **Organizing Details, pp. 217–221**
- **Interviewing Skills, p. 323**

Teaching Strategies

for CONSIDER YOUR AUDIENCE

HELPFUL HINT Remind students that, like Tina, they may want to compare the responses of different segments of their audience, such as girls and boys or different age groups. Explain that in order to do this, students must include at the beginning of their survey questions that elicit the respondents' age, gender, and so on.

for CHOOSE THE SIZE . . .

HELPFUL HINT You might suggest an audience size that you think is reasonable for students to survey; for example, students should not feel pressured to survey 100 people just because the model uses this number; however, caution students against inadvertently skewing their results by limiting their audience to their friends or to people they know well. Also, advise students to survey an equal number of people in each group they wish to compare, such as boys and girls, unless they want only the opinion of one group.

Writing
ON YOUR OWN

Public Opinion Survey

INVITATION TO Write

Tina Smith used a survey to find out what her classmates admired most in other people. Then she reported on her findings. You, too, can gather information about people's opinions by taking a survey.

Design a public opinion survey on a subject that interests you. Give the survey to a group of people, and then write a report about the results.

FINDING A FOCUS

1. Find a reason to take a survey. You can conduct a survey to get support for an idea—for example, that television violence is harmful to kids. You might use a survey to help you make a decision, such as which product to sell to raise money for your club. Perhaps you are simply curious about how other people think about an issue you care about, such as cafeteria menus or the length of the school day.

2. Consider your audience. Who will take your survey? That depends on what you want to learn. You may want to target certain groups, such as sports fans or skateboarders. On the other hand, you may simply want to survey students in general.

3. Choose the size of your survey. If, for example, you want to know how students feel about cafeteria menus, you would need to survey as many students as possible in order to get the most reliable information. If you want to know how the members of your club feel about meeting times, your survey would be limited to the club members.

130 Workshop 5

Literature Connection

Students might enjoy taking a survey about the kind of reading classmates do for pleasure. They could use broad categories, such as books, magazines, and comic books—or more specific ones, such as realistic fiction, science fiction, historical fiction, or nonfiction.

Music Connection

Interested students might take a survey to find out what musical instruments their classmates would like offered in the music curriculum. Students also could ask a librarian for help in finding music representative of several generations, then create a survey about attitudes toward the music.

CREATING YOUR SURVEY

1. Consider the form. What form works best for the type of survey you are doing? Tina asked people to rank qualities from least to most important. The resulting data gave her numbers that she could compare. Multiple-choice questions are another useful form. They can be used for issues such as which radio stations are more popular or what kinds of books students like to read.

2. Write the questions. Think about what you want to know. Brainstorm with some friends to come up with possible questions. Then try out different ways of wording the questions to make them as clear as possible.

3. Write directions. Tell people what you want them to do. Your directions need to be very clear or else you may get answers that you do not understand or cannot count. Sometimes a sample question and answer helps clarify directions for the people who take your survey.

4. Test your form. Try out your survey on a few of your classmates. Can they follow your directions? Do they understand your questions? If necessary, change the wording of questions or directions before giving your survey to a larger number of people.

COMPLETING THE SURVEY

1. Have people take the survey. Find a convenient time and place for people to read and complete your survey. Collect the completed forms and keep them together until you are ready to count the answers.

2. Keep track of the responses. Set up a chart or a list with which you can count responses and figure out the results of your survey.

Public
Opinion Survey   **131**

for CREATING YOUR SURVEY

INDIVIDUALIZING INSTRUCTION: INDEPENDENT LEARNERS These students should enjoy making up their own survey. Because independent learners usually prefer to trust their own judgment, however, they may need support in seeking the opinions of others. Therefore, you might want to pair such students with social learners who can help distribute or administer the survey.

for CONSIDER THE FORM

KEY TO UNDERSTANDING Tell students that their survey must be in a form that can be tabulated easily. For example, open-ended questions that require people to write their own answers cannot be tabulated easily. Therefore, whatever form the surveys take should provide answer choices. Their form might be like Tina's, or they might take the form of multiple-choice, yes-or-no, or true-or-false questions.

Students should also think about the length of their surveys. People often do not want to spend much time answering a lot of questions, and a survey of more than one page will be expensive to duplicate.

for WRITE THE QUESTIONS

HELPFUL HINT Caution students to phrase their questions as impartially as possible. Loaded language or false either/or reasoning can skew their results. To emphasize this point, ask students to critique this sample survey question:

> Schools load excessive
> homework on overworked
> students.   T   F

for TEST YOUR FORM

INDIVIDUALIZING INSTRUCTION: LEP STUDENTS Work individually with students who have difficulty in writing clear directions, or pair them with strong English speakers.

Stage 3
Present Responses and Examine Implications

1. Direct groups to plan presentations of their examples and their research findings. The presentations should include group members' personal responses.

2. Have students present video clips, photographs, print and video advertisements, newspaper and magazine clippings, and audiotapes. Have them comment on specific images they find repeated in various media. For example, did they find repeated images of teenagers as rebellious and irresponsible or of fathers as incompetent and foolish?

3. Afterward, invite students to discuss the effects that media images have on viewers' attitudes and expectations. Do media standards of beauty affect how they see themselves? Which images of families do they find to be realistic? Which seem false? Which images are offensive?

TEAM TEACHING

Language Arts Review oral presentation skills.

Social Studies Learn about the ways the media influence events. Use as examples presidential debates and war coverage.

Art Create posters and illustrations for presentations.

Math Gather statistics about the media. Study the TV rating system and learn how the numbers are computed (see *Resources, Stage 3*).

TEACHING TIPS
• Arrange for students to show video clips or to play audiotapes during their presentations.
• Invite social studies classes to attend the presentations.

Resources

STAGE 1

Television and the American Family by Jennings Bryant discusses the impact of television on families.

Dancing in the Dark: Youth, Popular Culture, and the Electronic Media by Quentin J. Schultze investigates how television and radio affect young people and popular culture.

Prime Time Kids: An Analysis of Children and Families on Television by Sally Steenland helps evaluate television images of children and families.

STAGE 2

Film by Richard Platt and *The TV Book* by Judy Fireman are large-format, heavily illustrated books tracing the history of the movies and of television. Both include many still photos that may give students ideas about which old movies and TV shows they might explore.

For reviews and other articles on media, check the *New York Times,* which dates back to 1851, and the *Chicago Tribune,* which dates to 1847.

The Writer's Craft, Grade 6, Writer's Workshop 6, "Responding to Literature," pages 140–160, teaches the writing of responses to written or visual materials.

STAGE 3

The Writer's Craft, Grade 6, Handbook 32, "Oral Reports," pages 324–325, can help students with their oral presentations.

Can You Believe TV Ratings? by Paula Apsell and Mike Tomlinson (Films for the Humanities and WGBH Television) is a TV program originally broadcast on *Nova.* It examines the methods used to measure audiences for TV shows.

Big World, Small Screen: The Role of Television in American Society by Aletha C. Huston discusses the impact of television on society.

Guerrilla Media: A Citizen's Guide to Using Electronic Media for Social Change (Films for the Humanities) by David Hoffman, Tony Schwartz, and Will Duggan gives examples of radio and TV spots and focuses on how the average person can use the media to promote social change.

How to Make a Speech, a McGraw-Hill video narrated by Steve Allen, offers a humorous introduction to creating and delivering effective oral presentations.

Statistical Abstract of the United States, published annually, includes statistics about families and about TV ownership.

Additional Projects

Young Tourists' Guide Ask students to use research, personal response writing, and other skills to create a guidebook to their community and the surrounding area. The guidebook should be intended for peers. Students should compile maps, photos, illustrations, descriptions, and reviews of their favorite and least favorite restaurants, amusement parks, outdoor recreation areas, local events, and so on. Students can donate a copy of the finished guidebook to the local department of tourism or chamber of commerce.

Reading Outreach Ask students to adopt a primary-school class and to visit regularly to read to the children and help them with reading skills. Between visits, students should survey young children's books in libraries and bookstores. Have students prepare reviews, with the primary students as an audience, of the books they think the children will like best. During visits, students should take turns presenting their reviews orally. Afterward, students may read the books to interested children.

The Best Pets Have students research information about specific breeds and types of animals commonly kept as pets. They should present their findings and add the findings to a class data center. Then ask students to choose favorite pet types or breeds; visit owners, breeders, and/or pet stores; and present "pet reviews" combining facts with their personal responses to this kind of pet.

Objective

- To use a visual prompt and writing prompts as springboards to informal writing

WRITING WARM-UPS

Encourage students to respond freely and informally to at least one of the Sketchbook prompts. Students may begin by brainstorming ideas or questions with the whole class and then exploring their ideas or questions by freewriting in their journals. Remind them that their responses will not be graded and may provide them with useful material for later assignments.

One way to respond to an object is to ask questions about that object. Students will also find this questioning technique helpful as they respond to a piece of literature in Writer's Workshop 6. Questioning can provide an inventory of what more they want to know or what they find puzzling. Asking questions and inventing histories can also suggest some engaging report topics for Writer's Workshop 7.

SHOW, DON'T TELL

The following is a sample for the first prompt that shows rather then tells about personal responses:

Everyone I know has his or her own special way of responding to music. My friend Jesse loves to dance to a rap beat, while my sister dreams away in her bedroom as she listens to tapes of classical piano. As for me, I can't wait to buy the latest country hit and try to play along on my guitar.

I and the Village (1911), Marc Chagall.

- What do you think about this painting? Jot down your reactions.
- Tell a story about what you see in this painting.
- Is there a book, a poem, a painting, a song, or another work of art that has a special meaning for you? Explain why.

Show, Don't Tell

When you respond to a story or a poem, you try to connect your own experiences to something in the literature. Using examples from your life, you can explain how a piece of literature makes you feel. Select one of the *telling* sentences below and turn it into a *showing* paragraph by using examples from your own experience.

- The character did something that I would do.
- The story made me sad.

140

6

Responding to Literature

Guided Assignment
Personal Response

Related Assignment
Book Review

Y ou've just been watching a TV show with friends. You're complaining about the ending, but someone else liked the actors. Still another remembers the funny lines. You're all responding to the show. Sharing your reactions is not only natural and fun, it also helps you understand your own thoughts and feelings about a work.

In this workshop you'll get a chance to write what you think and feel about a short work of literature. In a related assignment, you'll share your responses to a book you've read.

141

Links to THE LANGUAGE OF LITERATURE

Literature For more examples of short stories about growing up with various cultural and ethnic backgrounds, see *The Language of Literature,* Grade 6:
• Sandra Cisneros, "Eleven"
• Kristin Hunter, "The Scribe"
• Lensey Namioka, "The All-American Slurp"

• Francisco Jiménez, "The Circuit"

Writing This Guided Assignment on personal response to literature may be used as an extension of the Guided Assignment "Write a Personal Response" on page 86 of *The Language of Literature,* Grade 6.

6

Responding to Literature

Objectives

Guided Assignment

Personal Response To analyze a personal response to a short work of literature and to write a personal response essay on a short literary work of one's choice

Related Assignment

Book Review To evaluate a book review and to write a review of a book of one's choice

Teacher's Choice

Use the following guidelines to choose the assignment that best suits students' needs.

Personal Response This assignment will benefit all students by helping them express and explain their responses to a work of literature. Students are encouraged to explore their own feelings about the work as well as to explore the author's techniques. You may want to tie this assignment to writing activities in your literature program.

Book Review This assignment will be particularly challenging to students of limited English proficiency since they must read and evaluate an entire book; you may want to give these students the option of responding to a shorter work instead. For most students, this assignment may be used as an extension of the Guided Assignment in Workshop 5, "Sharing an Opinion."

Guided ASSIGNMENT — Personal Response

Guided
ASSIGNMENT

ASSIGNMENT RATIONALE

The ability to articulate a personal response to literature is not only a key to success in school, but also a skill that can increase students' enjoyment of literature and their awareness of the interactive relationship between the reader and the literary work. This assignment guides students in the process of evaluating a work of literature by relating it to their own experiences. It also offers practice in higher-level thinking skills, such as analyzing, inferring, making comparisons, and drawing conclusions.

Starting from LITERATURE

Motivate

Ask students if they have ever had to change schools because of a family move. Have them describe or speculate on the difficulties that such a move can present. Then ask how they would feel if they had to change homes and schools every year. Tell them that the story they will read is about a boy whose family moves several times a year.

Starting from LITERATURE

Imagine how it might feel to move often and to change schools frequently. What if people at school did not speak your language? Panchito has to face such situations. He and his family are farm workers from Mexico who follow the crops in southern California. As you read "The Circuit," notice what you are thinking and feeling. Use your journal to write down your thoughts, feelings, and questions as you read.

The Circuit
from

by Francisco Jiménez

IT WAS THAT TIME OF YEAR AGAIN. Ito, the strawberry sharecropper, did not smile. It was natural. The peak of the strawberry season was over, and the last few days the workers, most of them *braceros*,[1] were not picking as many boxes as they had during the months of June and July. . . .

Yes, it was that time of year. When I opened the front door to the shack, I stopped. Everything we owned was neatly packed in cardboard boxes. Suddenly I felt even more the weight of hours, days, weeks, and months of work. I sat down on a box. The thought of having to move to Fresno and knowing what was in store for me there brought tears to my eyes.

That night I could not sleep. I lay in bed thinking about how much I hated this move. . . .

   As we drove away, I felt
   a lump in my throat. I turned
   around and looked at our
    little shack for the last time.

At sunset we drove into a labor camp near Fresno. Since Papa did not speak English, Mama asked the camp foreman if he needed any more workers. "We don't need no more," said the foreman, scratching his head. "Check with Sullivan down the road. Can't miss him. He lives in a big white house with a fence around it."

When we got there, Mama walked up to the house. She went through a white gate, past a row of rose bushes, up the stairs to the front door. She rang the doorbell. The porch light went on and a tall, husky man came out. They exchanged a few words. After the man went in, Mama clasped her hands and hurried back to the car. "We have work! Mr. Sullivan said we can stay there the whole season," she said, gasping and pointing to an old garage near the stables. . . .

Early next morning Mr. Sullivan showed us where his crop was, and after breakfast, Papa, Roberto, and I headed for the vineyard to pick. . . .

After lunch we went back to work. The sun kept beating down. The buzzing

MORE ABOUT THE MODEL

Francisco Jiménez was born in Mexico. When he was four years old, his family moved to the United States to work as migrant farm laborers. He has written many autobiographical stories about his childhood. Jiménez writes in both English and Spanish. He explains, "Because I am bilingual and bicultural, I can move in and out of both American and Mexican cultures with ease; therefore, I have been able to write stories in both languages. I consider that a privilege."

insects, the wet sweat, and the hot dry dust made the afternoon seem to last forever. Finally the mountains around the valley reached out and swallowed the sun. Within an hour it was too dark to continue picking. The vines blanketed the grapes, making it difficult to see the bunches. *"Vamonos,"* [2] said Papa, signaling to us that it was time to quit work. Papa then took out a pencil and began to figure out how much we had earned our first day. He wrote down numbers, crossed some out, wrote down some more. *"Quince,"* [3] he murmured. . . .

The next morning I could hardly move. My body ached all over. I felt little control over my arms and legs. This feeling went on every morning for days until my muscles finally got used to the work.

It was Monday, the first week of November. The grape season was over, and I could now go to school. I woke up early that morning and lay in bed, looking at the stars and savoring the thought of not going to work and of starting sixth grade for the first time that year. Since I could not sleep, I decided to get up and join Papa and Roberto at breakfast. I sat at the table across from Roberto, but I kept my head down. I did not want to look up and face him. I knew he was sad. He was not going to school today. He was not going tomorrow, or next week, or next month.

He would not go until the cotton season was over, and that was sometime in February. I rubbed my hands together and watched the dry, acid-stained skin fall to the floor in little rolls.

When Papa and Roberto left for work, I felt relief. I walked to the top of a small grade next to the shack and watched the "Carcanchita" [4] disappear in the distance in a cloud of dust.

Two hours later, around eight o'clock, I stood by the side of the road waiting for school bus number twenty. When it arrived I climbed in. No one noticed me. Everyone was busy either talking or yelling. I sat in an empty seat in the back.

When the bus stopped in front of the school, I felt very nervous. I looked out the bus window and saw boys and girls carrying books under their arms. I felt empty. I put my hands in my pants pockets and walked to the principal's office. When I entered, I heard a woman's voice say, "May I help you?" I was startled. I had not heard English for months. For a few seconds I remained speechless. I looked at the lady who waited for an answer. My first instinct was to answer her in Spanish, but I held back. Finally, after struggling for English words, I managed to tell her that I wanted to enroll in the sixth grade. After answering many questions, I was led to the classroom.

Mr. Lema, the sixth-grade teacher, greeted me and assigned me a desk. He then introduced me to the class. I was so nervous and scared at that moment when everyone's eyes were on me that I wished I were with Papa and Roberto picking cotton. After taking roll, Mr. Lema gave the class the assignment for the first hour. "The first thing we have to do this morning is finish reading the story we began yesterday," he said enthusiastically. He walked up to me, handed me an English book, and asked me to read. "We are on page 125," he said politely. When I heard this, I felt my blood rush to my head. I felt dizzy. "Would you like to read?" he asked hesitantly. I opened the book to page 125. My mouth was dry. My eyes began to water. I could not begin. "You can read later," Mr. Lema said understandingly.

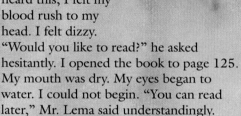

For the rest of the reading period I kept getting angrier and angrier with myself. I should have read, I thought to myself.

During recess I went into the restroom and opened my English book to page 125. I began to read in a low voice, pretending I was in class. There were many words I did not know. I closed the book and headed back to the classroom.

Mr. Lema was sitting at his desk correcting papers. When I entered he looked up at me and smiled. I felt better. I walked up to him and asked if he could help me with the new words. "Gladly," he said.

The rest of the month I spent my lunch hours working on English with Mr.

Lema, my best friend at school.

One Friday during lunch hour, Mr. Lema asked me to take a walk with him to the music room. "Do you like music?" he asked me as we entered the building. "Yes, I like Mexican *corridos*,"[5] I answered. He then picked up a trumpet, blew on it, and handed it to me. The sound gave me goose bumps. I knew that sound. I had heard it in many Mexican *corridos*. "How would you like to learn how to play it?" he asked. He must have read my face because before I could answer, he added: "I'll teach you how to play it during our lunch hours."

That day I could hardly wait to get home to tell Papa and Mama the great news. As I got off the bus, my little brothers and sisters ran up to meet me. They were yelling and screaming. I thought they were happy to see me, but when I opened the door to our shack, I saw that everything we owned was neatly packed in cardboard boxes.

---

1. **braceros** (brä sä´ rōs): *Spanish:* hired hands; day laborers.
2. **Vamonos** (vä´ mô nôs): *Spanish:* Let's go.
3. **quince** (kēn´ sä): *Spanish:* fifteen.
4. **"Carcanchita":** Papa's nickname for the old family car.
5. **corridos** (kô rē´ dôs): *Spanish:* ballads.

Think & Respond

How do you think Panchito feels about what happens at the end of the story? What are your thoughts and feelings about the story? **Freewrite** about your response to the whole story or to any part of it. Share your freewriting with your classmates.

145

Think & Respond

ELICIT PERSONAL RESPONSES

As a class or in small groups, have students discuss the questions in the Think & Respond box. Then have them write about their thoughts and feelings in their journals.

Students may say that Panchito felt sad, helpless, angry, or discouraged when he saw that he had to move once again.

EXPLORE THE AUTHOR'S TECHNIQUES

Point out to students that one reason "The Circuit" is such a powerful story is that Francisco Jiménez *shows*, rather than *tells*, what the life of migrant workers is like. Have students find examples from the story. (Samples: In paragraph 2 on page 143, instead of saying, "I found out we had to move again," the author describes what Panchito *saw*: "Everything we owned was neatly packed in cardboard boxes." In paragraph 3, instead of saying that Panchito was sorry to leave, the author describes the boy's physical sensation: "As we drove away, I felt a lump in my throat." On page 145, instead of saying Panchito was nervous about having to read aloud in class, the author again describes the boy's physical sensations: "My mouth was dry. My eyes began to water."

Music Connection

With the help of a music teacher, invite a volunteer to sing some popular Mexican corridos, or ballads. If that is not possible, find recordings of Mexican music and play them for your students. The popular singer Linda Ronstadt is of Mexican heritage and has recorded several albums of songs she heard when she was growing up, including *Mas Canciones* and *Frenesi*. You might also play folk songs about the lives of migrant farm workers. The folk singer Woody Guthrie recorded many of these, including the song "Deportee," which has also been recorded by Judy Collins, Arlo Guthrie, Pete Seeger, and the a cappella group Sweet Honey in the Rock.

The models that open this guided assignment differ from those in other workshop assignments; the Student Model is a personal response to the Professional Model. The Student Model is the final draft of the piece that students will see in process on the workshop pages that follow.

Motivate

Tell students about a reading experience you've had, when you said to yourself, "That's amazing! This author knows exactly how I feel; it's as if the writer has read my mind." Ask students if they have ever had this kind of experience, and encourage them to name authors or works that made them feel this way. Point out that writing a personal response essay is one way of expressing their feelings about stories and poems that make a deep impression on them.

BUILD ON PRIOR KNOWLEDGE

Ask students if there are any parts of the story "The Circuit" that they find especially sad or touching. What about those scenes really moves them? Tell students that those parts of a literary work that really touch them often echo their own experiences and are usually the ones that they themselves could write about most powerfully.

SET A PURPOSE

As students read the Student Model, have them notice which part of the story Vanessa focuses on, what details and dialogue she chooses from the story, and the reason why she focuses on those details.

One Student's Writing

Reading a
STUDENT MODEL

When Vanessa Ramirez, a sixth-grade student, read "The Circuit," she reacted strongly to one part of the story. That part seemed to touch her own life and experience. She decided to focus on her reaction in her paper. How does she show the reasons for her special response?

Responding to "The Circuit"
by Vanessa Ramirez

When I read and reread "The Circuit" by Francisco Jiménez, I didn't understand why it made me feel sad, but then I realized at the end that it reminded me of when I was small, when I first started school.

In the story a boy named Panchito can't go to school because he has to work in the fields to help his family. When he finally goes to school in November, he forgets how to speak in English.

Panchito says that when he entered the school office, he heard a voice say, "May I help you?" Then he says, "I had not heard English for months. For a few seconds I remained speechless." I put myself in Panchito's place when I read this, because I

English Class
Clase de Inglés

¿Qué tal?

HOLA!

Super!

LISA's COOL!

1226 Páginas Fáciles de Leer
1226 Easy-to Read Pages

Diccionario
ESPAÑOL/INGLÉS

ENGLISH/SPANISH
Dictiona

had already experienced it before. When I first started school, I spoke only Spanish, but my parents spoke for me. So that was a great relief.

The reason I say it was a great relief is because in my situation my parents spoke for me in order to enroll me and in his situation Panchito had to speak for himself to enroll in school. This part of the story hit my heart.

When people are used to talking in one language, it is very hard when they realize they're being told something in another language. It must be sad because they don't understand, or maybe they do, but they are embarrassed because they don't know how to speak the other language well. That's how Panchito felt when he went to enroll in school and when the teacher asked him to read in class.

I liked writing about this story because as I was writing, I was imagining that I was there in the story and because it kind of has to do with what happened to me.

Think & Respond

Respond as a Reader
▶ How was Vanessa able to tie the story to her own experience?

▶ In what way was Vanessa's reaction to the story the same as or different from yours?

Respond as a Writer
▶ What parts of Vanessa's essay made the strongest impression on you? Can you say why?

▶ How does the end of Vanessa's paper tie in with the beginning?

Think & Respond

RESPOND AS A READER
▶ Have students identify the part of the first sentence in which Vanessa states how the story relates to her own life. Then have students find examples in the body of her paper that explain or support her opening statement.

▶ Some ESL students may react as Vanessa did to the passages about first entering a school in which classes are conducted in English. Other students may identify more with the experience of moving to a new school or, more generally, with Panchito's experiences of dread, hope, excitement, and disappointment.

RESPOND AS A WRITER
▶ If students have difficulty explaining why a certain passage of Vanessa's essay impressed them, have them read the passage aloud. Then ask them questions to draw out their reasons for responding strongly to that passage.

▶ In both the introduction and the conclusion of her essay, Vanessa points out that Panchito's experiences reminded her of her own.

Draw Conclusions
To make sure students understand this introduction to writing a personal response to literature, challenge them to list the characteristics they have noted thus far. Responses may include the following:
- a clear statement of personal response to a specific work
- reasons from personal experience, and examples and quotations from the literary work
- a general conclusion

Social Studies Connection

Students who are interested in the culture and achievements of Mexican-Americans, as well as the social problems they face, might enjoy reading and reporting on the following books:

Cesar Chavez, by Ruth Franchere
Chicanos: The Story of Mexican-Americans, by Patricia De Garza

Famous Mexican-Americans, by Clarke Newlon
Henry Cisneros: Mexican-American Mayor, by Naurice Roberts
Soy Chicano: I Am Mexican-American, by Robert and Lynne Fitch

2. Organize your draft.   Here's one good approach:

- **Introduce the book.**   Give the title, the author, and perhaps something about the author's background. You may also want to state the main point you intend to make.
- **Summarize the book.**   Give readers a general idea about the content of the book, as Jeff does in his review. If the book is fiction, you might discuss plot, setting, and characters. Normally, you shouldn't give away the ending.
- **Evaluate the book.**   Tell why you admire or dislike the book. You may want to discuss the author's purpose. Did the book make you laugh or perhaps get you to accept a new idea? Support your reactions with specific examples from the book.
- **Conclude the review.**   You can restate your view or perhaps give a recommendation, as Jeff Hayden did.

REVIEWING YOUR WRITING

1. Think about your audience.   Have you given your readers enough information for them to decide whether they might like the book? Did you explain unfamiliar terms?

2. Apply the final touches.   Does your introduction draw the reader in? Is your conclusion convincing? Did you support your reactions? Did you check your grammar and punctuation?

PUBLISHING AND PRESENTING

- **Publish your review**.   Submit it to a magazine, as Jeff did, or to a class or school publication.
- **Make an advertisement.**   Use words and artwork—as in a movie poster—to show your reactions to the book you reviewed.
- **Hold a book-review round table.**   Get together with classmates to discuss, compare, and recommend various books.

PROBLEM SOLVING

"How can I get a good start on my draft?"

For help in getting started, see

- Handbook 2, "Finding a Starting Point," pages 197–202
- Handbook 6, "Drafting," pages 215–216

Grammar **TIP**

Check to be sure you have capitalized and spelled all proper names correctly.

Teaching Strategies

for EVALUATE THE BOOK
CRITICAL THINKING: EVALUATING
With the entire class, brainstorm a list of adjectives students might use to describe books they like and books they dislike. Add your own adjectives to the list to expand students' vocabularies. For example: LIKE: *funny, sad, fascinating, surprising, touching, exciting;* DISLIKE: *boring, predictable, outdated, confusing.* Encourage students to use applicable words in their reviews.

for THINK ABOUT YOUR AUDIENCE
PEER RESPONSE After students have had a chance to read each others' drafts, writers might ask readers to tell whether they would like to read the book themselves. If peer readers are not sure, writers can ask what additional information might help them form a definite opinion about the book. Writers may then want to make revisions in their drafts based on their peers' answers.

Guidelines for Evaluation
AN EFFECTIVE BOOK REVIEW
- identifies the book by title and author
- contains a brief summary of the book
- contains an evaluation of the book
- contains specific examples and quotations from the book that support the evaluation
- includes an attention-getting introduction and a convincing conclusion

Teaching Strategies

for SPEAKING AND LISTENING

MANAGEMENT TIP Have students who have read the same literary work meet in small groups. Each member of the group can recommend and read aloud a passage suitable for dramatization or oral interpretation. Tell groups to reach an agreement on which passage to present. Set aside class time for rehearsals and performances.

for MEDIA

COLLABORATIVE OPPORTUNITY Ask students if they have seen programs featuring pairs of movie reviewers who debate the merits of various films. Encourage pairs of students familiar with the format to collaborate in presenting and defending opposing views of the same work or works.

for FINE ARTS

HELPFUL HINT You may want to involve an art teacher in introducing students to various art techniques and in planning an exhibit of finished works.

Spring**boards**

Speaking and Listening
In a book, story, or play, find a scene that you think is particularly moving. Then, with the help of some of your classmates, act it out or present an oral interpretation.

MEDIA Imagine that you are the entertainment critic for your local TV station. Prepare a brief on-air presentation. It should give your personal response to a movie, play, television show, or literary work.

Music Think about current events and personalities in the news. Make up a rap or a folk song that tells your personal response to some person or event.

Reading
Write a "lit letter" to a friend. Describe a book you are reading. Tell your friend why you loved or hated the book.

fine **Arts** Make a
drawing, a collage, a painting, a sculpture, a mobile, or another piece of art that expresses your reaction to an event in your life or to a piece of literature. Write a paragraph to go with the art, telling what it means.

160

Reading Back and Forth

What do the words *eye, pop, dad, mom, noon,* and *civic* have in common?

They are all *palindromes*— words, phrases, or sentences that read the same way backward and forward. Try this one: *No lemon, no melon.*

An old joke says that Adam introduced himself to Eve with a palindrome: "Madam in Eden, I'm Adam."

Perhaps you've heard this famous one: "A man, a plan, a canal, Panama!"

Try reading these palindromes forward and backward.

- Rise to vote, sir.
- Never odd or even.

- Was it a rat I saw?
- Doc, note, I dissent. A fast never prevents a fatness. I diet on cod.
- Now, sir, a war is won.

What happens when you read the word *palindromes* backward? You get a *semordnilap,* a word that is another word in reverse. For example, *on* backward is *no, pots* backward is *stop,* and *star* backward is *rats.* Read *No evil repaid* backward, and you get *Diaper live on.*

Make your own list of palindromes or semordnilaps to share with friends. A dictionary can sometimes help. When you read back and forth, you never know what you might find.

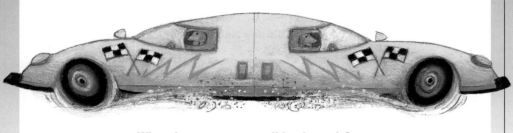

What does *race car* spell backwards?

When discussing this feature, point out to students that the name Eve is itself a palindrome. Ask if students can think of any other names that are palindromes. *(Bob, Nan, Anna, Otto, Ada, Asa)* Then ask if students can think of any proper names that are semordnilaps. *(Pam, Pat, Meg)*

Sentence Closers

Objectives
- To identify sentence closers
- To compose sentences with closers and punctuate the sentences correctly

Teaching Strategies

KEY TO UNDERSTANDING To help students identify closers, have a volunteer read each model sentence aloud without the closer. Point out that even without the closer, each model is a complete sentence. The closer simply adds descriptive details or other information to present a more complete picture.

Sentence Closers

At times, the last part of something is the best part—the finale of a fireworks display, dessert at the end of dinner, even the last part of a sentence. Like sentence openers, sentence closers are single words or groups of words that add important details to sentences.

> **Model A** The man was about fifty, <u>overweight but solid-looking</u>.
>
> **Frank Bonham, *Chief***
>
> **Model B** They were in the schoolroom again, <u>the five boys and Lina and the teacher</u>.
>
> **Meindert DeJong, *The Wheel on the School***
>
> **Model C** One of the pups came slowly toward me, <u>a round ball of fur that I could have held in my hand</u>.
>
> **Scott O'Dell, *Island of the Blue Dolphins***
>
> ▶ **ON THE MARK** Put a comma before a sentence closer to separate it from the rest of the sentence.

A. Combining Sentences Make a new sentence by adding the underlined part of the second sentence to the first sentence as a sentence closer. Write the complete sentence, putting a comma before the sentence closer.

1. My sister and I were working by our dock. We were <u>scraping and painting the little dinghy</u>. **Shirley Ann Grau, "The Land and the Water"**

2. I jumped to my feet. I was <u>completely thunderstruck</u>.
Antoine de Saint-Exupery, *The Little Prince*

3. She stayed behind because she thought it would be worthwhile trying the door of the wardrobe. She thought this <u>even though she felt almost sure that it would be locked</u>.
C. S. Lewis, *The Lion, the Witch, and the Wardrobe*

4. The pounding came up the stairs. It was <u>crashing on each step</u>.
Shirley Jackson, *The Haunting of Hill House*

5. They were the same kind of thunderheads as on the day of the ball game. The thunderheads were <u>white and piled up over the hills like a sky full of fresh dried laundry</u>. **Joseph Krumgold, *Onion John***

B. Unscrambling and Imitating Sentences Unscramble each set of sentence chunks below. Create a sentence that has a sentence closer and the same order of chunks and punctuation as the model. Then write a sentence of your own that imitates each model.

1. Model Mr. Underhill came out from under his hill, <u>smiling and breathing hard</u>. **Ursula K. Le Guin, "The Rule of Names"**

stood behind the cash register / the sales clerk / chatting and making change

2. Model They were eating borsch, <u>the rich, red soup with sour cream so dear to Russian palates</u>.
Richard Connell, "The Most Dangerous Game"

too difficult for many figure skaters / a dangerous, demanding move / she was practicing a triple jump

3. Model It was a good thing I had no homework that night, <u>for I could not possibly have concentrated</u>.
Jean Stafford, "Bad Characters"

because the storm would definitely have interfered / we took our hike this morning / it was a lucky break

Grammar Refresher Some sentence closers are appositives. To learn more about punctuating appositives, see Handbook 43, "Punctuation," pages 566–599.

Additional Resource
Sentence Composing Copy Masters, pp. 11–12

Answer Key

A. Combining Sentences
1. My sister and I were working by our dock, scraping and painting the little dinghy.
2. I jumped to my feet, completely thunderstruck.
3. She stayed behind because she thought it would be worthwhile trying the door of the wardrobe, even though she felt almost sure that it would be locked.
4. The pounding came up the stairs, crashing on each step.
5. They were the same kind of thunderheads as on the day of the ball game, white and piled up over the hills like a sky full of fresh dried laundry.

B. Unscrambling and Imitating Sentences
Unscrambled sentences are given. Students' imitations will vary but should follow the pattern of the model.
1. The sales clerk stood behind the cash register, chatting and making change.
2. She was practicing a triple jump, a dangerous, demanding move too difficult for many figure skaters.
3. It was a lucky break we took our hike this morning, because the storm would definitely have interfered.

for GRAMMAR REFRESHER
KEY TO UNDERSTANDING: APPOSITIVES An appositive is a noun or a noun phrase that identifies or gives more information about another word in the sentence, usually the word preceding it. Point out that the underlined words in Model 2 of Exercise B form an appositive phrase that defines *borsch*. Appositives are set off with commas when they provide nonessential information, but not when they provide essential information.

7

Informative Writing: Reports

Overview

Reports are longer pieces of informative writing that require research, analysis, and synthesis of information. Workshop 7 includes the following Guided and Related Assignments, as well as the interdisciplinary project described on page 163c–163d.

1. **Guided: Report of Information** calls on students to formulate questions, to research the answers, to analyze, synthesize, and paraphrase information as they take notes, and to draw conclusions to present in an interesting, informative, and logically organized report.

2. **Related: Family History** invites students to conduct interviews with family members, research documents and other primary sources from family history, and arrange details in a chronological narrative to share with the class and with family members.

Teaching Preview

Preparation Guide

1. Use the Overview on this page and the Teacher's Choice descriptions on page 165 as a basis for deciding which assignments to teach.

2. Preview the assignments and the teacher's notes and identify concepts that may require preteaching or extra support, given your class's abilities. The handbook mini-lessons suggested within the lesson may also provide guidance.

3. Preview the chart below for support materials in the Teacher's Resource File that may be used with this Workshop. Resources are for use with the Guided Assignment unless otherwise noted.

Support Materials

WRITER'S CRAFT RESOURCES

Prewrite and Explore
Thinking Skills Worksheets, p. 4, 10
Thinking Skills Transparencies, pp. 4–4a, 10–10a
Writing Resource Book, pp. 34–39

Draft and Discover
Elaboration, Revision, and Proofreading Practice, pp. 13–15
Elaboration, Revision, and Proofreading Transparencies, pp. 25–28
Writing Resource Book, pp. 40–41

Revise Your Writing
Elaboration, Revision, and Proofreading Practice, p. 16
Elaboration, Revision, and Proofreading Transparencies, pp. 29–30
Guidelines for Writing Assessment and Portfolio Use, pp. 20, 40–42

Peer Response Guides, pp. 19–20
Writing Resource Book, p. 42

Extension Activities
Sentence Composing Copymasters, pp. 13–14
Starting Points for Writing, pp. 29–30, 33–34, 38, 40
Writing from Literature, pp. 5–6, 15–18, 25–26
Standardized Test Practice

 Educational Technology
(available separately)
Writing Coach
Writer's DataBank
Electronic English Handbook
On Assignment! (videodisc)
The McDougal Littell Home Page at http://www.mcdougallittell.com

OTHER RESOURCES

Books and Journals
Elbow, Peter. "Breathing Experience into Expository Writing." *Writing with Power*. New York: Oxford U Press, 1981.
Hurst, C. O. "Writers, Research, and Report Writing." *Teaching PreK-8*. 23 (Aug./Sept. 1992): 150–152.

 Films and Videos
Peru. Altschul Group, 1992. (20 min.).
The Pueblo Dwellers. SRA, 1993. (21 min.)

Educational Technology
Intermediate Library Media Skills. Combase, 1986. Apple II Series.
The Multicultural Chronicles. MicroMedia Publishing, 1993. Hypercard.

DRAFT AND DISCOVER

1. Start writing any section you wish. You may want to begin drafting the part of your report you've learned the most about. However, if you have a clever idea for an introduction, then start at the very beginning and go from there.

2. Write one or more paragraphs for each main idea. Use your prewriting notes—your graphic and your note cards—as a guide to your writing.

3. Stay open to new ideas. As you write, you may find yourself heading off in unexpected directions. Go back to your sources for more information as you discover what you really want to say.

4. Assemble your draft. Put the pieces of your draft in an order that makes sense. Look again at Jonathan's final report on pages 167–169. You can see that he put his clusters of information in chronological, or time, order. Chronological order works well when you're describing events in history or when you're writing about someone's life. Other organizational patterns—such as order of importance or order of familiarity—may also work for the information you want to present.

5. Write an introduction and a conclusion. Your introduction should include a **thesis statement** that tells the main idea or purpose of your report. Your opening paragraph should also draw your readers into your writing and make them want to read on.

Your conclusion might summarize your main points, ask a question, or make a prediction. Notice how Jonathan's conclusion summarizes the importance of Jackie Robinson's contribution to baseball and to the fight for equality for all people.

6. Think about your draft. Do you want to share your draft with classmates now or work on it some more first? The following questions will help you and your readers review your report.

PROBLEM SOLVING

"What's the best way to organize my ideas? Would a more formal outline help?"

For help outlining your main ideas and ordering your details, see

- Appendix, page 608
- Handbook 7, "Organizing Details," pages 217–221

Objectives
- To draft a report of information
- To respond to one's own draft and that of a peer

Teaching Strategies

for WRITE ONE OR MORE PARAGRAPHS . . .

KEY TO UNDERSTANDING You might use Jonathan's cluster diagram on page 174 to point out that he used his plan flexibly. For example, he made "Work/Army," which is one item on his cluster, into two paragraphs; he put "Negro leagues" and "K.C. Monarchs," two items on the cluster, into one paragraph. Urge students to consider what information is most important and to expand those ideas, while combining or even eliminating less important details or items about which they have too little information.

for ASSEMBLE YOUR DRAFT

INDIVIDUALIZING INSTRUCTION: VISUAL AND KINESTHETIC LEARNERS You might suggest that these students try organizing with scissors and tape, cutting their paragraphs apart and trying them in different arrangements until they find an order that makes sense to them. Remind them that they may need to write new transitions when they reorder their reports.

TEACHER'S LOUNGE

"My class size is becoming a problem. By the time I've called roll, class is over."

NELSON

R E V I E W   Y O U R   W R I T I N G

Questions for Yourself
- What is the focus of my report?
- Did I find answers to the questions I had about my topic? What do I still need to research?
- Does my report read smoothly from beginning to end? Is anything missing? What parts should I rearrange?

Questions for Your Peer Readers
- What do you think is the main point of my report?
- Which parts interest you the most?
- Which parts need more explanation?

One Student's Process

Jonathan shared his draft with a friend whose comments appear in the margin.

Peer Reader Comments

> I've never heard of the Royals. Were they in the Major Leagues back then?

> It must have been awfully hard for him! What did Jackie do when he was treated so badly?

Before he could play in Brooklyn, Jackie had to play for the Montreal Royals. At first he was rejected by the Royals' fans and his teammates, but as time went on they accepted and liked him. Jackie became a hero in Montreal. Soon Jackie signed up with the Dodgers. Again the fans booed him, the team didn't like him, and other teams refused to play with him. But he began hitting and stealing more bases. The fans loved it! He was good at defence and hitting in pressure situations too, so the team liked him too!

R EVISE YOUR WRITING

1. Review your responses. Think about how you and your readers responded to your draft. What changes do you want to make? Will you add information and details? Will you take out information that's not related to your main focus?

One Student's Process

Jonathan thought about his friend's comments and added specific details and examples to support his ideas.

> for his great playing. When he played in other cities, though, the crowd and other teams made fun of Jackie or wouldn't play when he played.

Before he could play in Brooklyn, Jackie had to play for the Montreal Royals. At first he was the Dodgers' farm team, Jackie rejected by the Royals' fans and his teammates, but as time went on they accepted and liked him. Jackie became a hero in Montreal. Soon Jackie ¶ In 1947 signed up with the Dodgers. Again the fans a contract booed him, the team didn't like him, and other teams refused to play with him. But he began hitting and stealing more bases. The fans loved it! He was good at defence and hitting in pressure situations too, so the team liked him too.

> Jackie did what his manager wanted. He ignored the bad things other people said and did to him and tried his hardest to play well. Jackie

Paragraphs at Work Your outline, list, or cluster headings can help you see where your paragraph breaks should go. Remember these tips.
- Focus on one idea in each paragraph.
- Use a topic sentence to state the main idea.
- Include in each paragraph only those details and examples that support the main idea.

Report of Information **177**

for ONE STUDENT'S PROCESS

PEER RESPONSE Have students compare this portion of Jonathan's draft with the finished model paragraphs 4 and 5 on pages 168–169. Ask them how Jonathan's changes show that he understood and valued his peer reader's opinion. (He added details that responded directly to the questions the reader raised. For instance, he identified the Royals as "the Dodgers' farm team.") Remind students that Jonathan was free to disregard his reader's comments. Ask, "Did he make a good choice? Why?" (Sample: The additional details clarify passages that the reader would probably not have understood and add depth to Robinson's character.)

CRITICAL THINKING: SEQUENCING Another kind of transition that Jonathan frequently uses helps readers by showing how events are related in time. Have students point out words and phrases that tell when events happened. (Samples: "As he was growing up," "Throughout high school," "In 1942," "Before," and "During his baseball career") Ask students how these transitions help the reader. (They make the order of events clear.)

KEY TO UNDERSTANDING Discuss Jonathan's List of Sources (page 169) with students. Ask students to state the rule for writing the author's name (last name, comma, first name, period) and the order of information and its punctuation (Author. Title. Place: Publisher, Date.) Finally, have students explain the preferred form for a magazine article, a source with two authors, and an encyclopedia article.

Pᴿᴼᴼᶠᴿᴱᴬᴰ

Guidelines for Evaluation

IDEAS AND CONTENT
- focuses on a single topic
- supports main ideas with facts and details
- uses information from more than one source
- includes an effective introduction and conclusion

STRUCTURE AND FORM
- presents information in well-developed paragraphs
- employs appropriate transitions
- includes a List of Sources

GRAMMAR, USAGE, AND MECHANICS
- displays standard grammar, usage, and mechanics
- sets off transitions with commas when necessary

Standards for Evaluation

INFORMATIVE WRITING

A report
- has an interesting introduction that clearly states the subject
- focuses on a single topic
- includes facts and details to support main ideas
- uses information from more than one source and includes a List of Sources
- ends with a strong conclusion

LINKING GRAMMAR ᴬᴺᴰ WRITING

Using Transitions

You can show how your ideas are connected by using **transitions** between sentences and paragraphs. Words such as *however, also, therefore,* and *instead* are transitions that connect ideas. You can also repeat key words to link ideas. Transitions used at the beginning of a sentence are often followed by a comma. The transitions Jonathan uses to connect two paragraphs are underlined below.

Jackie was super in all the sports he played, and now professional scouts were observing him!
  However, Jackie never made a deal with these sports scouts. Instead, he took a job at a children's camp.

For more information about using transitions to connect ideas, see Handbook 11, "Using Transitions," pages 234–238.

2. Make an alphabetical List of Sources. Only list those books or articles you actually took notes from and used in writing your report. Also list any people you interviewed. Notice on page 169 how Jonathan prepared his List of Sources.

Pᴿᴼᴼᶠᴿᴱᴬᴰ

1. Proofread your report. Slowly and carefully reread your report. Correct any mistakes you might have made in grammar, spelling, capitalization, and punctuation.

2. Make a final copy. Read the Standards for Evaluation in the margin and decide if you were successful in completing the assignment. Make any additional changes you feel are necessary. Then write or print out a clean, final copy.

PUBLISH AND PRESENT

- **Present your report to another class.** Add visuals, such as models or graphs, to make your presentation more interesting.

- **Have a panel discussion.** If any classmates researched related topics, present these reports orally. You and the other presenters can then answer questions from the rest of the class.

- **Illustrate your report with drawings or photographs.** Then display your work on a class or school bulletin board.

REFLECT ON YOUR WRITING

I do a lot of research in books, and I read a lot of old diaries. There's an enormous amount of material available if one will take the time to get it.

Louis L'Amour, writer

1. Add your report to your portfolio. First, take some time to reflect on your writing process. Attach your answers to these questions to your final draft.

- How did I find my topic?
- What part of this project was most fun for me?
- What are the special strengths of my final draft?
- How have other types of writing I've done helped me to write this report?

2. Explore additional writing ideas. See the suggestions for researching and writing a family history on pages 182–184 and Springboards on page 185.

Jackie Robinson smashed a three-run home run against the Jersey City Giants during his minor league baseball debut, April 18, 1946. Here a teammate congratulates Robinson.

▶ FOR YOUR **PORTFOLIO**

Report of Information **179**

Reteaching

After students have completed their papers, assess the needs of students who were not successful in developing an effective report of information and assign the appropriate handbook mini-lessons, as well as the Workshop Support Materials listed in the Teaching Preview, pages 163a–163b. Concepts commonly requiring reteaching for this assignment are the following:

- Handbook 7, Organizing Details, pp. 217–221
- Handbook 10, Improving Paragraphs, pp. 230–233

The following suggestions and resources may also be useful:

Lack of Supporting Details Magazines such as *Faces* and *Cobblestone* contain articles that are essentially research reports. With students, read and informally analyze details that make an article interesting.

Weak Conclusions Use Handbook 15, "Conclusions," pages 250–252, to review writing conclusions. Have students examine the successful conclusion in the Strong Response for this workshop on page 40 in the *Guidelines for Writing Assessment and Portfolio Use* booklet in the Teacher's Resource File.

Extension and Enrichment

1. Have students work in pairs to research a topic, perhaps one that has emerged during the class's writing process.

2. Challenge students to collaborate on a class newsletter, working individually or in pairs to research and write reports about issues that relate to school life.

Closure: Reflect on Your Writing

If you had students share their reports, you may want to encourage further reflection by asking them to respond to these questions: "Now that you have heard (read) other people's reports, what would you change in your report *if you had time*? What might you do differently the next time?" Have students record their responses and attach them to their reports as reminders for future report writing.

Related
ASSIGNMENT

Starting from
LITERATURE

Objectives
• To respond to and analyze a family history
• To plan and research a family history
• To draft, revise, and present a family history

Motivate
Ask volunteers to tell stories about events in their families' histories. Explain that in this assignment, students will write their own family histories.

BUILD ON PRIOR KNOWLEDGE
Ask students how immigrants traveled to the United States one hundred years ago. (primarily via steamship) Ask what they think the journey might have been like. (Samples: long, slow, crowded, difficult) Ask students what problems they think the immigrants faced when they arrived. (Samples: language barriers, finding work, finding a place to live) Why might people have been willing to face such difficulties? (Sample: They thought they would have better opportunities.)

SET A PURPOSE
After students read Starting from Literature, ask them what kinds of experiences their family members talk about. Who tells these stories, and on what occasions? Why are these stories important in their families? As students read Merrill Wilk's family history, urge them to think about how she heard about this story for the first time and why it became important to her.

Related Family History
ASSIGNMENT

Starting from
LITERATURE

Parents, grand-parents, aunts, uncles, cousins. These are the people you call *family*. But what do you know about them? What were their lives like before you were born?

Researching and writing your family history, your family's story, connects you to the past. Writer Merrill Wilk researched her family's history and traced one side of her family back to Poland at the turn of the century. As you read, think about why she might have chosen to focus her family history on the immigration of her grandfather to the United States.

Finding Home

by
Merrill
Wilk

My grandfather Louis Zaremski (known now as Poppa Lou) was born in 1904 in a small, rural town in Poland. He was the first of six children born to Jacob and Molly Zaremski. Two other children, Frances and Morris, would be born in Poland before my family's dream of a better life in the United States finally came true.

Jacob was the first to arrive, settling in Chicago, Illinois, in 1910. He was a shoemaker by trade, as was his father before him. He set up shop and, by 1913, he had earned enough to send for his wife and children. Poppa Lou, then nine years old, still remembers the long journey to the United States.

Since they could only take with them what they could carry, Molly, Poppa Lou, Frances, and Morris packed their most precious belongings into a few small bags. Ironically, however, the day before my family was to leave Poland forever, their home burned to the ground. My family escaped with their lives, the clothes on their backs, and the money and passage papers Jacob had sent them. And on they went. . .

Social Studies Connection

Ellis Island Between 1892 and 1938, a majority of immigrants from Europe entered the United States through an immigration center on Ellis Island in New York Harbor. Students may wish to find out if any forebears entered the United States at this historic place, now part of Statue of Liberty National Monument.

for **FURTHER READING**

Books to Read Many young adult books, both fiction and nonfiction, deal with the experience of immigration. One novel students might enjoy is the Newbery Award-winning *Dragonwings,* by Laurence Yep. It tells of the experiences of a Chinese boy who enters the United States in the early 1900s.

Over two thousand immigrants spent more than two weeks in steerage, below the decks of the steamship New Amsterdam. Canvas hammocks for sleeping lined the walls. Benches and long tables filled the room. Each night, heaping platters of boiled herring were served family style, two or three to a table. One night a very large woman sat across from Poppa Lou, quickly eating as much as she could. When she thought no one was looking, she took a whole plate of herring and put it between her feet, hiding it under the skirts of her floor-length dress! My clever grandfather had watched her from the corner of his eye. When he thought she wasn't looking, he slid beneath the table, found the plate of herring, and put it back on the table for everyone to share.

After my family reached New York, they took a train into Chicago's La Salle Street Station. They arrived a day early, however, so Jacob wasn't there to meet them. A traveler's aide who spoke Yiddish and English helped Molly give directions to a driver who then took my family to Jacob's address. Unfortunately, Jacob wasn't home. The driver didn't know what to do, so he asked a police officer for help.

Unwilling to leave them on the street, the officer took my family to jail. Molly, Poppa Lou, Frances, and Morris spent their first night in Chicago on two cots in a jail cell on the second floor of the 48th Street Station. But when the officer brought my family breakfast the next morning before taking them to Jacob's shop, they knew a better life had already begun.

Think & Respond

What details does Merrill Wilk include to bring the characters—and the situations—to life for her readers? What sources might she have used to find this information about her family?

Ask students what kinds of information Merrill Wilk used to get and hold her readers' attention. (specific details, humorous anecdotes, unusual events) Suggest that as students research and write their own family histories, they try to uncover and include vivid details about their families' adventures.

Handbooks for Help and Practice

The following handbooks may be used as mini-lessons before students begin writing or as resources when problems arise.
• Show, Don't Tell, pp. 239–242
• Interviewing Skills, p. 323

Teaching Strategies

for PLANNING YOUR FAMILY HISTORY
STUMBLING BLOCK You may wish to confer with adopted or foster children privately and to assure them that the point of the assignment is to do research into the past, using people they know as a resource. They can write about their adopted or foster parents' families, or they might talk to other people they know. For example, an older neighbor might have a fascinating story to share.

INVITATION
═ TO ═
Write

Writing a family history, like the one Merrill Wilk wrote, makes connections between today and yesterday, between who you are and who your ancestors were. When you write a family history, you research your family's past and write about it in a report.

Gather information about one aspect of your family's past. Then write a family history based on your research.

PLANNING YOUR FAMILY HISTORY

1. Discover what you know. What interesting or funny stories about family members have you heard? What do you know about the lives of your grandparents or great grandparents? Your immediate family members may have much of the information you need. Ask them to go through family photograph albums or scrapbooks with you and to share stories about people and events.

2. Choose a focus. It would be nearly impossible to tell all there is to know about your family in one short report. You could probably fill several books with stories about their past! Instead, think about what part of your family's history you'd most like to write about.

Writer's Choice Would you like to focus on one person's story, as Merrill Wilk did? Would you rather write about the way your relatives' lives were changed by an event in history, such as a natural disaster? Perhaps you'd prefer to trace one side of your family back in time. The choice is yours!

RESEARCHING YOUR HISTORY

1. Begin your research. First, make a list of research questions. You may want to know, for example, when and where your ancestors lived and died, when they came to this country, and what kinds of work they did.

2. Talk to members of your extended family. Ask your parents for the names and phone numbers or addresses of other people you might contact. You could even send a questionnaire to family members who live far away. Be sure to include a letter explaining your purpose.

3. Gather documents written by your family members. Journals, diaries, and letters are wonderful sources of information about your family's past. As you review them, take notes on what's most interesting to you and what suits your focus.

WRITING YOUR FAMILY HISTORY

1. Tell your family's story. You don't want to only list the facts—the "who married whom and when" kind of information. These facts may be part of your report, but be sure to include some of the personal stories your family members shared. Don't just *tell about* what happened to someone; include the kinds of details that *show* what people actually experienced.

2. Share your draft with others. Before you write your next draft, you may wish to share your work with a friend or a family member. A friend might help you find ways to check your organization or make your writing more interesting. A family member might help you fix any mistakes you might have made or fill in any gaps in your story.

Writing TIP

You may wish to tape-record your interviews with family members. That way, you can replay the conversation later and write down the information you want to include in your report.

Ships such as the one shown in this poster ad carried hundreds of thousands of immigrants from Europe to the United States in the early 1900s.

Family History **183**

for BEGIN YOUR RESEARCH
HELPFUL HINT You might suggest that students ask "5W+H" questions (*Who? What? When? Where? Why?* and *How?*), to help them get started.

for GATHER DOCUMENTS...
HELPFUL HINT Encourage students to use material from journals, diaries, and letters to enliven their family histories. Remind them, however, to ask permission before disclosing private correspondence.

for WRITING TIP
INDIVIDUALIZING INSTRUCTION: LD STUDENTS If students have difficulty transcribing their interviews and assembling information into written form, you might encourage them to draft their family histories on tape recorders and to present their finished work orally.

for TELL YOUR FAMILY'S STORY
HELPFUL HINT: QUOTATIONS Explain to students that direct quotations can help make family histories more vivid. Allowing relatives to speak in their own words can give readers a better understanding of personalities. Quotations also can be an effective means of showing, rather than telling. If students need help with using quotation marks, you might refer them to pages 586–588 of Handbook 43, "Punctuation."

SPEAKING AND LISTENING

Suggest that students ask someone else to read their papers aloud to them. They should listen for places where their reader stumbles, then revise to make the writing flow smoothly.

MANAGING THE PAPER LOAD

You may wish to invite volunteers to present their family histories orally to the class and assess those presentations holistically. You might also consider holding a "Family History Day" in which different groups role-play important events in family members' lives.

Guidelines for Evaluation

AN EFFECTIVE FAMILY HISTORY

- focuses on a limited number of people and events
- includes personal details and anecdotes
- is supported by research
- uses transitions to show chronological order

REVIEWING YOUR HISTORY

1. Think about your limits. Check to see if you've tried to do too much in a short report. Are there too many names and dates? Does your history sound like a boring list of facts rather than an interesting story about interesting people? If so, think about how you can narrow your focus in your next draft. For example, you might zoom in on a smaller span of time, describing in detail what happened to two or three family members.

2. Does your story flow smoothly from beginning to end? Family histories are most often told in chronological order. Making a time line of the facts and events you've included can help you check your organization. Rereading your draft aloud is another way to see if the order of events is clear. Is any information out of place? Include any transitions, details, or stories that would make your history easier to follow.

TECHNOLOGY
— TIP —

You could turn your written family history into a multimedia presentation. For help, see pages 636-638 of the Access Guide.

European immigrants at Ellis Island, New York

PUBLISHING AND PRESENTING

- **Make copies of your family history.** Share your final piece with any family members who helped you with your research. You may also wish to send copies of your history to family members living far away.

- **Display your family history on a class bulletin board.** Include a drawing of your family tree and photographs of the people you've written about. Be sure to write a caption for each photo so your readers will be able to connect people's names with their faces.

184

What Do I Write About?

Finding a Starting Point

Ideas for writing can come to you in many ways. Sometimes you can see an idea in a photo, for example. What writing ideas can you get from this photo? Probably the best source of ideas, however, is *you*. Both your personal world and the larger world around you can provide an endless supply of ideas. All you need to do is learn how to tap into them.

W R I T E R T O W R I T E R

The first place I go to find ideas is in my head.

**Jaime Carr, student
York, Pennsylvania**

FINDING IDEAS

"I can't think of anything to write about." If you've said this to yourself, the problem may be that you don't know where to look for writing ideas. Here are some places you can begin your search.

for FURTHER READING

Books to Read Point out that viewing fine art can often spark writing ideas. Interested students might enjoy the following books:
- Robert Cumming, *Just Look: A Book About Paintings*
- Beryl Barr, *Wonders, Warriors, and Beasts Abounding*

In addition, allow interested students to peruse the Fine Art Transparency Pack in the Teacher's Resource File, which contains fourteen full-color transparencies of thought-provoking works, such as *The Flying Carriage* by Marc Chagall.

Finding a Starting Point

Objectives
- To identify various techniques for finding writing ideas
- To choose an appropriate technique and use it to find writing ideas for a given topic

▼ Related Mini-Lessons

For information on topics related to finding a starting point, see the following mini-lessons:
- **Thinking with Pictures, pp. 192–196**
- **Finding a Focus, pp. 203–204**

Teaching Strategies

GENERAL NOTE
HELPFUL HINT Explain to students that this handbook offers a variety of ways to find and explore writing ideas. Encourage students to experiment with each technique. Tell them that some of the techniques may not seem to fit their personal writing process at this point, but that they will find others that will work well for them.

for WRITER TO WRITER
PERSONAL TOUCH After reading aloud Jaime Carr's comment, share some of your own idea-finding strategies. Then invite students to share some of their favorite ways of finding writing ideas. For example, do any students have a favorite "thinking place"? Does it help to listen to a certain kind of music when they're searching for ideas? How many have found ideas in books, in stories, or from photographs of fine art? How many keep a writing journal or a page in their notebooks for recording writing ideas?

Writing
━TIP━

You might create a stockpile of writing ideas by making your own Top Ten lists of favorite persons, places, or things.

Your Personal World

The first place to look for writing ideas is in your personal world. Your daily life and all your memories, hobbies, and interests can be sources for writing ideas.

Your Daily Life　Your everyday experiences with family, friends, people you meet, things you read, and events you observe may be sources of writing ideas. Your experiences may make you surprised, excited, angry, or disappointed. Behind each of these experiences, there's a story waiting to be told.

Memories　How can you jar loose memories of experiences in your life? You might begin by reading your journal or by looking at photos. Talk with family members and friends about memories you share with them. What experiences and feelings come to mind?

Hobbies and Interests　You may not realize it, but you are an expert in something. Think about your skills, hobbies, and interests. What might your readers want to know more about?

The Larger World

What are people talking about? What's going on in your town and around the world? Look for things around you, in the news, or on TV that interest you, puzzle you, or concern

you. The special section of the newspaper shown here has articles about the Olympics, Columbus, and kids in Russia. Are there writing ideas here for you?

When you see interesting newspaper articles, ads, and photos, clip them out or copy them. Then save the clippings in a notebook, a folder, or a section of your journal. A clip file can be a gold mine of writing ideas.

198　Writing Handbook

WAYS TO TAP IDEAS

Now that you know where to look for writing ideas, you need to know how to dig into these idea sources. Here are some ways you can start getting ideas down on paper.

Freewriting

Just as the name says, **freewriting** means writing freely. You write down anything that comes to mind. Don't worry about spelling, grammar, punctuation, or even making sense. The goal is to discover what you are thinking about. A good way to start is to choose one idea and write for a set period of time— say three minutes. Try to keep your pencil moving, even if you can't think of anything. If you keep at it, something will come to mind.

Look at the example below. This student came up with a wide range of ideas. Notice how he kept finding ideas even after he thought he had run out.

> OK. I like science fiction. Books, movies— Terminator II, Star Trek, Android, Aliens—even comics—Flash Gordon, ray guns. Its funny to see the old movies with their bogus (special effects.) I saw one where the spaceship looked like a tin can on a string. Now what? My mind is blank. Empty, empty, empty. Outer space is empty. How big is outer space? (Are people living on other planets?) I can't think of anything else. Nothing. I could list my favorite (space movies.) I could rate all the movies I've seen. Time's up!

Student MODEL

How special effects have changed over the years could be a good topic.

I might want to do some more freewriting on this idea.

I could write a review of some space movies.

Finding a Starting Point **199**

SPICE BOX

The following activity requires preparation, but it can help students use freewriting to explore their imaginations. You will need an overhead projector, a glass pie pan, a glass of water, food coloring, and a seltzer tablet. Set the pie pan on the glass surface of the projector. Pour about an inch of water into the pie pan and turn on the projector.

Slowly add drops of food coloring to the water. Invite students to freewrite about whatever the swirling colors bring to mind. To give the "show" extra pizzazz, add a seltzer tablet.

Writing TIP

You can use freewriting anytime during the writing process to find ideas or to focus your thinking.

When you have finished freewriting, look over your paper and circle the ideas that catch your interest. Then freewrite on one of those ideas. This second freewriting is a good way to discover details about a subject. It also lets you decide whether you really like the topic enough to continue writing about it.

Talking with Others

A good way to examine a writing idea, and possibly to find a better idea, is to talk with other people. Try bouncing ideas off your classmates, friends, and family members. Give everyone a chance to talk. Build on one another's suggestions. If you listen carefully and ask questions, you may find new ways to look at your topic.

This is my idea . . .

What if we look at it this way?

What do you mean?

Listing

Another way to tap into writing ideas is to create a list. When you make a list, you start with a broad subject or idea. You then write examples or details related to the broad topic. Here is Lisa's list of things she and her friends collect.

COLLECTIONS

stamps
shells
comic books
bugs
rocks
baseball cards
compact discs
board games

After looking over her list, Lisa decided to explore one of the ideas. She made another list. Then she realized that she had enough ideas to begin drafting.

SHELLS

colors	jewelry
labels	conch shells
displays	cowrie shells
shapes	decorations

Drawing

You can also draw pictures, diagrams, and charts about people, places, and events that you might want to write about. Your drawings can help you "see" a subject and think about what you want to say. See Handbook 1, "Thinking with Pictures," pages 192–196, for more ideas on using graphic devices to explore ideas.

MAKING AN IDEA YOUR OWN

Writing becomes better when you care—when you have a reason for writing. Look for a personal connection to a topic. Don't just pick "my dog." Find an angle you care about. Was your dog your best friend at a time when you especially needed a friend?

For example, Luis was assigned to write a report on the history of a sport. He knew he wanted to write about baseball, but he wasn't sure where to go from there. To find an idea he truly wanted to write about, he thought about these questions.

- What is my personal experience with this topic?
- What special knowledge do I already have about this topic?
- What do I wish I knew more about?

for DRAWING

INDIVIDUALIZING INSTRUCTION: LD STUDENTS Some students who struggle with language may benefit especially from using drawings to generate ideas. To help them make the transition from drawing to writing, encourage them to label the parts of their drawings and to create captions.

for MAKING AN IDEA YOUR OWN

HELPFUL HINT Other questions that might help students find their own angles include the following:
- What's most important to me about this topic?
- How did I get interested in this topic?
- What does this topic have to do with my life?

For more information, refer students to Handbook 5, "Goals and Audience," on page 211.

for MAKING AN IDEA YOUR OWN

HELPFUL HINT Tell students that finding an angle they care about can help them enjoy writing and write better. Reassure students that if they ask in advance, most teachers will let them adapt an assigned topic to fit their interests.

ASSESSMENT Because these Practice Your Skills exercises are exploratory, you might check off students' responses rather than evaluate them. Suggest that students keep their responses in their writing journals for later use as idea sources.

Additional Resources

Writing Resource Book, pp. 46–48
Fine Art Transparency Pack
Thinking Skills Transparency Pack

Answers to Practice Your Skills

A. Answers will vary.

B. Answers will vary.

C. Answers will vary.

D. Answers will vary.

Here is the way Luis answered the questions.

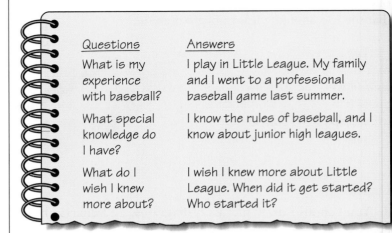

Questions	Answers
What is my experience with baseball?	I play in Little League. My family and I went to a professional baseball game last summer.
What special knowledge do I have?	I know the rules of baseball, and I know about junior high leagues.
What do I wish I knew more about?	I wish I knew more about Little League. When did it get started? Who started it?

For additional suggestions about how to make a topic your own, see Handbook 3, "Finding a Focus," pages 203–204.

Practice Your Skills

A. Look through a room in your house to trigger a memory of a person, a place, a conversation, or an experience. Then write about that memory.

B. Use listing, freewriting, or drawing to find writing ideas about a person, a place, an object, an event, or a conversation.

C. Use listing, freewriting, or drawing to find a list of writing ideas related to one of the following subjects.

heroes   school   summer   TV   clothes

D. Choose one of the following subjects. Use one or more of the methods you learned in this lesson to make the subject meaningful to you personally.

jobs   achievement   hobbies   travel   school

What's the Right Size for My Topic?

Finding a Focus

The shoes you wear, the soft drink you buy, and the TV you watch all come in sizes. You buy the size you need or want. In writing too, the size of your topic must fit your needs. To find the right size, think about what your purpose for writing is and what details you want to cover.

WRITING
HANDBOOK
3

NARROWING THE TOPIC

Asking questions and making graphic devices will help you divide a subject into parts. You may decide that you especially want to write about just one of the parts. On the other hand, you may see how several parts fit together to create a topic that you can manage.

Asking Questions

One student narrowed her topic on pets after asking these *who, what, when, where, why,* and *how* questions.

Writing
TIP
You can use the subheads in an encyclopedia article or the table of contents in a book to find the parts of a topic.

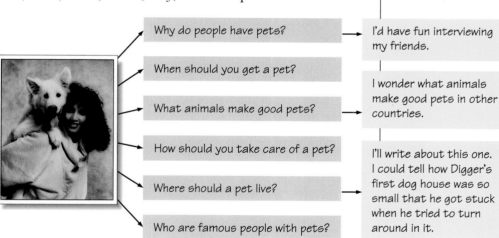

Why do people have pets?	I'd have fun interviewing my friends.
When should you get a pet?	
What animals make good pets?	I wonder what animals make good pets in other countries.
How should you take care of a pet?	I'll write about this one. I could tell how Digger's first dog house was so small that he got stuck when he tried to turn around in it.
Where should a pet live?	
Who are famous people with pets?	

Finding a Focus　**203**

Finding a Focus

Objectives
• To understand and use techniques for narrowing writing topics
• To narrow a writing topic appropriately for a given purpose

▼ Related Mini-Lessons

For information on topics related to finding a focus, see the following mini-lessons:
• **Thinking with Pictures, pp. 192–196**
• **Finding a Starting Point, pp. 197–202**

Teaching Strategies

GENERAL NOTE

KEY TO UNDERSTANDING Explain to students that their topic has to fit the length of their writing assignment. For example, a topic with four or five major parts would be too broad for a paragraph.

for ASKING QUESTIONS

INDIVIDUALIZING INSTRUCTION: ESL STUDENTS To use questioning to narrow a topic, these students need a clear understanding of the key words *who, what, when, where, why,* and *how.* Help by using each in sample sentences and translating, if possible.

for ASKING QUESTIONS

USING THE MODEL Call students' attention to the comments that the writer made in the margin. Her comments explore how she might work with the parts of her topic—how she might get information, which questions she has, and how she might use a memory.

Links to
LITERATURE & LANGUAGE

You might invite students to notice the author's focus in each of the following poems from *Literature and Language,* Grade 6:
• May Swenson, "Southbound on the Freeway"
• Carl Sandburg, "Fog"
• Issa, Three Haiku

Social Studies Connection

Tell students that *who, what, where, when, why,* and *how*—the 5W + H questions—can help them check their understanding of important historical or current events. Model the way they might tailor the questions to fit their needs: *Where* did the event occur? *Who* was involved? *When* did it occur? *Why* did it happen? *How* did it happen? *What* were its effects?

W R I T E R   T O   W R I T E R

I get started by making a web.

Kara DeCarolis, student
Golden, Colorado

Using Graphic Devices

You can also use graphic devices, such as clusters, diagrams, observation charts, lists, and drawings, to see the parts of a topic. Another student started the following cluster about storms. What would you add to the cluster? What do you think would be a good topic about storms for a two-page paper?

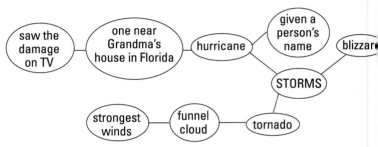

For more information on using graphic devices, see Handbook 1, "Thinking with Pictures," pages 192–196.

Practice Your Skills

A. Choose one of the topics below or one of your own. Then ask questions to focus the topic.

rock music   cars   art   holidays   comedy

B. Choose one of the topics below or one of your own. Then use a cluster, an observation chart, a list, or another graphic device to divide the topic into parts.

animals   snow   cities   sports   friends

How Do I Explore and Support My Ideas?

Developing a Topic

__The Wonderful Wizard of Oz:__ A tornado carries a girl and her dog from their home to another land.

Would you want to read *The Wonderful Wizard of Oz* on the basis of the summary above? If the summary included vivid details, however, you might want to read the book. Details about the tornado, the girl, her dog, their home, and the characters she meets would make the writing come alive. You too can learn ways to make your writing lively. Simply add details that explain, show, or illustrate your message.

KINDS OF SUPPORTING DETAILS

How would you describe the taste of a pizza? What is the nutritional value of pizza? Who invented pizza? To answer each of these questions, you would need to use different kinds of details. The details you choose will vary, depending upon what you want to accomplish. Here are some types of details that can help you in different writing situations.

Sensory Details

You can make descriptions easy to remember by using your senses. Think of ways to tell your readers how things look, sound, feel, smell, and taste. Look at the description of a picnic on the next page. The author could simply state that a delicious selection of food was gathered. But she does much more. (Be careful; her description could make you hungry.)

── TIP ──

You can explore your senses by making an observation chart. See Handbook 1, "Thinking with Pictures," pages 192–196.

PROFESSIONAL NOTEBOOK

Share the following advice from writer Anne Bernays: "Nice writing isn't enough. It isn't enough to have smooth and pretty language. You have to surprise the reader frequently, you can't just be nice all the time. Provoke the reader. Astonish the reader. Writing that has no surprises is as bland as oatmeal. Surprise the reader with the unexpected verb or adjective. Use one startling adjective per page."

Developing a Topic

Objectives
- To identify techniques for developing writing topics
- To choose an appropriate technique and develop a writing topic

▼ Related Mini-Lessons

For information related to developing a topic, see the following mini-lessons:
- **Thinking with Pictures, pp. 192–196**
- **Finding a Focus, pp. 203–204**
- **Organizing Details, pp. 217–221**
- **Show, Don't Tell, pp. 239–242**
- **Appealing to the Senses, pp. 266–273**

Teaching Strategies

GENERAL NOTE
KEY TO UNDERSTANDING Explain that effective details are specific ones. For example, "The boy held the money" is fairly general. "The five-year-old clutched the quarter" paints a vivid picture. As students work through the handbook, point out specific details in the models—colors and flavors in the piece by Maya Angelou; dates, addresses, and names in the model about Thomas Edison, and so on.

for SENSORY DETAILS
LINKING GRAMMAR AND WRITING Explain to students that they can bring sensory details to life by avoiding overuse of *is, was,* and other forms of *be.* Urge them to choose verbs that appeal to the senses. For example, on page 206, Maya Angelou writes that meat *sputtered* on the barbecue pit, not that it *was* on the barbecue pit. She writes, "Pound cakes *sagged* with their buttery weight," not that they *were* buttery and heavy.

USING THE MODEL Ask students which images from Angelou's description stand out most for them. Then have students name a favorite food. Ask volunteers to use sensory details to describe the food; urge them to be specific, as Angelou has been.

for FACTS

CRITICAL THINKING: DISTINGUISHING FACTS FROM OPINIONS Remind students that a fact can be proved. Ask them which of the following statements is a fact and which is an opinion. Then ask how each fact could be proved. (Most facts can be verified by checking an encyclopedia or other general reference work.)

- Thomas Edison was the world's greatest inventor. (O)
- The cotton gin was invented by Eli Whitney. (F)
- Navy Admiral Grace Hopper developed the computer language called COBOL. (F)
- Modern clothes would look very different if the zipper had never been invented. (O)

for REASONS

LINKING GRAMMAR AND WRITING Tell students that words such as *because, since, as a result,* and *therefore* are helpful in working reasons smoothly into sentences. To illustrate, share the following examples:

Our school should have an open campus policy at lunch time *because* many students need to go home for lunch.

Since Maria has the most experience with student government, I think she would make a good class president.

Literary
MODEL

Sense of sound ⎯
Sense of sight ⎯
Sense of taste ⎯
Sense of touch ⎯

On the barbecue pit, chickens and spareribs sputtered in their own fat. . . . Orange sponge cakes and dark brown mounds dripping chocolate stood layer to layer with ice-white coconuts and light brown caramels. Pound cakes sagged with their buttery weight, and small children could no more resist licking the icings than their mothers could avoid slapping the sticky fingers.

Maya Angelou, *I Know Why the Caged Bird Sings*

Facts

You can support your main idea with facts from experts or from reference books, such as encyclopedias and almanacs. A **fact** is any piece of information that can be proved true. The location of Edison's laboratories in New Jersey is a fact. What other facts does the paragraph below tell you about early movies?

Professional
MODEL

On February 1, 1893, Edison opened the world's first motion picture studio at his laboratories in West Orange, New Jersey. After producing numerous filmstrips to be viewed through the Kinetoscope [a box-like device for one viewer at a time], Edison opened the first movie theater on April 14, 1894, at 1155 Broadway, New York City. For a nickel, a customer could watch a brief filmstrip of the great bodybuilder Eugene Sandow lifting weights and performing gymnastics, or of Buffalo Bill mounting a horse and shooting his pistols. The new "theater" was a great success.

Charles Panati, *The Browser's Book of Beginnings*

Reasons

Don't leave your readers asking why. Give them reasons to support an opinion or tell why something happened. **Reasons** are explanations or logical arguments. The paragraph on the next page tells why scientists want to know when Merapi, a volcano in Indonesia, will erupt.

206 Writing Handbook

*L*inks to
*L*ITERATURE & LANGUAGE

Poem to Read Maya Angelou (1928–) is an African-American author who has written poems, songs, and a multivolume autobiography. The first volume, *I Know Why the Caged Bird Sings* (1970), covers her first sixteen years. You might read the poem "Life Doesn't Frighten Me" on page 359 of *Literature and Language,* Grade 6.

Like the book *I Know Why the Caged Bird Sings,* this poem draws on Angelou's personal struggle to succeed in an often hostile world. Ask students to identify the details that make this poem vivid and meaningful.

Why is it important to know when Merapi might blow? If many of the people living around the volcano's base don't leave in time, they could be killed. Hurricanes of 1,400-degree-Fahrenheit volcanic ash would burn the villagers and farmers. Or flows of mud caused by heavy rain mixed with the ash would bury them alive.

Brianna Politzer, "Magma P.I."

Professional
MODEL

— Main reason
— Supporting reasons

Examples

Sometimes the best way to help your readers understand a point is to give them an **example,** or instance of something. You can introduce an example with words such as *for instance,* or *to illustrate.* Look for examples in the paragraph below. Which ones support the main idea that the famous airplane pilot Amelia Earhart and her sister were athletic?

The celebrated aviator Amelia Earhart sits in the cockpit of her aircraft after setting a new altitude record, April 1931.

From an early age, Amelia and her sister were athletic. They turned a lawn swing into a jungle gym and hung by their knees on the top bar. They played baseball and football with equipment their father bought them. In the barn, they climbed on an old carriage where they took imaginary journeys behind teams of galloping horses while fighting off nonexistent attackers.

Ginger Wadsworth, "The Adventure Begins"

Professional
MODEL

Stories or Events

Another way to add details is to tell a story or describe an event that will help your readers understand your idea. A **story** or **event** can come from your experiences or from talking to others. It can also come from reading or from your imagination.

---

for EXAMPLES

HELPFUL HINT Explain that examples can be especially useful for helping readers understand a general statement. A strong paragraph might begin with a general topic sentence, then follow up with several examples to show exactly what the topic sentence means. Sometimes a paragraph begins with several specific examples and ends by summing them up in a general topic sentence.

for SECOND PROFESSIONAL MODEL

USING THE MODEL Lead students to see that the second and third sentences in the excerpt from "The Adventure Begins" support the idea that Amelia Earhart and her sister were athletic. To point out the wealth of specific details in these two sentences, ask how the excerpt would be different if Ginger Wadsworth had written instead, "They exercised on lawn furniture and played sports." What would we miss? (vivid examples that help the audience identify with the Earharts)

for EXAMPLES

CRITICAL THINKING: INTERPRETING Ask students to decide what the last sentence in Wadsworth's paragraph suggests about Amelia Earhart and her sister. (Samples: They had good imaginations; they liked to dream of adventure.)

---

for FURTHER READING

Books to Read Students interested in Amelia Earhart might enjoy reading about other adventurous women in the following books:
- Julie Fromer, *Jane Goodall: Living with the Chimps*
- Carole S. Briggs, *Women in Space: Reaching the Last Frontier*
- Charlene W. Billings, *Christa McAuliffe, Pioneer Space Teacher*
- Doreen Rappaport, *Living Dangerously: American Women Who Risked Their Lives for Adventure*

Professional
MODEL

The following paragraph tells a story about a real event that happened to Valerie Taylor, an Australian diver and underwater photographer. The details support the main idea that divers sometimes meet sharks unexpectedly.

Valerie remembers one such occasion many years ago. She was diving with two friends along the Great Barrier Reef near her home in Australia one sunny day. "Suddenly I sensed something swimming very close to me," she recalls. "Thinking it was one of the other divers, I looked around—straight into a large black eye. It belonged to a huge tiger shark, nearly fifteen feet long. I knew instinctively it was not going to hurt me. If it had wanted to bite, it would have done so before I ever saw it."

Judith E. Rinard, "Sharks Are Our Business"

Ways to Explore a Topic Further

During prewriting you explore your ideas and collect some details. To find out if you have enough details to support your ideas, ask yourself these questions:

- Can I accomplish my purpose with the details I have?
- Will the details I have get my ideas across clearly?
- Will my readers need more information to understand my ideas?

WRITER TO WRITER

The thing I like most about writing is the way it allows me to express myself.

Ben Everett, student
Charleston, Illinois

208   Writing Handbook

Perhaps you need more details for a paper on the knights of the Round Table. Try these strategies.

Common Ways to Find More Details

Recalling	Remember a movie you've seen about King Arthur and his knights. Have you read a book about Merlin the magician or about King Arthur's magic sword?
Observing	Study an illustrated book to learn about life during the time of King Arthur. Pay close attention to the way the people dressed and the places they lived.
Imagining	Ask yourself questions such as "What if I were a knight of the Round Table?" or "What if I were Guinevere's best friend?"
Interviewing	Plan to talk to your reading teacher or a librarian who knows about your subject. Write out the questions you want to ask. Then interview the person. Listen carefully and ask more questions if you don't understand.
Researching	Visit the library. Look for details in encyclopedias, in books such as *King Arthur and the Knights of the Round Table, The Tale of Sir Gawain,* and *The Legend of King Arthur.* Enjoy movies such as *Knights of the Round Table, Camelot,* and *The Sword in the Stone.*

Try to use several or all of these strategies. The more information you gather, the more familiar you will become with your topic. Then it will be easier for you to include interesting facts, stories, and specific details.

What can you do if you are writing a story about an imaginary character? You will probably rely on imagining. You might, however, blend in details from your memories, observations, and everyday experiences.

PROBLEM
SOLVING

"How do I know which facts, stories, and details to include?"

For more information on narrowing your topic and organizing details, see

- Handbook 1, "Thinking with Pictures," pages 192–196

- Handbook 3, "Finding a Focus," pages 203–204

- Handbook 7, "Organizing Details," pages 217–221

Developing a Topic **209**

for COMMON WAYS TO FIND MORE DETAILS
SPEAKING AND LISTENING To learn more about interviewing, students can turn to Handbook 31, "Interviewing Skills," on page 323.

for COMMON WAYS TO FIND MORE DETAILS
KEY TO UNDERSTANDING Point out that even if students are writing fiction stories, they may still need to research facts, observe specific sensory details, and so on, to bring their narratives to life. For example, to write a story about the knights of the Round Table, students might need to research the obligations of a knight.

Practice Your Skills

A. Imagine you are viewing the scene shown in this painting by Thomas Hart Benton. Write a description of everything that is happening around you. Use spatial organization to present your descriptive details so that your readers can picture the scene just as you see it.

Fire in the Barnyard (1944), Thomas Hart Benton.

B. Reorder each set of details below, using one of the organizational strategies shown in this handbook. Use the strategy that presents the details in the most logical order.

1. Soon the boy surfaced on the other side of the pool.
   Pedro stood poised on the high diving board and studied the water beneath him.
   He spouted water from his mouth as he let the air out of his lungs.
   The hometown crowd exploded into applause and wild cheers.
   He bounced once, lifted off the board, shot downward, and sliced through the water.
2. For one thing, skateboarding is fun, and just about anyone can do it.
   I think our town should reserve space in the park for a special skateboarding area.
   The most important reason, however, is that there are very few public places where kids are allowed to ride their skateboards.
   Also, it is very popular among junior-high students.
   Instead, dedicated skateboarders must skate in unsupervised, possibly dangerous places.

Organizing Details **221**

for PRACTICE YOUR SKILLS

ASSESSMENT Because this handbook focuses on organization, you might use primary trait scoring for the Practice Your Skills exercises, with structure as the primary trait. Content (elaboration) might be appropriate as a secondary trait.

Additional Resources

Writing Resource Book, pp. 53–56
Thinking Skills Transparency Pack

Answers to Practice Your Skills

A. Answers will vary. Descriptions should be spatially ordered, beginning at the teacher's right or left and moving around the room.

B.
1. (chronological order)
   Pedro stood poised on the high diving board and studied the water beneath him. He bounced once, lifted off the board, shot downward, and sliced through the water. Soon the boy surfaced on the other side of the pool. He spouted water from his mouth as he let the air out of his lungs. The hometown crowd exploded into applause and wild cheers.
2. (order of importance)
   I think our town should reserve space in the park for a special skateboarding area. For one thing, skateboarding is fun, and just about anyone can do it. Also, it is very popular among junior-high students. The most important reason, however, is that there are very few public places where kids are allowed to ride their skateboards. Instead, dedicated skateboarders must skate in unsupervised, possibly dangerous places.

Science Connection

Tell students that chronological and spatial order can be especially helpful in writing about topics in science. Chronological order is effective for writing about scientific processes, such as the life cycle of an insect or the way the heart pumps blood. Spatial order can be useful for scientific descriptions, such as a description of a plant or an animal, the solar system, or an ecosystem.

Examining
Paragraphs

Objectives
- To recognize the characteristics of a well-written paragraph
- To judge whether sentences in a paragraph develop its main idea
- To arrange details in a paragraph in a sensible order and to use transitional words

Related Mini-Lessons

For information on topics related to examining paragraphs, see the following mini-lessons:
- **Organizing Details, pp. 217–221**
- **Creating Paragraphs, pp. 226–229**
- **Improving Paragraphs, pp. 230–233**
- **Transitions, pp. 234–238**

Motivate
Retype one of the Starting from Literature models in the Writer's Workshop section of this book, eliminating all paragraph breaks. Duplicate the material and pass out copies to students. After they have read it, ask whether they found it easy to follow, or difficult. Then lead a discussion on the purpose and importance of paragraphing.

Teaching Strategies

for LITERARY MODEL

CRITICAL THINKING: INTERPRETING
Have students describe Sounder's bark in their own words and give details from the paragraph to support their answers. (Samples: loud, clear, musical, rich, full-bodied, echoing)

WRITING
HANDBOOK
8

Literary
MODEL

What Is a Paragraph?

Examining Paragraphs

A paragraph is as easy to spot as a zebra with purple polka dots. All you have to do is look for a group of sentences with the first line indented. However, a well-developed paragraph is more than just a series of sentences.

GOOD **PARAGRAPHS**

A **paragraph** is a group of sentences that all work together to express and develop the same main idea. In a well-written paragraph, the sentences are also arranged in an order that makes sense. Notice how all the sentences in the following model work together to describe a dog's bark.

> There was no price that could be put on Sounder's voice. It came out of the great chest cavity and broad jaws as though it had bounced off the walls of a cave. It mellowed into half-echo before it touched the air. It was louder and clearer than any purebred's voice. Each bark bounced from slope to slope in the foothills like a rubber ball. It was not an ordinary bark. It filled up the night and made music.
>
> **William Armstrong, *Sounder***

Literature Connection

Tell students to listen for the main idea as you read aloud the passage below from *Julie of the Wolves* by Jean Craighead George.

"Her house was not well built for she had never made one before, but it was cozy inside. She had windproofed it by sealing the sod bricks with mud from the pond at her door, and she had made it beautiful by spreading her caribou ground cloth on the floor. On this she had placed her sleeping skin, a moosehide bag lined with soft white rabbit skins. . . ."

Invite students to identify the main idea of the paragraph. (Sample: The character made herself a warm, cozy house.)

Developing a Main Idea

When you first draft a paragraph, just try to get down everything that comes to mind. Then, to improve your draft, you can do the following:

- Think about your main idea or purpose. What important idea do you want to get across?
- Take out any details that are not related directly to the main idea.
- Add details that help to develop the main idea further and make your paragraph more interesting.

Identify the main idea of the following paragraph. Then check to see whether or not all the details develop this idea.

> During the winter of 1838-39, U.S. troops forced fifteen thousand Cherokee men, women, and children to march from Georgia to Oklahoma through snow and bitter cold. Most were barefoot. All were hungry. Over a fourth of them died on the journey, which became known as the Trail of Tears. Many of the survivors started farms in Oklahoma. Farming was difficult, though, because cattle ranchers often drove their herds of cattle right across the Cherokees' fields.

The details about farming are interesting, but they have nothing to do with the Cherokees' forced march, which is the topic of the paragraph. When the sentences about farming are removed, the main idea comes across much more clearly as in this revised student model.

Student MODEL

> During the winter of 1838-39, U.S. troops forced fifteen thousand Cherokee men, women, and children to march from Georgia to Oklahoma through snow and bitter cold. Most were barefoot. All were hungry. Over a fourth of them died on the journey, which became known as the Trail of Tears.

Examining Paragraphs **223**

for DEVELOPING A MAIN IDEA

SPEAKING AND LISTENING After students read the instructional material up to the first sample paragraph, have them close their books and listen as you read the paragraph aloud. Ask them to raise their hands as soon as they hear any details that are not related directly to the main idea of the paragraph. Afterward, discuss with students why the last two sentences in the paragraph do not belong in it, and what the writer might do with them instead (delete them or use them in a new paragraph).

for DEVELOPING A MAIN IDEA

INDIVIDUALIZING INSTRUCTION: BASIC STUDENTS If these students have difficulty in identifying the sentences that do not belong in the paragraph, make two columns with the following headings on the board: *The March from Georgia* and *The New Life in Oklahoma*. Ask a volunteer to read the paragraph aloud. Then have students identify the heading under which each sentence belongs. Write each sentence in the appropriate column. Then tell students that the column with the most sentences represents the main idea of the paragraph and that the two sentences in the other column belong in another paragraph.

for STUDENT MODEL

HELPFUL HINT Have students read the revised Student Model. Then ask what kinds of details the writer might add to this paragraph to develop the main idea even further and make the paragraph more interesting. (Samples: the approximate temperatures, what the Cherokee men, women, and children ate, and how long the trip took)

for STUDENT MODEL

CRITICAL THINKING: CLASSIFYING

After students read the revised Student Model, direct their attention to the single words and the phrase in boldface type. Tell them that these are transitions that help the reader understand the order of the steps and the position of the ingredients in relation to one another. Point out that most of the boldfaced transitions in the revised Student Model indicate time order, but that one of the transitions signals spatial order. Have students identify this transition *(On this layer of sauce).*

for SECOND STUDENT MODEL

HELPFUL HINT To help students practice using transitional words that signal spatial order, have them write a brief description of what a finished snack-sized pizza would look like, from top to bottom. Have them use transitional words and phrases to help their readers visualize the pizza.

Arranging Sentences Sensibly

Once you have settled on the details you want to include in a paragraph, you need to arrange them in a way that makes sense. If you don't do this, you're likely to confuse your readers. For example, read the following paragraph.

> Snack-sized pizzas are easy to make. You just broil them for three to five minutes or until the cheese is melted. First, you have to toast and butter both halves of an English muffin. Then you can add extras such as cooked hamburger, onions, olives, and mushrooms. Don't forget to spread a thin layer of spaghetti sauce or pizza sauce on each half. Put mozzarella cheese on top.

Could you follow these directions? Do you know whether to put the sauce on before or after you add the extras? When do you put on the cheese? When do you broil the pizzas? Now see how much easier it is to follow the directions when the steps are presented in a sensible order.

Student
MODEL

The steps are arranged in chronological order.

Transitions help make the order of the steps clearer.

> Snack-sized pizzas are easy to make. **First,** toast and butter both halves of an English muffin. **Next,** spread a thin layer of spaghetti sauce or pizza sauce on each half. **On this layer of sauce,** add extras such as cooked hamburger, onions, olives, and mushrooms. **Then** put mozzarella cheese on top. **Finally,** broil them for three to five minutes or until the cheese is melted.

You can help your readers understand the arrangement of your sentences by using transitional words and phrases. Some of these words and phrases signal time: *soon, after a while.* Others signal place: *to the left, on top.* To learn more about transitions, see Handbook 11, "Transitions," on pages 234–238.

For help in finding the best ways to organize different types of details, you might want to review Handbook 7, "Organizing Details," on pages 217–221.

224 Writing Handbook

SPICE BOX

To give students practice in arranging ideas in chronological order, have them bring in comic strips from newspapers or magazines and cut apart the panels. Then have students trade panels with a partner and arrange them in correct order. Finally, have each student write a one-paragraph narrative summary of his or her strip, using transitional words that signal time order. Call on volunteers to read their summaries to the class.

Practice Your Skills

A. Decide which of these two examples is a weak paragraph. Then improve the weak paragraph by getting rid of the sentences that stray from its main idea.

1. People all over the world love baseball. Canadians love it enough to have two teams competing in the Major Leagues. People in many Latin American countries and in Japan love the game enough to have formed their own baseball leagues. What's more, in Japan a single baseball game often attracts more than fifty thousand fans.

2. Wolves communicate by using different types of howls. One kind of howl signals that a wolf wants to "talk." Another type of howl warns that danger is near. Many people think that wolves are vicious beasts, but they aren't. Wolves rarely attack people. In addition, they show mercy to one another. When wolves gather to hunt, they howl to greet one another. Then, to begin the hunt, they let out a wilder sort of howl. If you want to read a good book about wolves, read *Julie of the Wolves*.

B. Use what you've learned about good paragraphs to improve the following paragraph.

Some hot-air balloons hold only two passengers, but others hold more. Just how does a balloonist fly a hot-air balloon? Here are the basics. To take off, the balloonist lights a propane burner under the balloon. To land, the balloonist turns down the burner or opens the vent at the top of the balloon. To make the balloon go higher, the balloonist turns up the propane burner. A group of colorful balloons is quite a sight.

A propane burner heats the air inside a hot-air balloon, causing the air to expand. The balloon rises when the escape of some of the air decreases the overall weight of the balloon.

Examining Paragraphs **225**

for PRACTICE YOUR SKILLS

INDIVIDUALIZING INSTRUCTION: BASIC STUDENTS To help these students with Exercise A, point out that the first sentence in each of the paragraphs states the main idea. Have students read aloud each of the remaining sentences and tell whether it relates directly to the main idea stated in the first sentence.

Additional Resource

Writing Resource Book, pp. 60–61

Answers to Practice Your Skills

A.
1. No revision is needed.
2. Answers may vary. A sample revision is provided.

   Wolves communicate by using different types of howls. One kind of howl signals that a wolf wants to "talk." Another type of howl warns that danger is near. When wolves gather to hunt, they howl to greet one another. Then, to begin the hunt, they let out a wilder sort of howl.

B. Answers will vary. The first and last sentences, however, should be deleted as irrelevant and the remaining sentences rearranged in a sensible order. A sample revision is provided.

   Just how does a balloonist fly a hot-air balloon? Here are the basics. To take off, the balloonist lights a propane burner under the balloon. To make the balloon go higher, the balloonist turns up the propane burner. Finally, to land, the balloonist turns down the burner or opens the vent at the top of the balloon.

Creating Paragraphs

Objectives
- To write effective topic sentences
- To use supporting details—such as facts, statistics, reasons, and examples—to develop a paragraph

 Related Mini-Lessons

For information on topics related to creating paragraphs, see the following mini-lessons:
- **Developing a Topic, pp. 205–210**
- **Examining Paragraphs, pp. 222–225**
- **Improving Paragraphs, pp. 230–233**
- **Show, Don't Tell, pp. 239–242**

Motivate

To motivate students to write attention-getting topic sentences, read aloud the example topic sentences at the top of page 227 before you begin teaching the lesson. Ask students to imagine that these were the first sentences of magazine articles. Ask which sentences would make them want to read on, and why. Remind them that writing good topic sentences is an effective way to get their readers' attention.

Teaching Strategies

for DRAFTING TOPIC SENTENCES

INDIVIDUALIZING INSTRUCTION: ESL STUDENTS It may be helpful for some ESL writers to write a topic sentence and place it at the beginning of each paragraph they plan to develop. Although more sophisticated writers can often vary the placement of the topic sentence or even eliminate it entirely, beginning ESL writers often need the security and focus that a predictable pattern can give them.

Writing
TIP

If you put a topic sentence at the beginning of a paragraph, your readers will know right away what your paragraph is about.

How Do I Write a Paragraph?

Creating Paragraphs

Look over some of the paragraphs you've written. Which ones seem to work best? What makes them successful?

As you draft other paragraphs, keep in mind what has worked for you in the past. Also, consider using topic sentences and supporting details to express and develop your main ideas.

D RAFTING TOPIC SENTENCES

A **topic sentence** states the main idea or purpose of a paragraph. Here, for example, is the topic sentence from a paragraph about a computer game:

> If you've ever wanted to explore the universe with a crew of creatures from different planets, StarVoyager is the ideal game for you.

You don't have to put a topic sentence in every paragraph you write. However, including a topic sentence is a simple and direct way to make the main idea of a paragraph clear to readers. Furthermore, writing a topic sentence can help you stay focused on your main idea as you draft.

A good topic sentence can also get readers interested in your subject. To create attention-getting topic sentences, use the tips on the following page.

PROFESSIONAL NOTEBOOK

In her book *Errors and Expectations*, writing teacher Mina P. Shaughnessy recommends teaching students to write topic sentences by having them form generalizations about a group of pictures on a related subject: "Once aware that the term *topic sentence* implies a *relationship* among sentences, . . . the student should be ready to try developing his own governing statements by making inferences from small pools of data, preferably non-print data at first. . . ." She suggests using pictures of couples or of children at play. Students can use details from the pictures to create their topic sentences.

Writing Effective Topic Sentences

Bring your subject to life with vivid details.
Legend says that werewolves are people who develop fangs, fur, claws, and a thirst for blood when the moon is full.

Ask a question. What is life like on the ocean floor?

Talk to your readers. Imagine what it would be like to have an identical twin.

Include an interesting fact or statistic. Every second of every day, enough water splashes over Niagara Falls to fill four thousand bathtubs.

Set the scene. Horns blared and car doors slammed when the garbage truck blocked the intersection.

DEVELOPING PARAGRAPHS

A paragraph is more than just a topic sentence. As you learned in Handbook 8, "Examining Paragraphs," a paragraph is a group of sentences that develops one main idea. In a well-developed paragraph, these sentences contain the details needed to explain the main idea fully. They also support the main idea effectively.

As you develop your paragraphs, remember to do the following:

- Supply your readers with all the important information they need.

- Stay focused on your main idea.

- Explain and support your main idea with details such as facts, statistics, sensory details, incidents, examples, reasons, and quotations.

For more help in developing your ideas with supporting details, review Handbook 4, "Developing a Topic," pages 205–210, and Handbook 12, "Show, Don't Tell," pages 239–242.

Writing
TIP
Avoid using wordy phrases such as "This paragraph is about . . . ," "I am going to write about . . . ," or "My topic is. . . ." Instead, just start with what you want to say.

Creating Paragraphs **227**

What's the Best Way to Present My Information?

WRITING
HANDBOOK
12

Show, Don't Tell

Two friends are discussing a race one of them ran:

JAMIE: The other runner was gaining on me. She was getting closer and closer. I was afraid she would win.

MARIA: How could you tell she was getting closer? What did you do?

JAMIE: As I rounded the last bend, the crunching of footsteps on the cinder track got louder and louder. Then I felt the brush of her sleeve against mine as she tried to pass me. I pumped my arms and pushed my legs harder, thinking, You've got to do it! You've got to win!

Jamie's first description *tells* what happened in a general way, providing no details. Her second description *shows* what actually happened while she was running. By sharing the thoughts and feelings she experienced during the race, Jamie makes it possible for Maria to experience what happened too.

In writing, as in conversation, the details are what people care about. Whether you're writing a letter or a report for school, you can develop and expand your ideas by including interesting, lively details that capture and hold your readers' attention.

How to *Show* Rather Than *Tell*

Showing an Experience When you write about a personal experience, show what happened by using specific sensory details to bring the people and places to life. Look at the passage from "Baseball in April" on the next page. Notice how Gary Soto uses vivid description to show what he remembers about a visit to Disneyland.

Show, Don't Tell **239**

Literature Connection

Read aloud the following passage from *The Summer of the Swans* by Betsy Byars. Have students identify sensory details that show how scared a mentally handicapped boy feels when lost in the woods:

"The sound of the dogs seemed to him to be everywhere, all around him, so that he ran first in one direction, then in another, like a wild animal caught in a maze. He ran into a bush and the briers stung his face and arms, and he thought this was somehow connected with the dogs and thrashed his arms out wildly, not even feeling the cuts in his skin."

Show, Don't Tell

Objectives
- To recognize how sensory details, facts, examples, and reasons can improve various types of writing
- To write paragraphs that show, rather than tell, about a topic

 Related Mini-Lessons

For information on topics related to using show-don't-tell strategies, see the following mini-lessons:
- **Organizing Details, pp. 217–221**
- **Appealing to the Senses, pp. 266–273**

Motivate
On the board, write the sentences "I really liked the concert. It was great." Ask students what questions they might ask a friend who had made these statements, if they themselves wanted to find out more about the concert. Write their questions—and add some of your own—on the board. Point out that by providing vivid details in answering these questions, the friend could *show*, rather than *tell*, what the concert had been like.

Teaching Strategies

for SHOWING AN EXPERIENCE

HELPFUL HINT Some students may need to review what sensory details are. Have them list the five senses—sight, hearing, smell, taste, touch. Explain that sensory details appeal to these senses so that readers can imagine what an experience was like.

What does Disneyland look like? What's special about it? What fun things did you do?

Literary
MODEL

How do you get him to sit the first time? What do you repeat?

Professional
MODEL

Telling
Disneyland's a great place. Our trip there was fun.

Showing
Disneyland stood tall with castles and bright flags. The Matterhorn had wild dips and curves that took your breath away if you closed your eyes and screamed. The Pirates of the Caribbean didn't scare anyone but was fun anyway, and so were the teacups and It's a Small World. . . . Maria's younger sister, Irma, bought a Pinocchio coloring book and a candy bracelet. Her brothers, Rudy and John, spent their money on candy that made their teeth blue.

Gary Soto, "Baseball in April"

Showing a Process When you explain the steps in a process or give a set of directions, you need to be especially clear and complete. Notice how the telling sentence below leaves many questions unanswered. The showing paragraph includes all the important details.

Telling
To train your dog to sit, make him sit down, then repeat the command over and over.

Showing
Stand him on your left side, holding the leash fairly short, and command him to sit. As you give the verbal command, pull up slightly with the leash and push his hindquarters down. Do not let him lie down or stand up. Keep him in a sitting position for a moment, then release the pressure on the leash and praise him. Constantly repeat the command as you hold him in a sitting position, thus fitting the word to the action in his mind.

William D. Wescott, *How to Raise and Train a Keeshond*

240 Writing Handbook

PROFESSIONAL NOTEBOOK

Advice from the Authors Share with students Peter Elbow's explanation of "show, don't tell" in *Writing with Power:* "That is, if you want readers to feel something, it's no good telling them how to feel ('it was simply *terrifying*'). You have to show them things that will terrify them. . . . Direct all your efforts into experiencing—or re-experiencing—what you are writing about. . . . Be there. See it. *Participate* in whatever you are writing about. . . ."

WRITER TO WRITER

Let us understand your character by what happens to him. . . . Don't tell us that John Smith was angry. Show him kicking over a wastebasket.

Judson Phillips, writer

Showing an Opinion   Your opinions and beliefs are based on your experiences and on what you have learned from others. To show rather than tell your opinions, support them with facts, examples, or reasons. This student writer revised her telling sentence. She showed why she believes that solar energy is part of a solution to the world's environmental problems.

Telling
> We should rely more on solar energy because it's better for the environment.

Showing
> To save the environment, we need to rely more on solar energy. Solar energy—energy from the sun—is a cleaner form of energy than the energy that comes from burning fossil fuels, such as coal and oil. That means there will be less pollution and the air will be cleaner. The rate of global warming will slow down, and less wildlife will be displaced or killed by people searching the wilderness for new oil supplies.

Showing Information   Showing information in a report or essay means supporting each of your main points with plenty of facts, examples, and details.

Telling
> Animals play when they're young. That's how they learn survival skills.

Why is solar energy better for the environment? Better than what? How does it compare with other forms of energy?

Student
MODEL

A woman uses a solar box cooker to prepare food.

Which animals? What survival skills do they learn?

Show, Don't Tell   **241**

242 Writing Handbook

LINKING GRAMMAR TO WRITING

Tell students that using vivid verbs is one way to show readers what is happening. Point out the verbs *crouch, stalk,* and *pounce* in the passage. Ask readers who own cats if these actions are familiar to them. Have them describe the visual image each verb shows.

MANAGING THE PAPER LOAD

Assign the item that relates to the type of writing students are currently doing. If, for instance, students are writing descriptions, you might suggest they work on items 4 or 5.

Additional Resources

Writing Resource Book, pp. 63–64
Thinking Skills Worksheets
Thinking Skills Transparency Pack
Elaboration, Revision, and Proof-
    reading Practice
Elaboration, Revision, and
    Proofreading Transparency Pack

Answers to Practice Your Skills

A. Answers will vary. A sample revision is provided for paragraph 1.

The movie was disappointing. My favorite actor spoke a total of three lines and wore a clown mask the whole time. The two funny scenes that were in the coming-attractions trailer turned out to be the only laughs in the whole movie. The plot was so confusing that people in the audience kept turning to their friends and whispering questions about what was going on.

B. Answers will vary. A sample revision is provided for paragraph 3.

Our lunch period should be fifteen minutes longer. As soon as the bell rings, I race down to the cafeteria and wait in line for ten minutes. Then I spend another five minutes searching for a table and getting a drink. By the time I start eating, I only have fifteen minutes to gulp down my food and mumble hello to my friends. It is not a relaxing experience, and I usually end up with a stomachache by sixth period.

Professional
MODEL

Showing

Do animals really "play"? The next time you're at a zoo, watch how the lion cubs frolic. One will crouch low against the ground, stalk slowly toward its littermate, and then pounce on the surprised "victim." Such roughhouse sessions occur frequently among most carnivores such as wolves, tigers, cheetahs, raccoons, and coyotes. As they play, these young develop the abilities they need to become efficient predators.
Eugene J. Walter, Jr., "Why Do They Do What They Do?"

Practice Your Skills

A. Rewrite the following telling sentences, turning them into showing paragraphs. Use the writing strategies suggested in parentheses.

1. The movie was disappointing. (Show your opinion by supporting it with reasons and other evidence.)
2. There's a greeting card for every occasion. (Show why this is true by giving several examples.)
3. You need to know how to make a good first impression. (Show the steps in this process.)
4. The party was great. (Show the experience by using vivid sensory details to describe what happened.)
5. She stood out from the crowd. (Show this character by describing physical details and actions.)

B. Write a showing paragraph based on each of the following sentences.

1. It was a moment no one would forget.
2. I love making my favorite food. You can do it too.
3. Our lunch period should be fifteen minutes longer.
4. Junk food is being replaced by more healthful food choices for both snacks and meals.
5. I felt out of place.

Creating Longer Pieces of Writing

Exploring an idea can be like tugging on a magician's scarf: you start with one idea and it leads you to another, which leads to another, and so on. What then? If you want to write about all these ideas, you really can't do so in just one paragraph. After all, a good paragraph develops only one main idea. To explore a number of ideas, you write a composition.

WHAT IS A COMPOSITION?

A **composition** is a group of paragraphs that work together to develop a single topic. If this definition reminds you of the definition of a paragraph, that's because the two forms are very much alike. Just look at some of the similarities between a paragraph and a composition.

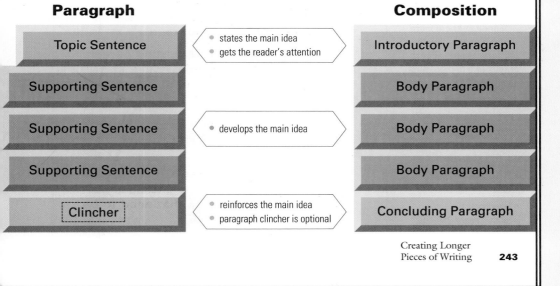

Paragraph		Composition
Topic Sentence	• states the main idea • gets the reader's attention	Introductory Paragraph
Supporting Sentence		Body Paragraph
Supporting Sentence	• develops the main idea	Body Paragraph
Supporting Sentence		Body Paragraph
Clincher	• reinforces the main idea • paragraph clincher is optional	Concluding Paragraph

Creating Longer
Pieces of Writing   **243**

Social Studies Connection

One place in which students are likely to find many examples of introduction-body-conclusion structure is in their social studies textbooks. Challenge students to find such a passage in their textbooks, one that is about five or six paragraphs long. Examine one or two examples as a class.

Creating Longer Pieces of Writing

Objectives
- To recognize how paragraphs work together in a composition
- To use strategies to create longer pieces of writing
- To use revising guidelines to improve a composition

> ### Related Mini-Lessons

For information on topics related to creating longer pieces of writing, see the following mini-lessons:
- **Improving Paragraphs, pp. 230–233**
- **Introductions, pp. 247–249**
- **Conclusions, pp. 250–252**

Motivate
Show students one frame from a popular comic strip. Ask students to point out the "parts" of the frame (characters, speech balloons, background). Then state that the single frame has all the "parts" of the complete strip and ask students if they would feel satisfied seeing only this one frame. (No; a single frame from a strip does not tell the whole story.) Then point out that a single paragraph from a composition no more tells the whole story than a single frame from a comic strip.

Teaching Strategies

for WHAT IS A COMPOSITION?

HELPFUL HINT You may want to point out that just as not all paragraphs rigidly follow one pattern, neither do all compositions. However, a successful composition will do what is described in the middle column of the chart.

HELPFUL HINT You may wish to point out that writers choose different ways to begin their compositions. The "best" way to begin differs according to the writer's personal choice and the writing topic. List a variety of choices on the board: 1. prepare detailed outlines; 2. work from rough notes; 3. work slowly and revise while writing; 4. write quickly and revise later; 5. write interesting parts first; 6. write from beginning to end; and so forth. Ask students for their own suggestions and add these to the list. (For more about drafting and editing, see Professional Notebook below.)

for REVISING A COMPOSITION

INDIVIDUALIZING INSTRUCTION: BASIC STUDENTS You may want to review the concepts of *main idea* and *topic* for these students. Students may be better able to distinguish between the concepts if they consider a specific example, such as the following:

Topic: video games

Main idea: Playing video games is a worthwhile hobby.

Writing TIP

You might want to make a rough outline of your composition. Then use each main point in your outline as the main idea of a paragraph.

PROBLEM SOLVING

"I need to know more about developing the different kinds of paragraphs in a composition."

For more information about developing paragraphs in a composition, see

- Handbook 4, "Developing a Topic," pages 205–210
- Handbook 14, "Introductions," pages 247–249
- Handbook 15, "Conclusions," pages 250–252

HOW DO I CREATE A COMPOSITION?

The strategies you use to write good paragraphs will also help you create strong compositions. So keep those techniques and guidelines in mind as you draft.

Drafting a Composition

When you start drafting, you may want just to explore and develop your ideas without giving any thought to how many paragraphs there will be. You can group and organize ideas later. On the other hand, you may know what your main ideas are, and you may want to develop each one as a paragraph. Refer to the guidelines for drafting paragraphs that appear in Handbook 10, "Improving Paragraphs," on pages 230–233.

Revising a Composition

Once you've gotten your ideas down on paper, you can improve your composition by following these guidelines.

Guidelines for Revising a Composition

- **Check to see that your first paragraph identifies your topic and gets your reader's attention.**

- **Make sure that each supporting paragraph develops only one main idea.** Break paragraphs overloaded with ideas into smaller paragraphs, each focusing on one main idea.

- **Check to see that the order of your paragraphs makes sense.** Rearrange paragraphs and add transitions as necessary.

- **Make sure that your last paragraph ties your ideas together effectively and does not introduce new thoughts that need to be developed or explained.**

PROFESSIONAL NOTEBOOK

Advice from the Authors Ask students if they agree with the following comment by Peter Elbow about editing during the drafting stage:

"Editing is usually necessary if we want to end up with something satisfactory. The problem is that editing goes on *at the same time* as producing. The editor is, as it were, constantly looking over the shoulder of the producer and constantly fiddling with what he's doing while he's in the middle of trying to do it. No wonder the producer gets nervous. . . . It's an unnecessary burden to try to think of words and also worry at the same time whether they're the right words."

How Can I Make My Writing Better?

Revising

You too can improve your writing by revising. Revising can be much more than taking out one unnecessary word, however. It is your chance to look back at your work and see what you like about it and what you want to change. You might want to reword a description or add to an explanation. You may even decide to start over again.

Keep in mind that writing is a very personal activity. Some writers like to revise as they go along. Others wait until they have completed a draft. Use whatever method is right for you.

STRATEGIES FOR REVISING

When you have completed a draft put it aside for a while. When you look at it again, you will be able to see it with fresh eyes. You may be surprised at the things you notice.

One good approach is to read your draft aloud. Hearing the sound of the words can help you decide how well you like your writing. Also, you may find places where you stumble as you read. Think about revising those passages.

Your peers can give you valuable advice for revising your writing. See Handbook 16, "Peer Response," on pages 253–256 for ways to get the best advice from others.

In addition, questions and suggestions like the ones shown on the next page might help you as you revise.

Revising   **257**

Objectives
• To learn strategies for revising
• To use revision guidelines to improve paragraphs and compositions

> **Related
> Mini-Lessons**

For information on topics related to revising, see the following mini-lessons:
• **Improving Paragraphs, pp. 230–233**
• **Transitions, pp. 234–238**
• **Peer Response, pp. 253–256**

Teaching Strategies

for STRATEGIES FOR REVISING
KEY TO UNDERSTANDING You may wish to emphasize that revising is seldom an orderly process. Writers may go over a piece of writing numerous times, making a few changes with each pass. Eventually, the piece may even become a mess of arrows, additions, and crossouts.

PROFESSIONAL NOTEBOOK

In her book *Errors and Expectations,* Mina Shaughnessy notes that beginning writers often do not understand the ways in which writing is different from speaking—particularly the necessity for the revision process. "Writers who are not aware of this," says Shaughnessy, "tend to think that the point in writing is to get everything right the first time and that the need to change things is the mark of the amateur." She urges teachers to encourage messiness, for "The messiness is indeed writing—the record of a remarkable interplay between the writer as creator and the writer as reader."

CRITICAL THINKING: EVALUATING

Have students write at least one more question that relates to each question in the first column. (Samples: What is my main idea? What are my supporting details? How does each sentence relate to the main idea? What transitions can I add? Which words or phrases can I make more vivid?)

for STUDENT MODEL

USING THE MODEL
To help students understand how the revisions relate to specific writing techniques, lead a discussion of the reasons why the student made these particular changes. For example, in the opening sentence, a question is more inviting because it draws the reader into the writing; the sentence beginning "At the center . . ." was moved because it was out of sequence.

COMPUTER TIP

A cut-and-paste function can be very helpful for moving or deleting sentences as you revise.

Student MODEL

Made introduction more interesting
Unimportant details deleted
New paragraph for a new main idea

Details added

Sentence moved

Transition added

Guidelines for Revising

Ask Yourself	Try This
• Is my main idea obvious?	• Rewrite your introduction or opening sentences.
• Have I included enough information to support my points?	• Add supporting details as needed to make your points clear.
• Should anything be taken out?	• Leave out details that don't develop your main idea.
• Is my writing easy to follow?	• Check the order in which you present information. Start a new paragraph for each main idea. Add transitions where needed.
• Is my writing interesting?	• Spice up your writing with vivid nouns, verbs, and modifiers.

One student made these revisions to a draft.

Have you ever
I've always wondered what was inside a baseball?
Yesterday I took one apart an old baseball I found in a to find out.
vacant lot. ¶ The first layer I took off was pieces of
leather. They were held together with red thread.
stitched   thick
Then I unwrapped layers of wool yarn wound very
yards and yards
tightly. At the center I discovered a small ball of
cork. That was covered by two layers of rubber. Now
Under the yarn I found
you won't have to destroy your own baseball to see
what's inside.

Practice Your Skills

A. The passages below need to be revised. Use the Guidelines for Revising on page 258 and make any changes you think are needed.

1.   Frank Drake, the President of the SETI Institute, said he thinks their new project will succeed. SETI stands for Search for Extraterrestrial Intelligence. SETI and NASA scientists are looking for intelligent life on other planets. They have started a 10-year, $100 million search for radio signals from space.

2.   What makes popcorn pop? The Native Americans were the first people to make popcorn. One way they made popcorn was to put an ear of corn on a stick and roast it over a fire. They gathered up the kernels that popped off the ear. The corn kernels that are used for popcorn contain a lot of water. When they are heated, the water expands and turns into steam. This causes the kernel to explode into a mass. The Native Americans scraped kernels from the cob and threw them directly into a fire. They ate the pieces that came out of the fire. One method was more complicated. They heated coarse sand in a shallow clay pan. When the sand was hot, they put corn kernels into it. The cooked kernels popped to the surface of the sand. There is nothing more tasty than fresh-popped popcorn. Eating popcorn became very popular with the explorers and settlers who came to America. Today people in the United States eat almost two pounds of popcorn per person a year.

B. Choose a piece of writing you completed recently, or something from your writer's portfolio. Revise it, using the ideas presented in this handbook. Then write a note to attach to the revised paper. Discuss the changes you made and the reasons you made them.

Additional Resources

Writing Resource Book, p. 70
Elaboration, Revision, and Proofreading Practice
Elaboration, Revision, and Proofreading Transparency Pack

Answers to Practice Your Skills

A. Answers will vary slightly. Sample revisions are shown below.

1.   "Our new project is bound to succeed," said Frank Drake, the President of the SETI Institute. SETI stands for Search for Extraterrestrial Intelligence. SETI and NASA scientists have started a 10-year, $100 million search for radio signals from space. They are looking for intelligent life on other planets.

2.   What makes popcorn pop? The corn kernels that are used for popcorn contain a lot of water. When they are heated, the water expands and turns into steam. This causes the kernel to explode into a puffy white mass.

   The Native Americans were the first people to make popcorn. They developed three ways to make it. One way was to put an ear of corn on a stick and roast it over a fire. Then they gathered up the kernels that popped off the ear. They also scraped kernels from the cob and threw them directly into a fire. They ate the pieces that popped out of the fire. The third method was more complicated. They heated coarse sand in a shallow clay pan. When the sand was hot, they stirred corn kernels into it. The cooked kernels popped to the surface of the sand.

   Eating popcorn became very popular with the explorers and settlers who came to America. Today people in the United States eat almost two pounds of popcorn per person a year.

B. Answers will vary.

Proofreading

Objectives
- To learn proofreading techniques and symbols
- To use a proofreading checklist and symbols to find and correct mistakes in grammar, capitalization, punctuation, and spelling

 Related Mini-Lessons

For information on topics related to proofreading, see the following mini-lessons:
- **Correcting Sentence Errors, pp. 281–284**
- **Capitalization, pp. 547–565**
- **Punctuation, pp. 567–598**

Teaching Strategies

GENERAL NOTE
KEY TO UNDERSTANDING
Emphasize to students the difference between proofreading and revising. Point out that revising involves changes in organization and content, whereas proofreading focuses on changes in grammar, punctuation, capitalization, and spelling.

for PROOFREADING STRATEGIES
HELPFUL HINT You might tell students that newspaper, magazine, and book publishers employ proofreaders, and that some people make proofreading a career. You might want to explain that the techniques outlined on the pupil page are the same ones that professional proofreaders use.

How Do I Know My Writing Is Correct?

Proofreading

What would you think if you saw this sign? If you're like most people, you would think that whoever created the sign needs a spelling lesson!

When you write, little errors like the one on the sign can take a reader's attention away from your message. By proofreading your work, you can find and correct errors in spelling, punctuation, capitalization, and grammar. You can help your readers concentrate on your writing, not on accidental mistakes.

PROOFREADING STRATEGIES

To catch the little mistakes in your writing that might slip by, you need to look carefully at your work. Here are some strategies you can try.

Proofread more than once. It's a good idea to read over your work several times. You can look for different kinds of mistakes each time. Put your paper aside between proofreadings. With fresh eyes, you may see errors you missed the first time.

TEACHER'S LOUNGE

A computer spell checker indeed hides hazards aplenty that lie in wait for the unwary. Share this little ditty with your students:

Spellbound
I have a spelling checker,
It came with my PC;
It plainly marks four my revue
Mistakes I cannot sea.
I've run this poem threw it,
I'm sure your please too no,
Its letter perfect in it's weigh,
My checker tolled me sew.

Read aloud for end punctuation. As you read your work aloud, pause where you think each sentence ends. Find the subject and verb. Be sure that you have used the correct end punctuation—a period, a question mark, or an exclamation point—for that type of sentence.

Read aloud for commas within sentences. Notice where you pause naturally. Such a pause may mean that a comma is needed. If you stumble over the words, you may be able to delete a comma that is not needed.

Proofread for initial capitals. Find the end punctuation mark of each sentence. Check to see that the next word begins with a capital letter.

Read your work backwards. Read backwards one word at a time to check your spelling. Circle any spellings you are unsure of. After you finish reading, check the spellings of the circled words in a dictionary.

Proofreading Checklist

Step 1: Look at your sentences.
Do all sentences express complete thoughts?
Are there any run-on sentences?
Do subjects and verbs agree?

Step 2: Look at your words.
Are words spelled correctly?
Have you used the correct forms of verbs to show tense?
Have you used the correct forms of pronouns?
Have you used adjectives and adverbs correctly?

Step 3: Look at your capitalization and punctuation.
Have you capitalized the first words of sentences?
Have you capitalized proper nouns and adjectives?
Have you used commas correctly?
Have you used end marks correctly?
Have you used other punctuation marks correctly?

Proofreading   **261**

for PROOFREADING STRATEGIES

PERSONAL TOUCH If you have a preferred proofreading technique, such as laying your work aside for a time between readings, reading from the bottom up, or asking someone else to proofread your work, share it with the class.

for PROOFREADING CHECKLIST

HELPFUL HINT Explain to students that when they proofread, they may need to look for each kind of mistake separately; that is, by making a separate and complete pass through their composition to answer each question under each step on the checklist. Assure students that professional proofreaders always work with a dictionary and a grammar handbook nearby and look up rules frequently to check their knowledge.

SPICE BOX

To stress the importance of a single comma, write these pairs of sentences on the board and have students answer the questions.
- In which case is Jean likely to be in trouble?
  Jean, our babysitter is two hours late!
  Jean, our babysitter, is two hours late!
- Which is more of a compliment?

Kay's little girl is a pretty, bright child.
Kay's little girl is a pretty bright child.
- Which shows the speaker knows the man well?
  He is the man I believe.
  He is the man, I believe.

Practice Your Skills

A. Recall the start of a race, a game, a concert, or some other event that you have participated in or observed. Try to relive the moment in your mind. Write down vivid sensory details that describe what you experienced. List the details under the four categories (1) sight, (2) sound, (3) touch, and (4) taste and smell. Use the details to write a description of your experience.

B. Practice describing different things. Choose three of the items below and describe each one in terms of two or three senses. For one item, try your hand at writing a simile or a metaphor to describe it.

1. a campfire   **4.** a pickle   **7.** a rose
2. a police siren   **5.** a fish   **8.** a bus
3. a caterpillar   **6.** a skyscraper   **9.** a baseball glove

C. Sensory details make any writing better—whether it is fiction or nonfiction. Write a story about a true or imaginary incident. Use details to make your writing lively and interesting. The following examples may give you some ideas.

1. A bee tries to land on your sandwich.
2. You are walking home in a rainstorm.
3. A tiny puppy tries to understand your commands.
4. You wait for the school bus on a cold day.
5. Your stomach lets you know it's lunch time.

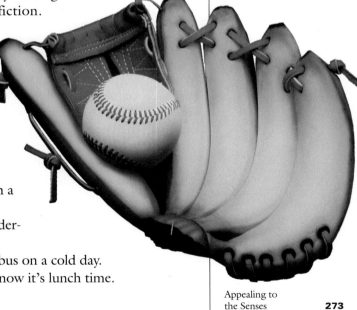

Appealing to the Senses   **273**

for PRACTICE YOUR SKILLS

HELPFUL HINT For Exercises A and C, suggest that students visualize the scenes before they begin to write. Those students who enjoy drawing might capture more details by sketching the scenes first.

for PRACTICE YOUR SKILLS

ASSESSMENT Each exercise involves writing a description that appeals to the senses. You might want to focus your grading on how well students appeal to more than one sense in their descriptions.

Additional Resources

Writing Resource Book, pp. 72–74
Spelling and Vocabulary Booklet

Answers to Practice Your Skills

A. Answers will vary.
B. Answers will vary.
C. Answers will vary.

WRITING
HANDBOOK
20

Levels of Language

Objectives

- To identify standard English, non-standard English, and slang
- To recognize the differences between formal and informal language
- To use language appropriate for one's audience and type of writing

Related Mini-Lessons

For information on topics related to levels of language, see the following mini-lessons:

- **Goals and Audience, pp. 211–213**
- **Personal Voice, pp. 276–277**
- **Using the Dictionary and the Thesaurus, pp. 308–311**
- **Oral Reports, pp. 324–325**

Motivate

Ask students how they expect to see people dressed in the following situations: at a wedding and at the beach. Explain that just as one's clothing should fit the social situation, so should one's language fit the writing situation.

Teaching Strategies

for CHOOSING THE RIGHT WORDS

INDIVIDUALIZING INSTRUCTION: LEP AND ESL STUDENTS You may have some students who have acquired English by hearing it spoken (by people in the neighborhood, for example, or on TV)—and who thus have never distinguished standard from nonstandard English. Be sensitive to the challenge these students face at this point; be prepared to work with them individually in a non-threatening atmosphere, to help them determine appropriate language choices.

WRITING
HANDBOOK
20

How Do I Make My Language Fit My Audience?

Levels of Language

> Propel, propel, propel your craft
> Smoothly down the liquid solution . . .
> **From *A Prairie Home Companion Folk Song Book***

Perhaps you would prefer to row, row, row your boat gently down the stream. In fact, the version of a well-known song quoted above would be much easier to understand if you replaced its formal vocabulary with more familiar words.

As you write and speak, you make choices about what words you will use. By thinking about your audience (a best friend, classmates, PTA members) and the kind of writing or situation (friendly letter or speech), you can learn to adjust your language to match any occasion.

CHOOSING THE RIGHT WORDS

Careful writers and speakers use **standard English,** language that follows the rules of grammar and usage. **Nonstandard English** is language that does not conform to rules of grammar and usage. Most of the time, you will be using standard English. When you use standard English, however, you will still need to make some decisions. Standard English can vary greatly in style, from formal to informal. **Slang,** for example, is a very informal kind of English used by a particular group. Choose language that is appropriate for your audience and type of writing.

Look at the chart on the next page. It shows some of the characteristics that distinguish formal language from informal language.

Levels of Language

	Formal	Informal
Characteristics	Advanced vocabulary, long sentences, no contractions	Simple vocabulary, shorter sentences, contractions
Type of writing	Report, business letter, speech, job application, letter to the editor	Friendly letter, journal entry, note to your best friend
Tone	Serious, reserved	Conversational, casual

Here are some examples of the differences between formal and informal language.

Formal   Students who wish to attend the concert should assemble in front of the gymnasium in the morning.

Informal   Students who want to go to the concert should meet in front of the gym in the morning.

Formal   If you cannot attend, please advise your teacher by 3:00 P.M. today.

Informal   If you can't make it, please tell your teacher by 3:00 P.M. today.

Practice Your Skills

Rewrite the passage below in a form appropriate for sending to the mayor of your town.

The kids on our block need your help. The streets are pretty busy here. There isn't a safe place to hang out. The old lot on Elm St. would be a great place for a playground. Right now, it's got heaps of trash. Suppose we kids clean up the lot. Could you OK the change for a playground and give us some equipment?

for LEVELS OF LANGUAGE
CRITICAL THINKING: COMPARING AND CONTRASTING
To make the difference between formal and informal language clear—and fun— ask students to come up with a situation in which informal language would be inappropriate—such as a summer-job interview. Then brainstorm a situation in which formal language would be inappropriate—such as a telephone call with their best friend. Then ask groups of students to generate sentences and alter them to fit each situation. For instance, "I like to watch soap operas" could become "I'm really into the soaps" or "I enjoy watching daytime drama."

Additional Resource
Writing Resource Book, p. 75

Answers to Practice Your Skills
Answers will vary. A possible revision is shown.

The young people in our neighborhood need your help. The streets are very busy, and there is no safe place for us to play. A vacant lot on Elm Street would make an excellent playground, but it is covered with trash. If my friends and I cleaned up the lot, could the city approve the use of the lot as a playground and provide some equipment?

Social Studies Connection

Choose a current news event, and ask two or three volunteers to role-play a discussion of it. Then ask them to role-play being broadcast journalists; tell them to write and then read aloud a one-paragraph story on the same event. Discuss the differences in language level between the two presentations.

WRITING
HANDBOOK
21

Personal Voice

Objectives
- To recognize that a writer has a personal voice
- To use journal writing, freewriting, and other strategies to develop a personal voice

 Related Mini-Lessons

For information on topics related to developing a personal voice, see the following mini-lessons:
- **Peer Response, pp. 253–256**
- **Levels of Language, pp. 274–275**

Motivate
To help students recognize that writers have individual voices, read aloud two poems that are very different. For example, you might choose "Fog" by Carl Sandburg and a stanza or two from "The Walrus and the Carpenter" by Lewis Carroll. Ask students whether they think both poems are likely to have been written by the same author. Encourage them to focus on some of the stylistic differences as they explain their answers.

Teaching Strategies

for YOUR OWN VOICE

USING THE MODEL Use questions such as these to help students understand why Lindsay's journal entry for September 15 has an unnatural voice:

What form of writing is this? (journal writing)

Who is the usual audience for journal writing? (oneself)

If you did not know that this is a journal entry, who would you think the audience is? (Samples: a teacher; the principal)

WRITING
HANDBOOK
21

How Can I Make My Writing Sound Like Me?

Personal Voice

When you call your friends on the phone, do you have to tell them who's calling? Of course not—they recognize your voice. How? Well, there is something unique about the way you sound and the way you put words together.

The same is true of your writing. You have a special way of choosing words and putting them together that is yours and yours alone. It's called your **writing voice.**

Your Own Voice

Have you ever tried to impress someone by using vocabulary or a formal way of talking that just isn't you? If you did, you most likely sounded unnatural—maybe even completely phony. The same thing can happen with your writing.

Young writers sometimes think they need to use big, important-sounding words and long, complicated sentences to make their writing sound grown-up and sophisticated. Often, though, their writing ends up sounding strained and unnatural. Here, for example, is how Lindsay wrote when she began keeping a journal for her writing class.

> **September 15**
> Today we have been assigned the task of keeping a writing journal. Through the coming months, we are to record our personal impressions and thoughts and use them as ideas for future writing projects. I shall attempt to observe the people and nature surrounding me and write about them in meaningful new ways.

At first, Lindsay's journal entries sounded unnatural, as if she were writing to impress some unknown reader. After several weeks, though, she began to find her own voice.

Compare this later journal entry with the first one. Which one sounds more natural to you?

November 9
> It seems like we spent all weekend raking leaves and cleaning up the yard for winter. Will and I piled up a HUGE mound of leaves, then we decided to jump in it like we did when we were little. The leaves went flying. They looked like a flock of red and yellow birds settling on the grass.

▼ Student MODEL

L EARN BY DOING

An effective way to discover and develop your writing voice is to write as often as you can. Try these strategies.

- **Write in your journal regularly.** When Lindsay finally relaxed and wrote just for herself in her journal, she discovered her own writing voice.

- **Freewrite at the start of every writing assignment.** You'll be expressing your ideas in your own words.

- **Read your writing aloud.** When you hear your writing spoken, you can more easily tell what sounds natural.

- **Write letters to friends.** Write in the same words you would use if you were speaking to your friends.

- **Use peer readers.** Have friends read your writing. After they finish, ask them, "Is it me? Do you know this writer?"

Practice Your Skills

Read this paragraph. How would *you* express the ideas in this paragraph? Rewrite the paragraph using your own voice.

> I urge all my fellow students to take part in the process of electing officials to govern our class. When one exercises the right to vote, one is taking part in one of our nation's most cherished traditions.

Personal Voice **277**

for LEARN BY DOING

INDIVIDUALIZING INSTRUCTION: LEP STUDENTS Encourage these students to find a writing voice by focusing on writing in their journals and on freewriting. Both of these types of writing activities allow students a chance to relax and explore their ideas without worrying about a reader's reactions.

BASIC STUDENTS If students' writing is stilted and wooden, you might suggest that they imagine a sympathetic reader who is interested only in what they want to say—not how they sound when they say it. If students can keep this reader in mind as they write, they will soon allow their natural voices to ring out.

Additional Resource
Writing Resource Book, p. 76

Answers to Practice Your Skills
Answers will vary.

TEACHER'S LOUNGE

"How come when you say we have a problem, I'm always the one who has the problem?"

Using Dialogue

Objectives
- To recognize that dialogue can provide information and show characters' personalities
- To write realistic dialogue that follows conventions of format and mechanics

 Related Mini-Lessons

For information on topics related to writing dialogue, see the following mini-lessons:
- **Show, Don't Tell, pp. 239–242**
- **Levels of Language, pp. 274–275**
- **Punctuation, pp. 586–588**

Teaching Strategies

for HOW TO USE DIALOGUE

STUMBLING BLOCK Some students may think that any passage with quotation marks around someone's words is dialogue. Emphasize that dialogue is a conversation that involves at least two people. An expert's opinion quoted in a research report is not dialogue.

Literary
MODEL

How Do I Make My Characters Sound Real?

Using Dialogue

Dialogue is conversation—people talking to each other. You can use dialogue in your writing to clearly *show* readers what happens and what people are like. Read the following paragraph. It doesn't use dialogue. It just tells about a conversation between two characters.

> Grandpa wanted to know how long I'd been saving the money. I told him it was two years. He was really surprised.

Now listen to the characters talking to each other.

> "How long have you been saving this?" he asked.
> "A long time, Grandpa," I said.
> "How long?" he asked.
> I told him, "Two years."
> His mouth flew open and in a loud voice he said, "Two years!"
>
> **Wilson Rawls, *Where the Red Fern Grows***

Dialogue makes the characters seem like real people. You "hear" how surprised Grandpa is. You can picture the scene between him and his grandson as if you were there.

HOW TO USE DIALOGUE

You can use dialogue in any kind of writing, from stories to newspaper articles. By presenting people's actual words, you can both provide information and show how the people think and feel.

Providing Information Dialogue can provide information about action, characters, and setting. What can you learn about these parts of a story from the following dialogue?

Literary
MODEL

> "Here I am trying to get home to cook me a bite to eat, and you snatch my pocketbook! Maybe you ain't been to your supper either, late as it be. Have you?"
>
> "There's nobody home at my house," said the boy.
>
> "Then we'll eat," said the woman. "I believe you're hungry—or been hungry—to try to snatch my pocketbook!"
>
> "I want a pair of blue suede shoes," said the boy.
>
> "Well, you didn't have to snatch my pocketbook to get some suede shoes," said Mrs. Luella Bates Washington Jones. "You could of asked me."
>
> **Langston Hughes, "Thank You, M'am"**

Showing Personalities Dialogue can also bring out the personalities of the characters and set the tone of your writing. For example, the tone could be humorous, angry, or sad. In the following example, the way the character speaks shows that he is used to ordering people around and that he is a little ridiculous. The dialogue gives the story its humorous tone.

Literary
MODEL

> "I want you to get the moon," said the King. "The Princess Lenore wants the moon. If she can have the moon, she will get well again."
>
> "The moon?" exclaimed the Lord High Chamberlain, his eyes widening. This made him look four times as wise as he really was.
>
> "Yes, the moon," said the King. "M-o-o-n, moon. Get it tonight, tomorrow at the latest."
>
> **James Thurber, "Many Moons"**

Using Dialogue **279**

MULTICULTURAL Connection

Dialect Sometimes writers use dialect in dialogue to make characters realistic and to give readers information about both characters and setting. Point out how Langston Hughes uses dialect in this passage from "Thank You, M'am."

---

for FIRST LITERARY MODEL
CRITICAL THINKING: INFERRING
After students read the model dialogue, ask them to infer what has just happened in the story. (A woman confronts a boy who has tried but failed to steal her pocketbook.) Then have students describe what they can tell about each of the two characters. (Samples: Mrs. Jones, a working woman, is firm but compassionate; the young thief may have a poor home life and wants a pair of blue suede shoes.) Write key information on the board. Note how much students were able to learn from a very brief passage of dialogue.

ADDING GROUPS OF WORDS TO SENTENCES

Sometimes a group of words in one sentence can add important information to another sentence. You can move the word group from one sentence to the other. If the words you move tell something about a person, a thing, or an action in the other sentence, put them near the name of the person, thing, or action.

Separate	Mom asked me to wash the dog. *She asked me twice today.*
Combined	Mom asked me **twice today** to wash the dog.

However, the group of words might make sense in more than one place in the new sentence.

> **Twice today,** Mom asked me to wash the dog.

Practice Your Skills

A. Combine each pair of sentences by moving a word group from one sentence to the other. Omit the words in italics.

1. The woman is my grandmother. *She is* wearing a ring.
2. Grandma moved here in 1940. *She came here* from Norway.
3. The most important thing she brought with her was a ring. *It is a* beautiful ruby *ring.*
4. Grandma lost her ring. *She lost it* the year I was born.

B. Combine each pair of sentences by adding important words from one sentence to the other sentence.

1. The postcard is from Grandfather. It is on the table.
2. He is visiting Mexico. He is there for the winter.
3. The card shows the ruins of an ancient city. The city is called Chichén Itzá.
4. Chichén Itzá was built by the Maya. They built the city hundreds of years ago.

Writing TIP

After you join two sentences, read the new sentence carefully. Words added in the wrong place can make a sentence confusing, wrong, or even funny—for example, "Mom asked me to wash the dog *twice today.*"

for ADDING GROUPS OF WORDS . . .

INDIVIDUALIZING INSTRUCTION: ESL STUDENTS Some ESL students may have difficulty with the idea that words or groups of words can be placed in various locations in a sentence. In some languages, such as German, grammar rules indicate clearly where such words or phrases should be placed. As a general guideline, tell students to place these words as close as possible to *me* words that are repeated in both sentences. As they gain fluency, students will learn to distinguish between adjectival and adverbial word groups.

Additional Resources

Writing Resource Book, p. 82
Sentence Composing Copy Masters, pp. 5–6

Answers to Practice Your Skills

A.
1. The woman wearing a ring is my grandmother.
2. Grandma moved here from Norway in 1940.
3. The most important thing she brought with her was a beautiful ruby ring.
4. Grandma lost her ring the year I was born.

B.
1. The postcard on the table is from Grandfather.
2. He is visiting Mexico for the winter.
3. The card shows the ruins of an ancient city called Chichén Itzá.
4. Chichén Itzá was built hundreds of years ago by the Maya. *or* Chichén Itzá was built by the Maya hundreds of years ago. *or* Hundreds of years ago, Chichén Itzá was built by the Maya.

Objective
• To use the book jackets and suggested writing prompts as springboards to informal writing

WRITING WARM-UPS
Use these writing prompts as risk-free ungraded activities that students can enjoy. Unless students wish (and have the time) to do more, suggest that each student respond to only one prompt. Before students begin, point out that all three prompts have a similar focus: students are asked to tell about something that keenly interests them. You might also point out that the authors of the three books in the illustration all chose to write about subjects that interested them individually.

• What kind of book would you like to write? Jot down some thoughts about what your book would be like.

• What fascinates you? Make a list of things you would like to find out more about.

• What is the most interesting thing you have learned in school this year? Tell why it is important to you.

292

Academic Skills

Whether you write them or read them, books can take you to new worlds. To get the most out of these worlds, you need to be able to read, study, think, and research effectively.

The handbooks that follow can teach you skills that will help you explore new worlds, in school and on your own.

Academic Skills

INTRODUCING THE HANDBOOKS

Here's a thought exercise you might use to introduce the Academic Skills Handbooks. Tell students to imagine that the pupil-edition page is in a foreign language they can't identify. Ask how they would go about learning what the page says.

First, of course, they would think about the problem and develop a strategy for solving it. They might consult a person with expertise in languages. They might also ask a librarian to help them find out what the language is. Perhaps the librarian could help them find a dictionary of that language. While translating the page, students would learn some words of the foreign language, and possibly some English words new to them, as well.

During the whole process just described, students would have used thinking skills, study and research skills, interviewing skills, library skills, dictionary skills, reading skills, and vocabulary skills. If, after succeeding in translating the page, they were to answer questions about their findings, orally and in writing, they would use skills from every mini-lesson in the Academic Skills section. Point out that these are general skills that can help people find information on any subject, from foreign languages to home cooking. They are also, of course, vital to succeeding in school!

Study and Research Skills

Objectives

- To use the KWL approach as a way to focus thinking when reading or researching
- To use a learning log to understand a subject better
- To recognize and apply effective techniques for studying and memorizing

▼ Related Mini-Lessons

For information on topics related to study and research skills, see the following mini-lessons:

- **Reading Skills, pp. 298–301**
- **Library Skills, pp. 312–319**
- **Thinking Skills, pp. 320–322**

Motivate

Ask volunteers to describe the biggest study problem they have—for example, scheduling study time. Is the study area noisy and distracting? Do they find memorizing hard? Do they spend a lot of time studying and still receive poor grades because their study methods are ineffective? Make a list of problems on the board and suggest that students look for solutions in this handbook.

Teaching Strategies

for THE KWL APPROACH

MODELING To help students understand the use of the KWL approach, model the first two steps, using a subject you yourself would like to study. On the board, make a "K" list of things you already know, then a "W" list of things you would like to know.

WRITING
HANDBOOK
25

How Can I Become a Better Student?

Study and Research Skills

Do you ever wish that it were possible just to open up your head and pour in knowledge? Unfortunately, learning doesn't work that way. To get the most out of your studies, you need to actively participate in the learning process. There are skills you can learn that will make your study time more efficient and enjoyable.

THE KWL APPROACH

Whether you are reading a textbook, doing a research report, or working on a project, using the KWL approach is a good way to focus your thinking. The letters stand for three questions you should ask yourself about your subject:

"What do I already know about my subject?" Before you start studying, make a list of everything you already know about the subject. The list will get you thinking about the subject and about what you don't yet know.

"What do I want to know?" Make a list of the things you would like to know about the subject. As you study, see if you find the answers to your questions.

"What did I learn?" After you have studied the subject, look back and list the things you have learned. Are there still things you want to know? Have your thoughts about the subject changed?

LEARNING LOGS

Writing about a subject helps you understand it better and often prompts you to think about things you hadn't noticed before. One of the best ways to take charge of your learning is to keep a learning log. A **learning log** is a journal you keep for one subject. Like your writing journal, your learning log is a place to record ideas, thoughts, and questions. You might want to keep separate learning logs for each of your subjects.

All sorts of things can go into a learning log. It is a perfect place to record your answers to the KWL questions and to note key facts about the subject. You can write about your reactions to the things you are learning and ask yourself questions about things you don't understand. You can also draw pictures or graphic aids to help you understand the subject.

Science Journal

4/13 Alligators and Crocodiles
K: reptiles, look like floating logs, dangerous huge teeth, short legs, alligators live in swamps in Florida
W: How are alligators and crocodiles different? How can you tell them apart? Do they both attack people?

4/14 Field trip to the zoo
L: I touched an alligator! Alligators aren't as ferocious as crocodiles. The zookeeper could hold the alligator's snout shut with one hand because the muscles to open the jaws are pretty weak. Alligators usually avoid people, but crocodiles will attack. One way to tell them apart is by the shape of the snout.

alligator snout:

crocodile snout:

It would be fun to actually see alligators in the wild! Where besides Florida could I find them?

Writing
TIP

Writing in your learning log is like thinking with a pencil. Remember, write for yourself—record what will be most useful to you.

Student MODEL

Things you already know

Things you want to know

What you have learned
Key facts

Drawings

Your feelings
Questions you still have

Study and Research Skills **295**

---

for LEARNING LOGS
HELPFUL HINT Students might like to color-code the KWL information in their learning logs. They might write in one color what they know; in a second color, what they want to know; and in a third color, what they have learned. Color-coding can help them locate different kinds of information in their logs quickly.

for LEARNING LOGS
INDIVIDUALIZING INSTRUCTION: LD STUDENTS To students who have difficulty with phrasing their ideas in writing, suggest using a tape recorder to keep a learning log.

ESL STUDENTS Because of the personal nature of learning logs, ESL students will probably prefer to use their first languages when recording ideas, thoughts, and questions. Tell these students that it is acceptable to use whatever language is more comfortable.

for STUDENT MODEL
USING THE MODEL Ask students what they might add to the list of "K" information and "W" questions. Emphasize the value of the drawings in the "L" part of the model, and note that some information can be conveyed more effectively through graphic aids.

PROFESSIONAL NOTEBOOK

In *The Young Learner's Handbook,* teacher and writer Stephen Tchudi offers this variation on keeping a learning log:

. . . Using a ruler as a guide, draw a line down the center of your notebook pages. Then write the facts in the left-hand column, leaving the right column free for your comments and questions to yourself.

296 Writing Handbook

Writing TIP

Your notes are for your eyes only. Don't worry about grammar, punctuation, and spelling. Feel free to use abbreviations and to make up symbols.

A crazy picture can help you remember that *core* is the innermost part of the earth.

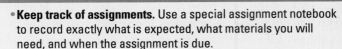

STAY ON TOP OF YOUR STUDIES

Try these ideas to make the most of your study time.

- **Keep track of assignments.** Use a special assignment notebook to record exactly what is expected, what materials you will need, and when the assignment is due.
- **Plan ahead.** Schedule your activities on a weekly calendar to make sure you have time for everything.
- **Keep a separate notebook or folder for each subject.**
- **Take notes as you study.** Include only the main ideas.
- **Review your notes as soon as you can.** Revise or add to them as needed, and highlight important points.

Memorizing

Do you think some people are born with good and bad memories, just as some people are tall and others short? Actually, there are skills anyone can learn to improve memory.

- **Write it, recite it.** The action of writing and the sound of your voice will help you remember information.
- **Find connections between items.** For example, remember items in the order they happened or recall items alphabetically.
- **Create a crazy picture.** Arrange the facts you want to remember in a vivid picture in your mind. Then, when you want to recall those facts, visualize the same picture.
- **Make up catchy sayings.** Develop a sentence or phrase using the initials of the words you want to memorize. For example, HOMES could help you remember the names of the Great Lakes: *H*uron, *O*ntario, *M*ichigan, *E*rie, and *S*uperior.

PROFESSIONAL NOTEBOOK

In *How to Sharpen Your Study Skills,* teacher and writer Sigmund Kalina offers these examples of "memory hooks":
- *word hooks.* In music, the spaces of the treble staff reading upward are f, a, c, e, which spell the word "face."
- *sentence hooks.* Make phrases or sentences that will help fix information in your memory. To remember which way to turn the clock at the start and end of Daylight Saving Time, remember that you "spring" *forward* and "fall" *backward.*

Base Words

The main word to which other word parts are added is called the **base word.** When you add a word part to a base word, you form a new word. For example, you can add the word part *mis-* to the base word *direct* to form *misdirect,* a word that means "to direct wrongly." In the same way, you can add the word part *-or* to the base word *direct* to form *director* a word that means "a person who directs."

direct   mis**direct**   **direct**or

Prefixes

A **prefix** is a word part that is added to the beginning of a base word. A prefix changes a base word to a new word with a new meaning. When you know the meanings of common prefixes, you can often figure out the meanings of unfamiliar words that contain those prefixes.

For example, look at the word *illegible.* The prefix *il-* means "not." The base word *legible* means "able to be read." So *illegible* means "not able to be read."

Here are some common prefixes and their meanings.

Prefixes	Meanings	Examples
il-, im-, in-, ir-	not	illegal, impossible, insane, irregular
mis-	wrong	mislead, misplace
non-	not, without	nonfat, nonsense
pre-	before	preheat, prehistory, preschool
re-	again	reappear, rebuild, recharge, reconsider
un-	not	unexpected, uncommon

for PREFIXES

STUMBLING BLOCK   Point out to students that sometimes, what looks like a familiar prefix is simply part of a word. For example, the word *reality* has nothing to do with the prefix *re-,* and the word *mister* does not contain the prefix *mis-.* To distinguish such words from ones that do contain prefixes, students need to look for an identifiable base word.

for PREFIXES

HELPFUL HINT   Ask students to define each of the example words in the chart by using the given meaning of the prefix. Have students generate and define other example words that include each prefix.

GENERAL NOTE

INDIVIDUALIZING INSTRUCTION: ESL STUDENTS   Some students for whom English is a second language might be unfamiliar with Latin or Greek-based prefixes and suffixes. Allow these students time to experiment with affixes in English, but expect errors as they learn to manipulate these word parts. Point out to them that memorizing the meanings of common prefixes and suffixes will expand their vocabulary considerably: they will be able to determine the definitions of many words that include them.

Writing
═══ TIP ═══

Sometimes the spelling of the base word changes when you add a suffix to it. If you're not sure about the spelling, check a dictionary.

Keep in mind that not all word parts that look like prefixes are prefixes. For example, the *mis-* in *missile* is not a prefix because *-sile* is not a base word. When you analyze word parts, watch out for prefix look-alikes.

Suffixes

A **suffix** is a word part that is added to the end of a base word. Like a prefix, a suffix changes a base word to a new word with a new meaning. For example, the suffix *-ous* means "full of" or "having." When *-ous* is added to the base word *danger,* the new word *dangerous* means "full of danger." When *-ous* is added to *courage,* the new word *courageous* means "having courage."

Here are some common suffixes and their meanings.

Suffixes	Meanings	Examples
-able, -ible	capable of being	washable, collapsible
-en	to make	lengthen, frighten
-er, -or	a person who does	teacher, governor
-ily	in what manner	speedily, happily
-ful, -ous	full of	successful, joyous
-hood, -ness	state of	falsehood, statehood, kindness, goodness
-less	without	heartless, restless
-like	relating to	childlike, lifelike

Practice Your Skills

A. Use the context clues in each sentence to write a definition of the word in italics. Check your definition in a dictionary.

1. Our new neighbor is a *polyglot*—that is, she can speak several languages.
2. They put the pottery in a *kiln,* or oven.
3. Some *condiments,* especially mustard, can really make food appealing.

4. The cages held *quetzals* and other tropical birds.

5. Sue is *ambidextrous*—that is, she can use both hands with equal ease.

6. Some *predators,* such as wolves and hyenas, hunt in packs.

7. The concert tickets were *complimentary;* in other words, she got them for free.

8. Some mythological creatures, like the *griffin,* combine the features of several different animals.

9. We heard a *quintet,* a group of five musicians, play folk songs.

10. *Carcinogens,* like cigarette smoke, are the focus of studies on the causes of cancer.

B. Look up the following words in a dictionary. Then use each word in a sentence that contains context clues to the meaning of the word.

   1. veranda   **2.** opulence   **3.** marsupial   **4.** artifact

C. Use what you learned about word parts in this handbook to answer the following questions.

   1. If *zeal* means "strong feelings" or "intense support for a cause," what does *zealous* mean?

   2. If *daunt* means "to discourage," what is a *dauntless* person?

   3. If *belligerent* means "ready to fight," what does *nonbelligerent* mean?

   4. If *classify* means "to place in a class or category," what does *reclassify* mean?

   5. If *attain* means "to gain through effort," what does *attainable* mean?

   6. If *natal* means "dating from birth," what does *prenatal* mean?

   7. If *toxic* means "poisonous," what does *nontoxic* mean?

   8. If *spite* means "feeling of anger or annoyance toward someone," what does *spiteful* mean?

4. quetzal—a kind of tropical bird
5. ambidextrous—able to use both hands equally well
6. predator—an animal that hunts
7. complimentary—free
8. griffin—a mythological creature that possesses the features of several different animals
9. quintet—a group of five musicians
10. carcinogens—substances that cause cancer

B. Sentences will vary. Context clues should, however, take the form of definitions, restatements, or examples.

C.
1. full of strong feelings
2. a person who cannot be discouraged
3. not ready to fight
4. to place in a category again
5. able to be gained through effort
6. dating from before birth
7. not poisonous; harmless
8. full of feelings of anger and annoyance

SPICE BOX

Form students into groups and write a base word, such as *place,* on the board. Set a timer for two minutes and have each group make a list of as many forms of the word as they can using prefixes, or suffixes or both. (Examples include *replace, displace, irreplaceable,* and *placement.*)

The group that forms the greatest number of actual words that are correctly spelled wins the round. Continue with other base words, such as *light* and *prove.*

Using the Dictionary and the Thesaurus

Objectives
- To recognize how a dictionary and a thesaurus are organized
- To find information in a dictionary
- To use a thesaurus to find synonyms

 Related Mini-Lessons

For information on topics related to using the dictionary and the thesaurus, see the following mini-lessons:
- **Study and Research Skills, pp. 294–297**
- **Vocabulary Skills, pp. 302–307**

Motivate
Call out an unfamiliar word—*whin, yeanling,* or *pilgarlic*—and have students find its meaning in classroom dictionaries. Ask the student who first locates a meaning to read it aloud and describe how he or she found it. Ask students whether they are aware that midgrade school dictionaries contain between 40,000 and 60,000 entries; high school dictionaries, between 75,000 and 100,000. The total number of English words now exceeds four million.

Teaching Strategies

for ALPHABETICAL ORDER
ASSESSMENT: SPOT CHECK To assess students' mastery of alphabetizing, have them number these words in alphabetical order: *cute* (3), *custom* (1), *cuticle* (4), *cutback* (2), *cutlass* (5).

WRITING
H A N D B O O K
28

Where Can I Find Information About Words?

Using the Dictionary and the Thesaurus

Mark Twain wrote, "The difference between the *almost right* word and the *right* word is . . . the difference between the lightning bug and the lightning." How can you capture lightning in your writing? A dictionary and a thesaurus can help you find just the right words.

USING A DICTIONARY

You know that a dictionary contains the spellings and definitions of words. There is, however, much more information packed into this helpful book. To use a dictionary effectively you first must know how it is organized.

Alphabetical Order

The words that appear in a dictionary are called **entry words.** Like the names in a phone book, the entry words in a dictionary are listed in alphabetical order—the order of the letters in the alphabet.

Words that begin with the same first letter, such as *elephant* and *envelope,* are alphabetized by the second letter. Words that have the same first and second letters, such as *festival* and *fertile,* are alphabetized by the third letter, and so on.

Guide Words

The two words in boldface type at the top of each page of a dictionary are called **guide words.** Guide words can help you find words in a dictionary quickly and easily.

The guide word on the left tells you the first entry word on that page. The guide word on the right tells you the last entry

---

Social Studies Connection

Suggest that students locate the glossary in their social studies textbook. Ask them to compare a typical glossary entry with a typical dictionary entry and to note the similarities and differences between the two.

word on that page. As you flip through a dictionary searching for a word, the guide words can help you quickly find the right page. When the word you're looking for falls alphabetically between two guide words, you're on the right page.

Dictionary Entries

The information a dictionary gives about an entry word is called a **dictionary entry.** Each entry has several parts, as you can see in the example at the top of the next page.

Entry Word The first part of a dictionary entry is the entry word. In most dictionaries, spaces or centered dots divide the entry word into syllables. Knowing how a word is divided into syllables enables you to hyphenate words correctly.

Pronunciation The next part of a dictionary entry is the **pronunciation guide,** often shown in parentheses. The pronunciation guide is a respelling of the word using symbols that stand for sounds. These symbols are explained in a **pronunciation key,** which often is found at the bottom of a dictionary's right-hand pages or at the front of the dictionary.

In the pronunciation guide, words of more than one syllable are shown with accent marks (´). These marks tell you which syllables to emphasize when you pronounce the word.

Part of Speech Most dictionaries tell you the part of speech of each entry word. Some words can be used as more than one part of speech. In those cases, the dictionary defines each part of speech separately. Notice in the dictionary entry on page 310 that *surprise* is defined first as a verb **(vt.).**

Word Origin Next the dictionary entry shows the origin of the word—how the word developed from words in other languages. In the entry for *surprise,* **ME** stands for Middle English, and **OFr** stands for Old French. The abbreviations used are explained in the front of the dictionary.

---

thread⟧ a coarse linen or cotton cloth with a diagonal weave, used for work clothes, uniforms, etc.
drill⁴(dril) *n.* ⟦< ? native term⟧ a short-tailed, bright-cheeked monkey *(Mandrillus leucophaeus)* native to W Africa, resembling the mandrill but smaller

---

Using the Dictionary
and the Thesaurus   **309**

---

for DICTIONARY ENTRIES

INDIVIDUALIZING INSTRUCTION: ESL STUDENTS Explain to your ESL students that English dictionaries do not generally list idioms as entry words. However, students may find idioms in their native language listed in a bilingual dictionary. Also explain that some English-language student dictionaries list idioms after the entry word for the main word in each idiom. For example, students can look within the entry for *cat* to find the meaning of "Don't let the *cat* out of the bag."

for DICTIONARY ENTRIES: PRONUNCIATION
SPEAKING AND LISTENING To familiarize students with the pronunciation key, write the phonetic spellings of several words on the board. Ask students to use the key in their class dictionary to sound out the pronunciation.

for DICTIONARY ENTRIES: PART OF SPEECH
KEY TO UNDERSTANDING To help students understand the part of speech entries in their dictionaries, make a list of common abbreviations on the board: noun *(n.)*, verb *(v.)*, pronoun *(pron.)*, adjective *(adj.)*, adverb *(adv.)*, preposition *(prep.)*, conjunction *(conj.)*, and interjection *(interj.)*. Then briefly review the meaning of each part of speech and elicit examples.

STUMBLING BLOCK
Ask students to share their own methods for finding an entry for a word whose spelling they are unsure of. (Samples: Try two or three different possible spellings; figure out the first few letters; ask someone else how to spell the word)

ASSESSMENT: SPOT CHECK
Have students use the dictionary to answer the following questions:

1. What does *e.g.* mean? (for example)
2. What kind of animal is a *fisher?* (a mammal of the weasel family)
3. What and where is *Ibiza?* (an island off Spain)
4. What is the etymology, or origin, of the word *galaxy?* (from the Greek *galaktos,* meaning "milk")

Ask volunteers to provide the answers and explain how they used the dictionary to find them.

KEY TO UNDERSTANDING
Make sure students are able to pronounce the word *thesaurus.* You might point out that this word comes from the same Greek root as the word *treasure.* Suggest that students think of a thesaurus as a "treasury of words."

COLLABORATIVE OPPORTUNITY
Ask students whether they have ever noticed that sportscasters seem to have an endless supply of synonyms for the verb *defeat* when they announce sporting events results. Write on the board these examples: *beat, blitz, conquer, topple.* Emphasize that synonyms have different shades of meaning and that choosing the exact synonym is an important writing skill. For example, of the words listed, which would they use in a headline to suggest that one team defeated another that had long been in first place? *(topple)* Which would they use to suggest that the winning team attacked quickly and never let up? *(blitz)* Which word suggests that even though one team won, the final score was close? *(beat)* Which word implies that the losing team will take a while to recover? *(conquer)*

Pronunciation guide | Part of speech | Word origin

Entry word — **sur·prise** (sər prīz´, sə prīz´) **vt. -prised´, -pris´ing** ⟦ME *surprysen* < OFr *surpris,* pp. of *sorprendre,* to surprise, take napping < *sur-* (see SUR-¹) + *prendre,* to take (see PRIZE²)⟧ **1** to come upon suddenly or
Definition — unexpectedly; take unawares **2** to attack or capture suddenly and without warning **3** *a)* to cause to feel wonder or astonishment by

Synonyms — **SYN.** —**surprise**, in this connection, implies an affecting with wonder because of being unexpected, unusual, etc. *[I'm surprised at your concern];* **astonish** implies a surprising with something that seems unbelievable *[to astonish with sleight of hand];* **amaze** suggests an astonishing that causes bewilderment or confusion *[amazed at the*

Definition   The definition tells you what the entry word means. Many words have more than one definition, and the different definitions are numbered. Usually the oldest definition is given first and the newest definition is given last.

Synonyms   Following the definition, a dictionary may provide **synonyms,** or words with similar meanings.

USING A THESAURUS

A thesaurus contains synonyms and antonyms for commonly used words. Synonyms are words that have similar meanings. **Antonyms** are words that have opposite meanings. A thesaurus can help you find the word that best expresses the meaning you have in mind.

Some thesauruses are organized alphabetically. Others have an index at the end. The index tells you where to find the synonyms for a specific word.

Suppose you have used the word *ran. Ran* is a general verb that means "to move quickly." Perhaps a more specific verb would make what you have written more interesting or exciting. Look at the thesaurus entry for *run* at the top of the next page.

TEACHER'S LOUNGE

That teachers must teach connotation and shades of meaning was brought home by the ninth-grader who had, as a vocabulary word, the word *tawdry.*

Looking it up in the dictionary, the youth found it defined as "cheap and tasteless."

The teacher found the word used in this sentence: "The cafeteria serves tawdry sandwiches."—from *Educator's Lifetime Library,* by P. Susan Mamchak and Steven R. Mamchak.

> **run,** *v.* [To go swiftly by physical effort] —*Syn.* rush, hurry, spring, bound, scurry, skitter, scramble, scoot, travel, run off *or* away, dash ahead *or* at *or* on, put on a burst of speed, go on the double, have effect, go on the double-quick, hasten (off), light out, have a free play, make tracks, dart (ahead), gallop, canter, lope, spring, trot, single-foot, amble, pace, flee, speed, spurt, swoop, bolt, race, shoot, tear, whisk, scamper, scuttle.

Words like *bound, scramble, dart,* and *scamper* are all more specific than the word *run. Bound,* for example, means "to move by leaping" and might be a better verb to describe the way a dog runs after a squirrel.

Practice Your Skills

A. Use a dictionary to to find the answer to each of the following questions.

1. From what language did the word *plumage* come? What did it mean originally?
2. What parts of speech can *record* be?
3. How would you pronounce *echidna?* What syllable would you emphasize?
4. What does *gregarious* mean?
5. What is a synonym for *ridiculous?*

B. For each of the following sentences, look up each word in italics in a thesaurus. Then rewrite each sentence using a more precise word.

1. The car *went* slowly up the mountain road.
2. The hungry children *ate* the pizza.
3. The detective *looked* at the footprints in the snow.
4. The exhausted marathon runner *walked* across the finish line.
5. She *carried* the overloaded suitcase through the airport.

Using the Dictionary and the Thesaurus **311**

MULTICULTURAL Connection

Students whose native language is not English might bring to class any bilingual dictionaries that they use to find the meanings of English words and idioms. Ask them to explain how the dictionaries are organized and to describe how they typically use them. Encourage English-speaking students to use the dictionaries to find words and expressions from another language that they would like to learn. Have them check their pronunciations of these words and expressions with their bilingual classmates.

WRITING HANDBOOK 29

Library Skills

Objectives
- To learn how books are arranged in the library
- To interpret the information on a catalog card or in a computerized catalog entry
- To identify the main uses of library reference materials

 Related Mini-Lesson

For information on topics related to using the library, see the following mini-lesson.
- **Study and Research Skills, pp. 294–297**

Motivate
Ask students to imagine that they have taken a time-machine trip to a community in the year 2200. One of the places they visit is a technologically advanced library. Ask students to imagine and describe the library of the future, noting how it is different from the typical library today. For instance, would people actually have to go to the library, or could they access most information from their homes?

Teaching Strategies

for THE SECTIONS OF THE LIBRARY

COOPERATIVE LEARNING Have students look at the layout of their school or local library, noting the location of the sections they use most frequently. Then suggest that they work together to draw a rough floor plan of the library, showing the relative locations of the sections they use or expect to use.

WRITING HANDBOOK 29

How Can I Find the Information I Need?

Library Skills

Imagine that there was one place where you could do all of these things: listen to a compact disc, use a computer, find a movie, see an art display, read a book. There is such a place—the library. You can find these resources and more in most libraries today. A world of information, ideas, and activities is available to you at the library.

THE SECTIONS OF THE LIBRARY

You may be surprised at what you can find in the library, if you just know where to look. Most libraries are arranged into the following sections.

Library Floor Plan

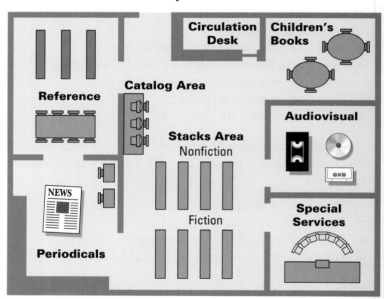

Guidelines for Oral Reports

Practicing

1. **Review your notes.** Read through your notes several times.

2. **Rehearse.** Tape-record your report and listen to see if you are speaking clearly and neither too quickly nor too slowly.

3. **Present your report before family members or friends.** Ask for honest feedback and helpful suggestions.

Presenting

1. **Stand up straight and look natural.** Take a deep breath before you begin. This will help you relax.

2. **Establish eye contact with your audience.** Look directly at your audience as much as possible.

3. **Use natural gestures and facial expressions.** Don't smile if you are talking about a sad subject. Keep any gestures simple and natural.

4. **Use your voice effectively.** Speak clearly and loudly enough to be understood by all your listeners. Pause briefly after you make an important point.

The Fourth of July Oration

Practice Your Skills

Prepare an oral report on a subject listed below or on one of your own choosing. Write down key ideas on your note cards before you rehearse your talk. Finally, present your report in front of your classmates.

how to care for a pet	a movie you have seen recently
robots	hurricanes

GENERAL NOTE

SPEAKING AND LISTENING
Interested students might enjoy listening to a recording of a gifted public speaker, such as Winston Churchill, John F. Kennedy, or Martin Luther King, Jr. These students can find recordings of the speaker of their choice, listen, and take notes on how the speaker used his or her voice effectively. Then allow students to share their recordings and analyses with the class.

for PRACTICE YOUR SKILLS
PEER RESPONSE Encourage students to practice their oral reports with a partner before presenting them to the class. Have the peer reviewers critique their partners' performances on the basis of the guidelines for presenting.

for PRACTICE YOUR SKILLS
SPEAKING, LISTENING, AND VIEWING If possible, videotape volunteers as they give their reports to the class. When students are finished, play back the videotape, so that they can observe their own work. Point out any movements or speech patterns that either detract from or add to students' deliveries.

Answers to Practice Your Skills
Students' reports will vary but should follow the guidelines for preparing an oral report.

Taking Tests

Objectives
- To recognize strategies for preparing for and taking classroom and standardized tests
- To recognize and apply strategies for answering different types of test questions

Related Mini-Lessons

For information on topics related to taking tests, see the following mini-lessons:
- **Study and Research Skills, pp. 294–297**
- **Reading Skills, pp. 298–301**

Teaching Strategies

for PREPARING FOR A TEST

PERSONAL TOUCH Describe for students a time when you felt especially well prepared for a test. Explain what you did to prepare. Then describe a time when you took a test for which you did not feel prepared. Invite volunteers to share their own test-taking experiences. You might also share with students your approach to composing and giving tests, including your reasons for using certain types of test.

for PREPARING FOR A TEST

HELPFUL HINT Point out to students that when their test preparation involves a lot of memorizing, they might find it useful to study with a partner. Partners can quiz each other on facts and can make sure that each of them knows the required material.

How Can I Score Better on Tests?

Taking Tests

No matter what Peppermint Patty says, taking tests doesn't have to be hard. You can improve your test scores by learning how to prepare for a test and how to answer different types of test questions.

PREPARING FOR A TEST

The secret to successful test-taking is careful preparation. The following strategies will help you take charge of any testing situation.

- **Know what to study.** Ask your teacher exactly what the test will cover. That way you can use your study time to focus on the most important information.

- **Make a study plan.** It helps to study a little bit every day. The night before the test, review what you have learned.

- **Review your materials.** Look over the notes you took in class, skim chapters you have read, and review any other materials you may have studied. Think of questions that you would ask if you were making up the test, and try to answer them.

- **Memorize important facts.** Look for and memorize important names, dates, events, vocabulary words, and other important information. For suggestions about how to memorize information, see Handbook 25, "Study and Research Skills," pages 294–297.

- **Rest and relax.** You will perform best when you are alert and well rested. Get a good night's sleep before test day. Then be confident as the test begins. If you studied well, you should do just fine.

TEACHER'S LOUNGE

TYPES OF TEST QUESTIONS

Studying the information that will be covered on a test is important. Just as important is knowing how to answer different types of test questions.

Some test questions ask you to choose one answer from among three or four. Other questions ask you to write a phrase or a sentence. Still others require an entire essay. You might be asked to decide whether a statement is true or false. The following guidelines will help you to recognize and answer different types of test questions. In the process, you will become a better test taker.

True-False Questions

To answer this type of test question, you must read a statement and decide whether it is true or false. The following strategies can help you decide.

- If *any* part of the statement is false, the answer is "false."
- Statements that include such words as *all, never, always,* and *none* are often, though not always, false.
- Statements that include such words as *generally, some, most, many,* and *usually* are often, though not always, true.

1. T (F) All reptiles are coldblooded and walk on four legs.

Although all reptiles are coldblooded, reptiles such as snakes do not have legs. Because the second part of the statement is false, the answer is "false."

Matching Questions

Matching questions ask you to match items in one column with related items in a second column.

for TYPES OF TEST QUESTIONS
CRITICAL THINKING: EXPRESSING OPINIONS Have students discuss which type of test question they prefer and why. Elicit opinions on which questions are most difficult and which are easiest. Explain to the class that knowing how to approach each type of question can make test-taking much less stressful.

for TRUE-FALSE QUESTIONS
ASSESSMENT: SPOT CHECK To be sure students understand the suggestions for answering true-false questions, write the following statements on the board and call on volunteers to label them *true* or *false.* Ask each volunteer to explain which strategy (if any) helped in answering the question.

Some sets of twins are identical.
(T)F

All animals that live in water are fish.
T(F)

Christopher Columbus sailed across the Atlantic Ocean in the 1400s and landed in what is now Massachusetts.
T(F)

Some people are allergic to bee stings.
(T)F

for MATCHING QUESTIONS

INDIVIDUALIZING INSTRUCTION: BASIC STUDENTS A matching test, with its long lists of items, can be overwhelming to some students. Stress to these students that if they are unable to match an item, they should come back to it after they have matched all items they are sure of. They may be able to find the correct answer by a process of elimination.

for MULTIPLE-CHOICE QUESTIONS

HELPFUL HINT Tell students that some multiple-choice questions have two possible answers that are quite similar. Often, one of these two answers is the correct one, as is the case with statements A and B in the example in the pupil book. It is important that they read the two answers carefully to determine how they differ and whether one is correct.

- First read all the items in both columns. Then match the ones you know for sure.
- Cross out the items as you match them. This way you won't be distracted by items you've already matched.

> **1.** Write the letter of the definition next to its term.
>
> __B__ **1.** index   **A.** a list of chapter titles and subheadings
>
> __C__ **2.** glossary   **B.** an alphabetical list of topics
>
> __A__ **3.** table of contents   **C.** an alphabetical list of terms and their definitions

Be sure to choose the most *exact* match for each item. For example, both an index and a glossary are alphabetical lists, but only a glossary includes definitions of terms.

Multiple-Choice Questions

A multiple-choice question asks you to choose the best answer from three or more possible answers.

- Read each choice carefully.
- Cross out any answers that are clearly wrong.
- Choose the answer that is most complete or correct.

> **1.** Which of the following best describes a river?
> **A.** a large stream of saltwater
> **B.** a large stream of water that empties into an ocean, a lake, or another body of water
> **C.** a large body of water separating two continents
> **D.** a body of water completely surrounded by land

Answers *C* and *D* are clearly incorrect. Answer *A* is only partly correct. Therefore, *B* is the correct answer.

Fill-in-the-Blank Questions

Fill-in-the-blank questions ask you to complete a sentence by adding an appropriate word or phrase.

- First fill in the answers that you know for sure.
- Then go back and try to answer the questions you left blank. An "educated guess" is better than no answer at all.
- Check each fill-in for correct capitalization and spelling. Also, be sure your answer fits grammatically with the rest of the sentence.

1. The first writing system was developed by the
   Sumerians .

This question requires an answer that tells *who* developed the first writing system. Telling *where, when,* or *how* writing was invented would be incorrect.

Short-Answer Questions

Short-answer questions ask you to write a brief answer, usually just a sentence or two.

- First read the directions to find out if each answer must be a complete sentence.
- If you must write a complete sentence, begin by restating the question. Then give the answer.
- Reread the answer to be sure you used correct grammar, spelling, punctuation, and capitalization.

1. Name the three social classes in ancient Rome.
   The three social classes in ancient Rome were the
   elite, the "more humble," and the slaves.

Notice how this answer first restates the question and then provides the answer.

Sumerian clay tablet, about 1980 B.C.

HELPFUL HINT To demonstrate how a fill-in-the-blank answer should fit grammatically with the rest of the sentence, discuss what is wrong with the following answer and tell how to correct it.

   Segregate is the separation of people
      by race.

Point out that because it is a verb, the word *segregate* is grammatically incorrect for this sentence. The answer must be a noun or pronoun because it is in the subject position in the sentence. *Segregation,* a noun, is the correct fill-in answer.

INDIVIDUALIZING INSTRUCTION: ADVANCED STUDENTS Some students may know more about a topic than is required for a short-answer question. Remind them that they should write only the answer to the question. Giving more than the required information will take time away from answering other questions and will not improve their grades.

Grammar Connection

When students take tests with short-answer questions, they must be able to recognize the difference between a sentence fragment and a complete sentence. Remind them to read test instructions carefully to determine whether they can answer in sentence fragments or they must write complete sentences. Refer students who need help in forming complete sentences to Handbook 34, "Understanding Sentences," pages 339–373.

Writing TIP

If you want to add additional information after you've finished writing, place it in the margin. Draw an arrow to indicate where the information should go in the paragraph.

Essay Questions

When you answer an essay question, you must write your answer as one or more paragraphs.

- First identify the topic you are to write about.
- Look for key words that tell how to answer the question, such as *compare, explain, describe, identify,* and *discuss.*
- Note the form you are supposed to use, such as a letter, an explanatory paragraph, or an essay.
- Note also whether your audience is your teacher, other students, or adults.
- Before you start writing, jot down some notes about the key points you want to make.
- Proofread your writing.

STANDARDIZED TESTS

In addition to the tests prepared by your teacher, you will also take standardized tests. These tests, sometimes called achievement tests, are used to measure your understanding of many subjects, including mathematics, reading comprehension, vocabulary, science, and social studies.

Standardized tests often include some of the same types of questions you have already studied. In addition, there are two other types of questions you may come across.

Reading Comprehension Questions

These questions test how well you understand something you have just read. You are given a passage to read, followed by one or more questions about the passage. For example, you might be asked to state the main idea of the passage, recall a detail, or draw a conclusion.

- Read the questions first, if you're allowed to. Then you will know what information to look for as you read.

330   Writing Handbook

- Read the passage carefully but quickly.
- Read each question carefully. Then select or write the best, most complete answer.
- If allowed, look back over the test to check answers you're unsure of.

Read the following passage carefully. Then answer the question that follows it.

> Jack London was an American adventurer and writer. Before he was twenty, he sailed the world. He achieved fame and fortune in his lifetime. His travels to Alaska spawned his most well-known adventure tales, *The Call of the Wild* and *White Fang*. London was a self-educated man who wrote about his concerns for the poor and the powerless. His novels and stories emphasize the cruel side of nature.
>
> 1. In his writing, what was Jack London concerned about?
>   **A.** fame and fortune   **C.** education
>   **B.** the poor and the powerless   **D.** sailing

Although all of the answers are mentioned in the passage, only *B* answers the question.

Vocabulary Questions   These questions test how well you know the meanings of words. **Synonym questions,** for example, ask you to find words that have the same, or almost the same, meanings as other words.

> Choose the phrase that is closest in meaning to the underlined phrase.
> 1. a <u>costly</u> computer
>   **A.** a cheap   **C.** a thrifty
>   **B.** an expensive **D.** an efficient

for READING COMPREHENSION QUESTIONS
USING THE MODEL   Have students carefully examine the passage about Jack London and the question that follows it. Ask volunteers to find the places in the passage where the incorrect answers are mentioned. Point out that in questions that ask for the main idea of a given passage, details from the passage are included in the answer choices; therefore students should read each question carefully to be sure they understand exactly what is being asked.

for VOCABULARY QUESTIONS
INDIVIDUALIZING INSTRUCTION: BASIC STUDENTS   Remind these students to use context clues and word parts to decipher unfamiliar words. Show them the base word *cost* in the example. Explain that they can determine the meaning of *costly* if they recognize the meaning of *cost* and the meaning of the suffix *-ly*. Refer students who need additional help to Handbook 27, "Vocabulary Skills," pages 302–307.

Literature Connection

Read students the passage below from *Hatchet* by Gary Paulsen. Then have each student write a reading comprehension question for the passage. Students can exchange papers and try to answer each other's questions.

"Brian Robeson stared out the window of the small plane at the endless green northern wilderness below. It was a small plane, a Cessna 406—a bush plane—and the engine was so loud, so roaring and consuming and loud, that it ruined any chance for conversation."

332 Writing Handbook

for ANTONYM QUESTIONS

STUMBLING BLOCK Point out to students that most antonym questions include in the answer choices at least one word that is a synonym of the under-lined word. Likewise, most synonym questions include one or more antonyms. Stress that reading the directions care-fully will help students see which the re-quired answers must be: antonyms or synonyms. In addition, point out that if students eliminate the synonyms or antonyms not asked for, they will better their chances of selecting the correct answer.

for TAKING A TEST

HELPFUL HINT Tell students that when they are taking a test, they might receive some instructions orally and should listen carefully. For example, a teacher might state that one part of the test will take fifteen minutes and one part will take thirty minutes. Being aware of this information can help students budget their time effectively.

Answer *A* is a word that means the opposite of *costly*. Answers *C* and *D* have different meanings than *costly*. Answer *B* is the word that is closest in meaning.

Antonym questions ask you to find words that have opposite meanings.

Choose the word that is opposite in meaning to the under-lined word.
1. a <u>fascinating</u> story
   A. interesting **C.** boring
   B. challenging **D.** attractive

Answers *A* and *D* both have meanings that are similar to *fascinating*. Answer *B* has a different meaning, but not an opposite meaning. Only *C* means the opposite of *fascinating*.

TAKING A TEST

When it's time to sit down and take a test, these tips can help you do well.

- **Look over the whole test.** See how long it is and what types of questions it includes.
- **Budget your time.** Read all the directions first. This will let you know whether you will need more time for one type of question, such as an essay.
- **Read the directions carefully.** Ask questions if you don't understand the directions. Follow the directions exactly.
- **Answer easy questions first.** Mark the questions you can't answer right away. Then go back to these questions later.
- **Mark answer sheets carefully.** If the test you're taking includes a computer-scored answer sheet, mark each answer in the correct space, filling in the answer circles or boxes neatly.

332 Writing Handbook

PROFESSIONAL NOTEBOOK

Writer and teacher Bertha Davis offers the follow-ing advice to standardized test-takers in her book, *How to Take a Test*.
"During timed tests:

> Keep Going
> KEEP GOING
> K E E P G O I N G

"'Keep going' does not mean rush. 'Keep going' means work calmly . . . in the recom-mended ways, at a steady pace. It is a two-word magic formula . . . . Adopt it as your own."
Remind students to skip any questions they cannot answer immediately, work through the entire test, and then try to answer them.

- **Review your answers.** Check that you have not left out any answers and that your answers make sense. Make any necessary changes.

Practice Your Skills

A. Answer the following questions.

1. T (F) Standardized tests always include reading-comprehension questions.
2. (T) F Before you begin a test you should look over the entire test, if this is allowed.
3. Questions that ask you to choose the best answer from three or more choices are _multiple-choice_ questions.
4. A word that means the opposite of a given word is an _antonym_ .

B. Read the following passage. Then answer the questions.

A desert is a hot, barren region that receives little rainfall. However, scientists do not agree on a specific definition. Some scientists define deserts by the amount of rainfall and evaporation. Some define them by the type of soil or plant life present. Others use a combination of all of these factors. The largest desert in the world is the Sahara in Africa. The Sahara covers an area about the same size as the United States.

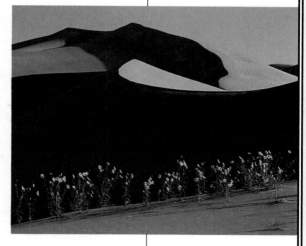

1. What factors do some scientists use to define deserts?
   A. rainfall and evaporation   **C.** plant life
   B. type of soil   (**D.**) all of the above
2. Which word is closest in meaning to the word *barren?*
   (**A.**) empty   **C.** tame
   B. fertile   **D.** rich

for REVIEW YOUR ANSWERS
HELPFUL HINT Sometimes, when students review their work, they are tempted to change several answers. Urge them to be sure of the correct answers before making changes. If they are uncertain of the correct answer to a question, they should stay with their original answer.

Additional Resources

Writing Resource Book, pp. 108–109
Tests and Writing Assessment
   Prompts

Answers to Practice Your Skills

A. Answers are shown on page.

B. Answers are shown on page.

MULTICULTURAL Connection

In some cultures, test-taking has far more importance than it does in the United States. For example, in Belgium, college students are often graded for the whole year on the basis of a single oral examination. Have interested students research the role of tests in the culture of their choice. They can report back to the class and lead a discussion on the differences and similarities they discovered.

ART NOTE In America, quilting has been a popular art form since the days of the earliest pioneers. Cloth was scarce in Colonial America. Therefore, women recycled clothing until it finally wore out; then they sewed usable scraps into colorful patterned quilts. Quilting remains a popular art form and hobby today, although most quilters do the work with the aid of machines, not strictly by hand.

An anonymous African-American woman worked long hours to produce this beautiful quilt. She was accomplished with a needle—probably a dressmaker who made hand-sewed clothes. She made the quilt from scraps of fine silk, using three techniques: piecing (sewing together scraps to form a large piece of cloth); appliqué (sewing pieces of cloth on top of other cloth); and embroidery (using colored threads to decorate cloth).

It isn't clear whether the quilter is showing the actual daily life of African-Americans of the time or depicting the way she imagines African-Americans will live after the end of slavery. The quilt alternates traditional diamond-shaped designs with "portraits" of log cabins and scenes of fashionably dressed African-Americans chopping wood, visiting, and courting.

You might point out that this quilter "built" her large quilt from scraps of fabric. Similarly, when students write, they create a large work from smaller units called sentences. Tell students that in this section of the text, they will study the basic parts of English sentences, which they'll piece together to build longer pieces of writing.

Detail of a pieced, appliquéd, and embroidered quilt, about 1870. The artist depicts over one hundred colorful log cabins, as well as scenes of community members engaged in a variety of daily tasks. Perhaps the quilt was made to show what life was like for African Americans after the abolition of slavery.

334

Social Studies Connection

Note that this quilt was made five years after the Civil War (1861–1865) ended and seven years after President Lincoln's Emancipation Proclamation (January 1, 1863). You might ask someone to report briefly on the Emancipation Proclamation, which freed only those slaves residing in the states that were rebelling against the Union. Have another student report on how and when slavery ended throughout the United States.

Grammar and Usage Handbook

MINI-LESSONS

Grammar and Usage Handbook

335

Skills

A S S E S S M E N T

PRETEST   Grammar Handbooks

Pretest

These tests enable you to assess your students' knowledge of grammar, usage, punctuation, spelling, and capitalization. The format of these tests is similar to that of some standardized tests. Use this assessment as a formal diagnostic tool or as an informal means of deciding which concepts in the Grammar and Usage Handbook you will emphasize.

Answer Key

Corrections for run-ons may vary.

1. **A**—grandpa
2. **A**—butterfly's
   B—folklore. There
3. **B**—are
4. **C**—safely
5. **B**—Ian and me
   C—cat's *or* cats'
6. **A**—these *or* those
   B—larger
7. **B**—his or her
   C—judge
8. **C**—fuel from
9. **A**—his or her
   B—Sitting
10. **D**
11. **B**—rode
12. **B**—Arlington, Virginia,
13. **B**—he
    C—had written
14. **B**—height
    C—Now,
15. **B**—ceiling. They

List of Skills Tested

1. **A**—capitalization—common/proper noun
   B—sentence fragment/run-on
   C—pronoun case
2. **A**—noun possessive
   B—sentence fragment/run-on
   C—noun plural
3. **A**—comparative adjective form
   B—subject-verb agreement
   C—noun plural
4. **A**—spelling
   B—spelling
   C—adjective/adverb confusion
5. **A**—punctuation—comma
   B—pronoun case
   C—punctuation—possessive

Directions   One or more of the underlined sections in the following sentences may contain an error in grammar, punctuation, spelling, or capitalization. Write the letter of each incorrect section. Then rewrite the section correctly. If there is no error in an item, write *D*.

> *Example*   The first navigator to sail <u>completely</u> around the world
> **A**
> was Juan Sebastián del Cano in <u>1522. Magellan</u> did not
> **B**
> <u>live. To complete</u> the expedition. <u>No error</u>
> **C**   **D**
>
> *Answer*   C—live to

1. We will visit my <u>Grandpa</u> in Mexico for the *posada* celebration before
   A
   <u>Christmas. He</u> will make piñatas for all of <u>us</u>. <u>No error</u>
   B   **C**   **D**

2. The <u>butterflys</u> name may have come from <u>folklore there</u> are stories about
   A   **B**
   <u>witches</u> taking the form of a butterfly to steal butter and milk. <u>No error</u>
   C   **D**

3. A drop of water is <u>smaller</u> than you might think. There <u>is</u> 120 <u>drops</u>
   A   **B**   **C**
   in a teaspoon. <u>No error</u>
                   D

4. The parachute was <u>invented</u> to help <u>people</u> jump out of burning buildings
   A   **B**
   <u>safe</u>. <u>No error</u>
   C   **D**

5. <u>First, the</u> veterinarian showed <u>Ian and I</u> how to clip the <u>cats</u> claws. <u>No error</u>
   A   **B**   **C**   **D**

6. Look at <u>them</u> two crystals. The <u>largest</u> one grew <u>more slowly</u> than the
   A   **B**   **C**
   other. <u>No error</u>
           D

THE SIMPLE PREDICATE, OR VERB

A **verb** is a word that tells about action or that tells what someone or something is. A verb is the most important word in a complete predicate.

You know that a sentence can be divided into two main parts. We call the subject part the **complete subject.** The complete subject includes all of the words that tell whom or what the sentence is about.

The predicate part of the sentence is called the **complete predicate.** The complete predicate includes all of the words that tell what the subject is, what the subject does or did, or what happened to the subject.

Read the following examples of complete subjects and complete predicates.

Complete Subject	Complete Predicate
A large silvery spacecraft	landed.
A large silvery spacecraft	landed in a field.
A large silvery spacecraft	landed in a field near school.
Hairy green aliens	invaded.
Hairy green aliens	invaded the planet..
Hairy green aliens	invaded the planet at midnight.

Look at each complete predicate above. What is the key word in each one? The most important word in the first three complete predicates is *landed.* The most important word in the last three complete predicates is *invaded.*

The most important part of every complete predicate is the **verb.** It is sometimes called the **simple predicate.** In this book, however, we will call the simple predicate the **verb.**

Objectives
- To identify the simple predicate and the complete predicate

Writing
- To use vivid verbs in sentences and paragraphs

Teaching Strategies

KEY TO UNDERSTANDING: PREDICATES Stress that the terms *simple predicate* and *verb* are both names for the same key word or words in the complete predicate of a sentence. Explain that a simple predicate or verb, however, may consist of more than one word. Give students examples of multiword linking verbs such as *will be, has been, have been,* and *had been*—and of multiword action verbs: *will kick, had been eating, might have been told.* Tell students that they will learn more about multiword verbs in Handbook 36, "Understanding Verbs." In the exercises in this lesson, however, most verbs are only one word.

INDIVIDUALIZING INSTRUCTION: SOCIAL LEARNERS Form these students into groups of four. Each group should then form two teams. Have each team create five original sentences and write them on an index card. Then have teams exchange cards and identify the complete subject, the complete predicate, and the verb (simple predicate) in each sentence.

**Writing Theme:
Strange Creatures in
Science Fiction**

Other related areas students might
wish to explore as writing topics include
the following:

- strange creatures in *Star Wars*
- Arthur C. Clarke, science fiction writer
- the stories of Ray Bradbury

Answers to Practice Your Skills

A. Concept Check
Verbs
Answers are shown on page.

══ TIP ══
Use specific action verbs to
make your writing vivid. For
example, say a spacecraft
zoomed, instead of saying it
moved.

Writing Theme
Strange Creatures in
Science Fiction

Types of Verbs

There are two types of verbs. Some verbs tell about an
action. These are **action verbs.**

> Mario *gazed* at the strange creature outside his window.
> The alien *leaped* toward the house.
> It *banged* on the door with its steel fist.

Other types of verbs may tell that something is, or they may
link the subject with words that describe it. These are called
state-of-being verbs. They are also called **linking verbs.**

> The space creature *is* small and chubby.
> Sara *seemed* surprised at the alien's sudden appearance.

Common Linking Verbs				
am	was	has been	seem	become
are	were	have been	look	feel
is	will be	had been	appear	taste

You will learn more about verbs in Grammar Handbook 36,
"Using Verbs," pages 394–430.

Practice Your Skills

A. CONCEPT CHECK

Verbs   Write each sentence on your paper. Underline the
complete predicate once. Draw a double line under the verb.

1. *The War of the Worlds* is a story about space monsters.
2. In the story creatures from Mars invade the earth.
3. These invaders are huge and ugly.
4. Their skin looks like wet leather.
5. The Martians carry powerful weapons.
6. They terrify people on the East Coast.
7. The monsters catch a common earth disease.
8. Deadly germs destroy the cruel Martians.
9. Not all aliens in science fiction are mean.

348   Grammar Handbook

Literature Connection

Slowly read aloud the following passage from
"The Circuit" by Francisco Jiménez. Have students identify the predicates, or verbs (underlined
below).

"I still <u>felt</u> a little dizzy when we <u>took</u> a break to
eat lunch. It <u>was</u> past two o'clock and we <u>sat</u>
underneath a large walnut tree that <u>was</u> on the
side of the road. While we <u>ate</u>, Papa <u>jotted</u> down
the number of boxes we <u>had picked</u>. Roberto
<u>drew</u> designs on the ground with a stick."

10. The alien in the movie *E.T.* is lovable and cute.
11. Children learn about friendship from this creature.
12. Many friendly, helpful aliens appeared on *Star Trek*.
13. For example, Mr. Spock worked closely with earth people.
14. He gave Captain Kirk good advice.
15. Like humans, aliens have been both good and evil.

B. REVISION SKILL

Using Vivid Verbs Write the following sentences. Replace each italicized word or phrase with a vivid verb from the list.

EXAMPLE   Weird monsters in science fiction *scare* people.
                 Weird monsters in science fiction *terrify* people.

craved	grew	starred	grabbed	caused
trudged	gobbled	oozed	invaded	stormed

16. Giant creatures without brains *moved* through the jungles on the planet Venus.
17. They *took* everything along the way.
18. In a story by Robert A. Heinlein, a speedy, eight-legged monster *went* across the earth.
19. This hungry alien *ate* metal.
20. It really *wanted* old cars for dinner.
21. The Blob *was* in a popular movie.
22. This famous monster *went into* a small town.
23. It *made* all kinds of trouble.
24. The slimy alien *came* slowly through the town.
25. With each human meal, the Blob *got* bigger and bigger.

C. APPLICATION IN WRITING

Science Fiction Story Write a story about a space creature that lands in your neighborhood. Be sure to describe the creature and its actions. In your story, use five of the vivid verbs in the following list.

rescue	struggle	search	invade
stare	scream	quarrel	command
topple	chuckle	explode	flee

FOR MORE PRACTICE
See page 367.

Understanding
Sentences   **349**

Objective

• To identify the simple subject

Teaching Strategies

KEY TO UNDERSTANDING: SIMPLE SUBJECTS Point out that sometimes a phrase containing one or more nouns can come between the simple subject and the verb in a sentence, as in the sample on the pupil page: *The red dragon **in the cave** thundered mightily.* Ask students to write on the board some sentences with this pattern of a phrase intervening between subject and verb. Have volunteers identify the simple subject in the sentence by finding the verb and then asking *who* or *what?* before the verb.

MANAGING THE PAPER LOAD To limit the number of written exercises to correct, you may wish to have your students complete Exercise A orally. If any students have difficulty in identifying simple subjects in this exercise, remind them to ask *who* or *what* before the verb.

Additional Resource

Grammar and Usage Practice Book, p. 6

The **simple subject** is the most important part of the complete subject.

In a complete sentence, every verb has a subject.

Complete Subject	Verb
The princess	danced.
The lovely princess	danced.
The lovely princess in the red gown	danced.
The prince	bowed.
The handsome prince	bowed.
The handsome prince from England	bowed.

Look at each complete subject above. What is the key word in each one? In the first group, the most important word is *princess;* in the second group, it is *prince.*

The most important word in a complete subject is called the **simple subject** of the sentence. Another name for the simple subject is the **subject of the verb.**

To find the subject of a verb, first find the verb. Then ask *who* or *what* before the verb. The answer indicates the simple subject of the sentence. Look at these examples:

The red dragon in the cave thundered mightily.
Verb: *thundered*
Who or what thundered?   dragon
Dragon is the subject of *thundered.*

The young girl spun gold from straw.
Verb: *spun*
Who or what spun? girl
Girl is the subject of *spun.*

Elves are magical beings in fairy tales.

Verb: *are*

Who or what are?   elves

Elves is the subject of *are*.

Practice Your Skills

A. CONCEPT CHECK

Simple Subjects   Write the verb and the simple subject of each of the following sentences.

1. Very few children's books existed before 1700.
2. Children learned lessons about good behavior from these first books.
3. Later stories entertained young readers.
4. Many early books were collections of fairy tales.
5. These tales are among the oldest kinds of literature.
6. People handed fairy tales down from generation to generation.
7. Two brothers collected German fairy tales during the early 1800s.
8. Their names were Jakob and Wilhelm Grimm.
9. German farmers told tales to the brothers.
10. The Grimms wrote down the farmers' exact words.
11. Then they published these ancient tales.
12. Their collection of fairy tales became very popular.
13. Authors in other countries published fairy tales too.
14. In Denmark, Hans Christian Andersen wrote 168 fairy tales.
15. Young readers around the world enjoy Andersen's magical tales.

Arthur Szyk illustrates Hans Christian Andersen's tale "The Nightingale" by showing the little bird singing to cheer an unhappy emperor.

Understanding
Sentences   **351**

B. Drafting Skill
Using Subjects and Verbs Creatively

Simple subjects and verbs are underlined on page. Student revisions will vary. Sample revisions are shown below.

16. The Pied Piper played his electric guitar for the homecoming celebration.
17. His inspiring rock-and-roll music charmed all the students at Coolville High School.
18. Unfortunately, the Rats, the Creepyville High School football team, overran their opponents.
19. The number of victories grew higher and higher.
20. The people of Coolville promised strong support for their team this year.
21. The street echoed with cheers of excitement.
22. The sound of the Pied Piper's rock-and-roll music drew people from every part of town.
23. The homecoming parade wound through the town.
24. Bunches of balloons floated through the air.
25. The people threw flowers at the Coolville football players.
26. The famous musician promised the team a victory.
27. During the game, the Pied Piper raced from song to song.
28. The music played faster and louder.
29. The Pied Piper led the team to victory with this music.
30. The townspeople of Creepyville cried over the defeat of their Rats.

C. Application in Writing
Fairy Tale

Answers will vary. Check to see that students have correctly used at least five of the nouns as simple subjects in their fairy tales.

B. DRAFTING SKILL

Using Subjects and Verbs Creatively   Find the simple subject and the verb in each sentence. Then rewrite the sentence. Keep the same simple subject and verb, but replace the other words to create a new fairy tale.

> EXAMPLE   The Pied Piper was a magical musician.
> The Pied Piper was a rock-and-roll star.

16. The Pied Piper played a magical fife.
17. His music charmed people and animals.
18. One day, rats overran the town of Hamelin, Germany.
19. The number of rats grew quickly.
20. The people of Hamelin promised the Pied Piper a rich reward for his help.
21. Soon every street echoed with the Pied Piper's magical fife music.
22. The sound of the music drew rats from every house in Hamelin.
23. A great parade of rats wound its way to the river.
24. Bunches of rats floated down the river.
25. Then the selfish people threw the piper out of town without a cent.
26. Angrily, the musician promised revenge.
27. The Pied Piper raced from the city.
28. Years later, the magical fife music again played in the town.
29. This time the Pied Piper led all the children away.
30. The townspeople cried over the loss of their children.

C. APPLICATION IN WRITING

Fairy Tale   Write a short fairy tale. Use at least five of the simple subjects below.

king	dragon	frog
forest	knight	princess
sword	horse	giant
apple	castle	cave
cottage	townspeople	countryside
crown	moon	raven

FOR MORE PRACTICE
See pages 367–368.

Writing Theme
Famous Mistakes in Architecture

A. Create a chart with two columns. Label one column *Simple Subject* and the other *Verb*. Write the simple subject and the verb of each sentence in the correct columns.

1. In July 1940, the <u>Tacoma Narrows Bridge</u> <u>opened</u> in the state of Washington.
2. This <u>bridge</u> <u>was</u> 2,800 feet long.
3. On a windy day, the <u>deck</u> of the bridge <u>bounced</u> up and down.
4. <u>Newspapers</u> <u>named</u> the wild bridge Galloping Gertie.
5. On Sunday afternoons, <u>traffic</u> <u>was</u> very heavy.
6. Many <u>people</u> <u>drove</u> across the bridge just for fun.
7. The <u>trip</u> <u>was</u> like a ride on a roller coaster.
8. However, the <u>fun</u> <u>stopped</u> in November 1940.
9. The <u>wind</u> <u>blew</u> at forty-two miles an hour.
10. Suddenly, the <u>bridge</u> <u>crashed</u> into the water below.

B. Write each of the following sentences. Draw one line under the <u>simple subject</u> and two lines under the <u>verb</u>.

11. Over eight hundred years ago, <u>architects</u> in Pisa, Italy, <u>designed</u> a beautiful marble tower.
12. However, <u>builders</u> soon <u>discovered</u> a big mistake.
13. The <u>foundation</u> under the tower <u>was</u> only ten feet thick.
14. <u>It</u> <u>was</u> not strong enough for the huge tower.
15. As a result, the <u>foundation</u> <u>sank</u> into the ground.
16. The whole <u>tower</u> <u>tilted</u> to one side.
17. Over the centuries, the <u>base</u> of the tower <u>settled</u> even more.
18. Today this unusual <u>building</u> still <u>tips</u> sideways.
19. <u>Tourists</u> <u>flock</u> to the Leaning Tower of Pisa.
20. Many <u>people</u> <u>consider</u> it one of the wonders of the world.

The Leaning Tower of Pisa, a bell tower, was begun in 1173 and completed between 1360 and 1370 in Pisa, Italy. Built on unstable soil, it tilts an additional twentieth of an inch each year.

Understanding Sentences **353**

Writing Theme: Famous Mistakes in Architecture

Other related areas students might wish to explore as writing topics include the following:

- the longest suspension bridge in the world
- the Taj Mahal in India
- the Eiffel Tower in Paris
- designing a dream house

MIXED REVIEW • PAGES 347–352

You may wish to use this activity to check students' mastery of the following concepts:

- the simple predicate, or verb
- the simple subject

A. Answers are shown on page. Student answers should be in columns.

B. Answers are shown on page.

Objectives
- To recognize subjects in unusual positions

Writing
- To vary the position of subjects in sentences

Teaching Strategies

INDIVIDUALIZING INSTRUCTION: KINESTHETIC LEARNERS Write the subject of each of the following sentences on blue index cards. Then write the rest of each sentence on a white card. Ask students to practice re-arranging the cards to place the subject in different positions.

After the race, flowers bloomed.

Through the woods raced the deer.

Here are the award-winning books.

Among the crowd appeared the winners.

LINKING GRAMMAR AND WRITING To determine whether the students' writing needs more sentence variety, suggest that they read their drafts aloud to themselves or to a partner. If the word order in a string of sentences sounds monotonous, they may be able to move a prepositional phrase or an adverb to precede the subject.

HELPFUL HINT Explain to students that *here* and *there* are never the subjects of sentences, even though these words often begin complete thoughts.

Additional Resource

Grammar and Usage Practice Book, p. 7

Writing
TIP

Give your sentences more variety by putting the subjects of some sentences in different positions.

The subject does not always come at the beginning of a sentence.

The subject is usually near the beginning of a sentence and before the verb. Writers, however, can change the order of sentences to add variety to their writing.

Animal paintings appear on the cave walls.
On the cave walls, animal paintings appear.
(The subject is near the end of the sentence but before the verb.)

On the cave walls appear animal paintings.
(The order of the subject and the verb is reversed.)

To find the subject of a sentence in which the order is unusual, first find the verb. Then ask *who* or *what* before the verb.

Who or what *appear? Paintings* appear.
Paintings is the subject of the sentence.

Sentences Beginning with *Here* and *There*

In a sentence beginning with the word *here* or *there*, the subject usually follows the verb.

There is the paintbrush.
    Verb: *is*
    Who or what is? paintbrush
    Paintbrush is the subject of *is*.

Here are the drawings.
    Verb: *are*
    Who or what are? drawings
    Drawings is the subject of *are*.

Practice Your Skills

A. CONCEPT CHECK

Subjects in Different Positions   Write each of the following sentences. Draw one line under the subject of the verb and two lines under the verb.

1. There is a wonderful cave in southern France.
2. Here are the world's oldest paintings.
3. Scientists from all over the world study the paintings in the Grotte de Lascaux.
4. On the walls and ceilings are pictures of animals.
5. Everywhere are creations from the distant past.
6. Inside the dark cave, a scientist imagines a scene from twenty thousand years ago.
7. In the middle of the cave sits an ancient artist.
8. Beside the artist are hollow bones.
9. These bones are the artist's paintbrushes.
10. Near him is a torch.
11. By firelight the artist begins his work.
12. Patiently, the artist draws a buffalo.
13. For early people, rock paintings had a magic purpose.
14. For example, they meant good luck to hunters.
15. Even today, there is mysterious power in these pictures.

B. REVISION SKILL

Varying the Positions of Subjects   Rewrite each sentence so that the subject comes after the verb.

16. Many examples of rock art are in southern Africa.
17. Many drawings are there from thousands of years ago.
18. Examples of rock art appear on the walls of cliffs in Rhodesia.
19. An animal scene is over here.
20. A deer comes from the forest.
21. A band of hunters gathers around the deer.
22. Bows and arrows are on the hunters' backs.
23. A huge rhinoceros is nearby.
24. Clouds of smoke are in the distance.
25. Other scenes of events in daily life are next to this drawing.

FOR MORE PRACTICE
See page 368.

Understanding Sentences   **355**

Writing Theme
Early Art

Writing Theme:
Early Art
Other related areas students might wish to explore as writing topics include the following:
- Egyptian tomb paintings
- Australian aboriginal art
- sculpture and painting in ancient Crete
- early cave painting at Altamira, Spain

Answers to Practice Your Skills

A. Concept Check
Subjects in Different Positions
Answers are shown on page.

B. Revision Skill
Varying the Positions of Subjects
Answers may vary slightly. Possible answers are given.
16. In southern Africa are many examples of rock art.
17. There are many drawings from thousands of years ago.
18. On the walls of cliffs in Rhodesia appear examples of rock art.
19. Over here is an animal scene.
20. From the forest comes a deer.
21. Around the deer gathers a band of hunters.
22. On the hunters' backs are bows and arrows.
23. Nearby is a huge rhinoceros.
24. In the distance are clouds of smoke.
25. Next to this drawing are other scenes of events in daily life.

C. Correcting Fragments and Run-ons Add words to each fragment to make a complete sentence. Rewrite each run-on as separate sentences. Write *Correct* if the sentence is correct.

26. Some advertisements twisted the truth about the West.
27. Newspaper editors also spread fabulous stories they made the West seem like a place in a dream.
28. Promised people in the East a better life.
29. The valleys were greener the skies were bluer.
30. Beets grew three feet thick, turnips measured five feet around.
31. Golden wheat with stems as thick as canes.
32. Mines with gold and silver.
33. Headed west in search of riches and adventure.
34. They believed the advertisements and newspaper stories.
35. However, few people became wealthy, many settlers on the Western frontier were poor.

D. Finding the Verb Write the <u>verb</u> in each sentence.

36. Many African Americans <u>were</u> pioneers during the 1800s.
37. For example, Biddy Mason <u>blazed</u> new trails for others.
38. She <u>found</u> adventure and freedom on the Western frontier.
39. Because of her courage, she <u>escaped</u> slavery in the South.
40. Her journey <u>began</u> in Mississippi during the early 1850s.
41. She <u>walked</u> all the way to California behind a wagon train.
42. Slavery <u>was</u> against the law in California.
43. In this free state, Biddy Mason finally <u>won</u> her freedom.
44. Later, she <u>became</u> a rich and powerful woman.
45. She <u>owned</u> businesses and land in Los Angeles.

E. Finding the Verb and Its Subject Write each of the following sentences. Draw two lines under the <u>verb</u> and one line under the <u>subject</u> of the verb.

46. <u>Pioneers</u> in a Kansas town <u>celebrated</u> on July 4, 1871.
47. <u>Harriet</u> <u>wrote</u> about the day's events in her diary.
48. At sunrise a <u>soldier</u> <u>fired</u> a cannon in the center of town.
49. <u>Families</u> in the area <u>decorated</u> their wagons and buggies.
50. Even <u>horses</u> <u>wore</u> tiny American flags.

C. Correcting Fragments and Run-ons
Some answers will vary. Sample answers are given.
26. Correct
27. Newspaper editors also spread fabulous stories. They made the West seem like a place in a dream.
28. These tales about the West promised people in the East a better life.
29. The valleys were greener. The skies were bluer.
30. Beets grew three feet thick. Turnips measured five feet around.
31. Golden wheat with stems as thick as canes covered the fields.
32. Mines with gold and silver offered the chance for wealth.
33. Many pioneers headed west in search of riches and adventure.
34. Correct
35. However, few people became wealthy. Many settlers on the Western frontier were poor.

D. Finding the Verb
Answers are shown on page.

E. Finding the Verb and Its Subject
Answers are shown on page.

51. The settlers rode into town for a day of fun.
52. By the courthouse the sheriff gave a patriotic speech.
53. Then the choir sang "The Star-Spangled Banner."
54. Many people brought food for a big picnic.
55. After lunch the boys played games.
56. Some men competed in wagon races and horse races.
57. At night, fireworks burst in the sky.

F. Finding Subjects in Different Positions Write the subject of each of the following sentences. Then tell whether it comes *before* or *after* the verb.

58. Here are some facts about education on the frontier.   A
59. At first there were no schools in the wilderness.   A
60. A pioneer woman usually taught boys and girls at home in her cabin.   B
61. Around her gathered a circle of children.   A
62. With a stick she scratched out numbers on the dirt floor.   B
63. Her students learned arithmetic and other subjects.   B
64. Later, pioneers built one-room schoolhouses.   B
65. There were many one-room schoolhouses in the Wild West.
66. Outside the schoolhouse door hung an iron bell.   A
67. Each morning the teacher rang the bell loudly.   B
68. Then the students rushed to their seats.   B
69. Along one side were rows of hard wooden benches.   A
70. In the front of the room was a blackboard.   A
71. Near the center of the room was a big potbellied stove.   A
72. There were students of all ages in the same classroom.   A

G. Identifying Kinds of Sentences Label each of the following sentences *Declarative, Imperative, Interrogative,* or *Exclamatory.* Then write the correct punctuation mark for the end of each sentence.

73. What was life like in Granite, Oklahoma
74. Are you ready for an adventure in history
75. Then take an imaginary journey in a time machine
76. Pretend you are a visitor to this frontier town
77. Pioneer families stop at the shops along Main Street

78. How busy the general store is

79. Horses gallop through the middle of town

80. So much action happens here

H. Finding Subjects and Verbs in Sentences Write each of the following sentences. Draw two lines under the verb and one line under the subject of the verb. If the subject *you* is understood, write it in parentheses.

81. Imagine a square dance in the 1800s.   (you)

82. Where is your partner?

83. Find one in a hurry!   (you)

84. What a fun time awaits you!

85. Listen to the caller.   (you)

86. "Are you all ready?"

87. "Swing your partner round and round."   (you)

88. "Form a star and then a chain."   (you)

89. "Now stampede!"   (you)

90. How loudly the dancers stamp their feet!

I. Finding Compound Subjects and Verbs Write each of the following sentences. Draw two lines under the verb(s) and one line under the subject(s).

91. Pioneer boys and girls had many chores.

92. On an ordinary day, most parents and their children woke up at four o'clock in the morning.

93. Younger children fed the chickens, gathered twigs, and picked berries.

94. Older children plowed the fields, planted the crops, and carried buckets of water.

95. Usually boys and their fathers worked in the fields.

96. In contrast, girls helped their mothers and worked at home.

97. They baked bread, washed clothes, and stitched embroidery.

98. Margaret Mitchell and her family were pioneers in Kansas during the 1870s.

99. As a young girl, she and her sisters trapped wild turkeys and hunted wolves.

100. Margaret, her parents, and her sisters built a log cabin.

Understanding
Sentences   **369**

GRAMMAR
HANDBOOK
34

REVIEW

These exercises may be used as a mixed review or as an informal evaluation of the skills presented in Handbook 34, "Understanding Sentences."

Additional Resources

Grammar and Usage Practice Book, p. 15
Tests and Writing Assessment Prompts, Mastery Test, pp. 9–12
Elaboration, Revision, and Proofreading Practice, p. 23

▶ **Writing Theme: Exploring Places**

Other related areas students might wish to explore as writing topics include the following:

• Francisco Coronado (1510–1544), Spanish explorer
• Prince Henry the Navigator of Portugal (1394–1460)
• Jacques Cartier (1491–1557), French explorer in Canada

A. Subjects and Predicates
Answers are shown on page.

B. Fragments and Run-ons
Some answers may vary. Sample answers are given.

16. Sentence
17. Run-on; One diver was a photographer. The other diver was a scientist.
18. Fragment; Suddenly, a shark floated near the divers.
19. Fragment; The photographer held a movie camera in front of the shark.
20. Sentence
21. Run-on; The camera surprised the shark. It remained very still.
22. Fragment; The shark stared peacefully at the divers.

23. Fragment; The shark's two dozen sharp teeth in the front of its lower jaw were scary.
24. Sentence
25. Run-on; However, the sharks in these caves are gentle. Their behavior here is very odd.
26. Run-on; Carlos Garcia discovered these caves and their unusually calm visitors. At first, the sharks seemed dead.

27. Fragment; The caves looked like a graveyard for sharks.
28. Sentence
29. Run-on; Sharks visit these caves. Then they become sleepy.
30. Fragment; The caves provide a restful place for sharks.

REVIEW

GRAMMAR
HANDBOOK
34

▶ **Writing Theme**
Exploring Places

A. Subjects and Predicates Write the italicized words in the following sentences. Label these words *Subject* or *Predicate*.

1. Your plane *circles above a snowy field.* P
2. You *see a land of lakes and streams from your window.* P
3. *Not a single road* is visible anywhere. S
4. *This huge, lonely, and wild land* is the tundra. S
5. The tundra *stretches north to the ice fields of the Arctic.* P
6. Your plane *lands near an icy patch of land.* P
7. With several other people, *you* explore this unusual place. S
8. Very few trees *grow here because of the cold weather.* P
9. However, *wild animals* roam everywhere. S
10. *Some animals, such as arctic hares and polar bears,* blend in with the snowy background. S
11. Reindeer *graze on the short grasses.* P
12. *A gray wolf* howls in the distance. S
13. Gulls *build their nests on the arctic cliffs.* P
14. Along the coast, *walruses* float on blocks of ice. S
15. *They* use their long white tusks as giant hooks. S

B. Fragments and Run-ons Label each numbered group of words *Sentence, Fragment,* or *Run-on.* Then correct the fragments and run-ons.

¹⁶Two deep-sea divers explored a cave off the eastern coast of Mexico. ¹⁷One diver was a photographer, the other diver was a scientist. ¹⁸Suddenly, a shark. ¹⁹Held a movie camera in front of the shark. ²⁰The shark almost bumped the photographer's face mask. ²¹The camera surprised the shark it remained very still. ²²Stared peacefully at the divers. ²³The shark's two dozen sharp teeth in the front of its lower jaw. ²⁴Sharks sometimes attack people. ²⁵However, the sharks in these caves are gentle their behavior here is very odd.

²⁶Carlos Garcia discovered these caves and their unusually calm visitors, at first, the sharks seemed dead. ²⁷Looked like a graveyard for sharks. ²⁸Actually, these caves are shark "hotels" under the sea. ²⁹Sharks visit these caves then they become sleepy. ³⁰Provide a restful place for sharks.

C. Simple Subjects and Verbs   Write the simple subject and verb of each sentence.

31. You follow a sandy path to the top of a hill.
32. At the top, great waves of sand seem endless.
33. These hills of sand are dunes on the Oregon coast.
34. The ocean piles the sand into huge dunes along the coast.
35. Their form changes often.
36. Violent winter winds reshape the dunes almost overnight.
37. Many dunes even "sing."
38. Sometimes the sand shifts in the wind.
39. Then the grains of sand brush across one another.
40. The movement sounds squeaky.

D. Types of Sentences   Label each complete sentence *Declarative, Interrogative, Imperative,* or *Exclamatory.* Correct the sentence fragments.

41. Explore the seas with Jacques-Yves Cousteau.
42. Discovered families of octopuses in a bay south of France.
43. Cousteau named this area Octopus City.
44. Dive beneath the ocean's surface.
45. What a strange world this is!
46. Where are the octopuses' homes?
47. Holes under those piles of rocks.
48. Is the octopus a terrible monster?
49. Frightens many people because of its scary appearance.
50. However, the octopus is really a very shy creature.

E. Subjects in Different Positions   Write each of the following sentences. Draw one line under the simple subject and two lines under the verb. Write understood subjects of imperative sentences in parentheses.

51. How adventurous are you?
52. Are you ready for a trip to the Southwest?
53. Explore the desert in Arizona.   (you)
54. Here is some important advice.
55. Bring canteens of water.   (you)

C. Simple Subjects and Verbs
Answers are shown on page.

D. Types of Sentences
Corrected fragments may vary. Sample answers are shown below.
41. Imperative
42. He discovered families of octopuses in a bay south of France
43. Declarative
44. Imperative
45. Exclamatory
46. Interrogative
47. Holes under those piles of rocks are their secret hiding places.
48. Interrogative
49. The octopus frightens many people because of its scary appearance.
50. Declarative

E. Subjects in Different Positions
Answers are shown on page.

Understanding
Sentences   **371**

71. You walk out on this glacier and inspect it.
72. The beauty and power are unmistakable.
73. The blue and green colors and the shapes are lovely.
74. Great cracks and towers develop in the ice.
75. Glaciers covered much of North America during the Ice Age and shaped the land.
76. Glaciers cut valleys, dug lakes, and carved mountains.
77. Alaska, Canada, and some Rocky Mountain states still have glaciers.
78. Mountains and polar regions are the homes of today's glaciers.
79. Glaciers begin as mounds of snow and grow slowly.
80. Snow falls and builds up each year.
81. The snow gets thicker and packs into ice.
82. The ice slides downhill and forms a glacier.
83. You go to the glacier's edge and see a mound of gravel.
84. The glacier scraped up rock and crushed it.
85. Only heat and the sea stop glaciers.

56. <u>Wear</u> long pants, high boots, and a hat with a brim.   (you)
57. Before your eyes <u>stretches</u> a beautiful <u>desert</u>.
58. How weird <u>it</u> <u>looks</u>!
59. The <u>desert</u> <u>reminds</u> me of a strange planet.
60. There <u>are</u> almost no <u>trees</u>.
61. Only ten <u>inches</u> of rain <u>fall</u> here every year.
62. How strong the <u>sun</u> <u>is</u>!
63. <u>Are</u> <u>you</u> too hot?
64. <u>Under</u> those rocks is a shady <u>place</u>.
65. <u>Be</u> careful!   (you)
66. Nearby <u>is</u> a <u>rattlesnake</u>.
67. The sharp <u>fangs</u> on that snake <u>are</u> really scary!
68. Where <u>are</u> the other <u>animals</u> in the desert?
69. <u>See</u> all the different holes in the ground.   (you)
70. <u>Creatures</u> in the desert <u>stay</u> cool underground.

F. Compound Subjects and Compound Predicates

Combine each group of sentences into one sentence by making a compound subject or a compound predicate.

71. You walk out on this glacier. You inspect it.
72. The beauty is unmistakable. The power is unmistakable.
73. The blue and green colors are lovely. The shapes are lovely.
74. Great cracks develop in the ice. Towers develop in the ice.
75. Glaciers covered much of North America during the Ice Age. Glaciers shaped the land.
76. Glaciers cut valleys. Glaciers dug lakes. Glaciers carved mountains.
77. Alaska still has glaciers. Canada still has glaciers. Some Rocky Mountain states still have glaciers.
78. Mountains are the homes of today's glaciers. Polar regions are the homes of today's glaciers.
79. Glaciers begin as mounds of snow. Glaciers grow slowly.
80. Snow falls. It builds up each year.
81. The snow gets thicker. It packs into ice.
82. The ice slides downhill. The ice forms a glacier.
83. You go to the glacier's edge. You see a mound of gravel.
84. The glacier scraped up rock. The glacier crushed it.
85. Only heat stops glaciers. Only the sea stops glaciers.

WRITING CONNECTIONS

Elaboration, Revision, and Proofreading

Revise the following draft about a personal experience by using the directions at the bottom of the page. Then proofread your revision for errors in grammar, capitalization, punctuation, and spelling. Pay special attention to sentence fragments and run-ons.

¹Lewis and I were always alike. ²We were the same age. ³Had the same interests. ⁴We were even the same size. ⁵We loved to play basketball against each other for hours at a time the games were always close. ⁶My favorite player is Michael Jordan. ⁷However, last year Lewis began to grow. ⁸He was beating me all the time. ⁹At first it made me mad. ¹⁰I accused him of cheating on the score. ¹¹I said he was fouling me, even when he wasn't. ¹²I couldn't beleive that he played basketball better than I did. ¹³My attitude changed last labor day, when our familys got together for a picnic. ¹⁴I looked at Lewis's parents and brothers, I noticed something for the first time. ¹⁵Everyone in his family is about a head taller than everyone in mine. ¹⁶The problem isn't that Lewis is better than I am. ¹⁷He's bigger. ¹⁸His height and wieght are things I cant change.

- Combine sentences 2 and 3 to correct the sentence fragment.
- Add the transition word "Soon" to the beginning of sentence 8 to make the order of events clearer.
- Add the phrase "than I am by six inches and twenty-five pounds" to sentence 17.
- Delete the sentence that doesn't belong.
- Divide the passage into two paragraphs.

Personal and Expressive Writing

Writing in your journal gives you a chance to explore your thoughts and to record your experiences. (See Workshop 1.) When you revise journal entries for others to read, you need to polish your rough ideas. Make sure that every sentence expresses a complete thought. Correct sentence fragments and run-ons, which may confuse your readers.

WRITING CONNECTIONS

Elaboration, Revision, and Proofreading

This activity will allow students to see some of the concepts presented in this handbook at work in a piece of personal and expressive writing. By revising and proofreading this passage, students will have the chance to correct sentence fragments and run-on sentences and to combine sentences.

You might have students work in small groups to revise the passage. Then discuss the completed revision with the entire class. Revisions may vary slightly. Typical revisions are shown below. Elements involving change are shown in boldface.

Lewis and I were always alike. **We were the same age and had the same interests.** We were even the same size. We loved to play basketball against each other for hours at a time. The games were always close. ~~My favorite player is Michael Jordan.~~ However, last year Lewis began to grow. **Soon** he was beating me all the time. At fist it made me mad. I accused him of cheating on the score. I said he was fouling me, even when he wasn't. I couldn't believe that he played basketball better than I did.

My attitude changed last Labor Day, when our families got together for a picnic. I looked at Lewis's parents and brothers. I noticed something for the first time. Everyone in his family is about a head taller than everyone in mine. The problem isn't that Lewis is better than I am. **He's bigger than I am by six inches and twenty-five pounds.** His height and weight are things I can't change.

Objective

• To use visual prompts and writing prompts as springboards to informal writing

WRITING WARM-UPS

These ungraded, spontaneous journal activities can be used imaginatively to introduce the concepts in this handbook. Suggest that students choose one prompt to respond to and that they save their responses in their writing folders.

You might begin by discussing the funny names and double meanings of the signs in the illustration. This leads naturally to the first prompt, in which students invent a fictional name for a town. Students using the other two prompts might also wish to include funny names as part of their writings.

• Invent your own town. Give it a name and then explain the meaning of the name.
• Make up the setting for a science fiction story. Write about the weird and wonderful objects in your setting.
• Imagine you have discovered the royal tomb of an Inca ruler. Tell about the fascinating artifacts you have found within it.

374

Understanding Nouns

A town can have an unusual name (Muleshoe, Texas) or a plain name (The Plains, Ohio). The names of persons and things can be just as simple or fancy. Dinosaur, Colorado, is a place. A dinosaur is (or was) a thing. Both names are nouns. You need nouns to name the people, places, things, and ideas you write about.

In this handbook you will study the different types of nouns. You will learn how you can use them to make your writing precise and interesting.

- **What Are Nouns?**
- **Common and Proper Nouns**
- **Singular and Plural Nouns**
- **Nouns That Show Possession**

Understanding Nouns

Objectives
- To identify nouns
- To distinguish between common and proper nouns
- To distinguish between singular and plural nouns
- To form plural nouns correctly
- To identify nouns that show possession
- To form possessive nouns correctly

Writing
- To use nouns that make writing more specific and precise
- To use proper nouns and possessive nouns correctly in writing

INTRODUCING THE HANDBOOK
Invite students to imagine what the world would be like if things didn't have names. They would have to point at everything. Warnings of danger—for example, "Car coming!"—would be almost impossible. People would scarcely be able to share information or to teach and learn skills.

Then introduce the term *noun*. Inform students that a *noun* is the name of one kind of word—a word that is the name of a thing, person, place, or idea. As students move into the handbook, encourage them to look for and to use specific, vivid nouns.

Objectives
- To identify nouns as words that name persons, places, things, or ideas

Writing
- To use precise nouns in writing

Teaching Strategies

LINKING GRAMMAR AND WRITING
Write on the board sentences such as the following and ask students to suggest precise nouns that create a clearer picture:

A <u>person</u> is walking a <u>dog.</u>

In front of the <u>building</u> is a <u>car.</u>

COLLABORATIVE OPPORTUNITY
You might divide the class into small groups and have each group suggest categories of things (for example, things that are made of metal). For each category, see which group can write the longest list in a limited time, perhaps two minutes. Make sure every item on the list is a noun. You might continue with categories of persons and places.

INDIVIDUALIZING INSTRUCTION: ESL STUDENTS
Extend students' vocabulary of English nouns by pairing them with native speakers to name objects pictured in magazines. Ask each student to take turns naming things that appear in the illustrations. To extend the vocabulary of ESL students, native speakers should supply nouns ESL students do not know.

Additional Resources

Tests and Writing Assessment Prompts, Pretest, pp. 13–14
Grammar and Usage Practice Book, p. 16

 Grammar Test Generator

Writing TIP

Notice how specific nouns in "Finding Home" on pages 180–181 record the persons, places, things, and ideas that were important to Merrill Wilk's family.

Data and Captain Picard from the television series *Star Trek: The Next Generation,* with Captain Kirk and Mr. Spock from the original *Star Trek.*

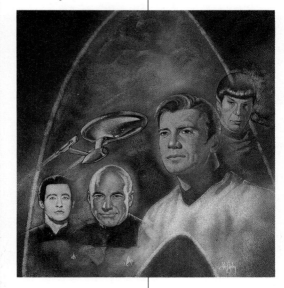

376 Grammar Handbook

A **noun** names a person, a place, a thing, or an idea.

Many names tell who you are. You may be an artist, a student, and a leader. These different names for you are nouns. Nouns are used to name persons, places, things, or ideas.

Many nouns name things that can be seen. Some examples are *spaceship, airport,* and *mountain.* Some nouns name things that can be neither seen nor touched. These include nouns such as *justice, courage, fear,* and *happiness.*

Here are some other examples of nouns.

Persons	Places	Things	Ideas
captain	desert	robot	loyalty
engineer	solar system	meteor	curiosity
Kirk	Asia	Eiffel Tower	knowledge
Uhura	Lima	*Enterprise*	love

A noun can name something in general, or it can be a precise name. Compare these sentences:

The travelers explored the area.
The astronauts explored the crater.

Did you notice how much more the second sentence tells in the same number of words? The word *astronauts* is more specific than *travelers,* helping a reader guess where these travelers might be. *Crater* gives a picture of the place, while the general term *area* does not. In your writing, always try to use specific nouns. They will make your ideas and descriptions clearer.

Practice Your Skills

A. APPLICATION IN LITERATURE

Nouns Write each of the italicized nouns and tell whether each refers to a *Person*, a *Place*, a *Thing*, or an *Idea*.

[1]In a far corner of the *universe,* on one of the forest *moons* of the planet *Endor,* there lived a *tribe* of small furry *folk* called *Ewoks.* [2]In a *village* perched high in the *branches* of the ancient *trees* they lived happy *lives,* with *love* and *goodwill* for their fellow Ewoks. . . .

[3]One of these young Ewoks was named *Teebo.* . . . [4]He could daydream and watch the *rivers* of color that flowed across the *sky.* [5]The sky *colors* seemed to sing a bright *song.* . . . [6]In these *songs* Teebo could hear different *voices.* [7]He could sense the *happiness* when the voices rejoiced at the planting of a new *birth-tree,* and the *sorrow* when the voices mourned the *end* of a tree's *lifetime.*

Joe Johnston, *The Adventures of Teebo*

B. DRAFTING SKILL

Using Precise Nouns Finish the following sentences. Using your imagination, complete each sentence with precise nouns.

8. Keisha rode her _____ to the _____.
9. When she reached the _____, she spoke to the _____.
10. Keisha didn't know that the _____ was from another _____ in the universe.
11. The _____ from his head made the _____ blink on and off.
12. Suddenly, a feeling of _____ came over Keisha as she ran to call the _____.

C. APPLICATION IN WRITING

Fantasy Imagine you are writing about a strange event that occurs in another universe. Before you begin writing, make a list of nouns you might use in your story. Go over your list to make each noun as specific as possible.

Writing Theme
Fantastic Fiction

Writing TIP

Choose the noun that names exactly what you mean. Do not say *tool* if you mean *hammer.* Do not write *boat* if you mean *canoe.*

FOR MORE PRACTICE
See page 388.

Understanding Nouns **377**

C. Using Plural Nouns   Write the following sentences. Correct all <u>errors</u> in the use of the plural forms of nouns.

26. There are many <u>formes</u> of animal communications.
27. <u>Cuckooes</u>, salmon, wolves, and other animals send messages.
28. You probably know that <u>gooses</u> honk, coyotes howl, and <u>sheeps</u> bleat, and that crickets sing by rubbing their two front wings together.
29. Did you know that male <u>deers</u> bellow to scare off rivals?
30. You've probably seen <u>fireflys</u> flashing to attract mates.
31. Different kinds of these insects flash different <u>patterns</u>.
32. One day <u>zookeeperes</u> were watching an elephant named Siri.
33. Siri was making <u>scratchs</u> on the floor with a rock.
34. The zoo employees got Siri paper, paints, and <u>brushs</u>.
35. Siri created <u>hundredes</u> of pages of drawings.
36. Some observers said that her work looked as though it came from art <u>studioes</u>.
37. Vervet <u>monkies</u> use various signals to communicate.
38. They have three main <u>enemys</u>: eagles, snakes, and leopards.
39. To escape leopards, the monkeys go far out on tree <u>branchs</u>, but to escape eagles, they stay close to the tree trunks.
40. Vervets use three different calls to tell one another which enemy is near so they will know how to save their <u>lifes</u>.

D. Writing Possessive Forms   Write the correct possessive form of each word in parentheses.

41. Humpback whales make (nature) most complex sounds.
42. The (humpbacks) sounds range from shrieks to groans.
43. Males sing songs during the (whales) mating season.
44. All humpbacks in each of the (ocean) regions sing one song.
45. The (group) song changes during the mating season.
46. Just as (people) taste in music changes, whales seem to get tired of singing the same song over and over.
47. Each (season) singing begins with last year's final song.
48. The songs seem to be a contest among a (region) males.
49. The (singers) breathing stops while they sing because whales cannot breathe and sing at the same time.
50. Most of the (performers) songs last ten to fifteen minutes.

C. Using Plural Nouns
   Errors are underlined on page.
Corrections are shown below.
26. forms
27. Cuckoos
28. geese, sheep
29. deer
30. fireflies
31. patterns
32. zookeepers
33. scratches
34. brushes
35. hundreds
36. studios
37. monkeys
38. enemies
39. branches
40. lives

D. Writing Possessive Forms
41. nature's
42. humpbacks'
43. whales'
44. ocean's
45. group's
46. people's
47. season's
48. region's
49. singers'
50. performers'

GRAMMAR HANDBOOK 35

REVIEW

These exercises may be used as a mixed review or as an informal evaluation of the skills presented in Handbook 35, "Using Nouns."

Additional Resources

Grammar and Usage Practice Book, p. 23

Tests and Writing Assessment Prompts, Mastery Test, pp. 15–16

Elaboration, Revision, and Proofreading Practice, p. 24

 Writing Theme: Tall Tales

Other related areas students might wish to explore as writing topics include the following:

- Pecos Bill and Slue-foot Sue
- John Henry
- Mike Fink
- an original tall tale, set in the present

A. Finding Common and Proper Nouns

Answers are shown on page. Student answers should be in columns.

B. Writing Singular and Plural Nouns

Errors are underlined on page. Corrections are shown below.

11. heroes
12. stories
13. achievements
14. impossibilities
15. children
16. mountains
17. wolves
18. bushes
19. raccoons
20. grizzlies

GRAMMAR HANDBOOK 35

Writing Theme
Tall Tales

A. Finding Common and Proper Nouns Label two columns *Common Nouns* and *Proper Nouns*. Write each noun from this paragraph in the correct column. Capitalize proper nouns. If a noun is used more than once, you need to list it only once.

[1]The story of paul bunyan is a famous tale that began in the united states. [2]People all over america have told the stories of a giant lumberjack who could perform great deeds. [3]The strength and abilities of this man were amazing! [4]He could cut down ten trees at a time with a single swipe of his ax. [5]Paul could drive the stumps into the ground with his bare fist. [6]Our hero could even squeeze water out of boulders. [7]paul dug the mississippi river and cleared the states of iowa and kansas for the farmers. [8]With a blue ox named babe, paul cleared western pastures so cattle could graze. [9]To give babe drinking water, the fantastic lumberjack scooped out the great lakes. [10]The adventures of paul bunyan are still enjoyed by americans.

B. Writing Singular and Plural Nouns Write the following sentences. Correct all errors in the plural forms of nouns.

11. Davy Crockett was one of many tall-tale heros.
12. He was real, but storys about him were bigger than life.
13. His strong opinions and the outrageous achievementes he claimed for himself made news everywhere.
14. Davy loved to exaggerate his adventures outrageously, and other people added more impossibilitys to his accounts.
15. The tales say he wasn't born like normal childs.
16. Davy was born on a meteor that crashed in the mountaines.
17. Many of the tales tell of fights Davy had, often with wild animals like mountain lions, wolfs, bears, and alligators.
18. Once he fought a huge mountain lion all night in the bushs, and by morning they had become lifelong friends.
19. All the raccoon knew that he was a great shot, so when they saw him they laid themselves down and gave up.
20. "When I was a baby," he claimed, "I could lick two grizzlys at once."

Literature Connection

Tall Tales to Read Students might enjoy hearing you read aloud Virginia Hamilton's story "Papa John's Tall Tale," from her collection of African-American folk tales *The People Could Fly.* Hamilton notes that in different regions of America, tall tales are called "toasties, gallyfloppers, windies, whoppers, and long bows." You might ask students what word, if any, they have been using to refer to these tales of exaggeration.

C. Writing Possessive Forms

Write the possessive form of each noun given in parentheses.

21. Back in the days of sailing ships, (sailors) lives were filled with hard work.
22. They often sang songs, or chanteys, while hoisting a (ship) sails, weighing anchor, or doing their other duties.
23. One of the (seafarers) favorite songs was "Old Stormalong."
24. The (chantey) hero was named Alfred Bulltop Stormalong.
25. Tales of (Stormy) adventures became popular.
26. This (hero) parents were unknown.
27. A tidal wave washed him onto (Cape Cod) coast, in New England, while he was still a baby.
28. Even then, Stormy was eighteen feet tall and drank milk by the barrel—to the (townsfolk) amazement.
29. When he grew up, many (ships) captains wanted him as a sailor.
30. He had numerous adventures on the seas and saved his fellow (crewmen) lives many times.

D. Proofreading

Write the following paragraph on your paper. Correct all errors in the use of proper nouns, plural forms, and possessive forms. (17 errors)

Of all this countries tall-tale heros, Mose was the first to come from a big city. He hailed from new york. People first heard about Mose in a broadway stage show called *A Glance at New York,* by B. A. Baker. From that time on, Mose' legend just grew and grew. Storys of his heroic deeds were told in newspapers and magazines.

Mose was a firefighter back when firefighters's dutys included pulling their wagones themselves. He was eight foot tall and was stronger than ten men. Once a horse-drawn trolley was caught in its track, blocking his fire trucks way. Mose unhooked the horses and picked up the trolley, with the trolleys' passengeres inside. He carried it across the street so that his team and their truck could get to the fire. Hearing a mothers crys, mose entered the burning building and soon carried out a baby—in his hat!

WRITING CONNECTIONS
Elaboration, Revision, and Proofreading

This activity will allow your students to see some of the concepts presented in this handbook at work in a piece of descriptive writing. By revising and proof-reading this passage, students will have the chance to use specific nouns and plural and possessive forms of nouns.

You might have students work in small groups to complete the revision; then discuss possible answers with the entire class.

Revisions will vary. A typical revision is shown below. Elements involving change are shown in boldface

A tradition at many celebrations in Mexico and other countries of Latin America is the breaking of a piñata. A piñata is a clay jug or a papier-mâché container covered with layers of brightly colored paper. Many piñatas are made in the shapes of animals, such as burros or birds. The piñata is dangled above the heads of guests. Each **guest** is blindfolded **and** gets three tries to break the piñata with a long stick. When someone succeeds, the piñata's contents **tumble** out. **Sweets, toys, and other small presents fall to the ground.** Everyone scurries to gather up the loot.

The tradition of breaking piñatas started in Spain. Today, it is carried on at celebrations for Christmas, Easter, and other occasions throughout the year. A piñata may also be an attraction at any party for children.

Observation and Description

A good way to learn about other cultures and customs is to describe them. (See Workshop 2.) When you revise this type of descriptive writing, look for ways to add vivid details. Using precise common and proper nouns will help you present information clearly.

Revise the following draft of a description by using the directio at the bottom of the page. Then proofread your work, looking espe cially for <u>errors</u> in the use of nouns. Also look for other errors in grammar, capitalization, punctuation, and spelling.

[1]A tradition at many celebrations in <u>mexico</u> and other <u>Countries</u> of <u>latin</u> <u>america</u> is the breaking of a piñata. [2]A piñata is a clay jug or a papier-mâché container covered with <u>layer's</u> of brightly colored paper. [3]Many piñatas are made in the shapes of animals, such as <u>burroes</u> or birds. [4]The piñata is dangled above the <u>head's</u> of guests. [5]Each one is blindfolded. [6]Each one gets three tries to break the piñata with a long stick. [7]When someone succeeds, the <u>piñatas</u> contents come out. [8]Everyone scurries to gather up the loot. [9]The tradition of breaking piñatas started in <u>spain</u>. [10]Today, it is carried on at celebrations for <u>christmas</u>, <u>easter</u>, and other <u>ocasions</u> throughout the year. [11]A piñata may also be an attraction at any party for <u>childs</u>.

1. In sentence 5, replace the vague pronoun "one" with the more precise noun "guest."

2. Combine sentences 5 and 6 to make a sentence with a compoun verb.

3. In sentence 7, replace the vague verb "come" with the more expressive "tumble."

4. Add this missing information after sentence 7: "Sweets, toys, an other small presents fall to the ground."

5. Divide the passage into two paragraphs.

Sniglets

Have you ever searched for just the right word to describe something—and found that the word you wanted was one you had to make up yourself? If so, then you've invented a **sniglet,** a word that doesn't appear in the dictionary but probably should. What sniglets can you add to this list?

cinemuck *(si' ne muk)* n. The combination of popcorn, soda, and melted chocolate that covers the floors of movie theaters.

glackett *(glak' it)* n. The noisy ball inside a spray-paint can.

oatgap *(oht' gap)* n. The empty space in a cereal box created by "settling during shipment."

pigslice *(pig' slys)* n. The last unclaimed piece of pizza that everyone is secretly dying for.

profanitype *(pro fan' i tipe)* n. The special symbols used by cartoonists to replace swear words (points, asterisks, stars, and so on).

snacktivity *(snak tiv' ih tee)* n. Any amusing table pastime (i.e., putting olives on the ends of one's fingers, "biting faces" into a slice of bread, etc.)

spork *(spork)* n. The combination spoon/fork you find in fast-food restaurants.

wondracide *(wun' druh side)* n. The act of murdering a piece of bread with a knife and cold butter.

Rich Hall and Friends

Have students work in pairs or small groups to come up with additional sniglets. (Maybe someone can even come up with another invented word for *sniglet.)* Suggest that students follow the dictionary-style format used in the text: the sniglet, then the parenthetical pronunciation guide, then the abbreviated part of speech, then the definition.

Students might be interested to know that in his humorous poem "The Owl and the Pussycat," the nineteenth-century English poet Edward Lear coined the sniglet *runcible spoon,* which is essentially the same thing as *spork:* "They dined on mince, and slices of quince, / Which they ate with a runcible spoon. . . . "

Objective
• To use a poem and writing prompts as springboards to informal writing

WRITING WARM-UPS

Start by reassuring students that they will not be graded for this assignment, which is designed to get them thinking imaginatively about some of the concepts in this Handbook. Most students will probably wish to respond to only one prompt, although some students may wish to write about them both.

For the first prompt, have small groups of students brainstorm what an elephant or another zoo animal might do after the zoo closes and the keepers go home for the night.

Suggest that students who select the second prompt begin by making a cluster diagram of ways in which they relax when there is no one to bother them. Finally, tell students that these prompts will require them to use vivid action words, which they will learn more about in this Handbook.

I wonder if the elephant
Is lonely in his stall
When all the boys and girls are gone
And there's no shout at all,
And there's no one to stamp before,
No one to note his might.
Does he hunch up, as I do,
Against the dark of night?

Gwendolyn Brooks
"PETE AT THE ZOO"

• Write a humorous description of what you think animals do when no one is around.
• Write about what you like to do when no one else is around.

394

Understanding Verbs

The people on this safari hope to shoot photos that will show all the activity of African wildlife: *running, grazing, stalking, playing, stampeding*—even *lounging* like these cheetahs. The photos will bring the African landscape to life for all who see them.

You can use verbs to make your writing come to life. Verbs are the engines that drive your sentences. They describe the action, tell that something exists, or link ideas.

In this handbook, you will learn ways to use verbs to capture the true spirit of the ideas you want to communicate.

Understanding Verbs

Objectives
- To identify action verbs and linking verbs
- To distinguish between main verbs and helping verbs
- To recognize direct objects of verbs
- To identify linking verbs and predicate words
- To recognize and form the present, past, and future tenses of verbs
- To identify the three principal parts of regular and irregular verbs
- To choose correct forms of these pairs of often-confused verbs: *can, may; let, leave; lie, lay; teach, learn; rise, raise; sit, set*

Writing
- To use vivid verbs in sentences and paragraphs
- To correct errors in verb tenses in sentences and paragraphs
- To use irregular verb forms and often-confused verbs correctly

INTRODUCING THE HANDBOOK
Call on volunteers to share their ideas about the art on this page. What actions does the photograph suggest? Call students' attention to the verbs they use to describe the scene. Then tell them that verbs are the core of written and spoken language, because they express actions or state the condition of people, objects, or ideas. Vivid, specific verbs are among a writer's most powerful tools.

Objectives
- To identify action verbs and linking verbs

Writing
- To use specific action verbs in a piece of writing

Teaching Strategies

KEY TO UNDERSTANDING: ACTION VERBS Students may have difficulty with the concept that some action verbs describe unseen actions. On the board, write some additional examples of verbs that express actions not perceived with the senses: for example, *remember, forget, guess,* and *sympathize.* Point out that many of these words relate to activities of the mind or of the emotions. Call on volunteers to compose sentences using these verbs.

HELPFUL HINT: LINKING VERBS To reinforce the concept that certain verbs work to connect the subject and predicate, use the following activity. Tell students that all the verbs at the bottom of page 396 are forms of the verb *to be.* Have students make up a sentence using each verb form. Then ask them to explain which words in each sentence are linked to the subject by the verb.

ASSESSMENT: SPOT CHECK To be sure students are able to recognize verbs in sentences, hand out clippings from a school or local newspaper. Ask students to identify the verb or verbs in each sentence. Write these verbs on the board. Then invite other students to classify each verb as an action verb or as a linking verb.

Verbs are words that tell about action or state that something *is.*

You use two kinds of verbs when you speak or write. These are **action verbs** and **state-of-being** or **linking verbs.**

Action Verbs

Some verbs tell about action you can see.

> The young boy *saddled* his pony.
> The two *galloped* across the field.

Other verbs tell about action you cannot see. That is, there is no physical movement.

> The boy *wished* for a long ride.
> He *enjoyed* the time with his pony.

State-of-Being or Linking Verbs

Some verbs do not show action. They tell what something is, or they link the subject with a word or words in the predicate. Such verbs are called **state-of-being verbs** or **linking verbs.** Since state-of-being verbs and linking verbs are very similar, we will refer to both of them as linking verbs from this point on. These are the most common linking verbs.

am	are	were	being
is	was	be	been

FRANK & ERNEST® by Bob Thaves

FRANK & ERNEST reprinted by permission of NEA, Inc.

Look at the linking verbs in the following sentences.

The pony *is* a reddish color.
He *was* a year old last month.
His movements *are* graceful.

These are some other familiar linking verbs.

look   appear   become   taste   seem
feel   sound   remain   smell

The clip-clop of the pony's hooves *sounds* hollow.
The pony *seems* relaxed now.
The pony *becomes* nervous around strangers.

Practice Your Skills

A. CONCEPT CHECK

Verbs   Write the verb from each of the following sentences.

1. Salinas, California, was John Steinbeck's home.
2. John wandered freely through the valley as a boy.
3. His family seemed warm and happy.
4. At age four, he received a Shetland pony.
5. Young John felt proud of this new responsibility.
6. Family friends traveled to the Pacific Ocean in summer.
7. John's family often made the trip by train.
8. The salty spray smelled wonderful to him.
9. Long hikes were a daily activity at the beach.
10. Starfish beckoned from tide pools.
11. Magnificent shells glittered in the sun.
12. The young children went for swims as often as possible.
13. John remained at the beach only part of the summer.
14. His uncle invited him to his ranch near King City.
15. The ranch appeared very different from the ocean.
16. The sun beat harshly on the hills and fields.
17. John searched for special places in the hills.
18. These places inspired special thoughts and feelings.
19. John used the ranch as the setting for his story "The Red Pony."
20. In the story, Jody seems much like young John.

Writing Theme
John Steinbeck

B. Application in Literature
Identifying Verbs

21. was, Linking
22. took, Action; stepped, Action
23. glittered, Action
24. touched, Action; rubbed, Action
25. relaxed, Action
26. brushed, Action
27. thought, Action
28. braided, Action
29. enter, Action
30. was, Linking; felt, Action

C. Application in Writing
Description

   Answers will vary.

B. APPLICATION IN LITERATURE

Identifying Verbs   Write the verbs in italics from the following passage. Label each verb *Action* or *Linking*. Notice how the writer mixes the use of action and linking verbs.

[21]Jody *was* glad when [the boys] had gone. [22]He *took* brush and currycomb from the wall, took down the barrier of the box stall and *stepped* cautiously in. [23]The pony's eyes *glittered,* and he edged around into kicking position. [24]But Jody *touched* him on the shoulder and *rubbed* his high arched neck. . . . [25]The pony gradually *relaxed* his tenseness. [26]Jody curried and *brushed* until a pile of dead hair lay in the stall and until the pony's coat had taken on a deep red shine. [27]Each time he finished he *thought* it might have been done better. [28]He *braided* the mane into a dozen little pigtails, and he braided the forelock, and then he undid them and brushed the hair out straight again.

[29]Jody did not hear his mother *enter* the barn. [30]She *was* angry when she came, but when she looked in at the pony and at Jody working over him, she *felt* a curious pride rise up in her.

John Steinbeck, "The Red Pony"

C. APPLICATION IN WRITING

Description   In the sentence "The girl went down the beach," *went* is a dull action verb. Notice how the sentence becomes livelier with a specific action verb that tells you just how the girl moved:

The girl *raced* down the beach.

Write a description of someone doing an activity, such as a friend playing with a pet or a family member enjoying a nice day. Use as many specific action verbs as you can.

FOR MORE PRACTICE
See page 423.

398   Grammar Handbook

PROFESSIONAL NOTEBOOK

As students revise for verb usage, share with them the advice of professional writing teacher William Zinsser:

   "Verbs are the most important of all your tools. They push the sentence forward and give it momentum. . . . Most verbs also carry somewhere in their imagery or in their sound a suggestion of what they mean: *flail, poke, dazzle, squash, beguile, pamper, swagger, wheedle, vex.* . . . Don't choose one that is dull or merely serviceable. Make active verbs activate your sentences."

from On Writing Well

C. PROOFREADING SKILL

Correcting Verb Tenses Write the following paragraph, correcting errors in verb tenses. Also correct errors in spelling, capitalization, and punctuation. (10 errors)

Jade is a semiprecious stone, and it came in too kinds—jadeite and nephrite. Today, jadeite will be the more valuable of the two. Both kinds of jade are used for jewlery. In 1990, a huge boulder of nephrite jade was found in northeastern china. The boulder will weigh 291 tons. and it was 23 feet long by 20 feet high. can you imagine wearing that around you're neck.

CHECK ✓ POINT
MIXED REVIEW · PAGES 408–411

Write the following sentences using the verb form given in parentheses.

1. I (past of *attend*) a horse show last Friday.
2. My friend Amy (past of *show*) her horse Gypsy.
3. Gypsy (present of *perform*) many beautiful movements for the appreciative crowd.
4. Amy (past of *work*) with Gypsy for a month preparing for Friday's show.
5. He (present of *bow*) and (present of *prance*) gracefully in front of the reviewing stand.
6. Before every show, Amy (future of *braid*) his tail.
7. Gypsy (present of *seem*) like a member of her family.
8. Some riders (future of *decorate*) their horses' manes with colorful satin ribbons.
9. Amy (past of *shudder*) when she learned about prehistoric people.
10. They (past of *hunt*) wild horses and ate the meat.
11. No one ever (future of *turn*) Gypsy into a ponyburger!
12. Almost any horse (future of *learn*) to obey commands.
13. Amy (present of *train*) Gypsy every day.
14. Sometimes Gypsy (present of *disobey*) her commands.
15. Amy simply (present of *repeat*) the command patiently.

FOR MORE PRACTICE
See page 425.

Writing Theme

Horses

C. Proofreading Skill
Correcting Verb Tenses

Errors in proofreading exercises are counted as follows: (a) A misspelled word is one error; two initials and a last name not capitalized are counted as three errors. (b) Run-on sentences and sentence fragments are each counted as one error, even though the correction involves both punctuation and capitalization.

Errors are shown on page. The correctly rewritten paragraph appears below.

Jade is a semiprecious stone, and it comes in two kinds—jadeite and nephrite. Today, jadeite is the more valuable of the two. Both kinds of jade are used for jewelry. In 1990, a huge boulder of nephrite jade was found in northeastern China. The boulder weighed 291 tons, and it was 23 feet long by 20 feet high. Can you imagine wearing that around your neck?

CHECK ✓ POINT

Writing Theme: Horses

Other related areas students might wish to explore as writing topics include the following:

• a famous horse, real or fictitious
• the remaining wild horses of the American West
• how the horse and the zebra are related
• workhorses today

MIXED REVIEW · PAGES 408–411

You may wish to use this activity to check students' mastery of the following concept:

• verb tenses

1. attended
2. showed
3. performs
4. worked
5. bows, prances
6. will braid
7. seems
8. will decorate
9. shuddered
10. hunted
11. will turn
12. will learn
13. trains
14. disobeys
15. repeats

Objectives
• To identify the three principal parts of regular verbs

Writing
• To use the various verb forms in writing

Teaching Strategies

KEY TO UNDERSTANDING: PAST PARTICIPLES Stress to students that there is a distinction between the *principal parts* of a verb and a verb's *tenses*. The first and second principal parts correspond to the present and past tense forms of a verb, but the past participle form does not express any one tense. On the contrary, a participle in a verb phrase is always used with one or more helping verbs. It is these helping verbs that determine the tense.

ASSESSMENT: SPOT CHECK Give students a list of five additional regular verbs, such as *pull, wave, sip, marry,* and *pounce.* Have them write the principal parts of these verbs on index cards. Then have students exchange cards with a neighbor and check the accuracy of each other's verb forms and spelling.

All verb tenses are made from the three **principal parts** of a verb: present, past, and past participle.

You have seen that every verb has many different forms. All of these different forms are made from just three **principal parts.** Look at the principal parts of the verbs below.

Present	Past	Past Participle
call	called	(have) called
halt	halted	(have) halted
print	printed	(have) printed
watch	watched	(have) watched
review	reviewed	(have) reviewed
carry	carried	(have) carried

The **present** part of the verb is its present tense. Add *-s* to form the singular. The present part used with *will* or *shall* forms the future tense.

The **past** part of the verb is its past tense. The spelling of the past tense of a verb may change if its present form ends in *y* or a consonant such as *-h, -d, -p,* or *-t.* For example, the past of *worry* is *worried;* the past of *snap* is *snapped.*

The **past participle** is always used with a helping verb such as *have.* Look at these other examples.

is called	has called	was being called
was called	have called	has been called
were called	had called	will have called
		will be called
		should have been called

Notice that with regular verbs, the past participle is the same as the past form. This is not always true of irregular verbs. You will learn more about the principal parts of irregular verbs later in this handbook.

Practice Your Skills

A. CONCEPT CHECK

Principal Parts of Verbs   Make three columns: *Present, Past,* and *Past Participle.* Write each of the following words in the *Present* column. Then write the past and past participle forms in their columns. Choose helping verbs to include with the past participles.

1. try	**6.** record	**11.** flub
2. produce	**7.** plan	**12.** vary
3. hurry	**8.** play	**13.** pick
4. act	**9.** edit	**14.** rehearse
5. learn	**10.** accept	**15.** shop

B. DRAFTING SKILL

Using the Principal Parts of Verbs   Write each sentence using the verb form given in parentheses.

16. Movies (past participle of *enjoy,* with *are*) by millions of people everywhere.
17. Movie making (present of *involve*) hundreds of people, from actors to costume designers to electricians.
18. Of course, no film ever (past of *start*) without a "property," or idea for a story.
19. The screenwriter's job never (present of *end*).
20. Scripts (past participle of *change,* with *must be*) often.
21. The director (present of *plan*) every detail.
22. His orders (past participle of *carry,* with *are*) out by the cast and crew.
23. For example, stunts (past participle of *practice,* with *should be*) many times for safety's sake.
24. In the past, stunt performers often (past of *injure*) themselves.
25. Today, safety equipment and procedures (present of *protect*) most stunt performers from harm during filming.

Writing Theme
Making Movies

FOR MORE PRACTICE
See page 425.

Understanding Verbs **413**

Additional Resource
Grammar and Usage Practice Book, p. 29

Writing Theme: Making Movies
Other related areas students might wish to explore as writing topics include the following:
- special effects in today's movies
- the role of the film editor
- changing black-and-white movies to color
- movies targeted for a young audience

Answers to Practice Your Skills

A. Concept Check
Principal Parts of Verbs

Helping verbs with the past participles may vary.

Present	Past	Past Participle
1. try	tried	(have) tried
2. produce	produced	(was) produced
3. hurry	hurried	(has) hurried
4. act	acted	(have) acted
5. learn	learned	(were) learned
6. record	recorded	(has) recorded
7. plan	planned	(are) planned
8. play	played	(will be) played
9. edit	edited	(had) edited
10. accept	accepted	(is) accepted
11. flub	flubbed	(have) flubbed
12. vary	varied	(have been) varied
13. pick	picked	(will have) picked
14. rehearse	rehearsed	(was) rehearsed
15. shop	shopped	(has) shopped

B. Drafting Skill
Using the Principal Parts of Verbs

Student answers should be in complete sentences.
16. are enjoyed
17. involves
18. started
19. ends
20. must be changed
21. plans
22. are carried
23. should be practiced
24. injured
25. protect

Objectives
- To identify the three principal parts of irregular verbs

Writing
- To use irregular verbs correctly in a piece of writing

Teaching Strategies

KEY TO UNDERSTANDING: IRREGULAR VERBS Tell students that verbs are irregular when they do not form the past tense by adding -d or -ed. To help students see the difference between regular and irregular verbs, write on the board the principal parts of the six regular verbs from the list on page 412 and six irregular verbs from the chart on page 415, and ask students to compare the forms.

MODELING Show students how to find the principal parts of irregular verbs. For example, have them look up the word *buy* in a dictionary. Point out and identify past tense and participle forms.

STUMBLING BLOCK Tell students that there are a few irregular verbs whose present tense, past tense, and past participle forms are the same. Write examples of these forms—such as *let, put, set, hit,* and *shut*—on the board. Tell students that the context in which a verb is used is the only clue as to whether the verb is in the past or the present tense. Give some examples of these verbs in sentences, such as "I always *let* (present) my hair grow in the winter" and "Yesterday I *let* (past) my dog run without his leash." Then have students offer some examples of their own in which the context indicates the present or past tense.

For some verbs, the past tense is formed by changing the spelling of the present form. These verbs are called **irregular verbs.**

You have already learned that the past form of all regular verbs is made by adding either -*d* or -*ed* to the present form of the verbs.

| race | rac*ed* | jump | jump*ed* | dip | dipp*ed* |

Some verbs, however, have past forms that are made by changing the spelling of the present form. These verbs are **irregular verbs.** Here are some examples.

| run | *ran* | sing | *sang* | go | *went* |

Sometimes, the past participle of an irregular verb is the same as the past form.

| said | *(has) said* | taught | *(have) taught* |

However, many irregular verbs have past participle forms that are different from the past forms.

| threw | *(were) thrown* | swam | *(have) swum* |

Remember these rules whenever you use regular or irregular verbs.

1. The past form of a verb is always used alone without a helping verb.

   The athlete *drank* the entire container of water.

2. The past participle must always be used with a helping verb.

   The athlete *had drunk* the entire container of water during the time out.

Here is a list of the principal parts of the most common irregular verbs. Refer to it whenever you are unsure about the proper form of an irregular verb. In addition, dictionaries list the principal parts of irregular verbs after the present form.

Principal Parts of Common Irregular Verbs

Present	Past	Past Participle
begin	began	(have) begun
break	broke	(have) broken
bring	brought	(have) brought
choose	chose	(have) chosen
come	came	(have) come
do	did	(have) done
drink	drank	(have) drunk
eat	ate	(have) eaten
fall	fell	(have) fallen
fly	flew	(have) flown
freeze	froze	(have) frozen
give	gave	(have) given
go	went	(have) gone
grow	grew	(have) grown
know	knew	(have) known
lay	laid	(have) laid
lie	lay	(have) lain
ride	rode	(have) ridden
rise	rose	(have) risen
run	ran	(have) run
say	said	(have) said
see	saw	(have) seen
sing	sang	(have) sung
sit	sat	(have) sat
speak	spoke	(have) spoken
steal	stole	(have) stolen
swim	swam	(have) swum
take	took	(have) taken
teach	taught	(have) taught
wear	wore	(have) worn
write	wrote	(have) written

CRITICAL THINKING: CLASSIFYING Point out to students that it may help them to master the chart of irregular verbs if they look for similar patterns of irregular forms. For example, *break, broke, broken* shows a pattern of changes similar to that of *speak, spoke, spoken*. Challenge students to identify other patterns, such as *teach, taught, taught* and *bring, brought, brought*. Have teams work on forming mini-lists of verbs with similar forms. Have students share their lists and quiz each other on the principal parts of verbs with similar forms.

INDIVIDUALIZING INSTRUCTION: ESL STUDENTS For many ESL students, it is frustrating to learn a language that always seems to "break the rules." Past tense irregular verb forms are especially difficult for these students because each form must be memorized separately. Pair ESL students with native English speakers to practice irregular verb forms orally. Below are some additional irregular verb forms that will be useful for ESL students to learn.

drive-drove	read-read
feel-felt	send-sent
forget-forgot	sleep-slept
lose-lost	tell-told
make-made	think-thought

Writing Theme: Record-setting Feats
Other related areas students might wish to explore as writing topics include the following:
• Charles Lindbergh, aviator
• Olympic records
• the *Guinness Book of World Records*
• baseball statistics

Answers to Practice Your Skills
A. Concept Check
Irregular Verbs

1. done	**9.** came
2. said	**10.** worn
3. chose	**11.** known
4. ran	**12.** lay
5. went	**13.** fell
6. broken	**14.** rose
7. taught	**15.** drunk
8. began	

B. Proofreading Skill
Using Irregular Verbs Correctly
Errors are shown on page. The correctly rewritten paragraph appears below.

In 1926, Gertrude Ederle stole the world's heart. She gave her best effort to a daunting task. At age nineteen, she swam the English Channel. Her time broke all previous records. The feat took fourteen hours and thirty-nine minutes. Other swimmers had nearly frozen in the cold water. Gertrude, however, wore a heavy coat of grease for warmth. Reporters had flown in from all over the world for the event. Some rode next to her in rowboats. In their articles, the reporters wrote about Gertrude's victory and sang her praises for the Olympic medals she had won earlier.

FOR MORE PRACTICE
See page 426.

Practice Your Skills

A. CONCEPT CHECK

Irregular Verbs   Write the correct form of the verb given in parentheses.

1. How many athletes have (past participle of *do*) what was thought to be impossible?
2. How many have (past participle of *say*), "I can do it"?
3. Sarah Covington-Fulcher (past of *choose*) a challenge that many believed impossible.
4. She (past of *run*) perhaps the longest distance ever.
5. She (past of *go*) 11,134 miles through 35 states.
6. Earlier records had now been (past participle of *break*).
7. This runner (past of *teach*) a lesson in endurance.
8. Her race (past of *begin*) on July 21, 1987.
9. It (past of *come*) to an end on October 2, 1988.
10. Twenty-six pairs of shoes were (past participle of *wear*) out during her run.
11. Could she have (past participle of *know*) the hazards?
12. Hazards, indeed, (past of *lie*) in wait along the route.
13. Once, the temperature (past of *fall*) way below zero!
14. In the desert, it (past of *rise*) to 124 degrees!
15. She must have (past participle of *drink*) lots of water!

B. PROOFREADING SKILL

Using Irregular Verbs Correctly   Write the paragraph. Correct all <u>errors</u>, especially those in the use of irregular verbs. (18 errors)

In 1926, gertrude ederle <u>stealed</u> the <u>worlds'</u> heart. She gave her best effort to a daunting task. At age <u>ninteen</u>, she <u>swum</u> the English Channel. Her time <u>breaked</u> all previous records<u>,</u> The feat <u>taked</u> fourteen hours and thirty-nine minutes. Other <u>Swimmers</u> had nearly frozen in the cold water. Gertrude, however, <u>weared</u> a heavy coat of <u>greese</u> for warmth. Reporters had <u>flew</u> in from all over the world for the event. Some <u>rided</u> next to her in rowboats. In <u>they're</u> articles, the reporters wrote about Gertrude's victory. <u>And</u> <u>singed</u> her praises for the Olympic <u>meddals</u> she had won earlier.

CHECK ✔ POINT

Write the correct form of the regular or irregular verb given in parentheses.

Writing Theme
Niagara Falls

1. Have you ever (saw, seen) Niagara Falls?
2. Each year, millions (visit, visited) the falls.
3. The water (runs, ran) violently over a rocky cliff.
4. Over time, the falls actually have (grew, grown) smaller.
5. Water (worn, wears) away part of the cliff.
6. This erosion (stolen, steals) an average of three inches from the cliff each year.
7. Still, water has (rush, rushed) over the cliff since the end of the Ice Age.
8. Visitors have (tell, told) of many amazing sights at Niagara.
9. Several times, for example, the falls have (freeze, frozen) in extremely cold weather.
10. Daredevils have also (try, tried) spectacular stunts.
11. Some have (went, gone) over the falls in barrels.
12. Most of them (fell, fallen) to disastrous ends.
13. A few, however, have (swam, swum) to safety.
14. In the 1800s, a famous French tightrope artist (gave, given) his greatest performance at Niagara.
15. People (came, come) from all over to see Blondin's performance.
16. Blondin (crossed, cross) above the falls on a thin wire several times.
17. During one crossing, he (wore, worn) a blindfold.
18. Another time, he (carried, carry) a man on his back.
19. At one point, he (sat, sit) calmly on the wire and (eat, ate) an omelet!
20. Officials have since (pass, passed) laws against such stunts.

Understanding Verbs **417**

Objectives

- To choose the correct form of these verbs: *can, may; let, leave; lie, lay*

Writing

- To use these verbs correctly in sentences

Teaching Strategies

KEY TO UNDERSTANDING: *CAN* AND *MAY* You may wish to share one or more of these notes with students: (a) *can* and *may* are almost always used as helping verbs; (b) while *can* has a past tense *(could)*, *may* is used only in the present tense; (c) *can* is often substituted for *may* in informal speech and dialogue. Point out, however, that it is important to use *can* and *may* correctly in formal writing.

INDIVIDUALIZING INSTRUCTION: VISUAL LEARNERS Encourage each student to think of a sentence for one of the following verbs: *can, may, let, leave, lie,* and *lay.* The sentence should be one that can be illustrated on a poster; for example, "You can stop forest fires." Then invite the students to create posters illustrating their sentences. Displaying the posters in the classroom will provide visual reinforcement of correct usage.

CONFUSING PAIRS OF VERBS

Several pairs of verbs are often confused. These include **can** and **may, let** and **leave,** and **lie** and **lay.**

Look at the correct way to use these confusing verbs.

Can and May

1. *Can* means "to be able."
2. *May* means "to be allowed to," "to be permitted to," or "to have the possibility of."

> Can you walk a tightrope?
> You may go to the circus.

Let and Leave

1. *Let* means "to allow" or "to permit."
2. *Leave* means "to depart" or "to let stay or let be."

Principal Parts   let, let, let
                            leave, left, left

> *Let* me see your ticket.
> What time do you *leave* for the show?
> Do not *leave* your ticket behind.

Lie and Lay

1. *Lie* means "to rest" or "to recline."
2. *Lay* means "to put or place something."

Principal Parts   lie, lay, lain
                            lay, laid, laid

> The elephant *lies* down upon command.
> The clown *lays* a red carpet in the ring.

Lay also means "to produce eggs": A hen *lays* eggs.

Practice Your Skills

A. CONCEPT CHECK

Confusing Verbs Write the <u>correct verb</u> from those given in parentheses.

1. I had just (laid, <u>lain</u>) down on the sofa for a nap.
2. Children's cries outside did not (<u>let</u>, leave) me sleep.
3. "(Can, <u>May</u>) I go to the circus?" cried a boy.
4. A girl cried, "(Leave, <u>Let</u>) me go too!"
5. I (<u>can</u>, may) imagine these same cries in ancient Rome.
6. The Romans (<u>laid</u>, lay) the foundations for the circus.
7. The circus's past also (<u>lies</u>, lays) in fairs and markets.
8. In the markets, vendors (lain, <u>laid</u>) out their goods.
9. I (<u>can</u>, may) picture the people shopping.
10. Vendors rarely (let, <u>left</u>) their stands.
11. Other people, though, would (lie, <u>lay</u>) down their purchases and watch jugglers, magicians, and minstrels.
12. Later, the idea of a market as a fair was (<u>left</u>, let) behind.
13. Fairs became separate celebrations that (left, <u>let</u>) people have fun.
14. People would (lie, <u>lay</u>) their troubles aside and laugh.
15. I (<u>can</u>, may) see why the children want to go to the circus!

B. REVISION SKILL

Using Verbs Correctly For each sentence, if a verb is incorrect, write the correct verb. If a verb is correct, write *Correct*.

16. Have you ever laid down with a ball on your nose?
17. Graduates of National Circus Project workshops claim they may juggle and perform other circus stunts.
18. Many schools let project members work with students.
19. The circus performers arrive and lie out the equipment.
20. They do not let students alone while learning.
21. Instead, they let students learn tricks and stunts.
22. Some find they may juggle balls easily after only one lesson.
23. For others, many balls still fall and lay on the floor.
24. By the time instructors leave, students feel confident.
25. Sometimes, schools may invite promising students back.

FOR MORE PRACTICE
See page 426.

Additional Resource
Grammar and Usage Practice Book, p. 36

Writing Theme
The Circus

Writing Theme: The Circus
Other related areas students might wish to explore as writing topics include the following:
- circus clowns
- big cats in circus acts
- circus buildings in ancient Rome
- the career of P.T. Barnum

Answers to Practice Your Skills

A. Concept Check
Confusing Verbs
  Answers are shown on page.

B. Revision Skill
Using Verbs Correctly
16. lain
17. can juggle
18. Correct
19. lay
20. leave
21. Correct
22. can juggle
23. lie
24. Correct
25. Correct

7. The <u>Falkland Islands</u> <u>lay</u> about three hundred miles to the <u>East</u> of
     A   **B**   **C**

Argentina. <u>No error</u>
          D

8. A woman in <u>Leeds, England</u>, is named <u>Ann Chovy can</u> you imagine having
             A   **B**

the name of a pizza <u>topping</u>. <u>No error</u>
               C   **D**

9. The tallest sea mountain <u>raises</u> 28,500 feet above the <u>ocean</u> floor. Yet its
                     A   **B**

peak is still 1,200 feet below the <u>water's</u> surface. <u>No error</u>
                     C   **D**

10. Shakespeare <u>wrote</u> *<u>The Merry Wives of Windsor</u>* in <u>fourteen</u> days. <u>No error</u>
           A   **B**   **C**   **D**

11. <u>Knifes</u> have been around much longer than <u>forks before</u> the invention
     A   **B**

of these tools, people ate with <u>their</u> fingers. <u>No error</u>
                     C   **D**

12. You probably don't think of <u>tomatoes</u> and <u>potatos</u> as foreign foods, but
                     A   **B**

originally the natives of South America <u>grown</u> them. <u>No error</u>
                     C   **D**

13. Famous authors have <u>wrote</u> many books on <u>typewriters, but</u> Mark Twain
                 A   **B**

was the first. <u>he</u> typed *The Adventures of Tom Sawyer* himself. <u>No error</u>
            C   **D**

14. We <u>seen</u> several camels in the <u>zoo's</u> Asian exhibit. One <u>drunk</u> a whole
      A   **B**   **C**

bucket of water while we watched. <u>No error</u>
                        D

15. Don't <u>raise</u> the curtain yet. <u>Niether</u> of the <u>pianoes</u> is working. <u>No error</u>
       A   **B**   **C**   **D**

Objective

- To use a photograph and writing prompts as springboards to informal writing

WRITING WARM-UPS

Begin by reminding students that they will not be graded on these sketchbook activities. The writing prompts and the photograph are intended as springboards to get students thinking imaginatively about the concepts in the handbook. Unless students volunteer to explore more than one prompt, have them work on a single response.

- You're in a baseball stadium when the home team scores the winning run. What happens? How does the crowd react?

- Tell about a time you were in a crowded place. It might have been a stadium, a theater, an elevator—anyplace where people are close together. Describe what you and the people around you were doing.

434

Understanding Pronouns

- **Pronouns and Antecedents**

- **Using Subject Pronouns**

- **Using Object Pronouns**

- **Possessive Pronouns**

- **Indefinite Pronouns**

A good team needs more than just starting players. It also needs substitute players on the bench who can come in to give the starters a rest. Nouns and pronouns work like a team too. You can use pronouns in your sentences as substitutes for nouns.

This handbook explains how pronouns can take the place of nouns and make your writing smoother and less repetitious.

Understanding Pronouns

Objectives
- To define pronouns and to identify pronouns and their antecedents in sentences
- To use pronouns correctly as subjects of sentences
- To use pronouns correctly after linking verbs
- To use pronouns correctly as objects in sentences
- To identify possessive pronouns and to use them correctly
- To distinguish between possessive pronouns and contractions
- To identify indefinite pronouns
- To use possessive pronouns that agree with indefinite pronoun antecedents

Writing
- To make writing smoother by using pronouns to avoid repetition of nouns and noun phrases
- To recognize errors and use pronouns correctly in writing

INTRODUCING THE HANDBOOK
You might ask students to discuss why teams need substitutes. (Regular players may get injured or overtired or may simply have a bad game.) Point out that just as a coach may want to replace an athlete, a writer may need to replace a word. If the same noun is used again and again in a short passage, the reader will find it monotonous.

Fortunately, there is a type of word that the writer can call upon to substitute for the overused noun. Introduce the term *pronoun;* tell students that they are about to study different kinds of pronouns and learn how to use them correctly.

Objectives
- To identify pronouns and their antecedents
- To use pronouns that agree in number with their antecedents

Writing
- To substitute pronouns for overused nouns in writing

Teaching Strategies

HELPFUL HINT: GENDER Explain that sometimes the gender of a singular antecedent is not stated. In such cases, the pronoun phrases *he or she* or *his or her* should be used. For example:

An *artist* may choose to frame *his or her* work in a variety of ways.

PRONOUNS AND ANTECEDENTS

A **pronoun** is a word used in place of a noun. An **antecedent** is the word or words a pronoun stands for.

Read these sentences:

Leo made *Leo's* own flip book so *Leo* could play with the book.

Leo made *his* own flip book so *he* could play with *it*.

The second sentence is less awkward than the first because some nouns have been replaced with pronouns. *His, he,* and *it* are **pronouns.** Pronouns take their meaning from the words they replace. *His* and *he* refer to *Leo. It* refers to *book.*

The word a pronoun stands for is the **antecedent** of the pronoun. In the examples above, *Leo* is the antecedent of both the pronouns *his* and *he. Book* is the antecedent of *it.*

Two nouns may also serve as the antecedent of a pronoun.

Leo and *Iris* made many flip books for *their* friends.
(*Leo* and *Iris* are both antecedents of *their.*)

Note that when a pronoun refers to the person speaking, there may not be a stated antecedent.

I flip the pages to make the characters move.

In most sentences, a pronoun appears after its antecedent. However, sometimes a pronoun and its antecedent may appear in separate sentences.

The *artists* arrived. *They* displayed *their* work.
(*Artists* is the antecedent of *They* and *their.*)

Sometimes the antecedent of a pronoun is another pronoun.

Did *you* watch Leo's cartoon in *your* room?
(*You* is the antecedent of the pronoun *your.*)

Literature Connection

Stress that good writers use pronouns to make their writing less repetitious and wordy. Have students identify the pronouns (underlined here) in this passage from *My Friend Flicka* by Mary O'Hara.

"Nell McLaughlin saw the change in Kennie and <u>her</u> hopes rose. <u>He</u> went to <u>his</u> books in the morning with determination and really studied. . . . Examples in arithmetic were neatly written out and, as <u>she</u> passed <u>his</u> door before breakfast, <u>she</u> often heard the monotonous drone of <u>his</u> voice as <u>he</u> read <u>his</u> American history aloud."

Pronouns can be either singular or plural. Pronouns may be used to refer to yourself, to someone you are addressing, or to other persons, places, or things.

Singular Pronouns

Person speaking	I	my, mine	me
Person spoken to	you	your, yours	you
Persons, places, and things spoken about	he	his	him
	she	her, hers	her
	it	its	it

Plural Pronouns

Person speaking	we	our, ours	us
Person spoken to	you	your, yours	you
Persons, places, and things spoken about	they	their, theirs	them

Pronoun and Antecedent Agreement

Use a singular pronoun when the antecedent is singular. Use a plural pronoun when the antecedent is plural. This is called making the pronoun **agree** with its antecedent in number.

The *cartoon* (singular) began. *It* (singular) was funny. *People* (plural) laughed. *They* (plural) were amused.

Practice Your Skills

A. CONCEPT CHECK

Pronouns   Write each pronoun in the following sentences. After the pronoun, write its antecedent if one is given.

> EXAMPLE   Cartoons and their creation interest me.
> their, Cartoons; me

1. I enjoy cartoons, but my friends think they are silly.
2. A cartoon may look simple, yet it is complicated to make.
3. At some time in your life, you have probably made your own flip book.

Writing Theme
Animated Cartoons

Understanding Pronouns   **437**

N:
se

Pronouns

..., Pretest, pp. 23–24
Grammar and Usage Practice Book, p. 43
 Grammar Test Generator

Writing Theme: Animated Cartoons

Suggest that students use these exercises as a springboard to writing. Other related areas that they might explore include the following:
- Walt Disney
- computer animation
- careers in art

Answers to Practice Your Skills

A. Concept Check
Pronouns
1. I; my, I; they, cartoons
2. it, cartoon
3. your, you; you; your, you

TEACHER'S LOUNGE

"Sure, I know what a pronoun is. It's a noun that plays for money."

4. We; our, We
5. their, Animators
6. He, Shamus Culhane
7. He, Shamus Culhane; us; his, He
8. they, Artists; them, sketches
9. his, artist; her, artist; its, sheet
10. they, pegs; it, drawing
11. it, table; he, artist; she, artist
12. their, animators
13. they, animators; them, cels
14. his, writer; her, writer; their, Artists
15. them, characters

B. Revision Skill
Substituting Pronouns for Nouns

Tom spends his free time in an animation studio. He is learning the skill of painting animation cels with opaque paint. This skill requires patience. It also requires careful attention to detail. The painter puts the opaque paint in the center of the area to be colored. Then he or she pushes it toward the outside of the area he or she is coloring. His or her hand must be very steady, and the strokes must be smooth. If they are not even, light can show through and ruin the cel. The work is sometimes very boring. To make it more fun, the artists often play practical jokes. They must be alert for upside-down paint jars on their desks or glue on their brushes.

As this work of the animator Arthur Babbitt illustrates, many drawings are necessary to create a simple walking sequence.

FOR MORE PRACTICE
See page 452.

4. We flip the pages and see figures move before our eyes.
5. Animators make their cartoons in a similar way.
6. Shamus Culhane is an animator. He is also an author.
7. He explains animation to us in his book *Animation from Script to Screen*.
8. Artists make many sketches for a simple movement, and they draw them on special sheets.
9. An artist draws his or her ideas on a transparent sheet, called a cel, that has holes along its top.
10. The holes fit on pegs, and they hold each drawing in the same place as the one before it.
11. The drawing table has a light under it, so the artist can see what he or she has drawn before.
12. The animators only draw key movements on their cels.
13. Assistant animators get the cels next, and they draw other movements on them.
14. Artists work closely with a writer, since his or her opinion of their drawings is important.
15. The writer invents characters, and the artists bring them to life.

B. REVISION SKILL

Substituting Pronouns for Nouns   Rewrite the following paragraph. Use pronouns in place of the words in italics to make the sentences flow smoothly.

Tom spends *Tom's* free time in an animation studio. *Tom* is learning the skill of painting animation cels with opaque paint. This skill requires patience. *This skill* also requires careful attention to detail. The painter puts the opaque paint in the center of the area to be colored. Then *the painter* pushes *the opaque paint* toward the outside of the area *the painter* is coloring. *The painter's* hand must be very steady, and the strokes must be smooth. If *the strokes* are not even, light can show through and ruin the cel. The work is sometimes very boring. To make *the work* more fun, the artists often play practical jokes. *Artists* must be alert for upside-down paint jars on *the artists'* desks or glue on *the artists'* brushes.

CHECK ✔ POINT

MIXED REVIEW • PAGES 436–438

APPLICATION IN LITERATURE

Write each pronoun in the following sentences. Write the antecedent of each pronoun if there is one.

1. "First you tell a diary all your secrets, then you publish it!"
   Richard Selzer

2. "Writing is more fun than ever. The longer I write, the easier it gets."
   Isaac Asimov

3. "You must write every single day of your life."
   Ray Bradbury

4. "Keeping a journal helps you get in touch with your own feelings."
   May Sarton

5. "I think writers—especially young writers—should want to read all the books they can get their hands on."
   Raymond Carver

6. "When we write, we make a contract: *My words are addressed to the outside world* . . ."
   Donald Hall

7. "People want to know why I do this, why I write such gross stuff. I like to tell them I have the heart of a small boy—and I keep it in a jar on my desk."
   Stephen King

8. "A writer doesn't so much choose a story as a story chooses him."
   Robert Penn Warren

9. "You were provided with an imagination. Use it. . . . For every new writer, every new year remains unexplored until he or she explores it."
   Irving Wallace

10. "I shoot the moment, capture feelings with my poems."
    Nikki Giovanni

11. "I don't tell; I don't explain. I show; I let my characters talk for me."
    Leo Tolstoy

12. "Sometimes young poets make the mistake of writing about things they think they ought to care about—they write about 'friendship' and 'peace' and the 'avenues of life' instead of about a certain friend, a certain day, a certain street. . . . The simple and particular way you talk with your friends is most likely the way you can best say what you want to."
    Kenneth Koch and Kate Farrell

Writing Theme
Writers on Writing

Understanding Pronouns **439**

CHECK ✔ POINT

MIXED REVIEW · PAGES 449–450

Write the <u>possessive pronoun</u> in parentheses that agrees with each indefinite pronoun.

1. Does anybody you know spend (<u>his or her</u>, their) time watching bats?
2. Many of the visitors come to see (his or her, <u>their</u>) favorite creatures living at Volo Bog near Chicago, Illinois.
3. Almost every one of the bats here makes (<u>its</u>, their) home in an old dairy barn.
4. Several of the visitors plan (his or her, <u>their</u>) evenings to see the bats fly from the dairy barn.
5. Everyone takes (<u>his or her</u>, their) place at sunset.
6. Many set up (his or her, <u>their</u>) cameras to take pictures.
7. Somebody raises (<u>his or her</u>, their) binoculars to get a closer look.
8. Several of the spectators clap (his or her, <u>their</u>) hands and cheer for the furry creatures.
9. Afterward, both of the tour guides give (his or her, <u>their</u>) daily speech about bats.
10. Neither misses (<u>his or her</u>, their) chance to praise bats.
11. Either explains bats' helpfulness in (<u>his or her</u>, their) talk.
12. Very few of the visitors discuss (his or her, <u>their</u>) fear of bats.
13. Nearly everybody shares (<u>his or her</u>, their) belief that bats are not creepy or dangerous.
14. Someone in the group enjoys (<u>his or her</u>, their) job taking care of bats at a nearby zoo.
15. Another has bats in (<u>his or her</u>, their) attic.

Writing Theme
Bats

Understanding Pronouns   **451**

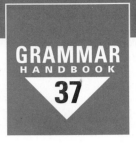

GRAMMAR
HANDBOOK
37

ADDITIONAL PRACTICE

Each of these exercises correlates to a section of Handbook 37, "Understanding Pronouns." The exercises may be used for more practice, for reteaching, or for review of the concepts presented.

Additional Resource

Grammar and Usage Practice Book, p. 49

 Writing Theme:
Water
Other related areas students might wish to explore as writing topics include the following:
• how animals survive in deserts
• glaciers
• how water filtration plants purify drinking water
• acid rain

A. Recognizing Pronouns
1. I; my, I
2. We, friends and I; our, We
3. her, Shinae
4. his, Tim
5. It, fire
6. our, friends and I; us, friends and I
7. them, wranglers
8. You; your, You
9. I; me, I; it, water
10. We; its, water

B. Using Subject Pronouns
   Answers are shown on page.

C. Using Object Pronouns
   Answers are shown on page.

GRAMMAR
HANDBOOK
37

Writing Theme
Water

A. Recognizing Pronouns   Write each pronoun—and its antecedent if there is one—in the following sentences.

1. I went hiking in the desert with my friends.
2. We lost our way in a large canyon.
3. By nightfall, only Shinae had water in her canteen.
4. Tim used his knife to cut scrub for a fire.
5. It was a wonderful fire.
6. Luckily, some wranglers saw our fire and found us.
7. The wranglers always carry extra water with them.
8. "You need a gallon of water for each day of your hike."
9. I only had two quarts of water with me, and it was gone.
10. We learned a lesson about water and its importance.

B. Using Subject Pronouns   Write the correct pronoun given in parentheses.

11. You and (I, me) may never know the secret of an ancient mummy called Otze.
12. (He, him) was found by a German couple.
13. Hiking in the Alps, (they, them) spotted him in a glacier.
14. "(She, Her) and (I, me) saw a human form in the ice."
15. Scientists and (they, them) were puzzled.
16. A frozen mystery was (he, him).
17. (He, Him) died suddenly, but (we, us) don't know why.
18. His tools and (he, him) are being studied.
19. Otze and (they, them) were buried for five thousand years.
20. "(We, Us) scientists are amazed at this discovery."

C. Using Object Pronouns   Write the correct pronoun given in parentheses.

21. Hard water affects (we, us) in many ways.
22. Water does not feel hard to you and (I, me).
23. It has mineral ions. Softeners remove (they, them).
24. Minerals make cloth feel stiff to you and (I, me).
25. These elements also stick to pipes and clog (they, them).
26. In the 1920s, an inventor gave a friend some zeolite and asked (he, him) to filter water through it.

---

27. He did, and it impressed his wife and (he, <u>him</u>).
28. It occurred to (they, <u>them</u>) to wash diapers in it.
29. The diapers felt softer to (she, <u>her</u>) and (he, <u>him</u>).
30. Today, many of (we, <u>us</u>) have soft water in our homes.

D. Using Possessive Pronouns   Write the sentences, correcting errors in possessive pronouns and contractions. If a sentence has no errors, write *Correct*.

31. Without water, its certain that you're going to die.
32. You're body needs water to turn food into energy.
33. Certain life forms do not have you're problem.
34. They're able to go long periods without water.
35. They're bodies shrivel up and look dead.
36. Add water and they regain their shape.
37. Their in a state of cryptobiosis.
38. Its a word that means "hidden life."
39. A life form's ability to "play dead" helps it's survival.
40. It's puzzling to scientists how cryptobiosis works.

E. Using Indefinite Pronouns   Write the correct possessive pronoun from those in parentheses.

41. Everyone is concerned about (<u>his or her</u>, their) future.
42. Many want (his or her, <u>their</u>) environment free of pollution.
43. Nobody wants (<u>his or her</u>, their) planet destroyed.
44. Several of the factories still dump (its, <u>their</u>) garbage.
45. A few of the local farmers spray (his or her, <u>their</u>) crops with poisonous bug spray.
46. Both of these practices have (its, <u>their</u>) dangerous effects on animals and humans.
47. For example, no one wants (<u>his or her</u>, their) drinking water to cause diseases.
48. Anybody worried about (<u>his or her</u>, their) health should try to solve this problem.
49. Someone wrote (<u>his or her</u>, their) solutions in a letter to the editor.
50. Almost everybody has (<u>his or her</u>, their) opinions about how to prevent water pollution.

D. Using Possessive Pronouns
31. Without water, it's certain that you're going to die.
32. Your body needs water to turn food into energy.
33. Certain life forms do not have your problem.
34. Correct
35. Their bodies shrivel up and look dead.
36. Correct
37. They're in a state of cryptobiosis.
38. It's a word that means "hidden life."
39. A life form's ability to "play dead" helps its survival.
40. Correct

E. Using Indefinite Pronouns
   Answers are shown on page.

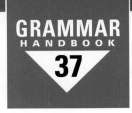

GRAMMAR
HANDBOOK
37

REVIEW

These exercises may be used as a mixed review or as an informal evaluation of the skills presented in Handbook 37, "Understanding Pronouns."

Additional Resources

Grammar and Usage Practice Book, p. 50
Tests and Writing Assessment Prompts, Mastery Test, pp. 25–28
Elaboration, Revision, and Proofreading Practice, p. 26

 Writing Theme: Mapmaking

Other related areas students might wish to explore as writing topics include the following:

- types of world maps
- computers in today's mapmaking
- weather maps
- how to read a road map

A. Finding Pronouns

1. you; your, you
2. his, Magellan
3. It, *Magellan*
4. it, *Magellan* (or satellite); their, Scientists
5. he, Francesco Bianchini
6. our
7. we; them, images
8. it, radar
9. their, scientists
10. We; it, crust

B. Using Subject and Object Pronouns
   Answers are shown on page.

GRAMMAR
HANDBOOK
37

Writing Theme
Mapmaking

A. Finding Pronouns Write the pronouns from the sentences. Then write each pronoun's antecedent if there is one.

1. Do you remember Magellan from your history lessons?
2. Well, a new *Magellan* has taken his place.
3. Modern-day *Magellan* is not a man. It is a satellite.
4. Scientists use it to make their maps of Venus.
5. In 1726, Francesco Bianchini drew the first map of Venus, but he was unable to make an accurate drawing.
6. The planet is hidden by clouds that block our view.
7. However, *Magellan's* radar makes images of Venus, and we can study them.
8. In eight months, it recorded 84 percent of the surface.
9. Now scientists can't make up their minds.
10. We don't know if Venus's crust is thick or if it is thin.

B. Using Subject and Object Pronouns Write the correct pronoun from those given in parentheses.

11. The sea floor is hidden from you and (I, me).
12. (We, Us) creatures of the land need to make maps of it.
13. Sailors mapped the ocean floor. (They, Them) lowered lead weights over the side of the ship.
14. Then mapmakers and (they, them) recorded the depths.
15. Later, the echo sounder gave (we, us) more information.
16. It allowed scientists and (we, us) to measure depths.
17. A mapmaker uses data that are valuable to (he, him) or (she, her).
18. With computers, (he, him) or (she, her) draws maps.
19. You and (I, me) can study the three-dimensional maps.
20. The maps allow (we, us) to see trenches and volcanoes.
21. Better technology is available to mapmakers and (we, us).
22. For example, a sonar device named *Gloria* has helped scientists and (they, them.)
23. A technician lowers this sensitive machine, and it sends (he, him) acoustic, or sound, pictures.
24. *Gloria* and (he, him) receive accurate "snapshots."
25. *Gloria's* pulses of sound fan out to both sides. Each sound wave bounces back to (we, us) from the ocean floor.

26. With computers, a picture appears before you and (I, <u>me</u>).
27. Line by line, the ocean floor is visible to (we, <u>us</u>).
28. Besides you and (I, <u>me</u>), other people also thought the ocean floor was flat.
29. However, *Gloria's* pictures show (they, <u>them</u>) and (we, <u>us</u>) mountains, trenches, and volcanoes.
30. (<u>We</u>, Us) land beings can now see the ocean bottom.

C. Using Possessive Pronouns and Contractions
Write the <u>correct</u> possessive pronoun or contraction for each sentence.

31. (Your, <u>You're</u>) not going to believe this.
32. Some people still cling to (<u>their</u>, they're) belief in a flat earth.
33. (Their, <u>They're</u>) known as the Flat Earth Society.
34. (<u>Its</u>, It's) leaders scorn all satellite pictures.
35. (Their, <u>They're</u>) sure the pictures are fakes.
36. They also scorn the moon landing and question (<u>its</u>, it's) truth.
37. According to them, (its, <u>it's</u>) a Hollywood trick.
38. Are you going to change (<u>your</u>, you're) mind?
39. Will you start (<u>your</u>, you're) subscription to the *Flat Earth News*?
40. (Your, <u>You're</u>) sure the earth is a sphere, right?

D. Using Indefinite Pronouns
Write the following sentences and correct all errors in agreement. If a sentence has no errors, write *Correct*.

41. Almost everyone checks their maps before a trip.
42. Many will even plot his or her route carefully.
43. If no one had their maps, would anyone travel?
44. Somebody had to take his or her chances and explore the unknown.
45. Each of the early explorers made maps for their country.
46. Several made their observations with instruments.
47. Not everybody knew how to use his or her tools well.
48. A few relied only on his compass and surveyor's chain.
49. Either of these instruments proved their value on expeditions.
50. However, neither was known for their accuracy.

C. Using Possessive Pronouns and Contractions
Answers are shown on page.

D. Using Indefinite Pronouns
41. Almost everyone checks his or her maps before a trip.
42. Many will even plot their route carefully.
43. If no one had his or her maps, would anyone travel?
44. Correct
45. Each of the early explorers made maps for his or her country.
46. Correct
47. Correct
48. A few relied only on their compass and surveyor's chain.
49. Either of these instruments proved its value on expeditions.
50. However, neither was known for its accuracy.

51. Correct
52. Correct
53. Anything used as a tool is given its own name.
54. Many of these tools, such as Gunter's chain, get their names from their inventors.
55. Anyone can learn to use his or her tools for mapping.

E. Proofreading

Errors are shown on page. The correctly rewritten paragraphs appear below.

56 The chances of discovering buried treasure in your back yard are slim. **57** You and I find secret maps and treasure only in adventure stories. **58** Correct **59** All that we treasure hunters have to do is bury some valuable-looking objects. **60** Marcus, Jen, and I have done this for fun. **61** Correct **62** Marcus and she found an antique watch and rhinestone costume jewelry. **63** Everybody searched his or her neighborhood for an old object that we could use as a treasure chest. **64** Someone had thrown away his or her old silverware, bowls, and other kitchen things. **65** Correct **66** Jen and I were in charge of figuring out distances. **67** She and I used a yardstick to measure the length and width of our back yard. **68** It's not very big. **69** This part of our plan was easy for her and me to do. **70** Correct **71** Next, Jen and Marcus drew a grid on their graph paper. **72** Jen and he added symbols to represent things in the back yard, such as the elm tree, the rosebushes, and the toolshed. **73** Their grid and map symbols looked pretty good. **74** It was up to Jen and him to pick the burial spot. **75** No one will guess it in his or her whole lifetime. **76** They're really excited about our secret burial ceremony!

---

51. Another was the astrolabe. Its purpose was to help explorers navigate at sea.
52. One could calculate his or her position by measuring the angles of stars above the horizon.
53. Anything used as a tool is given their own name.
54. Many of these tools, such as Gunter's chain, get its names from its inventors.
55. Anyone can learn to use their tools for mapping.

E. Proofreading

Rewrite the following sentences and correct all errors in the use of pronouns. If a sentence has no errors, write *Correct*.

56 The chances of discovering buried treasure in you're back yard are slim. **57** You and me find secret maps and treasure only in adventure stories. **58** Yet treasure can really be ours.

59 All that us treasure hunters have to do is bury some valuable-looking objects. **60** Marcus, Jen, and me have done this for fun. **61** They had the idea first. **62** Marcus and her found an antique watch and rhinestone costume jewelry. **63** Everybody searched their neighborhood for an old object that we could use as a treasure chest. **64** Someone had thrown away their old silverware, bowls, and other kitchen things. **65** Among them, we found an airtight container that was just the right size.

66 Jen and me were in charge of figuring out distances. **67** Her and I used a yardstick to measure the length and width of our back yard. **68** Its not very big. **69** This part of our plan was easy for she and me to do. **70** Then we made a scale for our map: one inch equaled one foot. **71** Next, Jen and Marcus drew a grid on they're graph paper. **72** Jen and him added symbols to represent things in the back yard, such as the elm tree, the rosebushes, and the toolshed. **73** They're grid and map symbols looked pretty good. **74** It was up to Jen and he to pick the burial spot. **75** No one will guess it in their whole lifetime. **76** Their really excited about our secret burial ceremony!

WRITING CONNECTIONS

Elaboration, Revision, and Proofreading

Revise the following draft of a friendly letter by using the directions below. Then proofread the letter for errors in the use of pronouns. Also correct any other errors in grammar, capitalization, punctuation, and spelling.

Dear Martin,

¹We had a great time on our vacation in arizona. ²My favrite place was Canyon de Chelly National Monument. ³First we drove along the rim of the canyon and looked at the scenery. ⁴Then Chuck and me went down a trail into the canyon. ⁵It cut back and fourth for about a mile, finally, we reached a stream at the bottom. ⁶Taking off our shoes and socks, we waded through the stream. ⁷On the other side, we saw the ruins of a village. ⁸Parts of the village were built into the cliff. ⁹There are other cliff dwellings at Mesa Verde National Park in Colorado. ¹⁰Some of the buildings still have all they're walls. ¹¹Even now the ruins look beatiful. ¹²Chuck and me wish you could have been there with us to see it.

Your friend,
Rick

1. In sentence 4, replace the weak verb "went" with the more precise verb "hiked."

2. Replace the vague pronoun "it" in sentence 5 with the more precise noun "the trail."

3. Add details to sentence 6 by describing the stream as "cool and clear."

4. Add this information after sentence 7: "The Anasazi Indians built the village about one thousand years ago."

5. Delete the sentence that doesn't belong.

Personal and Expressive Writing

Writing a friendly letter is a good way to share your feelings and experiences with others. (See Workshop 1.) When you revise a letter you have written, make sure you present all of the details your reader will want to know. By using pronouns effectively, you can make your writing flow smoothly and present information clearly.

WRITING CONNECTIONS

Elaboration, Revision, and Proofreading

This activity will allow your students to see some of the concepts presented in this Handbook at work in a piece of personal and expressive writing. By revising and proofreading this friendly letter, students will have the opportunity to replace vague pronouns with precise nouns, to use elaboration, and to correct errors in pronoun use.

You may wish to have students revise the passage independently, then meet in small groups for peer review. Then briefly discuss the changes as a class. Revisions may vary slightly. A typical revision is shown below. Elements involving change are shown in boldface.

Dear Martin,

We had a great time on our vacation in Arizona. My favorite place was Canyon de Chelly National Monument. First we drove along the rim of the canyon and looked at the scenery. Then Chuck and I **hiked** down a trail into the canyon. **The trail** cut back and forth for about a mile. Finally, we reached a stream at the bottom. Taking off our shoes and socks, we waded through the **cool and clear** stream. On the other side, we saw the ruins of a village. **The Anasazi Indians built the village about one thousand years ago.** Parts of the village were built into the cliff. ~~There are other cliff dwellings at Mesa Verde National Park in Colorado.~~ Some of the buildings still have all their walls. Even now the ruins look beautiful. Chuck and I wish you could have been there with us to see them.

Your friend,
Rick

Objective

• To use writing prompts and fine art as springboards to informal writing

WRITING WARM-UPS

Remind students that this assignment will not be graded. The art and writing prompts aim to help students begin thinking in a broad, imaginative way about the concepts in this Handbook. Unless students express an interest in more than one prompt, ask them to explore just one of these ideas.

For the first writing prompt, invite volunteers to suggest vivid words that describe Calder's creature. Have students close their eyes and imagine what it would look like in motion and how it would sound. Urge them to use such vivid words in writing their descriptions.

For the second writing prompt, remind students that a tall tale uses exaggeration to provide humor and entertainment. Point out that students' tall tales might make humorous exaggerations relating to size. Ask students to think about how the subject's size would affect movement, and how this person or thing might get along with people in an ordinary-sized world.

For the third writing prompt, tell students to focus on physical details. For example, ask students what they would do to avoid getting stepped on, if they were much smaller than everyone around them. How would they get enough to eat? Where would they go to get out of the rain? What other advantages or disadvantages would they have?

• Imagine you see this creature walking down the street. Write a vivid description so your readers will be able to see it too.

Chock (1972), Alexander Calder.

• Tell a tall tale about someone or something that is unusually big or small.

• Imagine that like Alice in Wonderland or Gulliver in the land of Lilliput, you have suddenly arrived in a place where you are much bigger or much smaller than all the things and people around you. Briefly describe your experience.

458

ART NOTE

Alexander Calder (1898–1976), the creator of the mobile, is famous for introducing motion into sculpture. Born near Philadelphia, Calder grew up in a family of artists and was making wire sculptures when he was only five. Later he studied engineering and attended art school in New York City and Paris. His first important works—such as an amusing wood carving called *The Flattest Cat*—often drew inspiration from the animal kingdom. In 1931 Calder devised his first mobile, or sculpture with moving parts. He created large and small mobiles, many of them for outdoor display.

Understanding Adjectives

- **What Are Adjectives?**
- **Kinds of Adjectives**
- **Articles and Demonstrative Adjectives**
- **Predicate Adjectives**
- **Making Comparisons with Adjectives**

Click! A photographer captures an image on film. The color, the texture, the size, the detail—all make whatever the camera records seem very real. Yet a writer can do even more. A writer can capture and share the way something feels, sounds, tastes, and smells.

Adjectives help writers create clear, detailed, lively images. In this handbook you will learn how to recognize adjectives and use them to add color and precision to your writing and speaking.

Understanding Adjectives **459**

Understanding Adjectives

Objectives
- To identify and use adjectives
- To distinguish between common and proper adjectives
- To determine whether an adjective tells *which one, what kind* or *how many* about a noun or pronoun
- To identify and use articles and demonstrative adjectives correctly
- To recognize predicate adjectives
- To identify and use correctly the comparative and superlative forms of adjectives

Writing
- To use adjectives to make descriptions more vivid and more precise

INTRODUCING THE HANDBOOK
Ask students if they agree with the expression "A picture is worth a thousand words." Elicit that although pictures may vividly capture objects and scenes that we see, writing can also capture what we see, smell, taste, hear, and touch. To illustrate, ask students to describe the smell of a freshly repaired asphalt street, the taste of a pizza, the sound of the classroom as school ends for the day, and how an ice cube feels in their bare hands. Write on the board the adjectives students use in describing these situations. Explain that in this handbook, they will learn how to use adjectives to make their writing vivid and effective.

Objectives

- To identify and use adjectives
- To distinguish between common and proper adjectives

Writing

- To use lively adjectives in writing

Teaching Strategies

STUMBLING BLOCK: PARTICIPLES
Students may have difficulty recognizing *aching* and *bruised* as adjectives. Point out that any word that describes a noun or pronoun is functioning as an adjective. Have students identify the noun or pronoun that *aching* and *bruised* modify. *(rider)* Then give students additional examples of similar forms:

I ate the *baked* potato.

The *bucking* broncos were angry.

Finally, ask students to generate their own examples of this type of adjective.

INDIVIDUALIZING INSTRUCTION: BASIC STUDENTS You may want to reinforce the use of proper nouns as adjectives by asking students to create sentences illustrating noun and adjective use of the sample words *African, Wyoming,* and *Independence Day.* (Samples: An *African* [noun] visited our school. Our *African* [adjective] visitor came from Senegal.)

Additional Resources

Tests and Writing Assessment
  Prompts, Pretest, pp. 29–30
Grammar and Usage Practice Book,
  p. 51

 Grammar
Test Generator

Writing
─ TIP ─

If a noun is used as a describer, it becomes an adjective. In the sentence "I need *ham* for my *ham* sandwich," the word *ham* is used first as a noun and then as an adjective.

W HAT ARE ADJECTIVES?

An **adjective** is a word that modifies, or describes, a noun or a pronoun.

Look at these sentences:

A bull charged around the arena.
An angry bull charged around the hot, dusty arena.

What words in the second sentence tell you more about the bull and the arena? *Angry* describes *bull. Hot* and *dusty* tell about the *arena.* Each word adds more specific information to the sentence.

These words are **adjectives.** Adjectives describe, or modify, nouns and pronouns.

Adjectives may be placed before or after a noun or pronoun. Two or more adjectives modifying the same word sometimes need to be separated with commas. Use a comma after each adjective except the last one.

The *young, startled* cowpoke tumbled from the saddle.

Adjectives may also follow the word they modify.

This rider, *aching* and *bruised,* limped from the arena.

Proper Adjectives

Some adjectives, such as *Texan,* are made by adding endings to proper nouns. These are called **proper adjectives.**

Always begin a proper adjective with a capital letter. Common adjectives, those not formed from proper nouns, are not capitalized.

Africa + *-n* = African   China + *-ese* = Chinese

Other proper adjectives do not have special endings.

Wyoming rodeo   *Independence Day* celebration

Practice Your Skills

A. CONCEPT CHECK

Adjectives For the following sentences, write each adjective and the word it modifies. Label each adjective *Common* or *Proper.* You should find a total of twenty-one adjectives.

1. Cowhands in the brush country of the Southwestern hills are often called vaqueros.
2. Once, the term referred only to Spanish and Mexican cowpunchers.
3. Quickly, however, it came to mean any ranch hands.
4. South American historical records mention cowhands too.
5. For example, an Argentinian cowpoke was a gaucho.
6. Gauchos were good singers and storytellers.
7. Home was often a rough shack made of mud and twigs.
8. A gaucho wore loose white pants, a wool shawl at the waist, a shirt of bright color, and leather boots.
9. The gaucho, strong and brave, no longer exists.
10. Barbed wire ended the reign of this colorful figure.

B. REVISION SKILL

Using Lively Adjectives Careful choice of adjectives can make your writing more interesting. Write the following sentences. Replace each of the underlined overused or vague adjectives with one that is more lively or precise. If a (P) follows the sentence, use a proper adjective.

11. The rodeo, which originated among working cowboys, is a U.S. tradition and a <u>nice</u> contest of skills.
12. Year-round, <u>big</u> crowds file into arenas throughout the United States.
13. Competing can be dangerous, so rodeos attract <u>good</u> riders.
14. Bronc riding and steer wrestling are two <u>good</u> events.
15. Bulls, mean and <u>mad</u>, also provide a challenge for riders.
16. Riding a bucking bull can result in a <u>bad</u> fall.
17. <u>Our</u> rodeos are not the only ones; Canada also has them. (P)
18. <u>Those</u> riders, our neighbors to the north, are also skilled. (P)
19. Cowboys in Mexico have <u>some</u> rodeos, or *charreadas.* (P)
20. Australia has ranches too, and <u>its</u> rodeos are popular. (P)

FOR MORE PRACTICE
See page 475.

Understanding
Adjectives   **461**

Objectives

- To identify and understand the three functions of adjectives

Writing

- To use adjectives with different functions in writing

Teaching Strategies

LINKING GRAMMAR AND WRITING Stress the importance of choosing adjectives that add clarity and interest to writing. Avoid the use of tired, overused adjectives. Have students suggest replacements for the tired adjective *nice* in these phrases: *a nice view, a nice street, a nice day, a nice boy, a nice party.*

INDIVIDUALIZING INSTRUCTION: ESL STUDENTS In Spanish and many other languages, adjectives that tell *what kind* often immediately follow the nouns they modify; in English, they rarely do (except as a predicate adjective or in sentences like "The car, red and shiny, sped away."). Help students understand that constructions such as "the sky blue" and "the woman old" are not used in English.

Additional Resource

Grammar and Usage Practice Book, p. 52

Writing
── **TIP** ──

Notice in "Yomarhi Purnima," pages 62–63, how the author Elizabeth Murphy-Melas uses adjectives to help the reader picture both Nepal and the thanksgiving festival she is describing.

I designed *those three red robot* masks in the *second* row.

KINDS OF ADJECTIVES

An **adjective** modifies a word by telling *what kind, how many,* or *which one.*

Every adjective has one of three functions. It tells *what kind, how many,* or *which one.*

Some Adjectives Tell *What Kind*

Some adjectives describe by telling *what kind.*

The *gold medal* winners waved to the *cheering* crowd from a *twenty-foot-long* float.

Many adjectives that tell *what kind* are formed by adding an adjective ending to a noun.

rain*y*	adventur*ous*
fear*less*	color*ful*
comfort*able*	gold*en*

Some Adjectives Tell *How Many*

Some adjectives limit by telling *how many.*

There are *two* astronauts who orbited the moon *ten* times.

Some Adjectives Tell *Which One*

Some adjectives point out specific members of groups by telling *which one* or *which ones.* Remember that possessive pronouns can be used as adjectives. A complete list of possessive pronouns appears on page 446.

Adjectives that tell *which one* or *how many* almost always come before the words they modify.

That woman riding in the *third* car is *our* senator.

A. Identifying Adjectives Label three columns on your paper *What Kind, How Many,* and *Which One.* Write the adjectives in each sentence in the correct columns. Ignore articles.

1. Before 1600, people didn't have cloth or paper napkins.
2. In those days, even the king went without any napkin at all.
3. However, a wealthy family would own one fine tablecloth.
4. These tablecloths were imported from Damascus in Syria.
5. The famous weavers in Damascus made wonderful tablecloths with marvelous flower and animal patterns.
6. The white cloth had red borders and gold fringe.
7. These expensive tablecloths were part of the royal treasure.
8. Few households could afford them.
9. Picture a gorgeous tablecloth spread on a feast table.
10. In those days, people ate with their fingers.
11. They wiped their greasy hands on the tablecloth.
12. After a few feasts, the lovely tablecloth was a mess.
13. Finally, someone decided to protect these tablecloths.
14. A towel was given to each guest.
15. These towels were the first napkins.

B. Using Articles and Demonstrative Adjectives Write the correct <u>word</u> from the ones given in parentheses.

16. Have you heard (a, <u>the</u>) warning "Don't eat with your fingers"?
17. (<u>This</u>, These) kind of warning would have seemed foolish when people ate everything with their fingers.
18. The use of (<u>a</u>, an) fork for eating began in Asia.
19. (<u>This</u>, These) custom spread to Europe very slowly.
20. By 1500 (<u>these</u>, them) utensils were common in Italy.
21. The English thought the Italians were too dainty and made fun of (those, <u>them</u>).
22. The English had (<u>a</u>, an) humble view that fingers were made to eat with.
23. (<u>This kind</u>, These kinds) of utensil caught on slowly in England and America.
24. A fork was (a, <u>an</u>) unusual item in most homes before 1800.
25. Until then, (<u>a</u>, an) person who used a fork was laughed at.

GRAMMAR
HANDBOOK
38

Writing Theme
Inventions

Understanding
Adjectives   **475**

B. Using Articles and Demonstrative Words
Answers are shown on page.

ADDITIONAL PRACTICE

Each of these exercises correlates to a section of Handbook 38, "Understanding Adjectives." The exercises may be used for practice, for reteaching, or for review of the concepts presented.

> **Additional Resource**
> Grammar and Usage Practice Book, p. 57

 Writing Theme: Inventions
Other related areas students might wish to explore as writing topics include the following:

- the history of a favorite invention
- a "new products" fair
- how to patent an invention
- a much-needed but not-yet-existing invention

A. Identifying Adjectives
Student answers will be in columns.
1. cloth, What Kind; paper, What Kind
2. those, Which One; any, How Many
3. wealthy, What Kind; one, How Many; fine, What Kind
4. These, Which One
5. famous, What Kind; wonderful, What Kind; marvelous, What Kind; flower, What Kind; animal, What Kind
6. white, What Kind; red, What Kind; gold, What Kind
7. These, Which One; expensive, What Kind; royal, What Kind
8. Few, How Many
9. gorgeous, What Kind; feast, What Kind
10. those, Which One; their, Which One
11. their, Which One; greasy, What Kind
12. few, How Many; lovely, What Kind
13. these, Which One
14. each, How Many or Which One
15. These, Which One; first, Which One

C. Identifying Predicate Adjectives

Answers are shown on page. Predicate adjectives are underlined once; the words they modify are underlined twice.

D. Making Comparisons with Adjectives

Answers are shown on page.

C. Identifying Predicate Adjectives   Write the following sentences. Draw one line under the predicate adjective or adjectives and two lines under the word that is modified.

26. Straight pins are very old.
27. Ice Age people were fond of fish-bone pins.
28. During the Bronze Age, people were happier with metal pins similar to today's safety pins.
29. Somehow through the years, the idea behind the efficient Bronze Age safety pin became unclear or lost.
30. Until 1849, straight pins remained popular.
31. That year, Walter Hunt became famous for his "invention," the safety pin.
32. Hunt's future looked bright.
33. However, his bank account remained small.
34. Furthermore, a friend of Hunt's was growing impatient about Hunt's unpaid fifteen-dollar loan.
35. The invention certainly appeared useful and practical.
36. The solution seemed obvious.
37. The friend would become rich from the ownership of the new invention.
38. Hunt would no longer be uncomfortable about his debt.
39. Furthermore, credit for the accomplishment would remain his.
40. Today, anyone with a missing button or a broken zipper is grateful to Walter Hunt.

D. Making Comparisons with Adjectives   Write the correct form of the adjective shown in parentheses.

41. The (earliest, most early) houses did not have windows.
42. Even great castles of the (powerfullest, most powerful) kings had only a hole in the roof of the kitchen to let out smoke from the cooking fire.
43. A window is much (better, best) than a smoke hole.
44. The first windows let some rain in and were (worse, worst) about letting in cold.
45. In later times, they were stuffed with straw or covered with canvas so homes would be (comfortabler, more comfortable) in bad weather.

A. Identifying Adjectives   Write the adjectives that modify each italicized noun in the sentences below. Include articles.

1. How would you like having a creepy *insect* living by your *bed?*
2. Strangely enough, many *people* enjoy having certain *kinds* of insects nearby.
3. These *bugs* that sing are often kept as pets.
4. Crickets and cicadas are two good *examples.*
5. They make wonderful *music.*
6. Chinese, Japanese, and Spanish *people* sometimes keep them.
7. These *owners* love their pets and give them special *care.*
8. Tiny *cages* are made for the *animals.*
9. An *owner* might keep several cricket *cages* near his or her *bed.*
10. The musical *crickets* then sing their *owner* to sleep.

B. Using Adjectives Correctly   Write the correct adjective from those given in parentheses.

11. Imagine waking up to (a, an) alarming cry—"*To-kay!*"
12. Your eyes open and you see a monster straight out of your (worse, worst) nightmare.
13. It's a gray, golden-eyed lizard with red dots, and it stretches a foot long—although right now it looks much (longer, more long).
14. It's staring down at you from (a, the) ceiling over your bed!
15. (Faster, More fast) than lightning, you leap from your bed.
16. But wait—now you remember. (This, That) monster up there is your new pet!
17. It's a tokay gecko, one of the (more common, more commoner) pets in Asia.
18. Some people in the United States like (these, them) unusual animals too.
19. Geckos have the (beautifullest, most beautiful) eyes.
20. They are also (more, most) useful than many other pets.
21. They're (better, more good) hunters than most lizards.
22. Nighttime, when they busily seek insects, finds them (more, most) active than daytime.
23. Most geckos are gentle, but the tokay doesn't like being handled and has the (worse, worst) bite of all.

GRAMMAR
HANDBOOK
38

Writing Theme
Unusual Pets

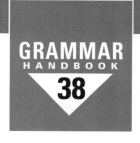

GRAMMAR
HANDBOOK
38

REVIEW

These exercises may be used as a mixed review or as an informal evaluation of the skills presented in Handbook 38, "Understanding Adjectives."

Additional Resources

Grammar and Usage Practice Book, p. 58
Tests and Writing Assessment Prompts, Mastery Test, pp. 31–34
Elaboration, Revision, and Proofreading Practice, p. 27

Writing Theme: Unusual Pets

Other related areas students might wish to explore as writing topics include the following:
- how crickets chirp
- unusual lizards
- mongooses as pets
- unusual pet birds

A. Identifying Adjectives
Answers are shown on page.

B. Using Adjectives Correctly
Answers are shown on page.

Understanding
Adjectives   **477**

C. Correcting Errors with Adjectives

31. What would be the best animal of all to have as a pet?

32. Of all pets, dogs and cats are the most typical.

33. Correct

34. If you're one of those people, you're in good company.

35. Correct

36. Perhaps the oddest was the alligator John Quincy Adams kept in the White House.

37. Those Adamses also kept silkworms.

38. Correct

39. Of all the presidents, Theodore Roosevelt may have had the largest assortment of creatures.

40. Parrots, snakes, lizards, pigeons, pigs, and rats—his children kept all those animals.

41. One of the best stories of all involves the snakes.

42. His son carried four of his newest snakes into a meeting.

43. Senators burst from the room, each trying to run faster than the others.

44. The Kennedy children also had a collection of pets. Theirs were less unusual than those in the Roosevelts' zoo.

45. The Kennedys' most remarkable pets were rabbits and hamsters.

---

24. The tokay is also the (largest, most large) gecko.

25. Because they have thousands of fine hairlike structures on the pads of their feet, (them, these) animals can walk up walls and across ceilings.

26. They can even walk across mirrors, as (this, that) one on the wall over there is doing.

27. Geckos are the (unusualest, most unusual) lizards because they are the only ones that talk.

28. The tokay, in its (loudest, most loud) voice, cries, *"To-kay!"*

29. (A, An) few geckos bark or quack, and some say *"Gecko!"*

30. Can you guess how (those, them) lizards got their name?

C. Correcting Errors with Adjectives Write each of the following sentences, correcting errors in the use of adjectives. If a sentence does not have an error, write *Correct.*

31. What would be the better animal of all to have as a pet?

32. Of all pets, dogs and cats are the more typical.

33. However, some people prefer more unusual animals.

34. If you're one of them people, you're in good company.

35. Some United States presidents chose stranger pets than you'd expect.

36. Perhaps the odder was the alligator John Quincy Adams kept in the White House.

37. Them Adamses also kept silkworms.

38. Silk was one of the costliest fabrics known, and Mrs. Adams's silkworms spun enough silk for her to make a dress.

39. Of all the presidents, Theodore Roosevelt may have had the larger assortment of creatures.

40. Parrots, snakes, lizards, pigeons, pigs, and rats—his children kept all them animals.

41. One of the better stories of all involves the snakes.

42. His son carried four of his most new snakes into a meeting.

43. Senators burst from the room, each trying to run more faster than the others.

44. The Kennedy children also had a collection of pets. Theirs were least unusual than those in the Roosevelts' zoo.

45. The Kennedys' more remarkable pets were rabbits and hamsters.

WRITING CONNECTIONS

Elaboration, Revision, and Proofreading

Revise the following draft of a description, using the directions at the bottom of the page. Then proofread the description, paying special attention to the use of adjectives. Also look for errors in grammar, capitalization, punctuation, and spelling.

¹Every year the recreation center is turned into a Haunted House for Halloween. ²As we approached the building this year, we heard sounds coming from inside. ³We walked to the door and timidly stepped into the dark and gloomy house. ⁴Ahead of us was a zigzag path that led us passed all sorts of creepy things. ⁵Arms reached out and grabed for us as we walked by. ⁶A Monster jumped in our path and then vanished. ⁷Compared to the monster, the swirling ghosts that swooped down from the rafters were definitately creepiest. ⁸A witch zoomed by on a broomstick. ⁹We reached the end. ¹⁰We all agreed this years' haunted house was more better than last years'.

1. Add one or more adjectives to tell what kind of "sounds" in sentence 2.

2. In sentence 5, add two adjectives that tell how the arms looked and felt.

3. In sentence 6, use adjectives to describe what the monster looked like.

4. Make the order of events clearer by adding a transition word to sentences that signal the next event.

5. Add "finally" to the beginning of sentence 9 to indicate the end of the description.

Observation and Description

Descriptive writing provides a chance to create a picture with words. (See Workshop 2.) When you revise descriptive writing, look for ways to use a variety of words that appeal to the senses. Using precise adjectives is one way to make your descriptions come alive.

WRITING CONNECTIONS

Elaboration, Revision, and Proofreading

This activity will allow your students to see some of the concepts presented in this handbook at work in a piece of descriptive writing. By revising and proofreading this passage, students will have the opportunity to improve clarity and elaboration by using precise, vivid adjectives.

You may wish to allow students to work in pairs to revise the passage. After students have completed their revisions, discuss the changes with the class.

Revisions may vary slightly. Errors are underlined on the page. See a typical revision below. Elements involving change and transition words are shown in boldface.

Every year the recreation center is turned into a haunted house for Halloween. As we approached the building this year, we heard **strange, scary** sounds coming from inside. **Then** we walked to the door and timidly stepped into the dark and gloomy house. Ahead of us was a zigzag path that led us past all sorts of creepy things. **Cold and slimy** arms reached out and grabbed for us as we walked by. **Next** a **hairy** monster, **drooling and red-eyed,** jumped in our path and then vanished. Compared to the monster, the swirling ghosts that swooped down from the rafters were definitely creepier. **Then** a witch zoomed by on a broomstick. **Finally** we reached the end. We all agreed this year's haunted house was better than last year's.

Objective

• To use writing prompts and a passage from literature as springboards to informal writing

WRITING WARM-UPS

Tell students that these activities will not be graded. They should have fun with writing while exploring, in an imaginative way, some of the concepts in this handbook. Urge students to choose at least one of the prompts to develop.

For the first writing prompt, explain that *A Connecticut Yankee in King Arthur's Court* is about a New Englander in Mark Twain's day (the late 1800s) who travels back in time to the days of King Arthur. Then have volunteers recall other books, films, or TV shows in which characters travel into the past. Tell students to keep these works in mind as they write.

Sketch Book

WRITING WARM-UPS

"Well, then," I said, "either I am a lunatic or something just as awful has happened. Now tell me, honest and true, where am I?"

"IN KING ARTHUR'S COURT."

I waited a minute, to let that idea shudder its way home, and then said:

"And according to your notions, what year is it now?"

"528— nineteenth of June."

Mark Twain
A CONNECTICUT YANKEE IN KING ARTHUR'S COURT

• What if you woke up one day and you were living in the past? It could be the time of King Arthur's court or the Roman Empire or any other time in history or legend. Write about how you would act, where you would go, and what you would do and see during your first day.

• Imagine you are a newspaper reporter witnessing an important event. Write a brief account for tomorrow's newspaper. Remember to include the five *w*'s—*who, what, when, where,* and *why.*

• How would you compare yourself to your best friend? What do you do better? What does your friend do better?

480

Literature Connection

Author Note Mark Twain (1835–1910) is the pen name of Samuel Langhorne Clemens, one of America's greatest writers. Twain grew up in the Mississippi River town of Hannibal, Missouri, and headed west after the Civil War. He first achieved fame with humorous tales about life on the rugged western frontier. *A Connecticut Yankee in* *King Arthur's Court* (1889) satirizes the romantic notions of King Arthur's day and the views of New Englanders in Twain's own time.

Understanding Adverbs

Camelot. The wizard Merlin. Sir Lancelot. Queen Guinevere. You are probably familiar with the legends of King Arthur and the knights of the Round Table. To retell rich tales such as these, you need to use rich language. By using adverbs, you can include details about how, when, and where actions take place.

In this handbook you will study ways you can use adverbs to make your writing precise and lively.

- **What Are Adverbs?**

- **Making Comparisons with Adverbs**

- **Adjective or Adverb?**

- **Double Negatives**

Understanding Adverbs

Objectives
- To recognize an adverb as a word that modifies a verb, an adjective, or another adverb
- To use the comparative and superlative forms of adverbs correctly
- To distinguish between adjectives and adverbs
- To avoid double negatives in speaking and writing

Writing
- To use adverbs to add clarity and precision to writing
- To recognize and correct errors in adverb usage

INTRODUCING THE HANDBOOK
If students are unfamiliar with the Arthurian legends, briefly explain that Arthur was a legendary King of Britain who invited the finest knights of his day to join him at his castle, Camelot. At his court, the knights were seated at a round table. Since no one knight sat at the head of the table, everyone felt equal. Merlin was Arthur's mentor and adviser; Guinevere was Arthur's wife; and Lancelot was one of the most famous knights of the Round Table. Ask students who have seen films or TV shows about King Arthur to describe the characters' actions. Point out that adverbs can help make such descriptions clearer and more vivid.

Objectives
- To identify adverbs and the information they provide

Writing
- To use adverbs to make writing more precise

Teaching Strategies

STUMBLING BLOCK Point out that some adjectives are often used incorrectly as adverbs. Write these sentences on the board; ask students what is wrong with each and how it should be corrected.

   The stagecoach traveled the route regular. (regularly)

   The impatient driver spoke loud to his horses. (loudly)

   Two days late, the stagecoach rumbled safe into town. (safely)

HELPFUL HINT: -LY ENDINGS
Point out that although the -ly ending is a clue that a word is an adverb, not all words ending in -ly are adverbs. Words such as *friendly, costly,* and *lovely* are adjectives: words such as *early* and *only* can be either.

LINKING GRAMMAR AND WRITING Note that when meaning isn't affected, adverbs can be placed in a variety of positions in sentences. For example, occasionally beginning a sentence with an adverb can make writing more interesting. Discuss the effect of the opening adverb in this sentence:

   Instantly, they were pursued by squadrons of bomber-shaped dragons, who gobbled them up.

   Jean Craighead George,
   The Talking Earth

Additional Resources

Test and Writing Assessment
   Prompts, Pretest, pp. 35–36
Grammar and Usage Practice Book,
   p. 59
 Grammar
   Test Generator

Writing
TIP

Adverbs can help make a story you're writing more specific. Use adverbs to tell more about the time, place, and extent of the action. See how adverbs add to this sentence.
   Bob saddled his horse.
   Bob *hurriedly* saddled his horse.

> An **adverb** modifies a verb, an adjective, or another adverb.

Adjectives add excitement and clarity to your sentences. Adverbs can help you be more precise.

An **adjective** modifies a noun or pronoun.

An **adverb** modifies a verb, an adjective, or another adverb.

   Mail moved *slowly.* (*Slowly* modifies the verb *moved.*)
   Postage was *extremely* expensive. (*Extremely* modifies the adjective *expensive.*)
   Settlers waited *very* impatiently for news. (*Very* modifies the adverb *impatiently.*)

An **adverb** tells *how, when, where,* or *to what extent* about the word it modifies.

   Bill Cody rode *swiftly.* (*Swiftly* tells *how* Bill rode.)
   He arrived *yesterday.* (*Yesterday* tells *when* he arrived.)
   The coach went *west.* (*West* tells *where* the coach went.)
   The rider was *completely* exhausted. (*Completely* tells *to what extent* the rider was exhausted.)

An adverb that modifies an adjective or another adverb often comes before the word it modifies.

   extremely steep   *very* carefully

An adverb that modifies a verb may be found in one of several positions.

   She wrote *often.*   She *often* wrote.   *Often,* she wrote.

Many common adverbs are formed by adding the ending -ly to adjectives. For example, the adjectives *quick* and *usual* become the adverbs *quickly* and *usually.*

   Other adverbs include *there, now, never, almost,* and *too.*

Literature Connection

Show students this passage from "The Circuit" by Francisco Jiménez and discuss how the adverbs (underlined) make characters' actions more vivid. Ask students to identify the word each adverb modifies. *(open, held; carefully, carried; out, carried; gently, placed; then, climbed; in, climbed; wearily, said)* "I held the front door <u>open</u> as Mamá <u>carefully</u> carried <u>out</u> her pot by both handles. . . . Papá <u>gently</u> placed it on the floor behind the front seat. All of us <u>then</u> climbed <u>in</u>. Papá sighed, wiped the sweat off his forehead with his sleeve, and said <u>wearily</u>: 'Es todo.' "

Practice Your Skills

A. CONCEPT CHECK

Adverbs Write each adverb and tell whether it answers *How, When, Where,* or *To what extent.* Then write the word it modifies.

> EXAMPLE   The stagecoach sped wildly downhill.
> wildly, How, sped; downhill, Where, sped

1. In the Old West, mail service was <u>unbelievably</u> slow.
2. Until 1858, California had <u>very</u> irregular mail service.
3. It <u>often</u> took two to three months for a letter to arrive.
4. <u>Finally</u>, the Butterfield Overland Mail Service began.
5. Stagecoaches carried passengers and mail <u>east</u> and <u>west</u>.
6. <u>Now</u>, imagine a trip to California in 1858.
7. You <u>eagerly</u> board the train in St. Louis.
8. After <u>nearly</u> 150 miles, you transfer to a stagecoach.
9. Hold on <u>tight</u>, because the ride is <u>really</u> rough.
10. You and the mail travel <u>almost</u> <u>constantly</u> <u>day</u> and <u>night</u>.
11. Sleep is <u>practically</u> impossible.
12. The coach <u>eventually</u> jolts to a stop in San Francisco.
13. <u>Shakily</u> you climb <u>down</u>.
14. You're <u>totally</u> exhausted.
15. <u>Just</u> think, your trip took <u>only</u> twenty-four days!

B. REVISION SKILL

Using Precise Adverbs Sometimes you can make a sentence more precise or change the meaning by changing an adverb. Write each sentence. Replace each adverb in italics with another adverb that answers the same question of *how, when, where,* or *to what extent.*

> EXAMPLE   The rider galloped *fearlessly* into the night.
> The rider galloped bravely into the night.

16. A Pony Express rider comes *quickly* into view.
17. A fresh rider and a horse stand *nearby*.
18. The first rider brings his horse *sharply* to a halt.
19. *Then* the new rider grabs the mail, leaps onto a waiting horse, and is off at top speed.

Understanding Adverbs   **483**

Writing Theme
The Old West and the
U. S. Mail

Writing Theme: The Old West and the U.S. Mail

Suggest that students use these exercises as a springboard to writing. Other related areas that they might explore include the following:

- smoke signals for communication
- the invention of the telegraph
- the introduction of postage stamps
- the introduction of zip code

Answers to Practice Your Skills

A. Concept Check
Adverbs

Adverbs are shown on page.
1. unbelievably, To what extent, slow
2. very, To what extent, irregular
3. often, When, took
4. Finally, When, began
5. east, Where, carried; west, Where, carried
6. Now, When, imagine
7. eagerly, How, board
8. nearly, To what extent, 150
9. tightly, How, Hold; really, To what extent, rough
10. almost, To what extent, constantly; constantly, How, travel; day, when, travel; night, When, travel
11. practically, To what extent, impossible
12. eventually, When, jolts
13. shakily, How, climb; down, Where, climb
14. totally, To what extent, exhausted
15. Just, To what extent, think; only, To what extent, twenty-four

B. Revision Skill
Using Precise Adverbs

Answers will vary. Sample adverbs are given below. Student answers should be in sentences.
16. swiftly
17. here
18. promptly
19. Soon

20. east
21. usually
22. steadily
23. rarely
24. constantly
25. seldom

C H E C K P O I N T

Writing Theme: Bullfighting

Suggest that students use these exercises as a springboard to writing. Other related areas that they might explore include the following:

- bullfighting in Spain or Mexico
- the history of bullfighting
- the running of the bulls in Pamplona, Spain
- famous bullfighters
- other workers in a bullring

MIXED REVIEW • PAGES 482-484

You may wish to use this activity to check students' mastery of the following concept:

- What are adverbs?

Application in Literature

Students need only list ten adverbs and the words they modify.

1. slowly, lifted; arrogantly, lifted
2. Back, came; again, controlled
3. back, looking
4. suddenly, charged; fast, charged; too, fast; fast, charged
5. None
6. up, tossed
7. None
8. automatically, acted
9. up, picked
10. backwards, ran; away, taking

FOR MORE PRACTICE
See page 495.

Writing Theme
Bullfighting

---

20. Riders carried mail 1,966 miles from St. Joseph, Missouri, to Sacramento, California, and then brought mail *back*.
21. Pony Express riders *always* rode as fast as possible.
22. They galloped *tirelessly* across the driest deserts.
23. They *scarcely* slowed down for steep mountain trails.
24. In deep snow, they *continually* urged their horses on.
25. Bad weather and rough trails *never* stopped them.

C H E C K P O I N T
MIXED REVIEW • PAGES 482–484

Application in Literature   Write ten <u>adverbs</u> from this paragraph and the word each modifies. If a sentence has no adverbs, write *None*. There are fourteen adverbs in all.

¹Juan . . . slowly, arrogantly, lifted the lure in both hands and let the animal charge under it. ²Back came the bull, and again, with quiet assurance, the boy controlled the animal's speed and direction. ³Without looking back, Juan walked towards Manolo. ⁴The animal seemed to have been nailed to the sand by the last pass, but suddenly it charged fast, too fast for Manolo to warn Juan. ⁵It happened in an instant. ⁶The boy was tossed up in the air and landed with a thud on the ground. ⁷The bull stomped the earth and moved his horns toward Juan, who had both arms thrown over his head. ⁸But Manolo . . . acted automatically with no thought of what he was doing. ⁹He picked up the muleta and waved it in front of the horns, and the horns charged the red cloth. ¹⁰Manolo ran backwards, taking the bull away from Juan.

Maia Wojciechowska, *Shadow of a Bull*

Literature Connection

Author Note   Poet, translator, and children's author Maia Wojciechowska (pronounced voi chə hov'skä) was born in Warsaw, Poland, in 1927. She escaped the Nazi occupation of her homeland and came to the United States when still a teenager. In her adventurous life, she has held dozens of jobs, including undercover agent, pro tennis player, and translator for Radio Free Europe; she has also raced motorcycles, parachuted from planes, and fought bulls. The last experience helped prompt *Shadow of a Bull* (1964), her Newbery Medal winner about the son of a bullfighter. Wojciechowska has also published works under the name Maia Rodman.

A. Finding Adverbs   Find every adverb in these sentences. Write the <u>adverb</u> and the word it modifies.

1. In the 1700s, bicycles were <u>pretty</u> crude and slow.
2. There were bikes <u>then</u>, but you'd <u>barely</u> recognize them.
3. In 1791, a French count invented a two-wheeled device that people <u>rather</u> <u>playfully</u> called a *célérifère,* which means "swift-footed."
4. It <u>more</u> or <u>less</u> resembled a bicycle.
5. It was designed <u>strangely</u>; it had two wheels but no pedals.
6. The rider <u>actually</u> ran while he or she sat on the thing.
7. The count <u>also</u> <u>somehow</u> left <u>off</u> any steering mechanism.
8. For a change in direction, a rider picked the célérifère <u>up</u> to move it.
9. The machine's wood wheels produced an <u>extremely</u> rough ride.
10. Célérifères were <u>somewhat</u> clumsy, but they were <u>much</u> faster than walking.

B. Using Adverbs Correctly   For each sentence, write the correct form of the adverb in parentheses.

11. Each year, engineering improvements create race cars that travel (<u>more</u>, most) rapidly than the previous year's models.
12. Certainly, early race cars traveled (<u>more slowly</u>, most slowly) than today's cars.
13. At the first automobile race, held in France in 1894, people were (<u>more curious</u>, most curious) about which cars would finish than about which car was fastest.
14. Of the twenty cars in the race, a car powered by a steam engine performed (more reliably, <u>most reliably</u>).
15. Not only was it reliable, but it ran the (faster, <u>fastest</u>).
16. Of the cars that finished, the winner puttered (more quickly, <u>most quickly</u>), averaging almost twelve miles per hour.
17. The other cars did (<u>worse</u>, worst), and most didn't finish.
18. The cars traveled (<u>less</u>, least) than seventy-five miles.
19. In 1895, the cars raced (<u>farther</u>, farthest) than they had the year before.
20. The car that ran (<u>best</u>, better) averaged fifteen miles per hour!

Understanding Adverbs   **495**

Writing Theme
Speed

ADDITIONAL PRACTICE

Each of these exercises correlates to a section of Handbook 39, "Understanding Adverbs." The exercises may be used for more practice, for reteaching, or for review of the concepts presented.

Additional Resource

Grammar and Usage Practice Book, p. 65

Writing Theme: Speed

Other related areas students might wish to explore as writing topics include the following:
- from sailing ships to steamships
- the invention of the airplane
- speed skating
- *Around the World in Eighty Days* by Jules Verne (book or film)

A. Finding Adverbs
Adverbs are shown on page.
1. pretty, crude, slow
2. then, were; barely, 'd (would) recognize
3. rather, playfully; playfully, called
4. more, resembled; less, resembled
5. strangely, was designed
6. actually, ran
7. also, left; somehow, left; off, left
8. up, picked
9. extremely, rough
10. somewhat, clumsy; much, faster

B. Using Adverbs Correctly
Answers are shown on page.

C. Choosing the Right Modifier

Correct modifiers are shown on page.

21. swiftly, travel, Adverb
22. good, horses, Adjective
23. really, fast, Adverb
24. frightening, trains, Adjective
25. real, blur, Adjective
26. rapidly, improved, Adverb
27. easily, broke, Adverb
28. unbelievable, It, Adjective
29. badly, do, Adverb
30. incredible, It, Adjective

D. Using Negatives Correctly

Answers may vary slightly. Typical answers are shown below.

31. No one had ever circled the world until Magellan did so in 1521.
32. His ships didn't make it in anything less than two years.
33. We have never quit trying to circle the globe faster.
34. The next noteworthy trip was made by nobody else but Nellie Bly, a reporter who in 1889 went around the world in about seventy-two days.
35. That record was nothing after people started flying.
36. In 1924, one plane had no trouble circling the earth in fifteen days.
37. Not even that record was safe, though.
38. Wiley Post and Harold Gatty took no time at all to break the record, taking less than eight days in 1931.
39. By 1957, the record was no more than two days.
40. None of these records means anything to space vehicles.

C. Choosing the Right Modifier   Write the <u>correct modifier</u>, the word it modifies, and whether it is an *Adjective* or *Adverb*.

> EXAMPLE   Trains can travel (safe, safely) at 120 mph.
> safely, travel, Adverb

21. Until recently, people didn't travel very (swift, <u>swiftly</u>).
22. If someone was in a hurry, horses were pretty (well, <u>good</u>).
23. Then trains made it possible for people to travel (real, <u>really</u>) fast.
24. To some people, early trains appeared (<u>frightening</u>, frighteningly).
25. An 1825 train seemed like a (<u>real</u>, really) blur at 7 mph.
26. Trains improved (rapid, <u>rapidly</u>), however.
27. By 1850, trains broke 60 miles per hour (easy, <u>easily</u>).
28. It may sound (<u>unbelievable</u>, unbelievably), but in 1955 a French train set a record by traveling 205 miles per hour.
29. At 160 mph, a Japanese train doesn't do so (bad, <u>badly</u>).
30. It seems (<u>incredible</u>, incredibly), but a United States rocket train that tests spacecraft parts reaches a rate of 3,090 mph.

D. Using Negatives Correctly   Write the following sentences, correcting all double negatives.

31. No one had never circled the world until Magellan did so in 1521.
32. His ships didn't make it in nothing less than two years.
33. We haven't never quit trying to circle the globe faster.
34. The next noteworthy trip wasn't made by nobody else but Nellie Bly, a reporter who in 1889 went around the world in about seventy-two days.
35. That record wasn't nothing after people started flying.
36. In 1924, one plane never had no trouble circling the earth in fifteen days.
37. Not even that record wasn't safe, though.
38. Wiley Post and Harold Gatty didn't take no time at all to break the record, taking less than eight days in 1931.
39. By 1957, the record wasn't no more than two days.
40. None of these records means nothing to space vehicles.

A. Identifying Adverbs

Write each <u>adverb</u> below. Also write whether the adverb tells *How, When, Where,* or *To what extent.*

1. A newborn bear is <u>usually</u> <u>only</u> seven or eight inches long.
2. The tiny cub <u>ordinarily</u> weighs <u>less</u> than a pound.
3. It is <u>completely</u> blind and lacks both teeth and hair.
4. It grows <u>quickly</u>, though, and <u>very</u> <u>soon</u> it is <u>not</u> helpless.
5. In <u>only</u> a few years, it may weigh 300 to 1,500 pounds.
6. Alaskan brown bears are the tallest—<u>sometimes</u> <u>nearly</u> nine feet high when standing <u>up</u> on two legs.
7. They are powerful and <u>dangerously</u> unpredictable animals.
8. Some bears can run <u>faster</u> than a horse for short distances.
9. Bears <u>once</u> lived <u>everywhere</u> in the United States.
10. <u>Now</u>, many black bears and a few grizzlies <u>still</u> live <u>here</u>.

B. Making Comparisons

Write the correct form of each adverb given in parentheses.

11. Of all Americans who have worked with animals, James Capen Adams may be the (well) known animal trainer.
12. People know him (well) as Grizzly Adams.
13. Adams had many jobs; the one he probably liked (little) was his first one as a shoemaker in Massachusetts.
14. In 1849, he joined the California Gold Rush, thinking he couldn't do (badly) as a prospector than he had done as a shoemaker.
15. He wanted (desperately) of all to work with animals.
16. He quit mining and traveled even (deep) into the mountains.
17. He caught and trained many animals; one, a bear he named Lady Washington, he trained the (carefully) of all.
18. Lady Washington fought back (hard) than a cub would have.
19. In time, Lady grew (much) gentle and they became friends.
20. Later, Grizzly captured a grizzly cub, which he named Benjamin Franklin; it was (easily) trained than Lady.
21. Ben had lived (briefly) as a wild animal than Lady.
22. Lady and Ben served Grizzly the (loyally) of all his animals.

GRAMMAR
HANDBOOK
39

REVIEW

These exercises may be used as a mixed review or as an informal evaluation of skills presented in Handbook 39, "Understanding Adverbs."

Additional Resources

Grammar and Usage Practice Book, p. 66
Tests and Writing Assessment Prompts, Mastery Test, pp. 37–38
Elaboration, Revision, and Proofreading Practice, p. 28

Writing Theme: Bears

Other related areas students might wish to explore as writing topics include the following:
- famous fictional bears
- pandas or koalas—bearlike animals

A. Identifying Adverbs
Adverbs are shown on page.
1. usually, When; only, To what extent
2. ordinarily, When; less, To what extent
3. completely, To what extent
4. quickly, How; very, To what extent; soon, When; not, To what extent
5. only, To what extent
6. sometimes, When; nearly, To what extent; up, How
7. dangerously, How
8. faster, How
9. once, When; everywhere, Where
10. Now, When; still, To what extent; here, Where

B. Making Comparisons
11. best	17. most carefully
12. better	18. harder
13. least	19. more
14. worse	20. more easily
15. most desperately	21. more briefly
16. deeper	22. most loyally

C. Using the Correct Modifier

23. Correct
24. These creatures survived very well everywhere west of Ohio and Kentucky.
25. Native Americans lived uneasily with them from the beginning.
26. Some groups would hunt the grizzly only if they needed food badly.
27. They respected the animal and felt bad when they killed one.
28. Correct
29. They were really sure that their ancestors had become bears.
30. Bears appear frequently in their legends and stories.
31. Correct
32. When angry, it could overtake a rider on horseback easily.
33. It could knock down both the rider and the horse with one remarkably powerful swipe.
34. Early pioneers never felt too safe with grizzlies near.
35. The settlers killed bears rather regularly.
36. Correct

D. Using Negatives

Answers are shown on page.

C. Using the Correct Modifier   Write the following sentences, correcting all errors in the use of adjectives and adverbs. If a sentence has no error, write *Correct*.

23. At one time, the sight of a grizzly bear was not unusual in North America.
24. These creatures survived very good everywhere west of Ohio and Kentucky.
25. Native Americans lived uneasy with them from the beginning.
26. Some groups would hunt the grizzly only if they needed food bad.
27. They respected the animal and felt badly when they killed one.
28. Others worshipped the awesome grizzly and never hunted it.
29. They were real sure that their ancestors had become bears.
30. Bears appear frequent in their legends and stories.
31. No doubt, this extremely deadly bear deserved its reputation.
32. When angry, it could overtake a rider on horseback easy.
33. It could knock down both the rider and the horse with one remarkable powerful swipe.
34. Early pioneers never felt too safely with grizzlies near.
35. The settlers killed bears rather regular.
36. Most grizzlies south of Canada have been gradually destroyed.

D. Using Negatives   For each sentence, write the <u>correct word</u> from those given in parentheses.

37. None of our presidents did (no, <u>any</u>) more to protect wilderness areas and wild animals than Theodore Roosevelt.
38. There wasn't (no one, <u>anyone</u>) who loved the outdoors more.
39. However, he wasn't in (<u>any</u>, no) way against hunting.
40. He didn't like (<u>anything</u>, nothing) much better than a bear hunt; but one time in Mississippi an old bear was caught.
41. Teddy didn't think (<u>anybody</u>, nobody) ought to shoot it.
42. He wouldn't (<u>ever</u>, never) shoot a helpless creature.
43. There wasn't (<u>anybody</u>, nobody) who ignored that story.
44. A toy maker (<u>could</u>, couldn't) not let the opportunity pass.
45. Nothing would sell (<u>any</u>, no) better than "Teddy" bears.
46. T.R. himself didn't have (<u>any</u>, no) objection to the toys.

WRITING CONNECTIONS

Elaboration, Revision, and Proofreading

Revise the following draft of an opinion paper by using the directions at the bottom of the page. Then proofread your paper, paying special attention to the use of adverbs. Also look for other grammatical errors and errors in capitalization, punctuation, and spelling.

¹Squirt guns don't seem like something for <u>no one</u> to get concerned about. ²They are just a way for kids to have some good, clean (and wet) fun. ³However, some people want to ban squirt guns. ⁴My cousin has a squirt gun. ⁵Why should all the kids who play safely with these toys be punished because a few kids act irresponsibly? ⁶The gun that people are worried about is a new, high-powered squirt gun. ⁷This gun holds more water. ⁸It shoots it more <u>forceful</u>. ⁹Critics say that if these guns are <u>missused</u>, they can be <u>dangrous</u> a few kids have been <u>injurd</u>. ¹⁰Yet any toy is <u>dangrous</u> if it is <u>missused</u>. ¹¹Some toys are too expensive. ¹²When these squirt guns are used properly, <u>theyre</u> a <u>blast</u>. And they are not unsafe.

1. Remove the two sentences that do not support the main idea.

2. Strengthen the argument by adding an example to sentence 10. "Even a tricycle can be dangerous if a child rides too fast or out into a street."

3. Improve the flow of sentences by combining 7 and 8 to make a sentence with a compound verb.

4. Replace the informal words *a blast* in sentence 12 with a more formal expression.

5. Make the conclusion of the paragraph stronger by placing sentence 5 after sentence 12.

Persuasive Writing

Stating your opinion allows you to share ideas on issues you feel strongly about. (See Workshop 5.) When you revise an opinion paper, look to see that you have stated your position clearly and supported it. Use adverbs to add details that tell *how, when, where,* and *to what extent.*

WRITING CONNECTIONS

Elaboration, Revision, and Proofreading

This activity will allow students to see some of the concepts presented in this Handbook at work in a piece of persuasive writing. By revising and proofreading this passage, students will have an opportunity to identify and correct errors in the use of adverbs. They will also become more aware of style.

You might have students work in small groups to revise the passage and then discuss the completed revision with the entire class. Revisions may vary slightly. See a typical revision below. Elements involving change are shown in boldface.

Squirt guns don't seem like something for anyone to get concerned about. They are just a way for kids to have some good, clean (and wet) fun. However, some people want to ban squirt guns. ~~My cousin has a squirt gun.~~ The gun that people are worried about is a new, high-powered squirt gun. **This gun holds more water and shoots it more forcefully.** Critics say that if these guns are misused, they can be dangerous. A few kids have been injured. Yet any toy is dangerous if it is misused. **Even a tricycle can be dangerous if a child rides too fast or out into a street.** ~~Some toys are too expensive.~~ When these squirt guns are used properly, they're **fun, and they are not unsafe. Why should all the kids who play safely with these toys be punished because a few kids act irresponsibly?**

Test 2

This test enables you to evaluate student mastery of the concepts taught in handbooks 37–39.

Additional Resource

Grammar and Usage Practice Book, pp. 67–68

Answer Key

Corrections for run-ons may vary.
1. **A**—aren't
   C—they're
2. **A**—really
3. **B**—well
4. **C**—her
5. **A**—its
6. **B**—most popular
7. **B**—his
8. **B**—most precious
9. **A**—Those
   B—anybody
10. **A**—August
    B—its name
11. **B**—he
12. **A**—This
13. **D**
14. **B**—poorly
    C—ever *or* don't need
15. **D**

Directions　One or more of the underlined sections in the following sentences may contain an error in grammar, punctuation, spelling, or capitalization. Write the letter of each incorrect section. Then rewrite the section correctly. If there is no error in an item, write *D*.

> **Example**　I watched the magician very <u>close</u>, but I don't understand.
> 　　　　　　　　　　　　　　　　　**A**
> How did <u>him</u> and his assistant make the rabbit <u>disappear</u>?
> 　　　　**B**　　　　　　　　　　　　　　　　　**C**
> <u>No error</u>
> **D**
>
> **Answer**　A—closely; B—he

1. Big animals <u>arent</u> always parents of big <u>babies</u>. Kangaroos are about an
   　　　　　　A　　　　　　　　　　　**B**
   inch long when <u>their</u> born.　<u>No error</u>
   　　　　　　　C　　　　　**D**

2. If a bus is going <u>real</u> fast and stops <u>suddenly</u>, it is the force of inertia that
   　　　　　　　　　A　　　　　　　**B**
   pushes <u>your</u> body forward.　<u>No error</u>
   　　　　C　　　　　　　**D**

3. A <u>bloodhound's</u> nose works really <u>good</u>. Some of these dogs can follow
   　　　A　　　　　　　　　　**B**
   a trail <u>that's</u> ten days old.　<u>No error</u>
   　　　　C　　　　　　　**D**

4. The song <u>"Happy Birthday"</u> was a gold mine for Mildred Hill. It was <u>written</u>
   　　　　　　A　　　　　　　　　　　　　　　　　　　　**B**
   by <u>she</u> and her sister Patty and has earned millions of dollars.　<u>No error</u>
   　　C　　　　　　　　　　　　　　　　　　　　　　　　**D**

5. If a salamander loses <u>it's</u> tail, <u>it</u> just <u>grows</u> a new one.　<u>No error</u>
   　　　　　　　　　　　A　　**B**　　**C**　　　　　　**D**

6. <u>There</u> are a great many people named John and Jim. Muhammad, however,
   　A
   is the <u>most popularest</u> name in the <u>world</u>.　<u>No error</u>
   　　　B　　　　　　　　　**C**　　**D**

7. Neither <u>John F. Kennedy</u> nor Warren G. Harding outlived <u>their</u> <u>father</u>.
        A   **B** **C**
<u>No error</u>
 D

8. <u>Rubies</u>, not diamonds, are currently the <u>more precious</u> stones on this
   A   **B**
<u>planet</u>. <u>No error</u>
 C   **D**

9. <u>Them</u> stingers on a queen bee won't hurt <u>nobody</u>. <u>They</u> are only used
   A   **B**   **C**
as weapons against other queen bees. <u>No error</u>
                                 D

10. July and <u>august</u> have something in common. Each got <u>their name</u> from
          A   **B**
a <u>Roman</u> emperor named Caesar—a Julius and an Augustus. <u>No error</u>
   C   **D**

11. My brother and <u>I</u> are twins, but <u>him</u> and my cousin <u>look</u> more alike than
               A   **B**   **C**
he and I do. <u>No error</u>
          D

12. <u>These</u> kind of penguin <u>grows</u> four feet tall and can weigh <u>nearly</u> one
   A   **B**   **C**
hundred pounds. <u>No error</u>
               D

13. Watch <u>out!</u> <u>Those</u> chili peppers are much <u>hotter</u> than bell peppers.
        A **B**   **C**
<u>No error</u>
 D

14. Two-thirds of all adult <u>Americans</u> see <u>poor</u> enough to need eyeglasses.
                        A   **B**
That leaves one third that don't <u>never</u> need to wear them. <u>No error</u>
                        C   **D**

15. Has everyone in the <u>string</u> section tuned <u>his or her</u> <u>instrument</u>? <u>No error</u>
                 A   **B**   **C**   **D**

List of Skills Tested

1. **A**—punctuation—apostrophe
   B—noun plural
   C—confusion of possessive pronoun and contraction
2. **A**—adjective/adverb confusion
   B—adjective/adverb confusion
   C—confusion of possessive pronoun and contraction
3. **A**—noun possessive
   B—good/well
   C—punctuation—apostrophe; subject-verb agreement
4. **A**—capitalization—title
   B—irregular verb form
   C—pronoun case
5. **A**—confusion of possessive pronoun and contraction
   B—pronoun-antecedent agreement
   C—subject-verb agreement
6. **A**—spelling
   B—comparative adjective form—more/most
   C—capitalization—common/proper noun
7. **A**—capitalization—initials
   B—agreement of possessive pronoun and indefinite pronoun
   C—capitalization—common/proper noun
8. **A**—noun plural
   B—comparative adjective form—more/most
   C—capitalization—common/proper noun
9. **A**—demonstrative adjective
   B—double negative
   C—pronoun case
10. **A**—capitalization—name of month
    B—agreement of possessive pronoun and indefinite pronoun
    C—capitalization—nationality
11. **A**—pronoun case
    B—pronoun case
    C—subject-verb agreement
12. **A**—demonstrative adjective
    B—subject-verb agreement
    C—adjective/adverb confusion
13. **A**—punctuation—end mark
    B—demonstrative adjective
    C—comparative adjective form
14. **A**—capitalization—nationality
    B—adjective/adverb confusion
    C—double negative
15. **A**—capitalization
    B—pronoun-antecedent agreement
    C—spelling

Objective

• To use visual writing prompts as springboards to informal writing

WRITING WARM-UPS

Encourage students to respond freely and informally to at least one of the Sketchbook prompts. Students may begin by discussing their reactions in small groups and then freewriting in their journals. Remind them that their responses will not be graded and will provide them with the opportunity to think creatively about the concepts presented in this handbook.

For the first writing prompt, elicit the response that information about color, shape, size, and location is especially useful in helping readers picture an unfamiliar object. Point out that phrases, or groups of words, often help clarify size (for example, *nearly three feet long*) and location (for example, *on the right* or *at the front*). Encourage students to use such phrases in their descriptions.

For the second writing prompt, suggest that students include in their written descriptions words and phrases that clarify the sequence of the episode's events: *at the start, next, after ten minutes,* and *near the end,* and so on.

For the third writing prompt, elicit the response that clear directions often include the following kinds of phrases about specific streets or roads (*on Main Street*), time (*in about fifteen minutes*), distance (*after ten miles*), and landmarks or sights along the way (*at the third light* or *by the middle school*). Tell students to include phrases like these in their directions.

Sketch Book

WRITING WARM-UPS

Extravaganza Televisione (1984), Kenny Scharf.

- This television gives new meaning to the question, What's on TV? Write a description of this television set. Use words that help you tell your readers exactly where things are located.
- Write about what happened in a recent episode of a television show you often watch.
- Imagine that you and a friend are going to meet at your home or some other specific place. Write directions to tell your friend how to get there.

502

ART NOTE

Do students agree that Kenny Scharf's TV sculpture is, in the words of one art critic, the "ultimate box"? Ask students how they would turn their headset, TV, or boom box into a work of art.

Prepositions and Conjunctions

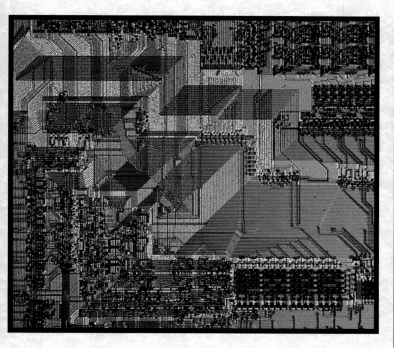

Circuits like this one provide the electrical connections that make a picture appear on your television set. When you write, you often need to provide connections between words and sentences.

In this handbook you will learn ways to use prepositions and conjunctions to show your readers how your ideas are connected and to add details to your writing.

- **What Are Prepositions?**

- **Using Prepositional Phrases**

- **Pronouns After Prepositions**

- **More About Prepositions**

- **What Are Conjunctions?**

- **Using Words as Different Parts of Speech**

Prepositions and Conjunctions

Objectives
- To identify prepositions and their objects
- To identify prepositional phrases
- To use object forms of pronouns as objects of prepositions
- To distinguish between prepositions and adverbs
- To use *between* and *among* correctly
- To identify conjunctions and the sentence parts they combine
- To identify the part of speech of a word by its use in a sentence

Writing
- To use prepositions, prepositional phrases, and conjunctions correctly in sentences
- To use prepositional phrases as a means of adding details to writing
- To combine sentences by reducing one sentence to a prepositional phrase and inserting it in another sentence
- To use conjunctions to combine sentences
- To use proofreading skills to correct errors in preposition and conjunction usage

INTRODUCING THE HANDBOOK
Ask students to name some of their favorite electronic devices—such as compact disc players and computers—and to tell what they find entertaining about each. Ask what happens when the devices are unplugged or the batteries go dead. Point out that without connections to electrical power, the devices are useless. Then explain that sentences have special words that make important connections between words and ideas. Tell students they will learn more about these useful words, called *prepositions* and *conjunctions,* in this handbook.

Objectives
• To recognize prepositions and their objects

Writing
• To use appropriate prepositions to complete sentences

Teaching Strategies

KEY TO UNDERSTANDING: OBJECTS OF PREPOSITIONS Have a volunteer answer the question preceding the chart by identifying the object of the preposition in each sample sentence. (the noun *table*) Stress the change in the relationship brought about by the change in prepositions.

To show how pronouns can also be objects of prepositions, ask what pronoun can replace the noun *tunnel* and its modifier *the* in the statement "We walked through the tunnel." *(it)* With the pronoun, the sentence will read, "We walked through *it.*"

INDIVIDUALIZING INSTRUCTION: ESL STUDENTS Urdu, Hindi, and other South Asian languages utilize postpositions, not prepositions (postpositions *follow* their objects). Point out to students who speak these languages that prepositions have the same function as postpositions—to show relationships between words in a sentence—but that in relation to their objects, prepositions' position in a sentence is different from that of postpositions.

Writing
TIP

Choose prepositions carefully to make your meaning clear. Often, by changing prepositions, you can change the relationship between words in a sentence.

WHAT ARE PREPOSITIONS?

A **preposition** shows how a noun or a pronoun relates to another word in a sentence. The noun or pronoun that follows a preposition is the **object of the preposition.**

The girl is *on* the table.

The girl is *above* the table.

Prepositions help to show relationships. For example, *on* and *above* show the relationship between the girl and the table. The noun or pronoun following a preposition is called the **object of the preposition.** Which word is the object in the captions below the pictures?

Commonly Used Prepositions

about	before	down	of	to
above	behind	during	off	toward
across	below	for	on	under
after	beneath	from	onto	underneath
against	beside	in	out	until
along	between	inside	outside	up
among	beyond	into	over	upon
around	but (except)	like	past	with
at	by	near	through	without

Practice Your Skills

A. CONCEPT CHECK

Prepositions Write the prepositions in the following sentences. Beside each preposition, write its object. Some sentences have more than one preposition and object.

1. Some magic tricks rely on appearances.
2. The laws of science are behind others.
3. Place a deck of cards on a table and cut the deck in half.
4. Look at the top card, show it to your audience, and then replace it.
5. Conceal a saltshaker in your pocket.
6. Reach inside that pocket.
7. Secretly coat the tip of your finger with salt and tap the top card with your finger.
8. Be sure you leave some salt on the surface of the top card.
9. Place one stack beneath the other.
10. The selected card seems lost in the middle of the deck.
11. Take a saltshaker from your pocket.
12. Sprinkle a little salt over the deck.
13. Also gently tap against the side of the deck with the shaker.
14. As if by magic, the deck will separate at the point where the selected card is.
15. Grains of salt on that card act like ball bearings, making the cards separate there.

B. DRAFTING SKILL

Using Prepositions Write prepositions that logically complete the following sentences.

[16]Stick a piece ____ double-sided sticky tape ____ the front edge of a table. [17]Show a six-inch piece of thread ____ your audience, then attach one end ____ the tape. [18]Take a comb ____ your pocket. [19]Run the comb ____ your hair. [20]Say, "Rope, rise ____ the air." [21]Hold the comb ____ the free end of the thread. [22]Draw the comb up ____ the air, and the thread mysteriously rises. [23]This trick is done ____ static electricity caused by rubbing the comb ____ your hair.

Writing Theme
Science and Magic

FOR MORE PRACTICE
See page 521.

Additional Resources

Tests and Writing Assessment Prompts, Pretest, pp. 39–40
Grammar and Usage Practice Book, p. 69
Grammar Test Generator

Writing Theme: Science and Magic

Suggest that students use these exercises as a springboard to writing. Other related areas that they might explore include the following:
- other card tricks
- how to perform a magic trick
- famous magicians
- famous scientific hoaxes
- scientific advances that might seem magical to a person from an earlier time

Answers to Practice Your Skills

A. Concept Check
Prepositions
    Answers are shown on page.

B. Drafting Skill
Using Prepositions
    Answers may vary. See typical answers below.
16. of; on, against, or to
17. to; to
18. from
19. through
20. into
21. over, above, or near
22. into or through
23. with; on, through, or in

Objectives
- To identify prepositional phrases

Writing
- To use prepositional phrases in writing
- To combine sentences by reducing one sentence to a prepositional phrase and inserting that phrase in another sentence

Teaching Strategies

LINKING GRAMMAR AND WRITING Explain that some prepositional phrases can be positioned in more than one place in a sentence. For example:

Many trees were cut *in the forest.*

In the forest many trees were cut.

Point out that writers sometimes place the prepositional phrase at the beginning of a sentence, for variety. Emphasize, however, that wherever a prepositional phrase is placed, the meaning of the sentences should remain clear and there should be no possibility of confusion for the reader.

INDIVIDUALIZING INSTRUCTION: ADVANCED STUDENTS Explain that an entire prepositional phrase works as a modifier to describe words functioning as nouns or verbs in a sentence. In the first sample sentence, *in the Southwest* describes the verb *live* by telling *where.* In the third sample sentence, *of the Pueblos* describes the noun *ancestors* by telling *which ones.* Ask what words the prepositional phrases in the other sample sentences describe. *(for many centuries, have lived; in high cliffs, made; in New Mexico . . . , settled; of stone and adobe, built; of stone and adobe, homes)*

Additional Resource
Grammar and Usage Practice Book, p. 70

Writing
─── **TIP** ───

Look at "The Circuit" on pages 142–145. Notice how the author Francisco Jiménez used prepositional phrases to add important details about events and places in the story.

A **prepositional phrase** is a group of words that begins with a preposition and ends with its object.

Look at the italicized prepositional phrases in the sentences below. Notice each preposition and its object.

Preposition | Object of Preposition

The Pueblo people live *in the Southwest.*

Preposition | Object of Preposition

They have lived there *for many centuries.*

In a prepositional phrase, one or more words that describe the object may come between the preposition and its object. The preposition, the object, and all the words that describe the object form the **prepositional phrase.**

Sentences often contain more than one prepositional phrase.

The ancestors *of the Pueblos,* the Anasazi, made their homes *in high cliffs.*

A preposition may have a **compound object** made up of two or more nouns or pronouns joined by *and* or *or.*

Object | Object | Object | Object

They settled *in New Mexico, Arizona, Utah, and Colorado.*

You can often make your writing smoother by reducing a sentence to a prepositional phrase and combining it with another sentence.

The Pueblos later built more elaborate homes. They built them *of stone and adobe.*

The Pueblos later built more elaborate homes *of stone and adobe.*

Always be sure to place the prepositional phrase close to the word or words it describes.

506 Grammar Handbook

Literature Connection

Point out to students that prepositional phrases, like other modifiers, can make writing more precise and vivid. Write on the board the following lines from "Lob's Girl" by Joan Aiken. Ask students to identify the prepositional phrases (underlined). Discuss how the phrases add precision and vividness to the writing.

The whole family was playing cards <u>by the fire</u> <u>in the front room</u> <u>after supper</u> when there was a loud thump and a crash <u>of china</u> <u>in the kitchen.</u>

3. In 1925, dog-sled teams proved their strength and value.
4. That year a diphtheria epidemic broke out in Nome, but the town was not prepared.
5. More serum was needed, or the town would face disaster.
6. Dog sleds and railroads combined their efforts.
7. Trains took the serum part of the way, and sleds carried it on to Nome.
8. Nineteen drivers and teams worked in a relay for a week.
9. Nome's residents cheered and celebrated the team's arrival.
10. Now every March the Iditarod Trail Sled Dog Race duplicates and honors that event.

B. DRAFTING SKILL

Sentence Combining   Combine each of the following sentence pairs into a single sentence. Choose a conjunction and use a comma if necessary. Omit words in italics.

11. Susan Butcher is a dog-sled racer. *She is* a four-time winner of the Iditarod race.
12. This famous race covers over 1,100 miles. *It* lasts many days.
13. Sled dogs in the race must be strong. They could not survive.
14. Early in one race, Butcher's sled got stuck in an icy creek. *The sled* broke in four places.
15. Her sled no longer steered properly. She continued anyway.
16. Later, a brutal snowstorm came up. *There were* fierce winds.
17. Butcher could wait out the storm. She could go on.
18. Two opponents were close. They were forced to stop.
19. She trusted her dogs. They trusted her.
20. She drove all night through the storm. *She* beat the second-place dog-sled by fourteen hours.

The four-time Iditarod winner Susan Butcher poses with a hard-working friend.

FOR MORE PRACTICE
See page 522.

Prepositions and Conjunctions   **517**

---

3. their strength and value; Object
4. That year a diphtheria epidemic broke out in Nome, but the town was not prepared; Sentence
5. More serum was needed, or the town would face disaster; Sentence
6. Dog sleds and railroads; Subject
7. Trains took the serum part of the way, and sleds carried it on to Nome; Sentence
8. drivers and teams; Subject
9. cheered and celebrated; Verb
10. duplicates and honors; Verb

B. Drafting Skill
Sentence Combining
     Answers may vary slightly. See typical answers below.
11. Susan Butcher is a dog-sled racer and a four-time winner of the Iditarod race.
12. This famous race covers over 1,100 miles and lasts many days.
13. Sled dogs in the race must be strong, or they could not survive.
14. Early in one race, Butcher's sled got stuck in an icy creek and broke in four places.
15. Her sled no longer steered properly, but she continued anyway.
16. Later, a brutal snowstorm and fierce winds came up.
17. Butcher could wait out the storm, or she could go on.
18. Two opponents were close, but they were forced to stop.
19. She trusted her dogs (*or* dogs,) and they trusted her.
20. She drove all night through the storm and beat the second-place dog sled by fourteen hours.

Objectives
• To identify the part of speech of given words

Writing
• To write sentences, using the same word as various parts of speech

Teaching Strategies

CRITICAL THINKING: ANALYZING
Have volunteers explain why *farm* is a noun in the first sample sentence (it names a place and serves as the object of a preposition), a verb in the second (it expresses action and shows what the subject does), and an adjective in the third (it describes the noun *machinery*, telling *what kind*).

SPEAKING AND LISTENING Point out that some words that can be either nouns or verbs change pronunciation when used as a different part of speech. For example, the noun *object* has the stress on the first syllable, but the verb *object* has the stress on the second. Have volunteers offer more examples and use them in sentences. (Some examples are *conduct, contest, convict, present, produce, project, refuse,* and *use*.)

Additional Resource

Grammar and Usage Practice Book, p. 74

Some words may be used as more than one part of speech. How a word is used in a sentence determines what part of speech it is.

On page 512 of this handbook, you learned that words like *up, down, around, in,* and *out* can be used either as prepositions or as adverbs. Many other words can function as more than one part of speech. Before you can determine what part of speech a word is, you must decide how the word is used in a sentence. Look at how the word *farm* is used in the following sentences.

As a noun
Josh and Jenna live on a *farm*.

As a verb
Their family first *farmed* that land a hundred years ago.

As an adjective
Josh and his father take care of the family's *farm* machinery.

Remember the rules for each part of speech when using words in different ways. For example, when you use *farm* as a noun, you add *-s* to form the plural *farms*. When you use *farm* as a verb, you add *-ed* to form the past tense *farmed*. To use *farm* in some tenses, you may need to add a helping verb such as *did* or *will*.

There is only one sure way to tell what part of speech a word is. Look at the sentence in which the word is used.

518   Grammar Handbook

Practice Your Skills

A. CONCEPT CHECK

Parts of Speech   Identify the part of speech of each word in italics. Write *Noun, Verb, Adjective, Adverb,* or *Preposition.*

1. Are you a good *weather* forecaster?
2. Certain signs have been used as *warning* signs of future weather for centuries.
3. Generally, *rain* is not likely if the wind is from the north.
4. In contrast, it will often *rain* or snow shortly after a south wind.
5. A *red* sky at sunrise can also be a warning of coming rain.
6. Red skies in the evening *promise* clear weather.
7. Trees with curling leaves are a *promise* of a coming storm.
8. If bees stay *inside* the hive, a storm is on the way.
9. Just before a storm, ordinary *daily* sounds are often louder.
10. With these tips you can predict the weather *daily.*

B. DRAFTING SKILL

Using Words as Different Parts of Speech   For each sentence, write your own sentence, using the word in italics. Use the italicized word as the part of speech shown in parentheses.

11. Many people *turn* to an almanac for information about the weather and other topics. (Noun)
12. Almanacs have been *around* for ages. (Preposition)
13. *In* fact, almanacs are among the earliest published works. (Adverb)
14. An almanac from ancient Egypt has *lists* of religious festivals and lucky and unlucky days. (Verb)
15. Later almanacs even forecasted the *weather.* (Adjective)
16. These forecasts helped guide explorers like Christopher Columbus *across* the seas. (Adverb)
17. The oldest almanac published in this *country* first appeared in 1792. (Adjective)
18. It offered numerous tips *on* planting. (Adverb)
19. Most almanacs *forecast* the weather months in advance. (Noun)
20. These *forecasts* are right eight times out of ten. (Verb)

Writing Theme
Weather and Almanacs

FOR MORE PRACTICE
See page 522.

Prepositions and Conjunctions   **519**

Writing Theme: Weather and Almanacs

Other related areas students might wish to explore as writing topics include the following:

- *The Old Farmer's Almanac*
- a meteorologist's training
- types of clouds
- how lightning forms
- the water cycle

Answers to Practice Your Skills

A. Concept Check
Parts of Speech

1. Adjective
2. Adjective
3. Noun
4. Verb
5. Adjective
6. Verb
7. Noun
8. Preposition
9. Adjective
10. Adverb

B. Drafting Skill
Using Words as Different Parts of Speech

Answers will vary. Sample answers are shown below.

11. It was not his *turn* to move his game piece.
12. She lives *around* the corner.
13. Bring the cat *in.*
14. The chart *lists* bestsellers.
15. Did you hear the *weather* report?
16. At this part of the stream, you need a boat to go *across.*
17. I like *country* music.
18. Turn the kettle *on.*
19. The weather *forecast* predicted snow.
20. A meteorologist *forecasts* the weather.

CHECK POINT

Writing Theme:
Adventure Stories

Other related areas students might wish to explore as writing topics include the following:

- *Twenty Thousand Leagues Under the Sea,* the Disney film, compared to the novel
- lost pirate treasures
- the novels of H. G. Wells
- the first submarines

MIXED REVIEW • PAGES 516–519

You may wish to use this activity to check students' mastery of the following concepts:

- What are conjunctions?
- using words as different parts of speech

A.
1. was attacking and sinking; Verb
2. Ned Land and a French professor; Subject
3. An explosion sent them overboard, but they were rescued; Sentence
4. Captain Nemo and the *Nautilus;* Object P
5. oxygen, electricity, and fuel; Object
6. Food and clothing; Subject
7. walked and hunted; Verb
8. For months they sailed around the world, and they experienced many adventures; Sentence
9. Nemo or the ship; Object P
10. submarines or atomic power; Object P

B.
11. sail, Verb
12. pirate, Noun
13. pirate, Adjective
14. plan, Verb
15. plan, Noun
16. sail, Noun
17. inside, Adverb
18. treasure, Noun
19. gold, Noun
20. gold, Adjective

CHECK ✔ POINT
MIXED REVIEW • PAGES 516–519

Writing Theme
Adventure Stories

A. In each of the following sentences, write and label the compound part as *Subject, Verb, Object,* or *Sentence.* For a compound object of a preposition, use the label *Object P.*

1. Apparently a monster was attacking and sinking ships.
2. Ned Land and a French professor tried unsuccessfully to destroy the monster.
3. An explosion sent them overboard, but they were rescued.
4. They had come up against Captain Nemo and the *Nautilus.*
5. The underwater ship had oxygen, electricity, and fuel.
6. Food and clothing came from the sea.
7. With special equipment they walked and hunted on the ocean floor.
8. For months they sailed around the world, and they experienced many adventures.
9. They woke up one morning on an island, with no sign of Nemo or the ship.
10. Jules Verne published the story *Twenty Thousand Leagues Under the Sea* in 1870, before submarines or atomic power.

B. Write the italicized words in the following sentences and identify the part of speech of each.

11. Armed with a treasure map, Jim Hawkins, Squire Trelawney, and Dr. Livesey *sail* off to find gold.
12. Long John Silver, the ship's cook, is really a *pirate,* however.
13. Several of his *pirate* friends are part of the crew.
14. They *plan* to take over the ship.
15. Jim, however, overhears their *plan.*
16. Shortly after going ashore, Jim looks back to see a skull-and-crossbones flag flying above the *sail.*
17. On the island, the pirates find a chest, but nothing is *inside.*
18. Ben Gunn, a pirate marooned on the island for three years, has already found the *treasure.*
19. Eventually Jim and his friends get the *gold.*
20. Long John Silver escapes with a bag of *gold* coins.

A. Recognizing Prepositions and Prepositional Phrases

Write the prepositional phrases in the following sentences. Underline the object or objects of each preposition.

1. Imagine a huge forest growing in a hot, steamy environment.
2. In a tropical rain forest, the tallest trees rise nearly two hundred feet above the ground.
3. Direct sunlight reaches only the highest of their branches.
4. Only dim light filters through the leaves to the ground.
5. Thundershowers occur often throughout the year.
6. However, few raindrops fall directly to the ground.
7. Water drips down tree trunks or falls from leaves.
8. The place teems with wildlife.
9. Many animals spend their entire lives in the trees.
10. Frogs, toads, lizards, and snakes dwell among the branches.
11. Flying squirrels and flying lemurs glide from tree to tree.
12. Monkeys scamper along branches or swing from vines.
13. Bats, gibbons, monkeys, squirrels, and toucans eat nuts and fruits from the highest branches.
14. Few low-growing plants can live in the dim light of the forest floor.
15. You could easily walk through most parts of such a forest, among the fallen leaves.

B. Using Pronouns as Objects of Prepositions

Write the correct form of the pronoun in parentheses.

16. One writer found an African rain forest quite useful to (he, him) as a setting for adventure stories.
17. Edgar Rice Burroughs wrote many books, but the most famous of (they, them) is *Tarzan of the Apes.*
18. The Tarzan stories are still familiar to (we, us) today.
19. The son of an English nobleman, Tarzan is lost as an infant in the jungle—where death waits for most people, but not for (he, him).
20. Instead, he is raised by a tribe of great apes, and an incredible series of exciting events unfold for Tarzan and (they, them).
21. It is easy for (he, him) to communicate with the animals.

Writing Theme
Rain Forests

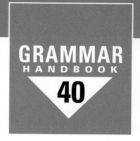

GRAMMAR
HANDBOOK
40

ADDITIONAL PRACTICE

Each of these exercises correlates to a section of Handbook 40, "Prepositions and Conjunctions." The exercises may be used for more practice, for reteaching, or for review of the concepts presented.

> **Additional Resource**
> Grammar and Usage Practice Book, p. 76

 Writing Theme:
Rain Forests
Other related areas students might wish to explore as writing topics include the following:

- native peoples of the Amazon rain forest
- plant life of the rain forests
- rain forests of the northwestern United States
- efforts to save the rain forests

A. **Recognizing Prepositions and Prepositional Phrases**
Answers are shown on page.

B. **Using Pronouns as Objects of Prepositions**
Answers are shown on page.

C. *Among* and *Between*
Answers are shown on page.

D. **Using Conjunctions**
Answers may vary slightly. See typical answers below.
31. The natives of the Amazon forest are highly inventive, and they also value generosity.
32. Some are farmers, but most are hunters and gatherers.
33. They invented the hammock and also created blowguns.
34. These forest dwellers have an interesting history, but their future is uncertain.
35. They could survive in many places, or they could disappear.

E. **Identifying Parts of Speech**
36. outside, Adjective; inside, Preposition
37. past, Preposition; past, Noun
38. along, Preposition; along, Adverb
39. over, Preposition; over, Adjective
40. On, Preposition; on, Adverb

22. Eventually Tarzan meets Jane and falls in love with (she, her).
23. The stories about (he, him) and (she, her) are widely read.
24. In the film version of the story, a chimpanzee named Cheeta lives in the jungle with Jane and (he, him).
25. Today, all this might seem unlikely to you and (I, me).

C. *Among* and *Between* Choose and write the correct preposition from the two given in parentheses.

26. (Among, Between) the world's tropical rain forests, the Amazon rain forest is the largest.
27. It lies (among, between) the Andes and the Atlantic.
28. It will be hard to keep a balance (between, among) protecting the environment and using the resources.
29. Scientists estimate that (between, among) 40 million and 60 million acres of rain forest are destroyed yearly.
30. Governments will have to choose (among, between) several different approaches to the problem.

D. Using Conjunctions Write each sentence pair as a single sentence, using *and, but,* or *or.* Add commas where needed.

31. The natives of the Amazon forest are highly inventive. They also value generosity.
32. Some are farmers. Most are hunters and gatherers.
33. They invented the hammock. They also created blowguns.
34. These forest dwellers have an interesting history. Their future is uncertain.
35. They could survive in many places. They could disappear.

E. Identifying Parts of Speech Write each italicized word and identify its part of speech.

36. The *outside* world knows little of life *inside* the forest.
37. The Amazon flows *past* the little villages as it did in the *past.*
38. However, times are changing *along* this river, and the forest people may have no choice but to go *along* with the changes.
39. The life they have lived *over* centuries may be almost *over.*
40. *On* the other hand, perhaps their traditions will live *on.*

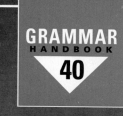

Writing Theme
Stone-Age Man

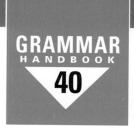

REVIEW

These exercises may be used as a mixed review or as an informal evaluation of the skills presented in Handbook 40, "Prepositions and Conjunctions."

Additional Resources

Grammar and Usage Practice Book, p. 77
Tests and Writing Assessment Prompts, Mastery Test, pp. 41–42
Elaboration, Revision, and Proofreading Practice, p. 29

Writing Theme:
Stone-Age Man

Other related areas students might wish to explore as writing topics include the following:
- characteristics of Stone Age civilization
- Neanderthal or Cro-Magnon Man
- methods used by archaeologists

A. Prepositional Phrases
Answers are shown on page.

B. Pronouns and Prepositions
Answers are shown on page.

A. Prepositional Phrases   Write the prepositional phrases in the following sentences. Underline the object or objects of each preposition.

1. In 1991, two hikers made a strange discovery in the Alps.
2. They were walking along a snow-covered mountain ridge.
3. They spotted part of a skull in a melting glacier.
4. To their surprise, the skull was part of a mummified body.
5. Scientists were soon at work on this cold, lonely site.
6. In a short while, a startling discovery was made.
7. The body was that of a prehistoric man who had died, and whose body had lain there for over 5,000 years.
8. Around the body were many of his belongings.
9. Among them were leather clothes, a bow, arrows, and an ax.
10. Without a doubt, this was one of the most important discoveries of its kind in recent years.

B. Pronouns and Prepositions   Write the correct pronoun or preposition given from the two in parentheses.

11. (Among, Between) the prehistoric man's belongings was a pair of shoes.
12. His shoes were different from those used by (we, us) today.
13. Scientists think that for (he, him) and others of his time, shoemaking may have been part of daily life.
14. Each shoe has a bottom sole and an upper flap, both of (them, they) made of leather.
15. (Among, Between) these parts is a socklike net sewn onto the sole.
16. Roswitha Goedecker-Ciolek is (among, between) the experts studying the shoes.
17. According to (she, her) and others on the team, the man stuffed grass into the nets so that the shoes would fit snugly.
18. It would have been easy for (he, him) to replace the grass when it became dirty or matted.
19. It seems clear to (she, her) that the man didn't remove his shoes often; they were too delicate.
20. These shoes may seem crude to you or (I, me), but they offered warmth and protection.

Prepositions and
Conjunctions   **523**

C. Conjunctions and Compound Constructions

Answers may vary slightly. See typical answers below.

21. Scientists do not know where this Stone Age man lived or why he was in the mountains.
22. A snowstorm or an avalanche probably killed him.
23. The man was 5 feet 4 inches tall and twenty-five to thirty-five years old.
24. Scientists may not be sure of the man's home, but they believe he was a herdsman or hunter from a nearby village.
25. There were many such villages, but scientists know little about them.
26. Most of the man's tools were made of copper or flint.
27. He carried a small box filled with leaves wrapped around pieces of charcoal, but we can only guess about their use.
28. The man probably carried glowing charcoal from his last fire and used it to start a fire at the next camp.

D. Words as Different Parts of Speech

29. about, Preposition
30. remain, Verb
31. about, Adverb
32. search, Adjective
33. search, Noun
34. use, Verb
35. use, Noun
36. around, Adverb
37. remains, Noun
38. Around, Preposition

C. Conjunctions and Compound Constructions Combine each of the following pairs of sentences to form a single sentence. Add conjunctions and commas where needed. Omit italicized words.

21. Scientists do not know where this Stone Age man lived. *They also do not know* why he was in the mountains.
22. A snowstorm probably killed him. *It might have been* an avalanche.
23. The man was 5 feet 4 inches tall. *He was* twenty-five to thirty-five years old.
24. Scientists may not be sure of the man's home. They believe he was a herdsman or hunter from a nearby village.
25. There were many such villages. Scientists know little about them.
26. Most of the man's tools were made of copper. *Some were of* flint.
27. He carried a small box filled with leaves wrapped around pieces of charcoal. We can only guess about their use.
28. The man probably carried glowing charcoal from his last fire. *He* used it to start a fire at the next camp.

D. Words as Different Parts of Speech. Write each word in italics. Identify its part of speech by writing *Noun, Verb, Adjective,* or *Preposition.*

29. Scientists believe the man died *about* 3000 B.C.
30. However, there *remain* many mysteries about this man.
31. For one thing, why was he walking *about* on this mountain?
32. Maybe he was part of a *search* party looking for copper.
33. Perhaps he was on a *search* for lost sheep or goats.
34. The man's bow is unfinished; clearly he did not *use* it.
35. An unfinished bow is of little *use* to anyone.
36. Possibly he was looking *around* for some materials to finish his bow.
37. As scientists study the man's *remains,* they may find the answers to their questions.
38. *Around* these mountains, they will also seek other clues to the ancient past.

WRITING CONNECTIONS
Elaboration, Revision, and Proofreading

On a separate sheet of paper, revise the following set of directions for assembling a pizza. Use the instructions given at the bottom of the page. Then proofread the directions for errors in grammar, capitalization, punctuation, and spelling. Notice the use of prepositions and conjunctions.

¹Use a mix to prepare pizza dough and <u>sauce or</u> make them from scratch. **²**Then follow these directions to assemble the pizza. **³**Sprinkle flour on a cutting board. **⁴**Put the pizza dough on the cutting board. **⁵**Flatten the dough. **⁶**Use a rolling pin. **⁷**Push the rolling pin in all directions to make the pizza as round as possible. **⁸**Add more flour as <u>necesary</u> to prevent the dough from sticking. **⁹**Sprinkle the <u>shreded Cheese</u> on top of the sauce. **¹⁰**Spoon the pizza sauce on the dough and spread it evenly. **¹¹**Finally, add your toppings. **¹²**Now <u>your</u> ready to put the pizza in the oven. **¹³**Bake it in an oven <u>heeted</u> to 425 degrees for ten to fifteen minutes. **¹⁴**You will know <u>you're</u> pizza is done when the crust turns golden <u>brown</u>.

1. Combine sentences 3 and 4, using the conjunction *and*.

2. Add the information in sentence 6 to sentence 5 as a prepositional phrase beginning with *with*.

3. Make sentence 8 clearer by adding the phrase "to the cutting board" at the end.

4. Add *next* to the beginning of sentence 10 to tell your readers you are moving on to a new step.

5. Switch the order of sentences 9 and 10 so that these steps are in the proper order.

Informative Writing: Explaining *How*

Writing directions involves giving step-by-step instructions. (See Workshop 4.) When you revise directions, look to see that you have included all the steps and have presented them in a clear order. Use prepositions and conjunctions to lead your readers clearly through the steps.

WRITING CONNECTIONS
Elaboration, Revision, and Proofreading

This activity will allow your students to see some of the concepts presented in this handbook at work in a piece of informative writing. By revising and proofreading the passage, students will have an opportunity to combine sentences using prepositions and conjunctions.

You may wish to make revision 1 with the class. Have students complete the remaining corrections and changes individually. Then read the passage line for line with the class, discussing the changes.

Rewritten paragraphs may vary slightly. See typical answer below. Proofreading errors are underscored on the page. Elements involving change are shown in boldface.

Use a mix to prepare pizza dough and sauce, or make them from scratch. Then follow these directions to assemble the pizza. **Sprinkle flour on a cutting board, and put the pizza dough on the board. Flatten the dough with a rolling pin.** Push the rolling pin in all directions to make the pizza as round as possible. Add more flour as necessary to prevent the dough from sticking **to the cutting board. Next, spoon the pizza sauce on the dough and spread it evenly. Sprinkle the shredded cheese on top of the sauce.** Finally, add your toppings. Now you're ready to put the pizza in the oven. Bake it in an oven heated to 425 degrees for ten to fifteen minutes. You will know your pizza is done when the crust turns golden brown.

Objective

• To use newspaper headlines as springboards to informal writing

WRITING WARM-UPS

Begin by reminding students that they will not be graded for this assignment. The headlines and the activities are intended as springboards to get them to think imaginatively about the concepts of this Handbook. Unless students volunteer to explore more than one prompt, have them work on a single activity.

Students who have difficulty in thinking of topics will probably choose the first prompt, which supplies the beginnings of headlines. Encourage students who choose the second prompt to invent as many wacky headlines as they can within a time span you decide on.

Dying planet
sends SOS to Earth

WOLF BITE TURNS
TEEN GIRL INTO
WEREWOLF!

Boy addicted to wood
eats baseball bats!

• How would you complete these headlines? Be as outrageous as you please.

Aliens from Outer Space _____

Escaped Gorilla _____

Dog with Two Heads _____

• Try creating some weird and wacky headlines of your own.

• What is the strangest thing you ever saw? Describe what happened.

526

Subject-Verb Agreement

WORLD TABLOID
Vol. 21, No. 4

Prehistoric crustacean terrorizes honeymoon cruise

Pet iguana rescues girl from burning building

Elvis spotted at Omaha drycleaner

Woman finds diamond bracelet in breakfast cereal

EXCLUSIVE

"What a crab!"
Cleveland couple cries.

- **Subject and Verb Agreement**
- **Agreement with Special Verbs**
- **Special Agreement Problems**
- **Agreement with Pronouns**

Y ou may not agree with the outrageous claims of these headlines. Yet the headlines are in agreement—their subjects and verbs work together. When you match singular subjects with singular verbs and plural subjects with plural verbs, your sentences are in agreement.

This handbook shows you how to avoid confusion in your sentences by making sure your subjects and verbs agree.

Subject-Verb
Agreement   527

Subject-Verb Agreement

Objectives
- To identify and use verbs that agree with their subjects
- To avoid agreement errors with verbs that have special forms
- To avoid agreement errors in sentences beginning with *There, Here,* and *Where*
- To use verbs that agree in number with compound subjects
- To avoid agreement errors when subject and verb are separated by a prepositional phrase
- To avoid agreement errors when certain pronouns are used as subjects

Writing
- To identify and correct errors in subject-verb agreement

INTRODUCING THE HANDBOOK
You might use the *World Tabloid* headlines as springboards by asking questions that involve alternate subject-verb numbers. For example, what if more than one woman found a diamond bracelet? Point out that the verb in the headline would change: "Women *find* diamond bracelets in breakfast cereal." Then introduce the term *subject-verb agreement,* and tell students that they are going to learn about this topic in the upcoming Handbook.

Objective

- To understand that subjects and verbs must agree in number

Writing

- To make subjects and verbs agree in sentences

Teaching Strategies

KEY TO UNDERSTANDING:
Remind students that the *subject* of a sentence is the word or words telling whom or what the sentence is about. The *verb* is the word or words telling what the subject does or is. Ask students to find the *subject* and *verb* in the following sentences:

The <u>girls</u> <u>ride</u> their bikes to school.

Lee's new mountain <u>bike</u> <u>is</u> black.

If students seem unsure about subject and verb, use pages 342–343 of Handbook 34, as a mini-lesson before beginning this Handbook.

INDIVIDUALIZING INSTRUCTION:
ESL STUDENTS In Vietnamese, Chinese, Japanese, and many other languages, there is only one form for each verb; therefore, verbs do not have to agree in number with their subjects. Be aware that some students are unaccustomed to the concept of subject-verb agreement. Offer them many opportunities to hear and use English sentences containing present-tense verbs.

Additional Resources

Tests and Writing Assessment
    Prompts, Pretest, pp. 43-44
Grammar and Usage Practice Book,
    p. 78

 Grammar
Test Generator

> Subjects and verbs in sentences must agree in number.

A singular noun stands for one person, place, thing, or idea.

> man   county   box   invention

A plural noun stands for more than one person, place, thing, or idea.

> men   counties   boxes   inventions

Verbs can also be singular or plural. A verb must **agree in number** with its subject. A subject and verb agree in number when they are both singular or both plural.

Singular	**Plural**
One *dog barks* at the bike.	Two *dogs bark* at the bike.
The *rider falls* off.	The *riders fall* off.

Singular verbs in the present tense usually end in *s* or *es*. In the sentences above, the verbs *barks* and *falls* are singular. They are used with the singular nouns *dog* and *rider*.

When the subject is plural, the verb must be plural too. Plural verbs in the present tense do not usually end in *s*. The noun *dogs* is plural. Therefore, the plural verb *bark* does not have an *s*. The noun *riders* is plural, so *fall* does not end in *s*.

Not all singular verbs are formed by adding -*s*. Here are some examples.

Singular	Plural
match*es*	mat*ch*
scurr*ies*	scurr*y*
miss*es*	mi*ss*
do*es*	d*o*

Practice Your Skills

A. CONCEPT CHECK

Subject and Verb Agreement   Write the verb in parentheses that agrees with the subject.

1. Some problems (<u>present</u>, presents) unusual challenges.
2. Often an unusual solution (solve, <u>solves</u>) them.
3. Snoring (result, <u>results</u>) from a blocked air passage.
4. Experts (<u>think</u>, thinks) thirty million Americans snore.
5. Inventors (<u>design</u>, designs) anti-snoring aids.
6. Muzzles (<u>hold</u>, holds) snorers' mouths closed.
7. One invention (keep, <u>keeps</u>) sleepers from turning over.
8. Another device (strap, <u>straps</u>) the forearm to the chin.
9. One plan (remove, <u>removes</u>) salt from the snorer's diet.
10. Some people (<u>try</u>, tries) hypnotism to stop snoring.
11. Snorers (<u>seek</u>, seeks) surgery to enlarge nasal passages.
12. Earplugs (<u>resolve</u>, resolves) the problem for people sleeping near snorers.

B. DRAFTING SKILL

Making Subjects and Verbs Agree   Write the following sentences, changing the verb in parentheses to the present tense. Make sure the verb agrees in number with the subject.

13. Inventions (helped) solve many practical problems.
14. A special book (presented) some fascinating inventions.
15. The book's title (attracted) readers: *Feminine Ingenuity: Women and Inventions in America.*
16. The book (showed) cyclists with a problem.
17. Some dogs (chased) bicycles recklessly.
18. A clever invention (repelled) the dogs.
19. Pepper boxes (attached) to the handlebars.
20. The rider (squeezed) a bulb on the box.
21. One squeeze (released) a cloud of pepper.
22. The sharp, spicy pepper (made) the dogs' eyes smart.
23. Also, the dogs (sneezed).
24. Just one dose (stopped) the dogs from chasing the bikes.
25. This unusual procedure (succeeded) in solving the problem.

FOR MORE PRACTICE
See page 539.

Subect-Verb Agreement   **529**

Writing Theme: Unusual Solutions
Suggest that students use these exercises as a springboard to writing. Other related areas that they might explore include the following:
- folk remedies
- the "inventions" of Rube Goldberg
- a personal experience with a problem and an unusual solution

Answers to Practice Your Skills
A. Concept Check
Subject and Verb Agreement
Answers are shown on page.

B. Drafting Skill
Making Subjects and Verbs Agree
13. Inventions help solve many practical problems.
14. A special book presents some fascinating inventions.
15. The book's title attracts readers: *Feminine Ingenuity: Women and Inventions in America.*
16. The book shows cyclists with a problem.
17. Some dogs chase bicycles recklessly.
18. A clever invention repels the dogs.
19. Pepper boxes attach to the handlebars.
20. The rider squeezes a bulb on the box.
21. One squeeze releases a cloud of pepper.
22. The sharp, spicy pepper makes the dogs' eyes smart.
23. Also, the dogs sneeze.
24. Just one dose stops the dogs from chasing the bikes.
25. This unusual procedure succeeds in solving the problem.

for FURTHER READING

Books to Read   Students interested in problem solving may enjoy the following books:
- Vaune Ainsworth-Land and Norma Fletcher, *Making Waves with Creative Problem Solving*
- Patricia Elwell, *Creative Problem-Solving for Teens*
- Diane Draze, *Think Tank*
- Rob Nelson and Robin Smith, eds., *Mind Benders*
- Ruth B. Noller and Ernest Mauthe, *Scratching the Surface of Creative Problem Solving*

Objectives

- To avoid agreement errors with verbs having special forms
- To avoid agreement errors in sentences that begin with *there, here,* or *where*

Writing

- To use verbs having special forms correctly in writing sentences

Teaching Strategies

CRITICAL THINKING: ANALYZING

After discussing the correct use of the forms of *be, have,* and *do* shown on the student page, have students help you list the negative contractions of these verb forms (*aren't, hasn't, doesn't,* and so on). Ask students which contractions would be correct with a singular subject and which with a plural one. Ask volunteers to use each contraction correctly in a sentence.

ASSESSMENT: SPOT CHECK

Before assigning the Practice Your Skills exercises, verify students' understanding by having them identify the subjects of the following sentences. (See single underlining below.)

Here (is/are) the pilot's gloves.

Where (is/are) the old biplanes?

There (is/are) one of them on the runway.

Then ask students to choose the correct verb form for each sentence. (See double underlining.) Have students share and explain their answers.

SPEAKING AND LISTENING In

informal speech, some people use the singular verb *is* with the words *There* and *Here,* regardless of the subject. In these situations errors, such as "There's too many boys in the auditorium," are commonplace. Emphasize to students that in writing, they must be sure that a verb that accompanies an initial *There* or *Here* agrees with the subject. Encourage students to find the subject by looking at the nouns or pronouns that follow the verb.

Writing
TIP

Remember to find the subject of the sentence when you use contractions.
  Wrong
    Here's the answers.
  Correct
    Here are the answers.

Additional Resource

Grammar and Usage Practice Book, p. 79

AGREEMENT WITH SPECIAL VERBS

Some verbs have special forms. Follow the rules of agreement for these verbs.

Special Forms of Certain Verbs

A few verbs have special forms. Make sure you choose the verb form that agrees in number with your subject.

Is, Was, Are, Were   The verb forms *is* and *was* are singular. The forms *are* and *were* are plural.

Singular   Lily *is* a detective. Lily *was* a detective.
Plural   The clues *are* here. The clues *were* here.

Has, Have   The verb form *has* is singular. *Have* is plural.

Singular   The investigator *has* no answer.
Plural   The investigators *have* no answer.

Does, Do   The verb form *does* is singular. *Do* is plural.

Singular   Lewis *does*n't like mysteries.
Plural   They *do*n't like mysteries.

There Is, Where Is, Here Is

Many sentences begin with *There, Where,* or *Here.* These words are never subjects of sentences. To decide whether to use a singular or plural form of a verb in such a sentence, first find the subject by asking *who* or *what* before the verb.

There (is, are) the planes.

Who or *what* is *there?* The planes are.
The word *planes* is the subject, and the word *planes* is plural.
Use the plural verb *are.*

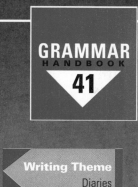

GRAMMAR
HANDBOOK
41

Writing Theme
Diaries

A. Making Subjects and Verbs Agree   Write the verb that agrees with the subject in number.

1. Diaries (preserves, preserve) thoughts and feelings.
2. Many people (keeps, keep) diaries and journals.
3. Famous people (has, have) published theirs.
4. Where else (does, do) people share their hopes and dreams and disappointments?
5. Where else (has, have) a reader become acquainted with a queen?
6. There (is, are) important lessons to be learned from diaries.
7. Here (is, are) one example from Queen Victoria's diary.
8. Even English queens (likes, like) parties.
9. One entry (tells, tell) about her dancing until 3 A.M.!
10. Other entries (reveals, reveal) her crush on Prince Albert.
11. (Does, Do) a queen get nervous before her wedding?
12. Queen Victoria (was, were) nervous and happy.
13. "The ceremony (was, were) very imposing," she wrote.
14. Other diaries (has, have) fascinating insights too.
15. Readers (shares, share) Davy Crockett's last days.
16. There (is, are) an account of the battle at the Alamo.
17. Provisions (was, were) running out.
18. The diary (shows, show) Crockett's great courage and determination.
19. Many paragraphs (describes, describe) the battle.
20. "Shells (has, have) been falling into the fort. . . ."
21. Another paragraph (states, state) a wish for freedom.
22. His diary (recounts, recount) his last day.
23. Crockett's last entry (was, were) "Liberty and independence forever!"
24. Here (is, are) stirring pieces of eyewitness accounts.
25. Without a doubt, diaries (makes, make) fascinating reading.

B. Using the Correct Verb   Write the correct present-tense form of the verb in parentheses.

26. Fame and money (be) only trifles to Thomas Edison.
27. Problems with dandruff (bother) him in July.
28. "Powerful itching of my head" (be) what he wrote.

Subject-Verb
Agreement   **541**

GRAMMAR
HANDBOOK
41

REVIEW

These exercises may be used as a mixed review or as an informal evaluation of the skills presented in Handbook 41, "Subject-Verb Agreement."

Additional Resources

Grammar and Usage Practice Book, p. 83
Tests and Writing Assessment Prompts, Mastery Test, pp. 45–46
Elaboration, Revision, and Proofreading Practice, p. 30

 Writing Theme: Diaries

Other related areas students might wish to explore as writing topics include the following:

- Robert F. Scott's South Pole diary
- the journals of Lewis and Clark
- notes from a naturalist's journal
- a personal memoir

A. Making Subjects and Verbs Agree
Answers are shown on page.

B. Using the Correct Verb
26. are
27. bother
28. is

29. tell
30. comes
31. are
32. are
33. does
34. haunts
35. are
36. fill
37. loves
38. has
39. do
40. has

C. Making Verbs and Pronouns Agree

Answers are shown on page.

29. Entries in Edison's diary (tell) us about the man.
30. The person behind the inventions (come) through in his plain, direct style.
31. Neither complaints nor embarrassing events (be) kept out of the diary.
32. Two keys on his piano (be) out of tune.
33. A clerk in a drugstore (do) not have peroxide.
34. A demon with eyes four hundred feet apart (haunt) his dreams.
35. Edison's comments and logic (be) keen.
36. Either nonfiction or novels (fill) part of every day for him.
37. This self-taught man of strong opinions (love) reading.
38. Lack of lessons or school (have) not discouraged or stopped him.
39. The walls of his office (do) not have diplomas.
40. He wonders if perhaps encyclopedia articles or the dictionary (have) facts about dandruff!

C. Making Verbs and Pronouns Agree   Write the correct verb.

41. I (is, am, are) the famous fly on the wall—a diary!
42. (Does, Do) you know of me?
43. I (saves, save) the thoughts of John Quincy Adams, our sixth president.
44. Nobody in Congress (escapes, escape) his sharp comments.
45. Each of Thomas Jefferson's tales (is, are) retold and made fun of.
46. Everyone (knows, know) about Jefferson's tendency to exaggerate.
47. One of Adams's dislikes (is, are) newspaper editors and their stories.
48. Everybody in Congress (has, have) the same dislike, he believes.
49. Anyone from Washington also (understand, understands) Adams's notes about summer heat.
50. Neither of his two sons (wish, wishes) to swim in the Potomac River to cool off, however.

WRITING CONNECTIONS
Elaboration, Revision, and Proofreading

Revise the following draft of a personal narrative by using the directions at the bottom of the page. Then proofread the narrative, making sure that all subjects and verbs agree in number. Also look for other errors in grammar, capitalization, punctuation, and spelling.

¹When we started our band, we had a problem. ²Bob's mom said we couldnt use there garage after just one session. ³Because we was too loud. ⁴None of the other parents even let us try. ⁵Then one day Keith said, "I found a great studio for us." ⁶He give us directions. ⁷He told us to meat him there the next afternoon. ⁸When Bob and I arrived, we was shocked. ⁹Our "studio" was the parking lot of an old gas station. ¹⁰"Don't worry," Keith said, "bands practices here all the time." ¹¹Then he pulled out his horn and blowed. ¹²"That really sound great," Bob said. ¹³"I like the way the sound echoes off the walls of the old building." ¹⁴In addition, there were no one living nearby to complane. ¹⁵We unpacked all of our gear. ¹⁶We begun to play to our audience of passing cars.

1. After sentence 1, add information to explain the problem the band had: finding a place to practice without disturbing the neighbors.

2. Combine sentences 6 and 7 to make one sentence with a compound verb.

3. Make sentence 14 more complete by adding the phrase "about the noise" to the end.

4. Add "anxiously" to the beginning of sentence 15 to show how the band members prepared to play.

5. Divide the passage into paragraphs.

Narrative and Literary Writing

Writing a personal narrative is a chance to share your experiences with others. (See Workshop 3.) When you revise a narrative, make sure you have presented events in the order in which they occurred. Also make sure your subjects and verbs agree so that your readers can easily follow your story.

WRITING CONNECTIONS
Elaboration, Revision, and Proofreading

This activity will allow students to see some of the concepts presented in this Handbook at work in a personal narrative. By revising and proofreading this passage, students will have the chance to identify and correct errors in subject-verb agreement. They also will become more aware of paragraphing and style.

You might have students work in small groups to revise the passage. Then discuss the completed revision with the entire class.

Revisions may vary slightly. See a typical revision below. Elements involving changes are shown in boldface. Proofreading errors are shown on page.

When we started our band, we had a problem **finding a place to practice without disturbing the neighbors.** Bob's mom said we couldn't use their garage after just one session because we were too loud. None of the other parents even let us try.

Then one day Keith said, "I found a great studio for us." He gave us **directions and told us** to meet him there the next afternoon. When Bob and I arrived, we were shocked. Our "studio" was the parking lot of an old gas station. "Don't worry," Keith said. "Bands practice here all the time." Then he pulled out his horn and blew.

"That really sounds great," Bob said. "I like the way the sound echoes off the walls of the old building." In addition, there was no one living nearby to complain **about the noise. Anxiously,** we unpacked all of our gear. We began to play to our audience of passing cars.

Skills

Test 3

This test enables you to evaluate student mastery of the concepts taught in handbooks 40–41.

Additional Resource

Grammar and Usage Practice Book, pp. 85–86

Answer Key

Corrections for run-ons may vary.

1. **D**
2. **B**—more loosely
   C—this
3. **D**
4. **D**
5. **A**—makes
   B—yellow. It *or* yellow; it
6. **B**—aunt
7. **A**—are
8. **A**—principal
   B—Middle School
9. **B**—lies
10. **C**—has
11. **C**—form
12. **C**—Cleveland and
13. **A**—There are
    B—children's
14. **B**—calories. When
15. **B**—is

Directions   One or more of the underlined sections in the following sentences may contain an error in grammar, punctuation, spelling, or capitalization. Write the letter of each incorrect section. Then rewrite the section correctly. If there is no error in an item, write *D*.

> **Example**   Palindromes <u>is</u> words or sentences that read the
>   A
> same forward and backward. <u>"Madam</u>, I'm Adam" is one
>   B
> of the <u>most famous</u>. <u>No error</u>
>   C   D
>
> **Answer**   A—are

1. Sometimes a flock of geese <u>flies</u> as high as <u>26,000</u> feet. That is almost five
                                   A   B
   <u>miles</u> above the earth! <u>No error</u>
     C   D

2. Which shoes <u>fit</u> <u>looser,</u> <u>these</u> kind or that kind? <u>No error</u>
               A   B   C   D

3. <u>There's</u> only one irregular verb in the <u>Turkish</u> language. That verb
      A   B
   is *imek,* and it means "to be." In English there <u>are</u> sixty-eight irregular
                                            C
   verbs. <u>No error</u>
          D

4. Where <u>are</u> the <u>science fiction</u> books shelved in this <u>library?</u> <u>No error</u>
         A   B   C   D

5. Neither of these spices <u>make</u> rice <u>yellow, it</u> is saffron that turns rice
                         A   B
   <u>golden</u>. <u>No error</u>
      C   D

6. Either our <u>neighbors</u> next door or my <u>Aunt</u> <u>feeds</u> our hamster when we
            A   B   C
   are away. <u>No error</u>
             D

7. Bud Abbott and Lou Costello <u>is</u> in the <u>Baseball Hall of Fame</u>, but neither
A   B
of them ever played professional <u>baseball. They</u> are honored for their
C
"Who's on First?" comedy routine.   <u>No error</u>
D

8. The <u>principle</u> said, "If it snows hard enough, everybody at John Wood
A
<u>middle school</u> <u>goes</u> home early."   <u>No error</u>
B   C   D

9. A fjord is a <u>long, narrow</u>, deep inlet of the sea. A fjord <u>lays</u> between
A   B
steep <u>cliffs</u>.   <u>No error</u>
C   D

10. <u>Neither</u> the <u>brushes</u> nor the paint for our project <u>have</u> arrived.   <u>No error</u>
A   B   C   D

11. <u>Bubbles</u> in <u>soda pop</u> <u>forms</u> where carbon dioxide gas is present.   <u>No error</u>
A   B   C   D

12. Only two presidents of the United States <u>have</u> entered the <u>White House</u>
A   B
as bachelors—Grover <u>Cleveland, and</u> James Buchanan.   <u>No error</u>
C   D

13. <u>There's</u> some <u>childrens'</u> television shows that are <u>really</u> educational. <u>No error</u>
A   B   C   D

14. Cream is <u>thicker</u> than milk and has more fat and <u>calories when</u> you weigh
A   B
each, however, milk is <u>heavier</u> than cream.   <u>No error</u>
C   D

15. Each of these computer <u>disks</u> <u>are</u> full. You <u>need</u> to get another disk.
A   B   C
<u>No error</u>
D

List of Skills Tested

1. **A**—subject-verb agreement
   B—punctuation—comma
   C—noun plural
2. **A**—subject-verb agreement
   B—comparative adjective form
   C—demonstrative adjective
3. **A**—subject-verb agreement
   B—capitalization—language
   C—subject-verb agreement
4. **A**—subject-verb agreement
   B—capitalization—common/proper noun
   C—punctuation—end marks
5. **A**—subject-verb agreement
   B—sentence fragment/run-on
   C—spelling
6. **A**—spelling
   B—capitalization—common/proper noun
   C—subject-verb agreement
7. **A**—subject-verb agreement
   B—capitalization—common/proper noun
   C—sentence fragment
8. **A**—spelling
   B—capitalization—common/proper noun
   C—subject-verb agreement
9. **A**—punctuation—comma
   B—confusing verb pairs
   C—noun plural
10. **A**—spelling
    B—noun plural
    C—subject-verb agreement
11. **A**—spelling
    B—capitalization—common/proper noun
    C—subject–verb agreement
12. **A**—subject-verb agreement
    B—capitalization—common/proper noun
    C—punctuation—comma
13. **A**—subject-verb agreement
    B—punctuation—possessive
    C—adjective/adverb confusion
14. **A**—comparative adjective form
    B—sentence fragment/run-on
    C—comparative adjective form
15. **A**—noun plural
    B—subject-verb agreement
    C—subject-verb agreement

Objective

- To use writing prompts as spring-boards to informal writing

WRITING WARM-UPS

Tell students that this page is intended to prompt informal written responses that will not be graded. The illustration and the text provide an imaginative intro-duction to concepts that will be devel-oped in the handbook. Allow students to work on one activity, unless they offer to respond to more than one prompt.

For the first writing prompt, have stu-dents brainstorm the names and some memorable attractions of theme parks they have visited or heard about. Ask one or two volunteers to name rides they par-ticularly liked. Then have individuals begin writing about an ideal theme park.

- Imagine you've been asked to develop a theme park like Safari Funland. Write a brief description of the park. What would it be called? What types of rides would the park have and what would you name them?

- Which movies or books do you like the best? Who do you think deserves to be called "great"? Make lists of movies, people, books, songs, products, or other items that are in your Top Ten.

546

Capitalization

- **Proper Nouns and Proper Adjectives**

- **More Proper Nouns**

- **First Words**

- **Outlines and Titles**

A musement park rides like the Zipper that spin 'round and 'round can make you really dizzy. Trying to remember all the rules for capitalization can make you really dizzy, too!

These rules, however, are important because capital letters are an important part of writing. Writers use them to name specific people, places, and things. This handbook will show you how to use capitalization in your writing.

Capitalization

Objectives
- To recognize and capitalize proper nouns and proper adjectives
- To capitalize the names of months, days, holidays, and historical events
- To capitalize the names of races, religions, nationalities, and languages
- To capitalize words referring to God and to religious scriptures
- To capitalize the names of clubs, organizations, and business firms
- To capitalize the first words of sentences and of most lines of poetry
- To capitalize the first words of entries in outlines and of titles

Writing
- To identify and correct capitalization errors in writing
- To use capital letters correctly in a piece of writing

INTRODUCING THE HANDBOOK
Explain that capital letters play an important role in making written prose easier to read. Point out that they guide the reader to the beginning of a sentence and to the names of specific people, places, and things. Tell students that in this handbook, they will learn rules that will help them use capital letters correctly in their writing.

Objectives
- To recognize proper nouns and adjectives and capitalize them correctly
- To apply capitalization rules to personal and official titles
- To capitalize the pronoun *I*

Writing
- To proofread paragraphs, correcting errors in capitalization
- To capitalize words correctly in writing

Teaching Strategies

KEY TO UNDERSTANDING Before introducing the definitions of common and proper nouns and adjectives, invite students to discuss connotations of the words *common* and *proper*. For instance, which word suggests formality, uprightness, and distinctiveness? *(proper)* Then have students look at the examples of nouns on the pupil page and try to formulate their own definitions of common and proper nouns. Finally, discuss the definitions in the text with these student-generated definitions in mind.

INDIVIDUALIZING INSTRUCTION: ESL STUDENTS The writing systems of languages such as Arabic, Hindi, Chinese, Korean, and Japanese do not distinguish between lowercase and capital letters. For students who speak these languages, provide extra help with English capitalization rules. Suggest that they write each rule in a notebook, for handy reference.

ADVANCED STUDENTS Challenge students to work in groups of three to compile lists of birds, animals, or trees whose names are made up of a proper adjective and a noun, such as the Douglas fir. Students may use prior knowledge, a dictionary, an encyclopedia, or magazine articles to find examples. Invite volunteers to tell the class about a particular item on their lists, explaining the origin or significance of the proper adjective.

Capitalize proper nouns and proper adjectives.

A **common noun** is a general name for a person, a place, a thing, or an idea. A **proper noun** names a particular person, place, thing, or idea. A **proper adjective** is made from a proper noun. All proper nouns and proper adjectives are capitalized.

Common Noun	Proper Noun	Proper Adjective
peninsula	Arabia	Arabian
country	Ireland	Irish

A proper noun may be made up of one or more words. Capitalize all important words in a proper noun.

Rocky **M**ountains   **L**incoln **P**ark **Z**oo   **P**eter the **G**reat

Proper adjectives are often used with common nouns. Do not capitalize the common noun.

Irish wolfhound   **B**urmese cat   **A**merican saddle horse

There are many kinds of proper nouns. These rules will help you recognize words that need to be capitalized.

Capitalize the names of people and pets.

Begin every word in a name with a capital letter. An initial stands for a name. Write initials as capital letters. Put a period after each initial.

Ken **G**riffey, **J**r.   **E**. **B**. **W**hite   **L**assie

Often, a word for a family relation is used in place of the name of a particular person, or as part of the name. *Dad* and *Aunt Jane* are two examples. Capitalize a word used in this way.

548   Grammar Handbook

MULTICULTURAL Connection

Some foreign languages include as part of a person's name a word (or words) that connects the first and last names. These short words are likely to begin with lowercase letters: Charles de Gaulle (French), Ludwig *van* Beethoven (German), Simon *van der* Meer (Dutch). Ask students to offer other examples of such names and to tell what the short words mean and whether or not they are capitalized.

Capitalize a personal title used with a person's name.

A **personal title** is a term of respect used in front of a name. Many titles have short forms called **abbreviations.** Capitalize abbreviations of personal titles. Follow an abbreviation with a period.

> **M**ister—**M**r.   **M**istress—**M**rs.   **D**octor—**D**r.

The title *Miss* has no abbreviated form. Do not use a period after this title. *Ms.* has no long form.

> **M**rs. **C**asey saw **C**aptain **G**etz and **D**r. **Y**ung at the zoo.

Do not capitalize a title that is used alone or that follows a person's name.

> The mayor met Joy Ortiz, the ambassador to China.

Capitalize the following titles when used before names, or when used alone to refer to the current holders of the positions.

> the **P**resident (of the United States)   **Q**ueen Elizabeth II
> the **V**ice-**P**resident (of the United States)   the **P**ope

Capitalize the word *I*.

> Clarice and **I** took our dogs to obedience classes.

Practice Your Skills

A. CONCEPT CHECK

Proper Nouns and Adjectives   Write the following sentences, using capital letters where necessary.

1. Yesterday i asked dad who he thought was the most popular fictional animal in the world.
2. He suggested garfield, the cartoon cat, but i think it is charlie brown's dog, snoopy.
3. The cartoonist charles m. schulz first drew this funny beagle over forty years ago, basing him on his own childhood dog, spike.

Writing Theme
Famous Animals

Practice Your Skills

CONCEPT CHECK

Titles and Outlines Write each item, using capital letters where needed. If the item is correct, write *Correct*.

1. what is your favorite type of story or poem?
2. Is it short stories like O. Henry's "hearts and hands"?
3. Do you prefer novels such as Cleary's *the luckiest girl?*
4. Do you like poems like David McCord's "rollercoaster"?
5. These authors share something with the writer of the *Iliad* of ancient Greece and reporters for today's *New York Times.* C
6. Whether they write for a textbook or for *sesame street*, most writers use a similar writing process.
7. Imagine that you are a reviewer for the *Chicago tribune.*
8. you are to write an article titled "my favorite movie."
9. you want to explain why *the wizard of oz* is your favorite.
10. first, you might brainstorm about the movie, then write your ideas in a draft you could title "working draft."
11. you might organize your article this way:
12. I. elements of the movie *the wizard of oz*
    A. plot, action, and special effects
    b. performances
        1. main characters
        2. minor characters
    II. my reaction to the movie
13. reread your draft and revise it so that it expresses just what you want to say about *the wizard of oz.*
14. You could research facts in a book like *The Oscar Movies.* C
15. You might add a comparison with a film like *star wars.*
16. You could write about the contribution "somewhere over the rainbow" and other songs make to the film.
17. After revising and proofreading, you would prepare a final draft of "my favorite movie" for publication.
18. Authors use this process whether writing an article for *Newsweek,* a school report, or a legal document. C
19. for example, Thomas Jefferson revised the declaration of independence many times before it was finally approved.
20. Now you can write a report titled "the writing process."

Writing Theme
The Writing Process

Capitalization **559**

Writing Theme
Poet, Biographer, Novelist

The poet, novelist, and biographer Eloise Greenfield.

CHECK ✔ POINT
MIXED REVIEW • PAGES 556–559

A. Write the sentences, using capital letters where necessary. If a sentence is correct, write *Correct.*

1. should Eloise Greenfield be called a poet or a novelist or a biographer—or simply a writer?
2. If you had read the *hartford times* back in 1963, you would have enjoyed her first published poem, "to a violin."
3. since then, she has had many other poems published, including a book of poems entitled *honey, i love.*
4. Her poems use words and rhythms to put the reader in the middle of a scene, as in "*rope rhyme.*"
5. It begins this way:
   get set, ready now, jump right in
   bounce and kick and giggle and spin. . . .
6. But Greenfield has also written novels, such as *sister.*
7. She has written biographies of famous African Americans too.   *C*
8. With her mother, Greenfield wrote the children's book *i can do it by myself.*
9. In addition to poems and books, she has written articles for magazines, including *ebony, Jr.*
10. Greenfield hopes her writing encourages young people to be proud of themselves, their heritage, and their abilities.   *C*

B. Application in Literature   Write this paragraph, using capital letters where necessary.

   i fell in love with langston terrace the very first time i saw it. our family had been living in two rooms of a three-story house when mama and daddy saw the newspaper article telling of the plans to build it. it was going to be a low-rent housing project in northeast washington, and it would be named in honor of john mercer langston, the famous black lawyer, educator, and congressman.
   Eloise Greenfield and Lessie Jones Little, "Childtimes"

A. Capitalizing Proper Nouns and Adjectives Write the following sentences, using capital letters where necessary.

1. Steven spielberg once said, "Like peter pan, i never wanted to grow up."
2. Audiences from north america to asia are glad he didn't.
3. spielberg was born in december 1947 to a jewish family.
4. His family moved from cincinnati, Ohio, east to new jersey, then west to Phoenix, and eventually to california.
5. Mr. and mrs. spielberg encouraged Steven's interest in movies.
6. He made a short film to earn a merit badge in the boy scouts.
7. By 1969, spielberg was a director at universal studios.
8. His first big american film was *Jaws* in 1975.
9. spielberg then wrote and directed the 1977 science fiction blockbuster *Close Encounters of the Third Kind*.
10. *Raiders of the Lost Ark*, in the summer of 1981, was the first of three films about the archaeologist indiana jones.
11. It takes place in the middle east just before world war II.
12. The lost ark is a box that contained the ten commandments written in stone as handed down from god to moses.
13. Indiana hopes to find it in a temple called the well of souls in the sahara desert.
14. Another film, *e.t.: The Extra-Terrestrial,* from 1982, may be spielberg's best-known movie.
15. People from austria to zaire love the tale of e.t. and elliot.

B. Capitalizing First Words Write the following sentences, capitalizing where necessary.

16. can you name the first full-length animated film?
17. it was *Snow White and the Seven Dwarfs.*
18. producer walt Disney introduced this classic in 1937.
19. later, disney produced other animated films of children's stories, including *Pinocchio* and *alice in Wonderland.*
20. eventually Disney combined live action with animation.
21. the movie *Mary Poppins* used this technique.
22. usually disney's composers wrote new song lyrics and music.
23. in *Alice in Wonderland,* however, one song used these lines from the poem "Jabberwocky" in lewis carroll's book:

GRAMMAR
H A N D B O O K
42

Writing Theme
Moviemakers

Capitalization **561**

GRAMMAR
H A N D B O O K
42

ADDITIONAL PRACTICE

Each of these exercises correlates to a section of Handbook 42, "Capitalization." The exercises may be used for more practice, for reteaching, or for review of the concepts presented.

Additional Resource
Grammar and Usage Practice Book, p. 92

Writing Theme: Moviemakers
Other related areas students might wish to explore as writing topics include the following:
• the adventures of Indiana Jones or another movie hero
• fantasy films
• special effects in filmmaking
• the role of the director in filmmaking

A. Capitalizing Proper Nouns and Adjectives
Words to be capitalized are shown on page.

B. Capitalizing First Words
Words to be capitalized are shown on page.

C. Capitalizing in Outlines and Titles

Words to be capitalized are shown on page.

24. 'twas brillig, and the slithy toves
    did gyre and gimble in the wabe;
all mimsy were the borogoves,
    and the mome raths outgrabe.

25. however, that lovable rodent mickey mouse was Disney's first great animated success!

C. Capitalizing in Outlines and Titles Write the following items, adding capital letters where needed.

26. the following outline shows some sources of popular movies:

27.   I. existing literature
      A. books
          1. children's books like *the wonderful wizard of oz*
          2. novels like *gone with the wind*
        b. fairy tales, legends, and other traditional stories
        c. stage plays, musicals, and operas
   II. original screenplays

28. many children's books, such as *heidi, treasure island,* and *sounder,* have been turned into movies starring child actors.

29. Others—for example, *the wind in the willows* and *aladdin*—were put on screen with animated characters.

30. films based on novels, such as *around the World in 80 days* and *Dances with wolves,* have won Oscars for best picture.

31. The animated film *cinderella* was based on the fairy tale.

32. another fairy tale, "beauty and the beast," has been made into two feature films, one with actors and the other animated.

33. the movie *oliver!* was the film version of the musical stage play *oliver!,* which was based on the book *oliver twist.*

34. its stars sang such songs as "who will buy?" and "consider yourself."

35. The movie (and musical) *annie* was based on a comic strip!

36. Most of the classic comedies, such as Laurel and Hardy's short film *the music box*, were original movie scripts.

37. *citizen kane* was loosely based on William Randolph Hearst.

38. He published the *san francisco examiner* and *harper's bazaar.*

39. *gandhi* was a more factual account of its subject's life.

40. whatever their source, movies are great entertainment!

A. Using Capitalization   Write the sentences, capitalizing where necessary. If a sentence is correct, write *Correct.*

1. Early flags of American colonies often showed a rattlesnake. C
2. The first flag for all the colonies joined thirteen red and white stripes with the british flag, called the Union Jack.
3. During the revolutionary war, patriots wanted a new flag.
4. Legend says Betsy Ross, a quaker seamstress, made the first u.s. flag in a house on arch street in philadelphia in 1776.
5. In her honor, the site is called the betsy ross house.
6. The new design replaced the union jack with thirteen white stars on a blue rectangle.
7. Records show that the continental congress adopted this flag on june 14, 1777, when it passed the Flag Resolution.
8. the new flag, the stars and stripes, was first used in a land battle on august 16, 1777, at the battle of bennington.
9. It was first flown at sea on november 1, 1777, on a ship commanded by captain john paul jones.
10. The Flag Act of 1818 set the number of stripes at thirteen, with the number of stars matching the number of states.   C
11. From 1791 till 1959, when a star was added for hawaii, the flag of the united states changed twenty-six times!
12. The flag that flew over fort mcHenry during the war of 1812 had fifteen stripes and fifteen stars.
13. this flag inspired francis scott key to write a poem.
14. Key was an american lawyer held on a british ship in chesapeake bay on tuesday, september 13, 1814.
15. He watched into the night as british ships shelled baltimore.
16. The next morning, overjoyed that the U.S. flag still flew over the fort, Key wrote some words that would soon be set to music: C
17. "oh! say, can you see, by the dawn's early light, what so proudly we hailed at the twilight's last gleaming?"
18. The title "The star-Spangled banner" comes from a line in the song: "oh! say, does that star-spangled banner yet wave."
19. On march 3, 1931, president herbert hoover signed a bill adopting the song as the united states' national anthem.
20. the very flag that inspired the song can be seen at the smithsonian institution in washington, d.c.

GRAMMAR
HANDBOOK
42

Writing Theme
Symbols of Patriotism

GRAMMAR
HANDBOOK
42

REVIEW

These exercises may be used as a mixed review or as an informal evaluation of the skills presented in Handbook 42, "Capitalization."

 **Writing Theme:
Symbols of Patriotism**

Other related areas students might wish to explore as writing topics include the following:

- the rattlesnake on early American flags
- the meaning of each color in the United States flag
- war memorials
- national anthems of countries around the world

A. Using Capitalization

Words to be capitalized are shown on page. Sentences 1, 10, and 16 are correct.

B. Mastering Capitalization
    Words to be capitalized are shown on page.

B. Mastering Capitalization   For each sentence and outline item, write correctly only the words lacking correct capitalization.

21samuel francis smith was a student at andover theological seminary in massachusetts. **22**he studied the bible and other religious subjects. **23**in 1831, lowell mason gave smith some german song books. **24**mason wanted smith to write songs for children, using melodies from the song books. **25**On a dreary winter day in february 1832, smith chose a melody and wrote these words:

> **26**my country! 'tis of thee, sweet land of liberty,
> of thee i sing. . .

27His patriotic song was introduced to the public on independence day in 1832. **28**four years later, the song was published in a book called *the boston academy* under the title "america, national hymn." **29**dr. smith eventually became the pastor of the first baptist church in newton, west of boston. **30**His song, "america," was being sung throughout the united states. **31**during the civil war, it was very popular among citizens of the North. **32**they sang it at rallies, in army camps, and at meetings.

33this patriotic song is still popular. **34**Some are surprised to learn that it has the same melody as the british national anthem. **35**Smith himself did not know he had chosen the melody of "god save the king." **36**the song from which he took the tune had german lyrics. **37**The result is that the melody appeals to the patriotism of people in two nations—the united kingdom and the united states.

38In 1914, Smith's son donated the original manuscript of "America" to the library at harvard university. **39**This manuscript is considered one of the treasures of the united states.

40The song "america"—a history
    I. Origin of the song "america"
        a. basic facts
            1. who, when, where
            2. what happened
        b. excerpt—first three lines
    II. the song's growth in popularity

WRITING CONNECTIONS

Elaboration, Revision, and Proofreading

Revise the following draft of a personal response to literature by using the directions at the bottom of the page. Then proofread your work, paying special attention to using capitalization correctly. Also look for errors in grammar, punctuation, and spelling.

¹Reading <u>The diary of a young girl</u> by Anne frank made me think about my reactions to writing in my own journal. ²Like anne, i sometimes wonders what the point is. ³Why would anyone want to read the scribblings of someone like me. ⁴On the one hand, her Dairy is a fascinating record of a terible time. ⁵It tells about all the things she endured with her Parents and her Sister. ⁶It also provide a chilling picture of what europe was like during world war II. ⁷Anne's writing shows me the value of just getting my thoughs out. ⁸Even if no one ever reads it, my thoughts have value for me. ⁹Writing is a way to relese my emotions. ¹⁰It is a way to figure out what I am thinking. ¹¹It is a way to figure out what I am feeling.

1. Add the following information after sentence 3 to introduce the sentences that follow. "Anne's diary gives two very powerful answers to that question."

2. Add emphasis to sentence 7 by beginning it with the phrase "more importantly, however."

3. Make sentence 8 clearer by replacing the vague pronoun "it" with the more precise "my journal."

4. Eliminate repetition by combining sentences 10 and 11 to make one sentence.

5. Divide the passage into three paragraphs.

Responding to Literature

Writing a personal response to literature allows you to share your thoughts and opinions about the things you read. (See Workshop 6.) When you revise this type of writing, make sure you present your reactions clearly and support them with specific details. Also check for errors in capitalization that could detract from your message.

WRITING CONNECTIONS

Elaboration, Revision, and Proofreading

This activity will allow students to see some of the concepts presented in this handbook at work in a personal response to literature. In revising and proofreading this passage, students will apply rules for capitalizing titles of books, the first words of sentences, and names of places. They will also be reminded of the ways in which using precise nouns and combining related sentences can strengthen a piece of writing.

Have students work in small groups to revise the passage. Finally, discuss the completed revisions with the entire class. Revisions may vary slightly. Typical changes are shown below. Elements involving change are shown in boldface.

Reading *The Diary of a Young Girl* by Anne Frank made me think about my reactions to writing in my own journal. Like Anne, I sometimes wonder what the point is. Why would anyone want to read the scribblings of someone like me? **Anne's diary gives two very powerful answers to that question.**

On the one hand, her diary is a fascinating record of a terrible time. It tells about all the things she endured with her parents and her sister. It also provides a chilling picture of what Europe was like during World War II.

More importantly, however, Anne's writing shows me the value of just getting my thoughts out. Even if no one ever reads **my journal,** my thoughts have value for me. Writing is a way to release my emotions. **It is a way to figure out what I am thinking and feeling.**

Objective
• To use writing prompts as springboards to informal writing

WRITING WARM-UPS
Begin by reminding students that they will not be graded for this assignment. The activities are intended as springboards to get them to think imaginatively about the concepts of this Handbook. Unless students volunteer to explore more than one prompt, have them work on a single activity.

For the first writing prompt, suggest that students imagine the alien. They might jot down a few descriptive words or phrases—or even draw this creature.

For the second writing prompt, have students recall some of the "other worlds" they remember from science fiction stories, movies, or TV shows. Then challenge students to imagine a science fiction setting that is completely different from these other alien worlds.

Sketch Book

• Imagine you just arrived in another world. Write the conversation you have with the first alien you meet.

• What is the biggest difference between this new world and the earth? Write a letter to your best friend, telling him or her about the wonders you've seen.

566

Punctuation

- **The Period**
- **The Question Mark and the Exclamation Point**
- **Commas That Separate Ideas**
- **Commas That Set Off Special Elements**
- **Other Uses of Commas**
- **The Apostrophe and the Hyphen**
- **The Colon and the Semicolon**
- **Quotation Marks**
- **Punctuating Titles**

No matter how you get your message across—with your voice, with your hands, or with your writing—you need to use signals. Punctuation marks are the signals you use when you write. They point out stops and starts. They add emphasis, join together words, or show how ideas are related.

In this handbook, you will learn ways you can use punctuation to clearly signal your meaning to your readers.

Punctuation

Objectives
- To use periods correctly in sentences, initials, abbreviations, outlines, and lists
- To use question marks and exclamation points correctly
- To use commas in a series, in compound sentences, to avoid confusion, to set off special elements in sentences and letters, and to set off direct quotations
- To use apostrophes to form possessives and contractions
- To use hyphens in word division, compound numbers, and fractions
- To use colons in business letters, expressions of time, and Biblical references
- To use semicolons to combine related sentences
- To punctuate quotations and titles correctly

Writing
- To correct punctuation errors
- To combine sentences, using correct punctuation
- To change indirect quotations to direct quotations

INTRODUCING THE HANDBOOK
To get students thinking about the effects of punctuation, play a brief recording of a conversation. Then have two volunteers come to the board and transcribe the recorded material while listening to it a second time. Are both transcriptions punctuated in the same way? Which of the punctuation marks indicate pauses or stops? Which suggest the speaker's tone of voice? Tell students that they will learn more about the role of punctuation as they work through Handbook 43.

Objectives
- To use a period after declarative sentences and most imperative sentences, after some abbreviations and all initials, and after numbers and letters in outlines and lists

Writing
- To revise writing by adding missing periods

Teaching Strategies

HELPFUL HINT Explain that when an imperative sentence states a strong command, it ends in an exclamation point (see page 571).

HELPFUL HINT Point out that abbreviations for government agencies and political organizations are usually written without periods, particularly if they are acronyms, abbreviations pronounced as words: NASA, NATO, UNICEF, OPEC.

After pointing out the abbreviation for *meter (m)*, you might go over some additional metric abbreviations. Reinforce that (as noted in the Writing Tip) such metric measures also usually appear without periods:

cm (centimeter)	**g** (gram)
km (kilometer)	**mg** (milligram)
cc (cubic centimeter)	**ml** (milliliter)

HELPFUL HINT Point out that the two-letter postal abbreviations for states are generally used only for addresses that include the zip code (for example, on an envelope or in the inside address of a business letter). Tell students to spell out state names in formal writing.

568 Grammar Handbook

THE PERIOD

Use a period after declarative sentences, after most imperative sentences, and after abbreviations, initials, and numbers and letters in lists.

Use a period at the end of declarative sentences and most imperative sentences.

A **declarative sentence** makes a statement.

Louis Pasteur developed the first rabies vaccine.

An **imperative sentence** states a command or a request.

Pour the solution into the beaker slowly.

Use a period after an abbreviation.

When taking notes or doing other kinds of informal writing, people often use shortened forms of words, or **abbreviations.** Notice how periods are used in these abbreviations:

P.O. (Post Office)	Co. (Company)
tsp. (teaspoon)	oz. (ounce)
Jan. (January)	Mon. (Monday)

Some abbreviations are written without periods.

FM (frequency modulation)	L (liter)
UPC (Universal Product Code)	m (meter)

The two-letter postal abbreviations of state names, such as *MA, AL,* and *CA,* are written with capital letters and no periods.

Dictionaries, newspapers, and magazines do not always punctuate abbreviations the same way. When deciding whether to use a period with an abbreviation, see what your teacher prefers or follow what your class dictionary says. Except for such abbreviations as *Mr., Mrs., Ms., Dr., A.M.,* and *P.M.,* avoid using abbreviations in formal writing.

MULTICULTURAL Connection

You might ask ESL students to share some common abbreviations from their first languages. For example, Spanish uses abbreviations for some terms not commonly abbreviated in English. In addition to all the words English typically abbreviated in English (months, weights and measures,

honorary titles, addresses, etc.), Spanish shortens the phrases used as the greetings and closings of letters:

B.S.M. *(beso sus manos):* with great respect
S.S.S. *(su seguro servidor):* your faithful servant
E.S.M. *(estrecho su mano):* I press your hand

Use a period after an initial.

An **initial** is the first letter of a person's name. It is used alone to stand for the name.

R. L. Carson—Rachel Louise Carson
Albert B. Sabin—Albert Bruce Sabin

Use a period after each number or letter in an outline. Use a period after each number in a list.

Astronomy
I. Galaxies and stars
  A. Types of galaxies
    1. Spiral
    2. Elliptical
    3. Irregular
  B. Types of stars
    1. Dwarf
    2. Giant
II. Solar system

Scientific Measurements
1. Volume
2. Mass and weight
3. Density
4. Temperature
5. Length

For information about the use of capital letters in outlines, see page 608.

Practice Your Skills

A. CONCEPT CHECK

Periods Copy each word, abbreviation, letter, or number that should be followed by a period. Then add the period.

1. Everyone in Mr Ramos's class had to do a science project
2. This chart shows the growth of plants for one project

Date	With Fertilizer	Without Fertilizer
Mon, Sept 21	7 cm	8 cm
Fri, Nov 20	12 cm	9.5 cm

3. T L Fabbri, M L Gibbons, and J T Ortez recorded the data
4. Dr Sharon Adams of Biotech Ltd was their advisor
5. Tom, Mary Lou, and J T gave both their plants the same amount of water and light but gave only one plant fertilizer

Punctuation   **569**

Writing
TIP

Do not use periods when abbreviating metric units of measurement. For example, use *g* for "gram" and *mm* for "millimeter."

Writing Theme
Science World

6. 1., 2., hr., min., 3., tsp.
7. growth.
8. I., II., A., B., III.
9. taller.
10. plants.

B. Revision Skill
Using Periods for Clarity
11. Tues., Sept., P.M.
12. E., St.
13. Co., Inc., St.
14. Dr., Mrs., B. J., eclipse.
15. Mt., difficult.
16. B. J., eclipse.
17. 1., sun., 2., projector.
18. IL.
19. Co., Inc., Mon., Tues., Oct., 4.
20. lb.
21. Ave.
22. P.M.

6. These are the measurements they used:
  1 Water—50 ml per day
  2 Sunlight—6 hr 30 min daily
  3 Fertilizer—1 tsp per week
7. For two months they carefully observed the plants' growth
8. They wrote a project report based on this outline:
  I What we thought would happen—our hypothesis
  II Our procedures
    A Daily watering and sunlight for both plants
    B Organic fertilizer for only one plant
  III Results and conclusions
9. Organic fertilizer caused one plant to grow taller
10. Use organic fertilizer if you want big, healthy plants

B. REVISION SKILL

Using Periods for Clarity All needed periods are missing from these notes. Copy each word, abbreviation, letter, or number that should be followed by a period, adding the period.

[11]The Science Club met Tues, Sept 6, at 7:00 PM [12]We were at 45 E Main St [13]I was asked to write to this address for a catalog:

  Science Equipment Co, Inc
  4652 Main St
  Beloit, WI 53511

[14]Dr Robert Alvin and Mrs B J Craig showed slides of their trip to Hawaii to see a solar eclipse [15]Clouds and ashes from the Mt Pinatubo eruption the previous June made viewing difficult [16]Yet B J Craig took fascinating pictures of the eclipse [17]She described safe ways to view a solar eclipse:
  1 Do not look directly at the sun
  2 Look through a special filter or use a pinhole projector
[18]Our next trip is to the Adler Planetarium, Chicago, IL [19]Alicia made arrangements with Corren Bus Co, Inc, for Mon and Tues, Oct 3 and 4 [20]The baggage weight limit for each person is 40 lb [21]We'll stay at the Hillcrest Hotel on Michigan Ave
  [22]The meeting ended at 9:30 PM

FOR MORE PRACTICE
See page 592.

Use apostrophes to show possession and to form contractions. Use hyphens to divide words at the end of lines and to write compound numbers and fractions.

Use an apostrophe to show possession. To form the possessive of a singular noun, add an apostrophe and *s.*

musician + 's = musician's   Charles + 's = Charles's

To form the possessive of a plural noun that does not end in *s,* add an apostrophe and *s.*

children + 's = children's   women + 's = women's

To form the possessive of a plural noun that ends in *s,* add only an apostrophe.

composers + ' = composers'   violins + ' = violins'

Use an apostrophe in a contraction.

A **contraction** is two words written as one, with one or more letters left out. An apostrophe replaces the missing letter or letters.

can + not = can't   she + will = she'll
I + am = I'm   he + had = he'd

Use a hyphen after the first part of a word divided at the end of a line. Then write the second part on the next line.

Musicians in the orchestra watched closely as the conductor raised her baton.

Divide a word only between syllables. Never divide a word of one syllable, such as *count* or *score.* A dictionary shows how to divide a word into syllables.

Punctuation   **581**

THE APOSTROPHE
AND THE HYPHEN

Objectives
- To use an apostrophe to show possession and to form contractions
- To use a hyphen to divide a word at the end of a line, in compound numbers, and in fractions

Writing
- To revise writing by adding necessary apostrophes and hyphens

Teaching Strategies

INDIVIDUALIZING INSTRUCTION: BASIC STUDENTS Explain that the first and third rules for forming possessives cover most English nouns. Provide the following additional examples:

glass + 's = glass's

doctors + 's = doctors'

ADVANCED STUDENTS Tell students that it is acceptable to add just an apostrophe to a singular noun if adding an additional *s* makes a word difficult to pronounce. Examples are words that contain more than one *s* or whose last syllable is pronounced *uz* or *eez.*

Jesus'   Achilles'
Moses'   Ulysses'

MODELING Write these contractions on the board and ask volunteers to provide the long form of each:

isn't   didn't   you're   we'd
aren't   wasn't   he'll   he's
don't   weren't   she'd   let's

Then have students state how each of the following words is shortened in a contraction: *not (n't), are ('re), will ('ll), had ('d), have ('ve), is ('s),* and *us ('s).* Usually, shortened forms are added to a verb or pronoun without any change in the first word's spelling. Ask students to think of exceptions. *(can't and won't)*

STUMBLING BLOCK Remind students that *it's* is the contraction of *it is,* but *its* is the possessive form of *it.* Add that *its* is a possessive pronoun and therefore does not need an apostrophe to show possession.

Punctuation **581**

Additional Resource

Grammar and Usage Practice Book, p. 99

 Writing Theme: Music

Other related areas students might wish to explore as writing topics include the following:

- great orchestras of the world
- a famous orchestra conductor, such as Arturo Toscanini, Leonard Bernstein, Herbert von Karajan, or Seiji Ozawa
- your school band or orchestra
- your response to a live concert or recording by an orchestra

Answers to Practice Your Skills

Concept Check
Apostrophes and Hyphens

1. ac-companied
2. audiences'
3. you've
4. conductor's, musicians'
5. conductor's
6. wouldn't
7. It's
8. orchestra's, player's
9. one-half, instru-ments
10. sixty-five
11. one-fourth
12. includ-ing
13. percussionist's
14. They're
15. Prokofiev's, children's

Writing Theme
Music

FOR MORE PRACTICE
See page 592.

Do not write a single letter at the end or the beginning of a line. These divisions would be wrong: *a- dapt, regga- e.*

Use hyphens in compound numbers from twenty-one through ninety-nine and in fractions.

eighty- eight piano keys   two-thirds of the audience

Practice Your Skills

CONCEPT CHECK

Apostrophes and Hyphens   Write the words that need apostrophes or hyphens in these sentences.

1. Originally, an orchestra was a group of musicians who ac companied opera performances.
2. Soon, audiences attention centered on the orchestras as much as on the opera singers.
3. If youve ever seen an orchestra play, then you know it has a leader, called a conductor.
4. A conductors baton and arm motions hold the musicians attention.
5. The conductors signals and gestures lead the orchestra.
6. Orchestra members wouldnt be able to play without direction.
7. Its important that the musicians play together as a group.
8. The orchestras success depends on each players skill and sense of cooperation.
9. More than one half of the musicians play stringed instru ments, such as violins, violas, double basses, and cellos.
10. For example, in an orchestra of one hundred members, about sixty five usually play stringed instruments.
11. About one fourth play brass instruments, such as trumpets, French horns, trombones, and tubas.
12. The rest of the musicians play either woodwinds—including clarinets, oboes, and flutes—or percussion instruments.
13. The timpani, or big kettledrums, are a percussionists most important instruments.
14. Theyre large, hollow copper kettles covered with drumheads.
15. Listening to Sergey Prokofievs *Peter and the Wolf* often builds childrens interest in the orchestra.

Use a colon after the greeting of a business letter and between hours and minutes in an expression of time. Use a semicolon to join two related sentences.

Use a colon after the greeting of a business letter.

Dear Mrs. DeMille: Dear Sir:

Use a colon between numerals representing hours and minutes. Also use a colon between chapter and verse in Biblical references.

10:14 A.M.   6:33 P.M.   Genesis 1:1–5

Remember to capitalize the letters and to use a period after each letter in the abbreviations A.M. and P.M.

Use a semicolon to combine two related sentences.

You can combine two related sentences into one by using a comma and a conjunction such as *and, but,* or *or* to connect the sentences.

We ran to the theater, but the show had already begun.

Another way to combine two related sentences is to use a semicolon (;). The semicolon takes the place of both the comma and the conjunction.

We ran to the theater; the show had already begun.
We ran to the theater; however, we were late.

You can use semicolons to avoid writing run-on sentences. For more about run-on sentences, see Handbook 34, pages 344–345.

Incorrect   The lights dimmed the movie began.
Correct   The lights dimmed; the movie began.

THE COLON

AND THE SEMICOLON

Objectives

- To use a colon after the greeting of a business letter, in expressions of time, and in Biblical references
- To use a semicolon to join two related sentences

Writing

- To combine sentences by using either a semicolon or a comma along with a conjunction

Teaching Strategies

KEY TO UNDERSTANDING Tell students to think of the semicolon as a cross between a comma and a period (which is exactly what it looks like). It signals a pause stronger than that of the comma but weaker than that of the period.

HELPFUL HINT The semicolon can also be used to avoid another common writing problem: the comma splice. A comma splice occurs when two sentences are combined ("spliced" together) with a comma—but no conjunction. To correct this problem (and still combine the sentences), a conjunction can be added, or the comma can be changed to a semicolon. Discuss these sentences with the class:

Incorrect: The train was pulling into the station, I ran to catch it.

Correct: The train was pulling into the station, and I ran to catch it.

Correct: The train was pulling into the station; I ran to catch it.

Additional Resource

Grammar and Usage Practice Book, p. 101

Writing Theme: Entertainment

Other related areas students might wish to explore as writing topics include the following:

- how to use a video camera
- a proposal for a new video
- an outstandingly funny home video
- your favorite music video

Answers to Practice Your Skills

A. Concept Check

Colons and Semicolons

¹ April 10, 19—
² Dear Ms. Velez:
   ³ Please put this announcement in the school paper. ⁴ Mr. Wu's sixth-grade class has made a video; it's called *On a Sunny Day.* ⁵ It's about summer sports, hobbies, and activities. ⁶ The video will be shown on Tuesday, April 28, at 11:00 A.M. and 2:00 P.M. ⁷ The movie is free; however, a donation for the Food Bank is welcome. ⁸ Cans of fruit, vegetables, and soup are needed. ⁹ We hope people come; the class has worked hard.
            ¹⁰ Sincerely yours,
                Andrea Giotti

B. Drafting Skill

Sentence Combining

11. Mr. Chandler's class made a video last fall; now they are making another one.
12. They discussed story ideas, and they chose one.
13. Anya wrote the script; Stacy helped her.
14. Class members are actors in the video, and (*or* or) they handle the technical jobs.
15. Jaina hopes to borrow her family's video camera, or Mr. Chandler may bring his camera.
16. Costumes are Sonya's job; she loves sewing.
17. Jason and Mike are collecting props, but they don't know where they will find a pair of stilts!
18. The actors must rehearse; they must learn lines.
19. The first rehearsals have been a little shaky, and everyone is nervous.
20. By the end of the month, everything must be ready; it will be time to start filming.

FOR MORE PRACTICE
See page 593.

Practice Your Skills

A. CONCEPT CHECK

Colons and Semicolons   Write the following business letter, adding colons, semicolons, and commas where necessary.

                        ¹April 10 19—
   ²Dear Ms. Velez
      ³Please put this announcement in the school paper. ⁴Mr. Wu's sixth-grade class has made a video it's called *On a Sunny Day.* ⁵It's about summer sports hobbies and activities. ⁶The video will be shown on Tuesday April 28 at 1100 A.M. and 200 P.M. ⁷The movie is free however a donation for the Food Bank is welcome. ⁸Cans of fruit vegetables and soup are needed. ⁹We hope people come the class has worked hard.
                        ¹⁰Sincerely yours
                        Andrea Giotti

B. DRAFTING SKILL

Sentence Combining   Combine each pair of sentences, using either a comma and a conjunction or a semicolon, as indicated in the parentheses.

11. Mr. Chandler's class made a video last fall. Now they are making another one. (semicolon)
12. They discussed story ideas. They chose one. (conjunction)
13. Anya wrote the script. Stacy helped her. (semicolon)
14. Class members are actors in the video. They handle the technical jobs. (conjunction)
15. Jaina hopes to borrow her family's video camera. Mr. Chandler may bring his camera. (conjunction)
16. Costumes are Sonya's job. She loves sewing. (semicolon)
17. Jason and Mike are collecting props. They don't know where they will find a pair of stilts! (conjunction)
18. The actors must rehearse. They must learn lines. (semicolon)
19. The first rehearsals have been a little shaky. Everyone is nervous. (conjunction)
20. By the end of the month, everything must be ready. It will be time to start filming. (semicolon)

A. Write the following business letter, adding apostrophes, hyphens, colons, semicolons, and commas where necessary.

Writing Theme
Mythical Animals

¹Dear Dr. Wasser

²Yesterday morning, about 600 A.M., I was walking on the beach near some cliffs when I saw the most incredible crea ture! ³It had an eagles head and wings and a lions tail and body. ⁴Ive heard youre an expert on unusual animals thats why I decided to write to you. ⁵You must be used to peoples imaginations running wild. ⁶However please dont tell me that I was dreaming. ⁷I was only twenty five feet away from this animal and I saw it clearly. ⁸I tried to get even closer but it flew away then. ⁹Please answer soon nobody else believes me!

¹⁰Sincerely
Alice Stein

B. Write the following reply. Add apostrophes, hyphens, colons, semicolons, and commas where necessary.

¹¹Dear Ms. Stein

¹²Thank you for writing to me I enjoy hearing about peoples unusual experiences. ¹³The animal you saw was a griffin but I have to tell you that its thought to be an imagi nary creature. ¹⁴Legend says that griffins lived in western Persia and guarded the gods gold mines from greedy humans. ¹⁵A griffin was supposed to be stronger than ninety nine eagles one could carry off and devour oxen elephants and even people. ¹⁶Griffins claws were thought to contain an antidote to poison and it is said that the claws were made into drinking cups.

¹⁷Please come to see me Id like to hear more about your ex perience on the beach. ¹⁸My office hours are 100 P.M. to 500 P.M. on Tuesdays and Fridays. ¹⁹Its not necessary to make an appointment.

²⁰Yours truly
Dr. Alvin Wasser

Writing Theme: Mythical Animals

Other related areas students might wish to explore as writing topics include the following:
- the sphinx or the manticore, two other mythological creatures that are part lion
- a creature from Greek mythology, such as the centaur, the Minotaur, or Pegasus
- the legendary unicorn or phoenix

MIXED REVIEW • PAGES 581–584

You may wish to use this activity to check students' mastery of the following concepts:
- the apostrophe and the hyphen
- the colon and the semicolon

A.
¹ Dear Dr. Wasser:
² Yesterday morning, about 6:00 A.M., I was walking on the beach near some cliffs when I saw the most incredible crea-ture! ³ It had an eagle's head and wings and a lion's tail and body. ⁴ I've heard you're an expert on unusual animals; that's why I decided to write to you. ⁵ You must be used to people's imaginations running wild. ⁶ However, please don't tell me that I was dreaming. ⁷ I was only twenty-five feet away from this animal, and I saw it clearly. ⁸ I tried to get even closer, but it flew away then. ⁹ Please answer soon; nobody else believes me!

¹⁰ Sincerely,
Alice Stein

B.
¹¹ Dear Ms. Stein:
¹² Thank you for writing to me; I enjoy hearing about people's unusual experiences. ¹³ The animal you saw was a griffin, but I have to tell you that it's thought to be an imagi-nary creature. ¹⁴ Legend says that griffins lived in western Persia and guarded the gods' gold mines from greedy humans. ¹⁵ A griffin was supposed to be stronger than ninety-nine eagles; one could carry off and devour oxen, elephants, and even people. ¹⁶ Griffins' claws were thought to contain an antidote to poison, and it is said that the claws were made into drinking cups.

¹⁷ Please come to see me; I'd like to hear more about your ex-perience on the beach. ¹⁸ My office hours are 1:00 P.M. to 5:00 P.M. on Tuesdays and Fridays. ¹⁹ It's not necessary to make an appointment.
²⁰ Yours truly,
Dr. Alvin Wasser

Objectives
- To use quotation marks at the beginning and end of direct quotations

Writing
- To revise sentences by changing indirect quotations to direct quotations

Teaching Strategies

INDIVIDUALIZING INSTRUCTION: BASIC AND LEP STUDENTS You may want to provide some additional pairs of sentences illustrating the difference between direct and indirect quotations. Point out, as well, that an indirect quotation is often signaled by the word *that*:

I said *that* I would do the job.

HELPFUL HINT Point out that in writing dialogue, a new paragraph should begin every time a new speaker is quoted. (For examples, direct students to the letters on pages 579 and 580 and the Thurber excerpt on page 589.) Tell students that if you are quoting more than one paragraph spoken by the same person quotation marks should be placed at the beginning of each paragraph but at the end of only the last paragraph. Ask students to look in newspapers, magazines, and books for passages that illustrate these rules for punctuating dialogue.

QUOTATION MARKS

Use quotation marks at the beginning and the end of a direct quotation.

When you write what a person has said, you are writing a **quotation**. A **direct quotation** is a restatement of the person's exact words. If you do not write the exact words, you are writing an **indirect quotation**. Here are examples:

Direct Quotation   Jenny said, "I've met the mayor."
Indirect Quotation   Jenny said that she had met the mayor.

Put quotation marks before and after the words of a direct quotation.

In the first sentence above, Jenny's exact words are set apart by quotation marks. The second sentence tells what Jenny said without using her exact words.

Place a period inside the quotation marks if the quotation ends the sentence.

Jenny said, "He shook my hand."

Use a comma, exclamation point, or question mark to separate explanatory words from a direct quotation.

"I was surprised," said Jenny.
"I couldn't think of anything to say!" Jenny exclaimed.

Place question marks and exclamation points inside quotation marks if they belong to the quotation itself.

Rita asked, "What did the mayor say to you?"
"I can't remember!" answered Jenny.

In the first sentence, the question is quoted. Therefore, the question mark is placed inside the quotation marks. In the second sentence, the speaker is showing strong emotion. The exclamation point is also placed inside the quotation marks.

MULTICULTURAL Connection

Punctuation style for quotations varies from language to language. For example, French, Spanish, Italian, and Russian have small angle marks called *guillemets* (« ») that enclose quotations. Dialogue, however, is set off by dashes. In German, quotations begin with inverted lowered quotation marks and end with inverted raised marks („ "). Even British style is somewhat different from American: commas are generally placed outside the closing quotation marks. Ask students to share examples of quotation styles from languages they are familiar with.

Place question marks and exclamation points outside quotation marks if they do not belong to the quotation.

Did Christopher say, "Sometime I would like to talk to the mayor myself"**?**

How amazing that Jenny said, "Maybe you can"**!**

Divided Quotations

Sometimes a quotation is divided. Explanatory words, like *he said* or *she asked,* are in the middle of the quotation.

"The interview," said Jenny, "is scheduled for Friday."

Notice that two sets of quotation marks are used for this quotation. This sentence has a comma after the explanatory words because the second part of the quotation does not begin a new sentence. Use a period after the explanatory words if the second part of the quotation is a new sentence.

"Today is Tuesday," said Paul. "That gives me three days to get my questions ready."

In this sentence, the second part of the quotation begins with a capital letter because it is a new sentence.

Practice Your Skills

A. CONCEPT CHECK

Quotation Marks Write the sentences, adding quotation marks and other punctuation where necessary. Write *Correct* if no additional punctuation is needed.

1. Our guests today announced the talk show host are two famous world leaders.
2. Ladies and gentlemen, please welcome Genghis Khan and Abraham Lincoln she said.
3. Mr. Lincoln she asked you are our sixteenth president. How do you lead people?
4. First of all, you must earn their respect Lincoln answered That's vital.
5. I disagree shouted Genghis You must show strength.

Punctuation   **587**

Writing
TIP

Use a variety of explanatory words when you write quotations. Some common explanatory words are *explained, shouted, asked, laughed,* and *replied.* Make sure the word you choose fits the situation.

Writing Theme
Interviews

Literature Connection

Ask students to find the vivid explanatory words (underlined) in this passage from "Miss Awful" by Arthur Cavanaugh.

"Such was Roger's distress that his mother offered to stop at the Schrafft's on Thirteenth Street and treat him to a soda. "Who's got time for sodas?" he <u>bleated</u>. "I have homework to do.

Punishment homework. Ten words, ten times each. On account of the . . . spelling test."

"Ten words, ten times each?" Mrs. Clark <u>repeated</u>. "How many words were on the test?"

"Ten," <u>moaned</u> Roger. "Every one wrong. Come on. I've got to hurry home. I don't have time to waste."

KEY TO UNDERSTANDING Remind students that commas and periods always go inside closing quotation marks. You might also point out that semicolons and colons go outside (see page 590):

Terry whispered, "I'm afraid," and then he burst into tears.

Terry whispered, "I'm afraid"; then he burst into tears.

LINKING GRAMMAR AND WRITING Suggest that students might occasionally use verbs other than *said* in tag lines, for example, *whined, shrieked, whispered, muttered.* Also point out that good writers vary not only the kinds of explanatory words they use, but also the placement of those words to introduce, interrupt, or conclude a quotation. (See examples in the Literature Connection, below.)

Additional Resource

Grammar and Usage Practice Book, p. 102

Writing Theme: Interviews

Other related areas students might wish to explore as writing topics include the following:

• an interview with a grandparent or other older person about his or her life
• an interview with a student leader
• an interview with a local store owner
• the life of a famous world leader

Answers to Practice Your Skills

A. Concept Check
Quotation Marks

1. "Our guests today," announced the talk show host, "are two famous world leaders."
2. "Ladies and gentlemen, please welcome Genghis Khan and Abraham Lincoln," she said.
3. "Mr. Lincoln," she asked, "you are our sixteenth president. How do you lead people?"
4. "First of all, you must earn their respect," Lincoln answered. "That's vital."
5. "I disagree!" shouted Genghis. "You must show strength."

Silly Signs

Signs are everywhere—on street corners and on diner counter tops, in store windows and in hotel lobbies. But do signs always mean what they say? Look at the examples below and judge for yourself. These signs appear in *English Well Speeched Here* by Nino Lo Bello.

WARNING: DOOR IS ALARMED

We Take Your Bags and Send Them in All Directions.

PLEASE DO NOT FEED THE ANIMALS. IF YOU HAVE ANY SUITABLE FOOD, GIVE IT TO THE GUARD ON DUTY.

If You Consider Our Help Impolite, You Should See the Manager.

Authentic Tie Cuisine

The Parade Will Take Place in the Morning If It Rains in the Afternoon.

Courteous and Efficient Self-Service

599

You might begin discussing this feature by making sure everyone in the class "gets" what makes these signs silly—and why they don't always say what they mean.

For example, what is the parade sign trying to say? ("The Parade Will Take Place in the Morning. If It Rains, It Will Take Place in the Afternoon.") What is the zoo sign apparently asking visitors to do? (Give suitable food to the guard so that he or she can feed it to the animals.) What's so nonsensical about the self-service sign?

Have students keep their eyes open for signs that could use some good editing or proofreading; then add them to your "bloopers" bulletin board (see page 263).

Test 4

This test enables you to evaluate student mastery of the concepts taught in handbooks 42–43.

Additional Resource

Grammar and Usage Practice Book, pp. 107–108

Answer Key
1. **A**—Captain Hook
2. **A**—ate, the
   B—*Nova*
3. **A**—Anchorage
   B—people, but
4. **B**—"Don't
5. **B**—It
6. **B**—P.M. The
   C—8:05
7. **B**—there
   C—stage.
8. **B**—Asian
9. **D**
10. **A**—Colorado River
11. **B**—liberty
12. **C**—God
13. **C**—"All Summer in a Day."
14. **D**
15. **A**—planets
    B—any room

Directions   One or more of the underlined sections in the following sentences may contain an error in grammar, punctuation, spelling, or capitalization. Write the letter of each incorrect section. Then rewrite the section correctly. If there is no error in an item, write *D*.

> **Example**   Sonja's grandmother came to the United States from
>   **A**   **B**
> Norway in 1932 mine came from Ireland the same year. No error
>   **C**   **D**
>
> **Answer**   C—1932. Mine

1. Peter Pan fans all recognize the name captain Hook, but few know that
                                           A
   Hook's first name was James. No error
     B   **C**   **D**

2. After we ate the electricity went off, so we couldn't watch *nova* on
            A   **B**
   public television. No error
        C   **D**

3. The biggest city in the United States is anchorage, Alaska. It doesn't
                                           A
   have the most people but it covers the largest area. No error
             B   **C**   **D**

4. "The bus leaves in two hours," the guide said. "don't be late or you'll
                       A   **B**
   be left behind!" No error
       C   **D**

5. The woolly mammoth had tusks sixteen feet long. it has been extinct since
        A   **B**
   the Ice Age. No error
      C   **D**

6. The brochure says the museum closes at 8:00 P.M. the doors are locked
                       A   **B**
   at 8 05. No error
     C   **D**

7. The usher at the concert told Eric and <u>us</u> that <u>"There</u> might be a few seats
                                        A   **B**

    near the <u>stage."</u> <u>No error</u>
             C   **D**

8. African elephants are larger and <u>more dangerous</u> than <u>asian</u> elephants.
                                   A   **B**

    African elephants also <u>have</u> larger ears. <u>No error</u>
                         C   **D**

9. Charles Dickens named one of the <u>worst</u> villains in his stories after his best
                                     A

    friend, Bob <u>Fagin. Fortunately,</u> Fagin had a sense of humor. <u>No error</u>
    B   **C**   **D**

10. The <u>colorado river</u> is important to millions of <u>Americans. It</u> is the major
         A   **B**

    source of water for all the states in the <u>Southwest</u>. <u>No error</u>
                               C   **D**

11. Who <u>shouted,</u> <u>"Give</u> me <u>Liberty</u> or give me <u>death</u>"? <u>No error</u>
         A   **B**   **C**   **D**

12. On every U.S. coin <u>there</u> <u>is</u> the motto "In <u>god</u> we trust." <u>No error</u>
                     A **B**   **C**   **D**

13. One of my favorite short stories by <u>Ray Bradbury</u> <u>is</u>
                                   A   **B**

    <u>"All summer in a Day."</u> <u>No error</u>
             C   **D**

14. Some bristlecone pine trees in <u>California</u> are four thousand years old.
                                     A

    <u>They're</u> believed to be the <u>oldest</u> living things in the world. <u>No error</u>
    B   **C**   **D**

15. The planet Jupiter is so large that all the other <u>planet's</u> in our solar system
                                           A

    could be placed inside it if it were hollow. However, there wouldn't be

    <u>no room</u> for all of the <u>planets'</u> moons. <u>No error</u>
    B   **C**   **D**

List of Skills Tested

1. **A**—capitalization—title with name
   B—punctuation—possession
   C—capitalization—common/proper noun
2. **A**—punctuation—comma
   B—capitalization—title
   C—capitalization—common/proper noun
3. **A**—capitalization—place name
   B—punctuation—comma
   C—comparative adjective form
4. **A**—punctuation—quotation
   B—capitalization—quotation
   C—punctuation—quotation
5. **A**—capitalization—common/proper noun
   B—capitalization—first word
   C—capitalization—time period
6. **A**—capitalization—common/proper noun
   B—capitalization—first word
   C—punctuation—colon
7. **A**—pronoun case
   B—punctuation—quotation/indirect quotation
   C—punctuation—quotation
8. **A**—comparative adjective form
   B—capitalization—nationality
   C—subject-verb agreement
9. **A**—comparative adjective form
   B—spelling
   C—punctuation—end mark
10. **A**—capitalization—river
   B—capitalization—first word
   C—capitalization—geographic region
11. **A**—punctuation—quotation
   B—capitalization—common/proper noun
   C—punctuation—quotation
12. **A**—spelling
   B—subject-verb agreement
   C—capitalization—deity
13. **A**—capitalization—common/proper noun
   B—subject-verb agreement
   C—capitalization—title
14. **A**—capitalization—common/proper noun
   B—punctuation—contraction
   C—comparative adjective form
15. **A**—noun plural
   B—double negative
   C—plural possessive

Skills

Post-Test

This test assesses your students' mastery of skills acquired in the Grammar and Usage Handbook.

Answer Key

Corrections for run-ons may vary.

1. **C**—he
2. **B**—Paris, France,
   C—Ontario?
3. **A**—are
   B—confusing. Can
4. **B**—telegraph, was
5. **C**—country"?
6. **A**—uncle
   B—likes
7. **B**—knows
   C—its *or* her
8. **A**—sits
9. **B**—indoors to
   C—mice
10. **A**—well
    C—poorly
11. **A**—lie
    B—north
12. **C**—me
13. **C**—bicycling
14. **D**
15. **D**

Directions   One or more of the underlined sections in the following sentences may contain an error in grammar, punctuation, spelling, or capitalization. Write the letter of each incorrect section. Then rewrite the section correctly. If there is no error in an item, write *D.*

> **Example**   The statue of Crazy Horse in <u>south dakota</u> will be the largest
>   **A**
> sculpture in the world when it is <u>completed</u>. It is being carved out of a
>   **B**
> <u>mountain</u>. <u>No error</u>
>   **C**   **D**
>
> **Answer**   A—South Dakota

1. Christopher <u>Columbus's</u> younger brother Bartholomew helped the famous
                A
   navigator plan his <u>voyages. Christopher</u> and <u>him</u> were very close. <u>No error</u>
                 B   **C**   **D**

2. Was the letter <u>addressed</u> to <u>Paris France</u> or Paris, <u>Ontario.</u> <u>No error</u>
               A   **B**   **C**   **D**

3. The instructions for operating this VCR <u>is</u> very <u>confusing can</u> you help
                          A   **B**
   me <u>please?</u> <u>No error</u>
      C   **D**

4. At first, Samuel B. <u>Morse, the</u> inventor of the <u>telegraph was</u> <u>better</u> known
                    A   **B**   **C**
   as a painter than as an inventor. <u>No error</u>
                             D

5. Was it Nathan Hale who <u>said, "</u>I regret that <u>I</u> have but one life to give
                     A   **B**
   for my <u>country?"</u> <u>No error</u>
        C   **D**

6. My <u>Uncle</u> has two pet ferrets. One of them <u>like</u> to eat French fried
      A   **B**
   <u>potatoes.</u> <u>No error</u>
     C   **D**

7. Somehow each of the ewes in that large flock of <u>sheep</u> <u>know</u> how to find
A   B

<u>their</u> lambs. <u>No error</u>
C   D

8. Mount Kenya <u>sets</u> right along the Equator, but because of <u>its</u> <u>height</u>—over
A   B   C

17,000 feet—the top is covered with snow. <u>No error</u>
D

9. Rural households in ancient <u>Greece</u> often kept snakes <u>indoors. To</u> control
A   B

rats and <u>mouses.</u> <u>No error</u>
C   D

10. Most metals conduct electricity <u>good</u>. On the other hand, <u>substances</u>
A   B

made of nonmetal conduct electricity <u>poor</u>. <u>No error</u>
C   D

11. Parts of Scotland <u>lay</u> as far <u>North</u> in latitude as southern Alaska, but warm
A   B

air from the <u>Gulf Stream</u> makes Scotland's climate quite mild. <u>No error</u>
C   D

12. Stalactites <u>hung</u> all around <u>us</u>, and a bat flew at Tom and <u>I</u>. <u>No error</u>
A   B   C   D

13. The triathlon participants had <u>swum</u> a <u>mile, but</u> they still had the
A   B

<u>bycycling</u> and running events ahead of them. <u>No error</u>
C   D

14. On <u>December 7, 1941,</u> millions of Americans turned on <u>their</u> <u>radios</u> and
A   B   C

heard about the Japanese attack on Pearl Harbor. <u>No error</u>
D

15. Stevland Morris is a great musician. However, most people <u>wouldn't</u>
A

recognize that <u>name. They</u> know <u>him</u> as Stevie Wonder. <u>No error</u>
B   C   D

List of Skills Tested

1. **A**—punctuation—possessive
   B—sentence fragment/run-on
   C—pronoun case
2. **A**—spelling
   B—punctuation—comma
   C—punctuation—end mark
3. **A**—subject-verb agreement
   B—run-on sentence
   C—punctuation—end mark
4. **A**—punctuation—comma
   B—punctuation—comma
   C—comparison form
5. **A**—punctuation—quotation marks
   B—pronoun case
   C—punctuation—quotation marks
6. **A**—capitalization—common/proper noun
   B—subject-verb agreement
   C—noun plural
7. **A**—noun plural
   B—subject-verb agreement
   C—agreement of possessive pronoun and indefinite pronoun
8. **A**—confusing verb pairs
   B—possessive pronoun
   C—spelling
9. **A**—capitalization—common/proper noun
   B—sentence fragment/run-on
   C—noun plural
10. **A**—adjective/adverb confusion
    B—noun plural
    C—adjective/adverb confusion
11. **A**—confusing verb pairs
    B—capitalization—common/proper noun
    C—capitalization—common/proper noun
12. **A**—irregular verb form
    B—pronoun case
    C—pronoun case
13. **A**—irregular verb form
    B—punctuation—comma
    C—spelling
14. **A**—punctuation—comma
    B—pronoun-antecedent agreement
    C—noun plural
15. **A**—punctuation—apostrophe
    B—sentence fragment/run-on
    C—pronoun case

ART NOTE Help students unfamiliar with Asia to understand that Asia is the home of diverse cultures and religions. In some countries, such as Nepal, Buddhist and Hindu festivals and traditions intermingle.

The three papier-mâché masks shown here are used in various joyful religious festivals in Indonesia, Nepal, and Hong Kong. The upper mask and the one at the right portray a lion and a dragon.

Upper Mask. This ceremonial mask of a lion is from Bali. (Note the striped ears, fierce teeth, and leonine nose.) In Asia, lion-head masks are sometimes thought to bring good luck and wealth.

Lower Right Mask. On Chinese New Year, men snake through the streets, performing the dragon dance. The first dancer carries an elaborate dragon mask like the one shown here. According to Chinese mythology, four dragon kings rule the four seas surrounding the earth and also control rainfall. Lakes and rivers are ruled by local dragon kings, and people place a small dragon-king statue by each well. To the Chinese, the dragon is well-meaning and is a powerful symbol.

Lower Left Mask. This devil mask was photographed at a winter religious festival in Katmandu, the capital of Nepal (a country in the Himalayas between Tibet and India). This mask may have been used in either a Buddhist or a Hindu festival.

Encourage students to find and tell (or read aloud) a myth or folk tale from the Nepalese tradition.

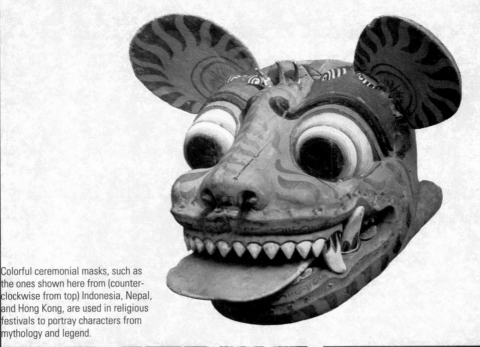

Colorful ceremonial masks, such as the ones shown here from (counterclockwise from top) Indonesia, Nepal, and Hong Kong, are used in religious festivals to portray characters from mythology and legend.

604

ACCESS GUIDE

Access Guide

Sharing your writing with others is a good way to get encouragement and new ideas. It is also a way to find out what things your readers like in your writing and what ideas may not be clear. Here are some techniques to help you get the responses you need to improve your writing.

Sharing

How to Use   Share your writing with your peer readers by asking them to read or listen to it. Hearing how your words sound may help you and your peer readers discover new ideas or places where more details are needed.

At this stage your peer readers serve as your friendly audience. They should not evaluate your writing.

When to Use   You may use this technique when you are exploring ideas. You may also use it to celebrate a finished piece of writing.

Pointing

How to Use   Ask your readers to tell you about the things they like best in your writing. Ask them to be specific and to avoid simply saying, "I like it."

Have readers point out the words and phrases that create an image or express an idea clearly.

When to Use   Use this technique when you want to find out what ideas are getting through to your readers. Also use it when you want encouragement and support for your writing.

Summarizing

How to Use   Ask readers to tell you the main idea in your writing. If readers stray from the main idea and start to talk about specific parts that they like or that confuse them, you might say, "For now, I want to know if I got my idea across to you."

Remind readers that at this stage you are not asking for an evaluation of your writing.

When to Use   Use this technique when you want to know if your main idea or goals are getting through to readers.

Telling

How to Use   Ask readers to tell you how they felt as they read your words. For example, did they feel sad or happy at any parts of your story? Did they get the characters mixed up? Did anything make them laugh?

As readers describe their feelings, ask them to point out the parts of the story that caused their reactions.

When to Use   Use this technique when you want to find out which words and phrases are creating the effect you want and which ones are confusing your readers.

Identifying

How to Use   Ask for feedback about things the readers don't understand, things they want to know more about, and questions that came to mind as they read.

Ask specific questions, such as these: What part was most interesting to you? Is there anything you'd like to know more about? Was anything confusing? How can I improve the organization? What are your views on this topic?

When to Use   Use this technique to identify strengths and weaknesses in your writing.

Techniques for
Peer Response   **607**

OUTLINING

An outline helps you plan your writing and take notes. In an outline main ideas are listed as headings. Details are shown as subpoints. A **sentence outline** uses complete sentences for the main ideas and details. A **topic outline** uses words or phrases, as in this model.

Sign Language

Thesis Statement: Sign language is a system of gestures and hand symbols developed to help hearing-impaired people communicate.

I. Types of sign language (Main idea)
  A. American Sign Language (Subpoint for I)
    1. Based on ideas, not words (Detail for A)
    2. Expresses ideas in gestures
  B. American Manual Alphabet
    1. Based on the alphabet (Detail for B)
    2. Uses finger symbols for letters
    3. Combines finger symbols with gestures
II. Uses of sign language
  A. By deaf people (Subpoint for II)
  B. By hearing-impaired people
  C. By non-hearing-impaired people

Correct Outline Form

1. Write the title at the top of the outline.
2. Arrange main ideas and details as shown in the model.
3. Indent each division of the outline.
4. Break down each heading into at least two details. For example, if there is a 1 under A, there must be a 2.
5. In a topic outline, use the same form for items of the same rank. If A is a noun, then B and C should be nouns.
6. Begin each item with a capital letter. Do not use end punctuation in a topic outline.

Adjectives

Write an adjective on a slanted line below the word it modifies. Treat possessive nouns and pronouns as adjectives.

The explorers searched a secret cave.

Adverbs

Write an adverb on a slanted line below the word it modifies.

Cats pounce silently.

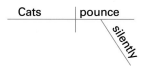

Prepositional Phrases

A prepositional phrase acts as an adjective or an adverb, so diagram it in a similar way. Draw an angled line below the word modified. Write the preposition on the slanted part and its object on the horizontal part. Put any modifiers on slanted lines below the object.

Fish darted through a coral tunnel.

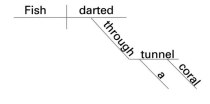

GLOSSARY FOR WRITERS

ADJECTIVE   a word that modifies a noun or pronoun: *one* day.

ADVERB   a word that modifies a verb, an adjective, or another adverb; in "She smiles often," *often* is an adverb modifying the verb *smiles*.

AUDIENCE   your readers or listeners.

BRAINSTORMING   a way of finding ideas that involves listing them without stopping to judge them.

CHRONOLOGICAL   arranged in order of occurrence.

CLICHÉ   an overused expression, such as "sly as a fox."

CLUSTER   a kind of map made up of circled groupings of related details.

COHERENCE   in paragraphs, logical flow from one sentence to the next; in compositions, logical ties between paragraphs.

CONJUNCTION   a word or pair of words that connects other words or groups of words: Glenna *and* Gary won.

DIALECT   a form of a language that has a distinctive pronunciation, vocabulary, and word order.

DIALOGUE   spoken conversation; the conversation in novels, stories, plays, poems, and essays.

ELABORATION   the support or development of a main idea with details, incidents, examples, or quotations.

FIGURATIVE LANGUAGE   the imaginative and poetic use of words; writing that contains such figures of speech as similes, metaphors, and personification.

FREEWRITING   a way of exploring ideas, thoughts, or feelings by writing down everything that comes to mind within a specific length of time.

GLEANING a way of finding ideas for writing by jotting down things you see, hear, read, do, think, and feel as they catch your attention.

GRAPHIC DEVICE a visual presentation of details; graphic devices include charts, graphs, outlines, clusters, and idea trees.

IDEA TREE a graphic device in which main ideas are written on "branches" and details related to them are noted on "twigs."

INTERJECTION a word or phrase used to express strong feeling.

JOURNAL a personal notebook in which you can freewrite, collect ideas, and record thoughts, feelings, and experiences.

LEARNING LOG a kind of journal in which you record and reflect on what you have learned and note problems and questions to which you want to find answers.

METAPHOR a figure of speech in which a comparison is made without the word *like* or *as;* "life is a journey" is a metaphor.

NONSEXIST LANGUAGE language that includes both men and women when referring to a role or group made up of people of both sexes; "A coach shares his or her skills and experience" and "Coaches share their skills and experience" are two nonsexist ways of expressing the same idea.

NOUN a word that names a person, a place, a thing, or an idea.

PARAGRAPH a group of related sentences that develop a single main idea or accomplish a single purpose.

PEER RESPONSE suggestions and comments on a piece of writing, provided by peers, or classmates.

PERSONIFICATION a figure of speech in which human qualities are given to nonhuman things.

PORTFOLIO a container (usually a folder) for notes on work in progress, drafts and revisions, finished pieces, and peer responses.

PREPOSITION   a word that relates its object to some other word in the sentence; in "Alec waited near the fence," *near* is a preposition.

PRONOUN   a word that is used to take the place of a noun or another pronoun; in "He will help us," *he* and *us* are pronouns.

RUN-ON SENTENCE   two or more sentences incorrectly written as one.

SENSORY DETAILS   words that show the way something looks, sounds, smells, tastes, or feels.

SENTENCE FRAGMENT   a group of words that does not express a complete idea.

SIMILE   a figure of speech in which the word *like* or *as* is used to make a comparison; "hands like ice" is a simile.

SPATIAL ORDER   organization in which details are arranged in the order they appear in space, such as from left to right, front to back, top to bottom, or inside to outside.

TOPIC SENTENCE   a sentence that states the main idea of a paragraph.

TRANSITION   a connecting word or phrase that clarifies relationships between details, sentences, or paragraphs.

UNITY   in a paragraph, the working together of all the sentences to support the same main idea; in a composition, the working together of all the paragraphs to support the overall goal.

VERB   a word that expresses an action, a condition, or a state of being; in "The clown painted his face," *painted* is a verb.

WRITING VOICE   the personality of the writer as it comes across through word choice and sentence structure.

Reading and Writing Across the Curriculum

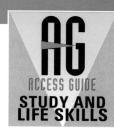

You probably already know and use many strategies for reading and studying, such as previewing your reading, reading actively, looking for main ideas and key terms, and reviewing your notes. (See Writing Handbooks 25 and 26, pages 294–301, if you wish to review these strategies.)

As you may recall, one especially useful strategy is the KWL method, which gives you a three-question approach:

K: What do I already **know** about the topic?
W: What do I **want** to find out about it?
L: What did I **learn** about the topic?

By answering these questions in a learning log, you can improve your recall and understanding of material you read.

In addition to these general strategies, you may find it helpful to try the following special tips and strategies for reading and writing about social studies, math, and science.

SOCIAL STUDIES

- When reading a chapter or studying for a test, create a time line to help you understand the chronological order of events.
- Ask "what-if" questions to explore the impact of historical events. For example, if Lincoln had not been assassinated, how might he have helped the nation recover from the Civil War?
- Use a Venn diagram to show the commonalities and differences between people, places, or events.
- Study the charts, photos, graphics, and maps found in a lesson. As you examine maps, consider the influence of geography upon historical events, such as the migration of a people or the conflicts between two countries.
- Think about connections between the events you are studying and other situations you have studied or observed. What events taking place today remind you of those you are reading about?

Writing with Computers

Word-processing programs allow you to draft, revise, edit, and format your writing and to produce neat, professional-looking papers. They also allow you to share your writing with others.

PREWRITING AND DRAFTING

A computer makes it easy to experiment with different ways of expressing and organizing your ideas. You can use it to keep an electronic journal or portfolio, to organize your notes in files, or to access templates for special writing formats. It also allows you to store multiple drafts of a paper and even to add graphics to clarify and enhance your message.

CREATING VISUALS

Charts, graphs, diagrams, and pictures often communicate information more effectively than words alone do. You can use visuals—graphs, tables, time lines, diagrams, and flow charts—to illustrate complex concepts and processes or to make a page look more interesting.

The visuals you choose will depend on the type of information you want to present to your readers. Take time to explore ways to display your data to determine which visual format best suits your purpose. Here are some options you might consider.

Tables, Graphs, and Charts Many word-processing programs have table and graphic functions you can access through the tool bar to help you create these kinds of graphics with ease.

- Use tables to arrange facts or numbers into rows and columns so that your readers can compare information more easily.
- Use a graph or chart to help communicate complex information in a clear visual image. Choose a different color or a different shade of gray for each part of a pie chart or graph.

What You'll Need

- computer
- word-processing program
- printer
- a graphics program to create visuals
- access to clip-art files from a CD-ROM, a computer disk, or an on-line service

COMPUTER TIP

Create a separate file to use as a writing notebook. Keep all of your story starters, ideas to research, and other writing ideas in this file.

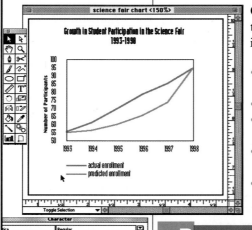

Other Visuals Art and design programs allow you to create visuals for your writing. Many programs include the following features:

- drawing tools that allow you to draw, color, and shade pictures like the one at the left
- clip art that you can copy into your document
- page borders that you can use to decorate title pages, invitations, or brochures
- text options that allow you to combine words with your illustrations
- tools for making geometric shapes in flow charts, time lines, and process diagrams

REVISING AND EDITING

Improving the quality of your writing becomes easier when you use a word-processing program to revise and edit.

Revising a Document

Most word-processing programs allow you to do more than just add and delete words in your draft. Writing electronically makes it easy to move text from one location in your document to another. You can try out different ideas and save them by making multiple drafts of the same work, saving each document with a new name. You can even merge parts of several documents to create a new document.

Peer Editing on a Computer

The writer and the reader can both benefit from the convenience of peer editing "on screen," or at the computer. Some programs, like Writing Coach, have a split-screen function that provides space for a peer reader or your teacher to comment on your writing. The reader might also type comments or suggestions in a different typeface or type style within your text.

If you use a computer, be sure to save your current draft and then copy it for each of your peer readers. Also, ask each reader who responds on-line to include his or her initials in the file name.

634 Access Guide

Peer Editing on a Printout

Some peer readers prefer to respond to a draft on paper rather than on the computer. If you type your document in a compact form, remember to respace it just before printing. It is common to double-space or triple-space your document and leave extra-wide margins to give peer readers room to note their reactions and suggestions. Provide a separate printout for each reader.

Editing a Document

Many word-processing programs have the following kinds of features to help you catch errors and polish your writing:

- The spell checker and grammar checker automatically find possible errors in your writing and suggest corrections. Evaluate each suggestion carefully to make sure it is appropriate before making changes in your text.
- The thesaurus suggests synonyms to improve your writing.
- The search-and-replace feature searches your document and corrects every occurrence of something you want to change.

TECHNOLOGY
—— TIP ——

Some word-processing programs or other software provide preset templates, or patterns, for writing outlines, memos, letters, or invitations. If you use one of these templates, you will not need to adjust the formatting.

FORMATTING AND PUBLISHING

Format refers to the layout and appearance of your writing on the page. You can use a computer to manipulate the type size, typeface, and position of your text to show the importance and organization of ideas. The screen at the right shows some of your options. Keep your format simple. Remember that your goal is to create an attractive document that is easy to read.

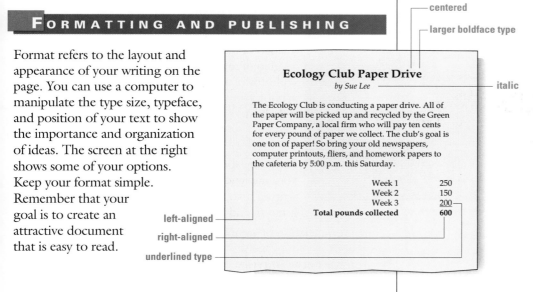

centered

larger boldface type

Ecology Club Paper Drive
by Sue Lee — italic

The Ecology Club is conducting a paper drive. All of the paper will be picked up and recycled by the Green Paper Company, a local firm who will pay ten cents for every pound of paper we collect. The club's goal is one ton of paper! So bring your old newspapers, computer printouts, fliers, and homework papers to the cafeteria by 5:00 p.m. this Saturday.

Week 1	250
Week 2	150
Week 3	200
Total pounds collected	**600**

left-aligned

right-aligned

underlined type

Technology   **635**

Creating a Multimedia Presentation

What You'll Need

- Individual programs to create and edit the text, graphics, sound, and videos you will use

- A multimedia authoring program that allows you to combine these elements and create links between the screens

A multimedia presentation is a combination of text, sound, and visuals such as photographs, videos, and animation. You can combine these elements in an interactive presentation—one in which the user chooses a path to follow in exploring the information.

LEARNING ABOUT MULTIMEDIA

To start planning a multimedia presentation, you need to know the options available to you. Ask your school's technology adviser which of the following elements you could include.

Photos and Videos

Photographs and live-action video clips can make your subject come alive. Here are some examples of visuals that can be downloaded or scanned in:

- video of news coverage of a historical event
- video of music, dance, or theater performances
- photos of an artist's work
- photos or video of a setting that is important to the text

Sound

Including sound in your presentation can help your audience understand information in your written text. For example, the user may be able to listen to and learn from

- the pronunciation of an unfamiliar or foreign word
- a speech
- a recorded news interview
- a musical selection
- a dramatic reading of a work of literature

636   Access Guide

Animation

Many graphics programs allow you to add animation, or movement, to the visuals in your presentation. Animated figures add to the user's enjoyment and understanding of what you present. You can use animation to illustrate

- the steps in a process
- changes in a chart, graph, or diagram
- ways your user can explore information in your presentation

PLANNING YOUR PRESENTATION

To plan a multimedia presentation, first choose your topic and decide what you want to include. For example, instead of writing a family history (see pages 180–184), Merrill might create a multimedia presentation about her grandfather's arrival in the United States. She could include the following items:

- introductory text describing her grandfather
- a videotaped interview with him
- a letter he wrote after his arrival in America
- a photo gallery with written captions
- a drawing of the family tree
- a poster ad from the early 1900s showing the kind of ship that carried immigrants from Europe to the United States

Next plan how you want your user to move through your presentation. You can choose one of the following ways to organize your presentation:

- step by step with only one path, or order, in which the user can see and hear the information.
- a branching path that allows users to make some choices about what they will see and hear, and in what order

If you choose the second way—an interactive presentation—you need to map out your presentation in a flow chart, or navigation map. This will help you plan the links among your screens so that your user can choose a path through your presentation. Each box in the navigation map on the following page represents a screen in Merrill's presentation.

TECHNOLOGY TIP

You can download many photos, sound clips, and video clips from Internet sources onto your computer. This process allows you to add elements to your multimedia presentation that would usually require complex editing equipment. There are also CD-ROMs with extensive collections of video and audio clips.

Writing TIP

If you want to copy materials, you usually need permission from the copyright owner. You do not need permission, however, if you are not making money from your presentation, if you use it only for educational purposes, and if you use only a small percentage of the original material.

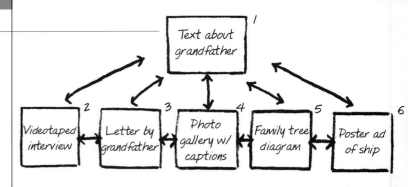

You could follow screens 1–6 in order, or you could keep returning to the contents, or menu, on the first screen. This would allow you to choose the order in which you follow the presentation.

CREATING YOUR PRESENTATION

As you create your multimedia presentation, use the navigation map as a guide.

When you have decided on the content of a screen, it is helpful to sketch the screen out. Remember to include in your sketch the links you will create to other screens in your presentation. Refer to the navigation map to see what links you need to add to each screen.

This example shows screen 1 from the navigation map above.

This screen includes a photograph that has been scanned in.

The user clicks on an underlined heading to move to a different screen.

FINDING HOME

My grandfather Louis Zaremski was born in 1904 in a small town in Poland.

Click on the headings below to find out about his immigration to the United States.

Videotaped interview
Letter by grandfather
Photo gallery
Family tree diagram
Poster ad of immigrant ship

C

social studies, 67, 89, 623
speaking and listening, 137
Culture and customs, 64–66
beginnings and endings, 66
compiling an anthology, 66
describing, 65
drafting, 65
exploring, 64–65
multicultural calendar, 66
publishing, 66
reenacting, 66
reviewing, 66

D
Dates
capitalization in, 552
commas in, 576
Declarative sentences, 356, 568
Definition, in dictionary, 310
Definitions and restatements, 303–304
Demonstrative adjectives, 465–66
Describing people and places, 50–61
beginnings and endings, 58
drafting, 56–57
ideas for writing, 54–55
metaphors with, 58
organization, 56
prewriting, 54–55
proofreading, 60
publishing and presenting, 60–61
reflecting, 61
reviewing, 57
revising, 58–59
sensory details with, 58
similes with, 58
standards for evaluation, 60
topics, 54–55
Details, 17, 43, 56, 209, 223, 227
organizing, 217–21
see also Elaboration; Sensory details
Dewey Decimal System, 313–14
Diagraming sentences, 617–19
Diagrams, 109, 192, 300
Dialect, 620
Dialogue, 78, 82, 620
guidelines for, 82, 280
to provide information, 279
punctuating, 586–87
skits, 83
to show personalities, 279
writing, 278–80
Dictionary, 308–11
alphabetical order, 308

definition, 310
entry words, 309
guide words, 308–309
part of speech, 309
pronunciation guide, 309
pronunciation key, 309
synonyms, 310
word origin, 309
Direct objects, 403
diagraming, 618
Directions, 94–105
audience, 100
brainstorming, 99
drafting, 100–01
exploring topics, 98–99
organization, 100
pictures, 100
prewriting, 98–99
proofreading, 104
public opinion survey, 131–32
publishing and presenting, 104–05
reflecting, 105
reviewing, 101
revising, 102–03
transitions, 102
Discovery, writing for, 13–23
drafting and discovering, 18–19
ideas for writing, 16–17
organization, 18–19
prewriting and exploring, 16–17
proofreading, 20
publishing and presenting, 21
reflecting, 21
revising, 19–20
topics, 16–17
see also Drafting
Discussion, 127
Divided quotations, 587
does, do, 530
Double negatives, 492
Drafting, 8, 18–19, 215–16
book review, 158–59
in describing people and places, 56–57
directions, 100–101
family history, 183
information reports, 175
journal writing, 35
opinion, 122–23
personal narrative, 78
personal response, 150
poetry writing, 87
public opinion survey, 131
with computer, 633
Drama. *See* Plays